Ontario and Quebec's Irish Pioneers

ALSO BY LUCILLE H. CAMPEY

Atlantic Canada's Irish Immigrants:
A Fish and Timber Story

Ignored But Not Forgotten:
Canada's English Immigrants

Seeking a Better Future:
The English Pioneers of Ontario and Quebec

Planters, Paupers, and Pioneers:
English Settlers in Atlantic Canada

An Unstoppable Force:
The Scottish Exodus to Canada

"A Very Fine Class of Immigrants":
Prince Edward Island's Scottish Pioneers, 1770–1850

"Fast Sailing and Copper-Bottomed":
Aberdeen Sailing Ships and the Emigrant Scots They Carried to Canada, 1774–1855

The Silver Chief:
Lord Selkirk and the Scottish Pioneers of Belfast, Baldoon and Red River

After the Hector*:*
The Scottish Pioneers of Nova Scotia and Cape Breton, 1773–1852

The Scottish Pioneers of Upper Canada, 1784–1855;
Glengarry and Beyond

Les Écossais:
The Scottish Pioneers of Lower Canada, 1763–1855

With Axe and Bible:
The Scottish Pioneers of New Brunswick, 1784–1874

Lucille H. Campey

Ontario and Quebec's Irish Pioneers

Farmers, Labourers, and Lumberjacks

THE IRISH IN CANADA

DUNDURN
TORONTO

Cover design: Laura Boyle
Front cover image: Merrickville, Montague Township (Lanark County), on the Rideau River. This watercolour, painted in 1838 by Philip J. Bainbridge (1817–1881), shows immigrants in a small boat rowing towards the Merrickville settlement, having arrived in the Rideau Canal steamer shown on the left. Merrickville's population was predominately Irish at the time and remained so for many decades. Courtesy Library and Archives Canada Acc. No. 1983-47-60. Back cover: Gravestones of Irish settlers at Saint-Columban, north of Montreal. Photograph by Geoff Campey. Printer: Webcom

Library and Archives Canada Cataloguing in Publication

Campey, Lucille H., author
    Ontario and Quebec's Irish pioneers : farmers, labourers, and lumberjacks / Lucille H. Campey.

(The Irish in Canada)
Includes bibliographical references and index.
Issued in print and electronic formats.
ISBN 978-1-4597-4084-6 (softcover).--ISBN 978-1-4597-4085-3 (PDF).--
ISBN 978-1-4597-4086-0 (EPUB)

    1. Irish--Ontario--History. 2. Irish--Québec (Province)--History. 3. Immigrants--Ontario--History. 4. Immigrants--Québec (Province)--History. 5. Ontario--Emigration and immigration--History. 6. Québec (Province)--Emigration and immigration--History. 7. Ireland--Emigration and immigration--History. I. Title. II. Series: Campey, Lucille H. Irish in Canada.

FC106.I6C36 2018   971.3004'9162   C2018-903097-6
                                                 C2018-903098-4

1 2 3 4 5   22 21 20 19 18

Conseil des Arts du Canada | Canada Council for the Arts | Canadä | ONTARIO ARTS COUNCIL CONSEIL DES ARTS DE L'ONTARIO an Ontario government agency un organisme du gouvernement de l'Ontario

We acknowledge the support of the **Canada Council for the Arts**, which last year invested $153 million to bring the arts to Canadians throughout the country, and the **Ontario Arts Council** for our publishing program. We also acknowledge the financial support of the **Government of Ontario**, through the **Ontario Book Publishing Tax Credit** and the **Ontario Media Development Corporation**, and the **Government of Canada**.

Nous remercions le **Conseil des arts du Canada** de son soutien. L'an dernier, le Conseil a investi 153 millions de dollars pour mettre de l'art dans la vie des Canadiennes et des Canadiens de tout le pays.

Care has been taken to trace the ownership of copyright material used in this book. The author and the publisher welcome any information enabling them to rectify any references or credits in subsequent editions.
— *J. Kirk Howard, President*

The publisher is not responsible for websites or their content unless they are owned by the publisher.

Printed and bound in Canada.

VISIT US AT

dundurn.com | @dundurnpress | dundurnpress | dundurnpress

Dundurn
3 Church Street, Suite 500
Toronto, Ontario, Canada
M5E 1M2

To Geoff, with all my love

CONTENTS

LIST OF MAPS

❧

*All maps are © Geoff Campey, 2018

LIST OF TABLES

PREFACE

*O*ntario and Quebec's Irish Pioneers is the second book in the Irish in Canada series. It describes the great influx of Irish people to Ontario and Quebec during the eighteenth and nineteenth centuries and identifies the push/pull factors that were at work. It reveals the considerable pioneering achievements of the Irish and describes the ships that they sailed in, while debunking the victim-ridden interpretations of more recent times.

I was fortunate in having access to Cecil Houston and William Smyth's *Irish Emigration and Canadian Settlement*, which provides an excellent grounding on the subject. Donald MacKay's *Flight from Famine* and Bruce Elliott's *Irish Migrants in the Canadas* were invaluable as general reference books. On a provincial level, Robert Grace's *The Irish in Quebec,* containing bibliographic references to the many Irish settlements that were founded, was of immense help. *The Untold Story: The Irish in Canada,* edited by Robert O'Driscoll and Lorna Reynolds, is another invaluable source, particularly for regional and township studies. Much has been published on Irish settlements in different parts of Ontario. Donald Akenson's *The Irish in Ontario: A Study in Rural History*, concentrating on Leeds and Lansdowne townships in eastern Ontario, Catharine Anne Wilson's *A New Lease on Life: Landlords, Tenants, and Immigrants in Ireland and Canada,* dealing with an Irish group who settled at Amherst Island near Kingston, and Aidan Manning's *Between the Runways*, relating to Irish Catholic settlements in Peel County west of Toronto are but three examples. Many Ontario township studies of Irish settlement have been documented both as journal articles and as dissertations. My book's bibliography reveals the extent and wide-ranging nature of this material.

The Irish were early birds. They arrived in mid-Canada long before the English, and became assimilated in the wider population much sooner. They had left their homeland to achieve a better standard of living and be part of a more egalitarian society, and they were phenomenally successful. By 1871 they were the largest immigrant group in Ontario, and in Quebec, outnumbering the combined total of Scottish and English immigrants. They founded a host of communities and had an immense impact on the economic development of both provinces. Since Ontario and Quebec offered differing opportunities, the immigrant streams from Ireland worked differently and to different timescales. A practice adopted widely by the Irish was to use a remittance system, whereby people funded their sea crossings through money sent by family and friends who had already settled in Canada.

Ontario and Quebec's Irish Pioneers: Farmers, Labourers, and Lumberjacks describes the Irish communities that formed in the different regions of Ontario and Quebec, while tracing where the immigrants had originated from in Ireland and why they chose their particular locations. Until 1830 they mainly sailed from Ulster ports in the north of Ireland, most being Protestants, but afterward departed increasingly from the south and west of Ireland, most being Catholics. Letters home and diaries are used extensively to reveal immigrant views on what they found and to better describe the conditions they faced in the outback. A consideration of the famine years of the mid-1840s is followed by an examination of the shipping services that were used by the Irish. Contrary to popular perceptions, they were good. Most of the Irish travelled in good-quality ships.

The Irish settled in many parts of Ontario and Quebec and were for the most part fairly ordinary people who sought the better life that was theirs for the taking. Catholics experienced widespread prejudice in their new country, and the Irish in general were often treated as an underclass. The Irish labourers who dug the canals and built the railways are the unsung heroes, since no one else at the time could have done this arduous work. Many labourers saved their wages to launch themselves into farming — which proved to be a very bumpy ride, since few had the necessary skills and had to learn them the hard way.

This is a book about good and talented people who made an enormous contribution to Canada's early development.

ABBREVIATIONS

BAnQ	Bibliothèque et Archives Nationales du Québec
BPP	British Parliamentary Papers
DCB	*Dictionary of Canadian Biography*
DERO	Derbyshire Record Office
JLA	*Journal of the Legislative Assembly of the Province of Canada*
LAC	Library and Archives Canada
MCFMS	Mellon Centre for Migration Studies
NAB	National Archives of Britain
NAI	National Archives of Ireland
NAS	National Archives of Scotland
OA	Ontario Archives
PRONI	Public Records Office, Northern Ireland
RHL	Oxford University: Rhodes House Library

CHAPTER 1

✧

Mid-Canada's Appeal to the Irish

The Kirkpatrick boys has got a situation six days after they landed and like this place very much.... There is nothing got here but by sore industry, but you will get in for the earning here. People lives a great deal more comfortable here than they do at home.[1]

Having arrived safely in Montreal, Charlotte Bacon writes to her father in Londonderry telling him that she will pay back the money lent to her by her grandmother for her sea crossing, and she also encloses money given to her by another Montreal immigrant, which is to be handed to his family in Ireland. Charlotte makes two very important points. First, Irish immigrants must work hard in the New World if they are to succeed, and second, she identifies herself as one of the many Irish people who acted as go-betweens in funding passages. Her father will give the money, entrusted to his safekeeping, to a Londonderry family, who will use it to finance their passage to Quebec. As the Irish politician John Maguire pointed out, "emigration will never cease with Irish families as long as any portion of them remain at each side of the Atlantic."[2]

Most nineteenth-century Irish immigration was financed by so-called remittances — funds that were sent from North America to Ireland.[3] In their 1848 report, the Colonial Land and Emigration Commissioners noted how in that year "a considerable part of the expense of emigration from Ireland is defrayed by money remitted to Ireland from North America by parties who have previously emigrated."[4] That had been typical of most years. No other immigrant group adopted this practice to such an extent. In 1868, John Maguire estimated that colossal sums had crossed the Atlantic eastward as Irish settlements continued to grow in North America. "In the history of the world there is nothing to match this."[5] A top priority for a new arrival was to save money to send back to a loved one in Ireland so that he or she might follow. Charlotte Bacon and her father played their part, and countless others did as well.

Many of the Irish who came to Canada were labourers, finding employment as canal diggers, lumberjacks, and general servants. Labourers, being much in demand, could command far higher pay than was the case in Ireland. Moreover, they could enjoy the freedom and benefits of a more egalitarian society while gaining materially. Those with a farming background hoped to acquire land more or less immediately and were at a great advantage over the general labourers, who had to learn their farming skills the hard way.

Henry Johnson, having left County Antrim in 1848 to live in Niagara, said that he felt a kind of independence "you can never have in the Old Country."[6] However, when William Graves visited Upper Canada nearly thirty years earlier to assess its farming opportunities, he was advised by Dr. William Baldwin, a prominent politician, to remain at home. Baldwin told him that "it often grieved him to find some, whom he knew left comfortable homes with a view of bettering their circumstances, and are now sadly disappointed."[7] Someone of Graves's high social rank and affluence would almost certainly join the ranks of the disappointed; but most immigrants, being of more modest means, would hope to benefit from the New World. Johnston Neilson, an Armagh teacher, was so desperate to join his father and brother in Upper Canada that he asked the Colonial Office to lend him £20 to £30 to pay for his passage and onward travel. He wanted his elderly mother, who still lived with him in County Armagh, to share in the benefits of the New World.[8] A great many people felt the way he did. Yet, so often this Irish immigration saga has been shrouded in negative imagery.

Although Irish people had strong positive motives for relocating to Canada, their story has been hijacked by doom-mongers who would have us believe that they were all victims of one dreadful happening. The immigration that took place during the Great Irish Famine of the mid-1840s, when many thousands of Irish people died, has become the story. Scenes have been conjured up of distraught people forced to leave Ireland by cruel landlords, while a sinister role is painted of the British government's alleged role in forcing this upon them. This claptrap may well suit supporters of the Irish republican cause, but it has nothing to do with the truth. Very few Irish people were compelled by force or famine to leave Ireland. In any case, most of mid-Canada's Irish population began arriving in the early 1800s — long before the famine struck. The sudden surge in numbers during the famine period occurred at the tail end of the influx, not its beginning. Most Irish chose of their own free will to relocate to Canada and it is easy to see why this was the case.

With its rapidly growing population and the increasing subdivision of its landholdings, Ireland's agricultural system had become unsustainable. The land tenure system was chaotic, there was no security of tenure, and landlords had no contractual obligations toward their tenants. People were stuck with the age-old problems of unproductive land and overpopulation.

Conditions were also desperate for Ulster's textile workers. Because hand-weaving was a cottage-based, labour-intensive industry, workers were vulnerable to the structural changes taking place in the early nineteenth century as a result of increasing mechanization. Thousands of Ulster linen weavers were thrown out of work or had to survive on pitiable rates of pay, thus creating another great stimulus for emigration.[9]

The first Irish influx came from France, not Ireland. Having become incensed by the British government's brutal suppression of the Irish Catholic rebellion against English rule in 1641, many Irishmen moved to France, where they joined a foreign legion, known as the Irish Brigade, and fought on the French side in battles against the British.[10] When the St. Lawrence Valley became colonized by the French, the Irish who had settled in France contributed to the population of the future New France,

Irish cabin scene, circa 1880–1900. Photographed by Robert French, 1841–1917.

and on the eve of the British Conquest in 1763, around 100 Irish-born families were residing there. Despite having fought on the losing side in the Seven Years' War, most of the ex–Irish Brigade men remained in New France — later renamed Quebec.

The second influx of Irish immigrants, who came from the United States, brought pro-British settlers. They actively sought to live under the British Crown. After Britain's defeat in the American War of Independence (1775–83), people from Ulster who had previously settled in the New England States headed north so that they could live in British-held territory.

The principal Irish influx began shortly after the end of the Napoleonic Wars in 1815, when the United Kingdom was plunged into a deep economic depression. Until 1830 Irish immigrants mainly originated from Ulster in the north, many being Protestants, but afterward increasingly came from the south and west, many being Catholics (Map 1).

Having been remarkably well-informed about Quebec's agricultural opportunities, around 1820 the Irish headed for the farming regions lying north and south of Quebec City and Montreal, where there was

Map 1: Reference Map of Ireland When United with Great Britain (pre-1922)

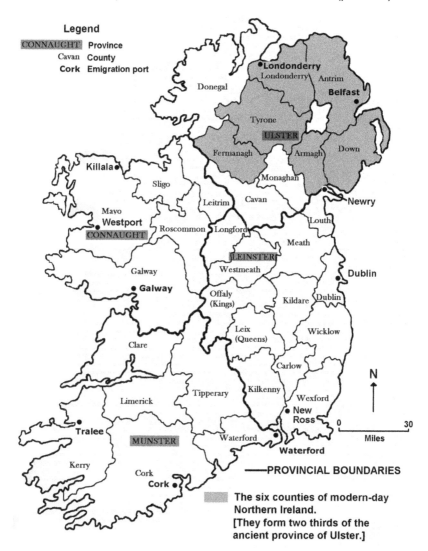

Legend

CONNAUGHT Province
Cavan County
Cork Emigration port

PROVINCIAL BOUNDARIES

The six counties of modern-day Northern Ireland.
[They form two thirds of the ancient province of Ulster.]

an abundance of vacant wilderness land. Some of the land had belonged to the Catholic Church and had reverted to the Crown, some had been granted to disbanded soldiers who failed to take up their holdings, while some belonged to seigneurs who ran their estates for country pursuits or to further their business interests and took little interest in turning their land into productive use.

Thanks to the colonizing efforts of John Neilson, a Quebec politician and landowner who was also editor of the *Quebec Gazette*, huge swathes of land located behind the long-settled French communities lining the St. Lawrence River north and west of Quebec City became Irish strongholds (Map 2). Being able to settle within the city's hinterland, where jobs in the rapidly expanding timber trade and shipbuilding industries were plentiful and where there was also an abundance of fertile farmland, encouraged many to come, although the cold climate and remoteness of the area were serious drawbacks. Settling on seigneurial land, which they could only rent, not buy, and sharing their lives with people who spoke a different language from theirs and in many cases followed a different religion, they formed extensive Irish communities of mixed religion along the major river frontages. Most were farmers, though some had to supplement their incomes with seasonal employment in the lumber camps to make ends meet. The fact is that it was only the Irish who possessed the necessary fundraising and networking skills to get themselves to such areas, although their numbers were relatively small.

Meanwhile, a major catalyst to settlement south of Quebec City was the opening of the Craig's Road in the early nineteenth century, which made the fertile farmland on the south side of the St. Lawrence accessible

Map 2: Reference Map of Upper and Lower Canada

to immigrants. Being quick off the mark yet again, some Irish Catholics headed to Frampton Township, where they were able to find vacant land and soon founded the settlement they dubbed St. Malachie. The Beaurivage seigneury, just to the west of it, became another Irish stronghold. In 1851, 70 percent of its population was Irish. With the help of Craig's Road, the Irish made even greater strides in the Eastern Townships

Because of their well-known farming skills, Ulster immigrants were highly prized. Their takeover of three Megantic County townships in the northern half of the Eastern Townships owes much to Alexander Buchanan's persuasive talents. As the Quebec immigration agent, he was well placed to do a bit of talent-spotting. Listening for Ulster accents as people disembarked from their ships in the late 1820s, he managed to persuade a good number to take up land in Megantic County. However, although they founded viable farming communities, they did not attract followers, since the region could not compete with the better opportunities to be had in Ontario. The irony is that, while Megantic County was losing its Ulster Irish, the towns of Sherbrooke and Richmond in the south were attracting ever more immigrants from Ireland, many of whom were Catholics. Twenty years later, when a railway line reached Richmond, even more Irish came to the area. At the time, Irish Catholics in Canada were just about tolerated and often viewed with suspicion, but they came to Canada despite the government's indifference to them.

The Montreal area was another major Irish stronghold. The Irish were the city's principal canal diggers, railway builders, and factory workers. With the wages earned from such activities, many went on to launch themselves into farming, principally in locations south of Montreal. The jobs made available by the construction of the Lachine Canal in the early 1820s, the Chambly Canal in the 1830s, and the Beauharnois Canal ten years later gave these labourers the springboard they needed to finance their route to farming. By 1851 large numbers of Quebec's Irish farmers were concentrated in Huntingdon County or the Beauharnois seigneury, the former being mainly Protestant and the latter of mixed religion. On the other hand, their settlements north of Montreal were far more scattered, with the earliest being St. Columban (present-day spelling is St. Colomban), founded in the 1820s under the guidance of Father Patrick

Phelan, a Montreal priest. Its settlers came from Griffintown, an Irish shantytown in Montreal known for its poverty and shabbiness. They were helped by a caring priest and given government funds to launch a farming community that thrived until the mid-nineteenth century. However, their settlements had a fixed lifespan. Few Irish came to the area after the mid-nineteenth century, while established settlers left to take advantage of the better opportunities to be had in Ontario and the United States.

The Irish influx north and south of the St. Lawrence River between Quebec City and Montreal pales in significance when compared with what took place west of Montreal in the Ottawa Valley. By 1881 people of Irish ancestry dominated 53 townships in an almost continuous line of settlements that straddled eight counties. This region was at the very heart of the timber trade, which was the prime force that fuelled mid Canada's economic expansion. As timber felling began in earnest in 1815, the Irish poured into the region, establishing their many settlements along both sides of the Ottawa, Gatineau, and Rideau rivers. They worked as lumberjacks or in sawmills and in other wide-ranging forestry activities. The Irish were also an important part of the workforce that dug the Rideau Canal, linking the St. Lawrence River with the Ottawa River. After it was completed in 1832, townships lining its route suddenly acquired large numbers of redundant Irish canal workers as settlers. However, the Irish had been well ensconced in this region long before the Rideau Canal had even been contemplated.

In 1809 a small group who originated from the southeast of Ireland acquired land in Leeds and Lansdowne — a prime township site that fronted on the St. Lawrence River. They were followed by others from the same area soon after 1815, thus sowing the seeds of a major settlement coup. The area attracted hundreds more Irish, who headed north toward the Ottawa River to settle on the vast stretches of vacant land between the St. Lawrence and Ottawa rivers. Yet again, the Irish were the early birds, but their first inroads may date back even farther than 1809. This was the region where Irish ex-soldiers who had fought in the American War of Independence were allocated land. So, it's possible that Irish Loyalists arriving in 1784 were the first group to lay claim to land in Leeds and Lansdowne Township and subsequently attract followers.

By 1851 Quebec's Irish immigrant population was twice that of the English and Scottish immigrant populations combined. One third of the Irish lived in Montreal and Quebec City, while the remainder were primarily concentrated in the farming districts of the Upper Ottawa Valley, the Beauharnois region south of Montreal, and the Eastern Townships. However, by this time Ontario had overtaken Quebec as the prime destination for Irish immigrants, having become more accessible through the building of roads and waterways. Quebec could no longer compete with Ontario's better land, job prospects, and climate, while Atlantic Canada increasingly lost many of its already-established Irish settlers to it. Once again, the Irish were the early birds. They arrived in the area in large numbers between 1817 and 1825, even before Upper Canada's internal routes had been built, but this time they had help. They had three colonization leaders and financial backing from the British government.

In 1821, Peter Robinson, brother of the Upper Canada attorney general, led 500 Irish Catholics, mainly from County Cork, to the Ottawa Valley. Two years later he led another Cork group of 2,000 to the Peterborough region. In 1818, Richard Talbot, an Irish military officer, took charge of two much smaller groups of County Tipperary Anglicans — sending one to the Ottawa Valley and the other to London Township in Middlesex County. Working behind the scenes, James Buchanan, the British consul in New York City and brother of Alexander, Quebec's immigration agent, was in many ways the most effective of the three leaders. In 1816–17 he recruited "great numbers" of Irish immigrants living in New York who wished to relocate to Ontario, offering them free transportation and land on which to settle.[11] It was claimed that he recruited up to 7,000 immigrants who were mainly Irish, most being from Ulster. He offered one group land in Durham County to the west of where Peter Robinson's Peterborough group would later settle and a second group land in Peel County. The Durham County venture attracted many Irish followers who eventually spread themselves across Peterborough, Victoria, Durham, Northumberland, and Hastings counties, principally occupying the back townships, lying some distance away from the river frontages. They included the County Clare tenants of Colonel George Wyndham and the Wicklow tenants of the Earl of

Fitzwilliam, the former settling mainly in Northumberland County and the latter in Hastings County.

Meanwhile, James Buchanan also offered some of his Irish recruits land in Peel County, a prime location west of the future city of Toronto. Unlike Peter Robinson's Catholic settlers, who had to cope with the isolation and long-distance travel associated with life in the back townships of the Ottawa Valley and Peterborough regions, Buchanan's Peel settlers were relatively close to Lake Ontario and to the towns along it. This guaranteed them relatively easy access to the gristmills where their corn would be ground and to the markets where their flour and other produce could be sold. Nevertheless, despite its remoteness, the Lake Simcoe region, some thirty miles north of Lake Ontario, became the number one Irish destination, surpassing Peel County and everywhere else in Ontario.

Simcoe County's Irish influx was a do-it-yourself operation, driven entirely by self-funded immigrants and word-of-mouth recommendations. The rapid growth of York, the future Toronto, stimulated by the building of the Erie Canal, had been the major catalyst in enticing Irish immigrants to the area. After its completion in 1826, a good many of the canal diggers, who were Irish immigrants living in New York, ventured north to Toronto looking for work. Later, some of them moved to the Simcoe region, where they established themselves as pioneer farmers. Before long, members of extended families and friends arrived from Ireland and turned the region into a major Irish enclave. By 1881 Simcoe County's southern half was 60 percent Irish and the county had the highest proportion of Irish in the whole of Ontario.

Farther to the west, the placement of Richard Talbot's Irish settlers in London Township (Middlesex County) in 1818 was to have far-reaching consequences. Because of its fertile land and excellent location, the township filled up quickly, causing the Irish to snap up the adjacent vacant land to the north of it in Biddulph and McGillivray townships in Huron County. This provided land both for further arrivals from Ireland and the many Irish who, having previously settled in the Ottawa Valley and elsewhere in eastern Ontario, sought better locations.

The townships were situated at the southern end of the Canada Company's vast Huron Tract on either side of a major colonization road, while a local company agent ensured that Irish Protestants and Catholics were kept separate from each other in both townships. By 1881, 80 percent of Biddulph's population was Irish, making it the largest Irish stronghold in the Huron Tract. From these beginnings the Irish advanced north through the Huron Tract and beyond, eventually predominating over large swathes of Huron, Perth, Wellington, Bruce, and Grey counties. Many brought their practical pioneering skills with them, having previously settled in eastern Ontario, or in some cases Quebec.

Lambton County, on the southwest extremity of Ontario, became another Irish stronghold after the discovery of oil there in 1858, when Petrolia became Canada's major oil-producing centre. Twenty years later, the Irish were the largest ethnic group in six Lambton County townships, one having been named Enniskillen, commemorating a town in the north of Ireland.

The Irish planted their Shannon, Kilkenny, Kildare, New Erin, St. Malachie, and countless "Irish Settlements" in the more remote areas of Quebec and Ontario, but few survived as distinctly Irish communities beyond the 1850s. Little trace has been left of their settlements in the more densely populated regions of mid-Canada where the Irish had to share locations with other ethnic groups. However, they left their mark very distinctly in the cities where they were able to acquire living accommodation near to their places of work. Montreal had a "Griffintown," Toronto a "Corktown and "Cabbagetown," and Hamilton a "Corktown," each bringing a tiny bit of Ireland to the New World. To the general public, their shantytowns were sordid slums needing to be demolished; but they were havens to the Irish — places that kept alive memories and acted as reminders of their beloved culture and homeland.

Irish Catholics brought their St. Patrick's Societies with them to Canada, while Irish Protestants brought their Orange Order. St. Patrick's Day parades, celebrating Ireland's patron saint, commemorated an Irish homeland but evoked a distant past that has largely been lost. A typical parade, held in Richmond in 1906, had been preceded by a religious service and was followed later that day by an evening concert:

> Bedecked with their handsome gold and green regalia, fairly glistening in the sun, with national standards

and banners flaunting in the breeze, to the strains of the "Wearing of the Green" and other popular airs, the men of the St. Patrick's Society, 100 strong, paraded the streets of Richmond on Saturday, March 17th. The fitful gusts of the wind and the flurrying snow only added to their patriotic ardour. Acting Grand Marshall William McDerby, assisted by A.P. Campbell, rode at the head of the procession, which was over a quarter of a mile long and included: the pupils of the Brother's School, the members of the Catholic Order of Foresters, the members of the Catholic Mutual Benefit Association, the members of the Saint-Jean-Baptiste Society, each under their respective marshals and headed by their distinctive banners. The officers of the society, President Dr. John Hayes and his guest Mr. John Hall Kelly brought up the rear.[12]

Religious observance was an important support mechanism for the uprooted Irish, who were coming to terms with their strange new

St. Patrick's Day Parade, Quebec City, 1924. Photographed by Andrew Merrilees.

environment. However, unlike the Scots, who were served by Presbyterian missionaries sent from Scotland,[13] and the English, who had the Anglican missionaries sent by the London-based Society for the Propagation of the Gospel,[14] the Irish were left high and dry. They had no equivalent support system. Church of Ireland worshippers might join the Anglican Church or the Presbyterian Church, where they would have been seen as outsiders, or they might have been attracted by Methodism and the other non-conformist sects, which were growing in popularity. And Irish Catholics, who were served by a few priests who travelled considerable distances to reach their congregations, had to rely on their own fundraising to build churches.

Sometimes the local clergymen were Irish, as was the case with Dublin-born priest Father Edward Gordon, who looked after an area that comprised most of Peel County, part of Halton County, and the southern townships of Simcoe County.[15] The Reverend Samuel B. Ardagh, an Irish-born Anglican missionary, presided over much of Simcoe County from his base near Barrie, regularly travelling up to 100 miles to bring the word of God to his flock.[16] Arriving at the age of sixty, the Dublin-born Reverend James Magrath became one of Toronto Township's Anglican ministers. Acquiring large landholdings, he built up an estate, which he named "Erindale," a name adopted later by Irish immigrants who settled along the Credit River.[17]

The Kilkenny-born Father Patrick Phelan, based in Montreal, was so concerned by the squalid conditions being endured by the Irish families living in Griffintown that he masterminded their relocation to St. Columban in 1820, having obtained land from the Gentlemen of St. Sulpice and raising the necessary funds.

The Reverend James Burton, an Anglican missionary based at Rawdon, north of Montreal, also involved himself with the progress of settlement by acting as the local land agent. No doubt, he had been given this job to encourage Protestant settlers to come to this area, but his was a losing battle. It was mainly Irish Catholics who wished to settle in Quebec, but when their numbers greatly exceeded other ethnic groups, trouble often arose. French Canadians living in St. Sylvestre, south of Quebec City, during the 1850s, objected when Irish Catholics insisted that their community should have an Irish priest rather than a

French one to reflect the greater size of the Irish Catholic population. The size of the Irish Catholic community seemed threatening to local Irish Protestants, as well, and this led to violent conflicts between Irish Catholics and Irish Protestants. A recurring theme in this saga is the tensions felt between Irish Protestants and Irish Catholics. They had carried the bitter resentment they felt toward one another with them from the Old Country to Canada, thus creating tensions that often led to violence. A bone of contention was the tendency of Irish Protestants to publicly extol what they saw as Protestant supremacy. This was extremely irksome to Catholics. The Orangemen's parades, which commemorate the victory of the Protestant King William over the Catholic King James at the Battle of the Boyne in 1690, understandably incited riots from time to time. However, when the Orange Order expanded beyond its Irish origins in Canada, to eventually embrace all Protestants, it transformed itself into a British men's social club, whose principal role was to extol British values and provide mutual support to its members.

Although Catholics were meant to enjoy equality before the law, day-to-day living proved otherwise. Irish Catholics were often openly denigrated by Protestants and denied sought-after jobs. Even the well-off Irish were berated and subjected to negative stereotyping. They were the ones who drank too much, fought too much, and wasted too much time. According to Kirby Miller, even "well-educated, middle-class Irish Catholics experienced religious barriers to success and respect."[18] Irish Catholics were generally viewed with disdain and judged to be wanting in basic farming skills. Rather than being regarded as hard-working people on a learning curve, they were despised for their inexperience and poor performance as farmers. However, the Irish learned to overcome the prejudice they encountered, and they prospered. As Nicholas Flood Davin, the Limerick-born journalist and politician, pointed out,

> Men have come here, who were unable to spell, who never tasted meat, who never knew what it was to have a shoe to their foot in Ireland, and they tell me they are masters of 1,000 or 2,000 or 3,000 acres, as the case may be, of the finest land in Canada.[19]

Orangemen's Day Parade, Ottawa, 1953. Photographed by Rosemary Gilliat Easton, 1919–2004.

By the mid-nineteenth century, the Irish outnumbered the Scots and English and had established a great many of Quebec and Ontario's founding communities. The famine came and went, but was only a small part of their story. The Irish memorials that have been erected at Grosse Île and at the sites of the former immigration sheds are a reminder of this harrowing time. However, the accomplishments of the Irish who arrived and thrived as pioneers must also be acknowledged and celebrated. This book tells their many differing stories.

CHAPTER 2

৶৻

Early Arrivals

Given the fact that an estimated 40,000 Irish men, women and children were emigrating to France during the seventeenth century, a period during which she [France] was colonizing the St. Lawrence Valley, it is perhaps not surprising that we find some Irish in New France in that period.[1]

Most of the first wave of Irish settlers to reach what would become Quebec Province (New France) came not from Ireland but from the Continent. Religious persecution against Irish Catholics by the English had caused a large-scale exodus to France. Oliver Cromwell's brutal suppression of the rebellion of Irish Catholics against English rule in 1649–50 galvanized people in a mass movement from Ireland to France. Once there, Irishmen joined a foreign legion known as the Irish Brigade, the so-called "wild geese," which fought on France's side in its various battles across Europe.[2] Others settled down as civilians. However, once the business and farming opportunities to be had in the St. Lawrence Valley, then being colonized by France, became more widely known, many of those Irish set sail for Quebec City. By the late 1600s there were said to be about 100 Irish-born families and an additional 30 with mixed Irish and French backgrounds living in New France.[3] Only 10 colonists had arrived from Ireland directly.

The influx began as just a trickle. Records of Quebec City's court cases, considered in the first half of the eighteenth century, provide some examples of New France's Irish residents at the time: Jean Layahe was taken to court in 1714 for manufacturing counterfeit money; Charles Kennedy, Andre McBair, and Denis Quanillon were accused in 1755 of stealing "during the night"; and Edouard Farel was charged three years later with stealing money from a Quebec surgeon.[4] There was also Edward Hamilton, working as a stoker for the Forges du Saint Maurice, an iron production company near Trois Rivières, who was taken to court in 1742 over financial irregularities.[5] However, with the outbreak of the Seven Years' War (1756–63) between Britain and France, the situation changed dramatically. Many Irishmen living in France who went to New France to fight in the war on the French side, remained in the St. Lawrence Valley after Britain's victory.[6] This they did despite having backed the losing side. Some took French wives and disguised their names in the hope of seeming less threatening to the Protestant elite who were now in charge. Nevertheless, they openly professed their Irishness. Just two years after the taking of New France by the British, Quebec City experienced the first of many St. Patrick's Day celebrations, an event that was duly recorded in the *Quebec Gazette.*[7]

Britain's victory over France in the Seven Years' War gave her a new colony — the province of Quebec. Its population of some 120,000 people, who were mainly French-speaking Roman Catholics, were the inhabitants of long-established communities, with their own distinctive language, culture, and religion.[8] They could not be expected to surrender their way of life willingly. Faced with this political reality, Britain allowed the French regime to continue largely unchanged. The French population was given the right to follow their traditional practices and laws and Quebec became the only place in the entire British Empire where Catholics and Protestants had equal status. This ruling gave Irish Catholics a safe haven and helps to explain why so many Irish ex-soldiers who had fought for France in the Seven Years' War decided to remain in Quebec. This was the one part of North America where Catholics could enjoy the benefits of the New World without suffering religious discrimination.

The influx from the United States that followed Britain's defeat in the American War of Independence, officially recognized by the Treaty of Paris in 1783, brought the next wave of Irish people to mid Canada. Known collectively as Loyalists, the Irish were among the refugees from the former British colonies who streamed out of the United States after the war ended. Many of them were so-called Ulster Presbyterians — people who could trace their ancestry back to the Scottish Lowlands.[9] Having left Ulster for North America starting in the early 1700s to escape religious discrimination in Ireland and benefit from the New World's enticing farming opportunities, they headed north in 1784 following Britain's defeat.[10] Deciding to stay under the umbrella of the devil they knew, they sought sanctuary in the remaining British-held colonies. Writing in the early nineteenth century, a visitor to the future Upper Canada noted the prevalence of Irish settlers, who came "chiefly from the Ulster counties of Down, Antrim, Londonderry, Tyrone and Donegal."[11]

Loyalist resettlement was carried out at the British government's expense, both for humanitarian reasons and to bolster British North America's population and defensive capabilities. A relatively small group of 5,000 or so Loyalists went to the old province of Quebec, with the overwhelming majority, some 35,000, being resettled in the Maritime region.[12] The Quebec Loyalists were sent initially to the military camps and garrisons being established at Sorel and Machiche (now Yamachiche), near Trois Rivières, and along the strategically important Richelieu River, notably at Chambly, St. Jean, Noyan, Foucault, and St. Armand (Map 3).[13] In 1775, American soldiers used the Richelieu to try to capture Montreal, and later travelled along the Chaudière River to lay siege to Quebec. Both assaults were thwarted.[14] Despite anxieties they may have had over future attacks, the authorities encouraged the Loyalists to move west when the war ended in 1783. They were granted land far afield in the vacant wilderness along the Upper St. Lawrence River, just to the west of the French seigneuries.[15] When, in 1791, the old province of Quebec was divided into Upper and Lower Canada, these holdings would be located in Upper Canada. Thus most of the original Quebec Loyalists ended up in Upper Canada.

Loyalists were allocated land in accordance with the British government's defence concerns. The St. Lawrence River, Lake Ontario, and

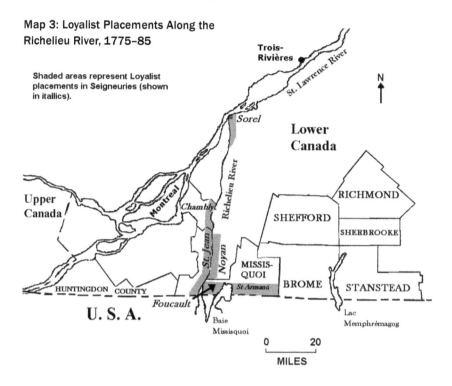

Map 3: Loyalist Placements Along the Richelieu River, 1775–85

Shaded areas represent Loyalist placements in Seigneuries (shown in itallics).

Niagara regions were all vitally important boundary areas that were considered vulnerable to attack from the United States. Priority was given initially to defending the St. Lawrence River territory. Ex-soldiers from the main regiments that had fought in the war were granted land between present-day Cornwall and Kingston. The main units were the King's Royal Regiment of New York (Royal Greens), the Butler's Rangers, Major Edward Jessop's Corps, the King's Rangers, the King's Loyal Americans, the Queen's Loyal Rangers, the Volunteers of Ireland,[16] and the Royal Highland Emigrants Regiment. The different units were allocated land in one or more of the eight adjacent townships that had been set aside, all having river frontages: Charlottenburg (Glengarry County), Cornwall and Osnabruck (Stormont County), Williamsburgh and Matilda (Dundas County), Edwardsburgh and Augusta (Grenville County), and Elizabethtown (Leeds County).[17] Five additional townships were laid out for the Loyalist units in the Bay of Quinte region at the eastern end of Lake Ontario (Map 4).[18]

Map 4: Loyalists in Upper Canada

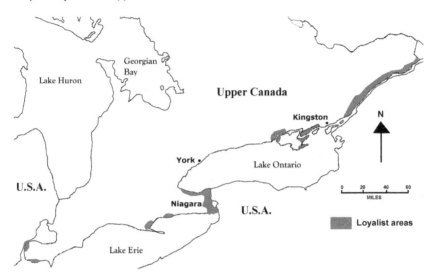

Having served in the King's Royal Regiment of New York, the largest of the Loyalist units, the Irish would have been allocated land in Glengarry, Stormont, and Dundas counties.[19] And having served also in the Jessop's Corps, they would have been allocated land in Grenville and Leeds counties.[20] Glengarry and the surrounding area later became a major Scottish Highland stronghold, thus making it an unlikely Irish destination. On the other hand, later census data reveals that a substantial Irish population became concentrated in Leeds and Grenville counties. No doubt, having been able to launch themselves in prime river locations from the late eighteenth century, they had an excellent base from which to attract followers.

Unlike the other units, the Volunteers of Ireland regiment was not allocated land in Upper Canada. Instead, its former soldiers obtained their land grants in Nova Scotia.[21] However, there is reason to believe that some may have settled in Lower Canada. Rawdon Township, north of Montreal, was named after Sir Francis Rawdon, the Irish lord who commanded the Volunteers of Ireland in the American War of Independence.[22] Although there was no question of any official allocations of land having been made, it looks as if some of the unit's ex-soldiers may have established a community that they named after their commanding officer. In 1832, Joseph Bouchette commented on the "few Irish immigrants" in Rawdon

Encampment of Loyalists at Johnston, on the banks of the St. Lawrence River, June 6, 1784. Watercolour by James Peachey. The principal Loyalist military leader was Sir John Johnson from the Mohawk Valley of New York, who commanded the King's Royal Regiment of New York.

"who have, without any legal authority, settled promiscuously in various parts."[23] Possibly they were traceable back to the ex-soldiers from this unit. As Catholics, it would certainly have suited them to settle in this area.[24]

Loyalists had a tough beginning. Most were unprepared for the extreme rigours of pioneer life. Because sites were chosen more for their military value rather than the fertility of the land, they often had to cope with poor farming prospects. Delays frequently occurred in administering land grants. Greatly disillusioned, some simply gave up and went back to the United States. Those who remained often sought a better location. Before long, Loyalists were moving westward along Lake Ontario to York (later Toronto) and beyond that to Niagara and the north side of Lake Erie (Map 4). All the while they were being joined by Americans who were crossing the border in search of land. This was not an expression of loyalty to Britain. Americans simply wanted to benefit from the free land grants.[25]

The British government welcomed the steady arrival of American colonists, since it was loath to see its own people lost to the North American colonies.[26] In any case, the war between Britain and France from 1793 to 1801 and the later Napoleonic Wars, which began in 1803 and ended in 1815, made transatlantic travel extremely hazardous and uninviting. As a consequence, much of Upper Canada's population growth before 1815 can be attributed to American immigration. By as early as 1799, American settlers had penetrated vast swathes of southwestern Upper Canada, becoming concentrated mainly in York, Wentworth, Lincoln, Welland, Norfolk, and Kent counties.[27] Judging from the fact that the population reached 71,000 in 1806, the influx must have been considerable, involving several thousand people.

While the Loyalist influx had strengthened Upper Canada defensively and provided its first immigrant communities, the situation in Lower Canada had been totally different. The authorities there had resisted pressure from Loyalists to settle, fearing that this would antagonize the resident French population. Lower Canada had a large and long-established French population, with its own religion, language, and land tenure system, and a way of life that had continued virtually unchanged since the British Conquest of 1763. While the French pressed for the status quo, Anglophone merchants had wanted British institutions and customs to be imposed on the French. They desired an elected assembly and wanted to see the end of the French seigneuries, which only allowed for tenancies rather than freeholds. This, the merchants argued, was harmful to the spirit of commercial enterprise that needed to develop. However, the merchants lost the argument, and with the passing of the Quebec Act of 1774, recognizing the right of the French to uphold their culture and seigneurial land tenure, life carried on as usual.[28] Co-operation had been won.

When the Americans attacked during the War of Independence, most French Canadians remained neutral, and during the War of 1812 they were staunch supporters of the British side.[29]

However, despite Governor Haldimand's misgivings, Loyalists were allowed to settle along the Richelieu River in three seigneuries: Foucault,[30] Noyan, and St. Armand. Foucault was owned by Major Henry Caldwell, an Irishman, while Noyan and St. Armand were under the control of English seigneurs.[31] This development suited Loyalists, who were desperate to find land, and would have been welcomed by the government as well. American forces had launched an attack along the Richelieu River in 1775 and might strike again. Haldimand reasoned that loyal settlers

Swiss-born Sir Frederick Haldimand was Quebec governor from 1778 to 1786. A military officer, he served in the British Army during the Seven Years' War and the American Revolutionary War.

could play an invaluable role in helping to safeguard this strategically important region of Lower Canada.

Major Caldwell's advertisement, which was published in the *Belfast Newsletter* in 1774, stressed the fertility of his land in the Foucault seigneury. Interested parties were asked to contact agents in Tyrone, Down, and Londonderry, Ulster counties that had historically lost people to the North American colonies. If sufficient numbers came forward, Caldwell would charter a ship to sail from Londonderry in the spring:

But no person need apply that has not a sufficiency to pay the usual passage to America, to set themselves up in a little way as farmers and maintain them[selves] for a year after their arrival, as before that time they will not be able to grow as much grain and potatoes as will support them: which will require a capital to each family of from £30 to £40, provisions of all kinds being cheap in that country.[32]

While mainly seeking affluent farmers, Caldwell also indicated that he would offer employment to a few labourers, "who can be well recommended," such as a millwright and a blacksmith. Census data reveals that Caldwell's Manor had a substantial Irish-Protestant population in 1851, suggesting that his earlier recruitment efforts had been successful. The Irish Catholics who were living in the nearby seigneuries of Sabrevois and Monnoir by the 1830s were unlikely to have had any connection with Caldwell's scheme, since it targeted Ulster Protestants.[33]

Accustomed to the egalitarian ideals of the New World, Loyalists would have preferred freeholds, but accepted seigneurial land out of necessity.[34] Facing economic hardship and a shortage of land on which to settle, they grabbed what they could. Happily for them, the situation soon changed in their favour. With the creation of the Lower Canada Assembly in 1791, new townships were opened up around the existing seigneuries.[35] This was a major shift in policy. It provided freehold tenure to Loyalists and the many New Englanders who flocked across the border, as well as to later immigrants. It also laid the foundations for the future colonization of the vast stretches of the Eastern Townships.

Although Loyalists were initially unwelcome in much of Quebec, a concerted effort had been made to establish small numbers of them well to the north in the very remote Gaspé Peninsula. Its strategic location at the entrance to the St. Lawrence River made it a prime defensive site. With this in mind, and having received favourable reports about the Gaspé's farming and fishing opportunities, Governor Haldimand had arranged for around 400 Loyalists to be sent to the north side of Baie-des-Chaleurs, along the border between Lower Canada and New Brunswick (Map 5).[36] Most settled in the area between Pointe au Maquereau (Point Mackerel)

Map 5: Loyalists in the Gaspé Peninsula

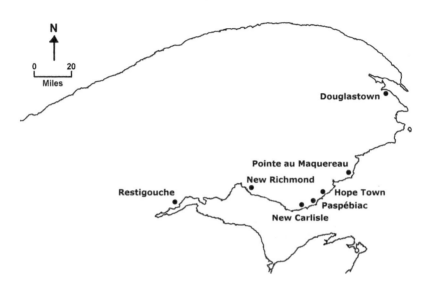

The United Empire Loyalists' postage stamp introduced in 1934. Loyalists were later known as United Empire Loyalists in recognition of their loyalty to the Crown after the British defeat.

and Restigouche, with the largest concentrations developing initially in and around Paspébiac (near New Carlisle).[37] Some Loyalists joined small, already-established communities at New Richmond and Restigouche, while the Paspébiac colonists went on to found another community on the east side of the peninsula that they called Douglastown. Later, Douglastown would become predominately Irish, but this was due to a late-nineteenth-century influx of fishery workers.[38]

A larger-than-life character from Cork by the name of William Willcocks tried unsuccessfully in 1792 to lead a group of Irish settlers to a prime site in Whitby Township (Ontario County) that had been granted to him by the government. Britain's war with France in the following year and various bureaucratic bungles meant that he lost what few settlers he had been able to recruit to the United States.[39] Hugh Hovel Farmar, a Cork merchant, also had great plans that came to nothing. He intended to assist Irish Catholics to relocate to Upper Canada in 1794, but failed to secure the backing of the British government, which largely ignored him. Farmar offered to recruit settlers and organize their transport but was met with a wall of silence.[40] Seven years later, Thomas Douglas, fifth Earl of Selkirk, also tried to steer the British government into supporting a scheme for assisting Irish Catholics to relocate to Upper Canada, but he, too, was rebuffed.[41]

At this stage, emigration was regarded as being detrimental to Britain's interests and there was no question of public funds being provided to assist it. However, the government had a rude shock when it nearly lost Canada to the United States in the hard-fought War of 1812–14. Such were its defence concerns after this that the previously unthinkable idea of using public funds to subsidize emigration suddenly became official policy.

A gentleman farmer, Robert Baldwin, did not seek financial assistance when he relocated to Upper Canada in 1798. Also from Cork and a neighbour of Hugh Farmar, he got the shock of his life when he reached his destination. Possibly Farmar had given him an over-optimistic account of what to expect. His first impressions were terrible:

> At night they [Baldwin and his family] crossed the Bay
> of Toronto arriving at the celebrated town [of York] and
> finding it composed of a dozen or so houses — a dreary
> dismal place — not even possessing the characteristics
> of a village. There was no church or schoolhouse or in
> fact any of the ordinary signs of civilization, but being in
> fact a mere settlement.[42]

Robert Baldwin had imagined that he would see the bustling town of York, but instead found a wilderness. Not realizing how primitive conditions would be, he had brought his family "without properly arranging for their comfort." Home was going to be "a small log hut with a bark roof and a chimney made of sticks and clay."[43] As Baldwin would discover the hard way, early arrivals had to improvise and withstand unspeakable hardships on their way to becoming successful farmers.

Settlers from the United States continued to stream into Upper Canada during the 1790s, having been encouraged by Lieutenant Colonel John Graves Simcoe, the first lieutenant governor. In his grand design for the province, Simcoe fervently believed that Americans could be persuaded to show allegiance to Britain. This was a naïve and vain hope. Wedded to egalitarian ideals, Americans had little time for the elitist and class-based ways of the mother country. They certainly did not wish to have the feudal constraints of the Old World imposed upon them.

Meanwhile, as Upper Canada wrestled with its land policy and road-building program, problems of a more serious nature were brewing. Defended by only a few regular soldiers and having a mainly American population whose loyalty to Britain was doubtful, Upper Canada was attacked by the United States in 1812. Thanks to its small but efficient army, and having control over the St. Lawrence River, Great Lakes, and coastal waters, Britain was able to defeat American forces in 1814. Crucially, the Lower Canada Assembly had voted funds for the British military and raised a 6,000-strong militia.[44]

On a positive note, the War of 1812 had brought men like Lieutenant James Prendergast to Upper Canada. Having served in the 99th Regiment of Foot, he obtained a land grant in Clarendon Township (Pontiac County) in the Ottawa Valley and later went on to persuade some of his fellow soldiers to join him.[45] Possibly, like him, they were Irishmen who had been born in County Monaghan. John Woolsey, whose father had arrived from Armagh shortly after the British Conquest of New France, served in the Militia during the War of 1812 and later became one of Quebec's leading merchants.[46] Many other Irishmen would be quick to spot Canada's economic potential and, after establishing themselves in business, play their part in public service.

The War of 1812–14 left Upper and Lower Canada with a clearer sense of their own identity; it also made them more wary of the continuing threat they faced from their republican neighbours. The war had demonstrated the importance of holding fast to the British tie for protection and it also identified the folly of relying mainly on American immigration to grow the population. Both lessons had been learned. There was an obvious need to encourage immigration from Britain and Ireland.

Atlantic Canada had received the first wave of immigrants, but, as mid Canada's much better land and job opportunities became widely known and transport facilities improved, Upper and Lower Canada became the preferred destinations. The Irish arrived in Upper Canada in increasing numbers from the 1820s although they had been taking up city jobs in Lower Canada long before this. Arriving in Quebec City and Montreal in appreciable numbers from the late eighteenth century, they soon moved to nearby rural areas to establish themselves in farming. Settling on seigniorial land, alongside the long-established French-Canadian population, they founded distinctive Irish communities. Although there were language differences and they could not purchase land, many shared a common religion with the local inhabitants. This was the one part of British North America where being Roman Catholic was not a disadvantage.

CHAPTER 3

༄

Quebec City and Rural Areas to the North and South

In the Laurentides, the poor soil could only be tackled by people who had no fear of hardship — the Irish or the French.... Between 1820 and 1830 a garland of Irish settlements festooned the southern rim of the region. At Stoneham, Valcartier and Lake Beauport little colonies of people originating from Ireland were established; in 1820 they spilled over from Valcartier into Fossambault, where they founded Ste. Catherine [-de-la-Jacques-Cartier] the first parish in the Laurentides (1832) and thence they spread [west] towards St. Raymond.[1]

The "garland of Irish settlements" described so eloquently by the French geographer Raoul Blanchard was situated north of Quebec City, some distance beyond the French-Canadian settlements that lined the St. Lawrence River bank. The Irish first arrived around 1820 and, following their early success, attracted family and friends to join them over a period of some thirty years. This pattern was repeated again when Irish settlers occupied vacant land on the south side of Quebec City behind the long-settled French communities that lined the riverside (Map 6).

With the building of colonization roads these areas had suddenly become accessible to immigrants. However, this, too, was a short-lived influx. Few Irish arrived in Lower Canada after the mid-nineteenth century, and many left the region as the better opportunities to be had in Upper Canada and the United States became more widely known.

The Irish settled in large numbers north and south of Quebec City despite having to rent land from a feudal seigneur. The seigneurial land tenure system barred settlers from ever owning their own land. And, while Irish Catholics benefited from living in a part of British North America where their religion was tolerated, the opposite was true for Irish Protestants. They were outsiders. Yet, regardless of having to rent land and live among people who spoke a different language, and in some cases followed a different religion, the Irish came to the Quebec region in large numbers. The motivation was financial. The prospect of settling within the hinterland of Quebec City, where jobs in the timber trade and shipbuilding were plentiful, where the land was fertile and where a market for goods was readily available, proved irresistible. Thus, for economic reasons, the region north and south of Quebec City attracted many Irish people, irrespective of their religion.

Large areas of uncultivated land within Quebec City's hinterland remained unsettled by the turn of the nineteenth century. French-Canadian farmers were nowhere to be found in some areas because the land had never been made available to them. Some of it was Crown land that had formerly been the property of the Catholic Church. Some of it had been granted to disbanded British and Irish soldiers who failed to settle on it and grasp its opportunities. In some cases seigneuries were being used by their owners as bases for country pursuits and to further business interests. Few had any interest in attracting settlers. Thus vacant land in prime locations that could be rented on reasonable terms and conditions was theirs for the asking. It just needed someone to organize the first settlement. John Neilson,[2] a businessman and politician, told the Select Committee on the Civil Government of Canada, which met in 1828, how he, working together with two Quebec City lawyers, had been that someone.

In 1816, Neilson, together with Andrew Stewart and Louis Moquin, his business partners, purchased a large quantity of seigneurial land from the

John Neilson (1776–1848), photographed circa 1840, was a businessman and politician. A Scot, he became editor of the bilingual *Quebec Gazette* at the age of twenty-one and held this post for fifty years. He was active politically for much of his life and latterly became the Quebec County representative in the Legislative Assembly, formed after the Lower and Upper Canada rebellions of 1837–1838.

Crown. It was located beyond the French-Canadian communities "at the back of the people by whom I am elected." Having been owned formerly by the Jesuits, who had never developed it, it was a huge swathe of wilderness "lying in a lump." The fact that it was a continuous stretch of land, in what is now Quebec County, was crucially important to Neilson, since he realized that potential colonizers would wish to transplant themselves as whole communities. As Neilson pointed out, the primary aim of a newly arrived immigrant was to settle close to a friendly face: "He has his sixteenth cousin or somebody from the same parish or neighbourhood, and from whom he has heard by letter, and he goes and sits down beside them if possible." However, the location was considered to be "too much to the north" and "we could not get anybody from the vicinity to commence the settlement."[3]

Neilson employed three Americans to undertake the initial forest clearing and "the moment that opening was made there came people from

Scotland and England and we gave them lots and they settled on the land likewise and now that settlement and vicinity contains about 500 souls. They are all Scotch or Irish, with perhaps a few English and one or two Americans." Neilson also gave population figures for "the Protestant settlements" but gave no details of the Roman Catholic numbers.[4] As other evidence indicates, the settlers were primarily Irish and a good many were Roman Catholics. No doubt, appreciating the British government's preference for Protestants, Neilson was dodging the truth. Three years later, as if to counter negative propaganda concerning the rising number of Irish Catholics in Quebec City, he wrote this piece in the *Quebec Gazette*: "Numbers of Irish have remained in the towns of Quebec and Montreal, where many of them are thriving and their general conduct, far from being exceptional, leaves little doubt but that they will prove peaceable and useful citizens of their adopted country."[5]

In the end, Neilson claimed that he had been "more instrumental in introducing people from Europe than anybody else in Lower Canada" and "has been the cause of upwards of 1,000 of these persons being settled in the county which I represent [Quebec] and in the adjoining county [Portneuf]."[6]

While he had sought to recruit English, Scottish, and Irish immigrants, only the Irish responded in significant numbers. It seems that the prospect of starting a new life in an isolated northern wilderness made sense to the Irish, but was unpalatable to the English and Scots. As Raoul Blanchard pointed out, they were people "who had no fear of hardships."[7] The Irish responded to the challenge and turned to each other for support. Knowledge of the region's economic potential was spread through grapevines in Ireland and Quebec. Funds to pay for ship crossings were raised both by the immigrants themselves and friends and families who had already settled in Lower Canada. There were no government-funded colonization schemes and no one organized their settlements when they arrived. The Irish planned and executed these colonization projects themselves. At the beginning of the nineteenth century they mainly came from the north of Ireland and were for the most part Protestant farmers. However, beginning in the mid-1830s most were Roman Catholic labourers who originated from the south and west of Ireland.[8]

Alexander Buchanan, the Quebec immigration agent, provides irrefutable evidence that the Irish were the region's principal colonizers.[9] In 1832 he reported that the communities forming "on the north side of the St. Lawrence and in the district and vicinity of Quebec, are the settlements of Beauport, Stoneham, Tewkesbury, Valcartier, Jacques Cartier, Deschambault, and Portneuf [, which] are principally Irish."[10] And he also noted, "their settlements are thriving."[11] He went on to report that the new settlements that were forming on the south side of the St. Lawrence were "principally Irish," and he singled out Lotbinière County as a place where "proprietors are offering encouragement."[12] The 1851 Census would later confirm Buchanan's assessment that this was a major Irish influx.

The Irish possessed the necessary networking and money-raising skills to actually get themselves to these areas. Once early footholds had been established, they attracted followers from their part of Ireland. This co-operative spirit produced distinctive communities that could take strength from a shared culture and social values. Those Irish, who arrived in large numbers in the 1830s and 1840s, had access to a scheme that enabled them to finance their ship crossings. They used a remittance system whereby their family and friends who had already settled in Canada forwarded them the required funds. In 1832, Alexander Buchanan noted how "the working emigrants of the last and preceding seasons find opportunities to get transmitted their little earnings to the United Kingdom to aid their friends coming out to join them."

Ten years later, Alexander Buchanan, nephew of the earlier Alexander, reported "the remarkable feature in the immigration of the past year has been the very large proportion [of Irish] who have come out to their relations. I estimate it at a full three-fourths of the whole."[13] Over the years, millions of pounds and dollars crossed the Atlantic eastward following major Irish settlement in North America.

Between 1820 and 1850 a steady stream of farmers, tradesmen, and labourers, who originated initially from the north of Ireland and later the south, headed for Portneuf, Quebec, and Montmorency counties on the north side of the St. Lawrence and Lotbinière and Dorchester counties on the south, turning parts of them into major Irish enclaves (Map 6). Some came as urban dwellers and later established themselves in farming. Being very poor, they needed jobs in the city to accumulate funds to enable them to make this transition. Some new arrivals opted for full-time employment as lumberjacks while others acquired land with the intention of supplementing their farming income from seasonal employment in the lumber camps.

Map 6: Irish Communities to the North and South of Quebec City, 1851

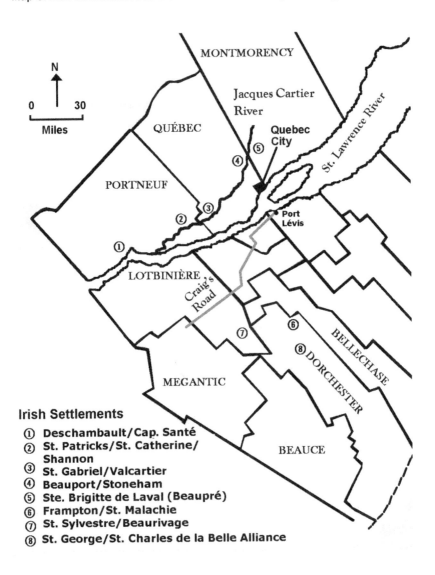

Irish Settlements

① **Deschambault/Cap. Santé**
② **St. Patricks/St. Catherine/Shannon**
③ **St. Gabriel/Valcartier**
④ **Beauport/Stoneham**
⑤ **Ste. Brigitte de Laval (Beaupré)**
⑥ **Frampton/St. Malachie**
⑦ **St. Sylvestre/Beaurivage**
⑧ **St. George/St. Charles de la Belle Alliance**

The rapid growth in the St. Lawrence timber trade brought afford-able and regular sea crossings within the grasp of the average immigrant. Following the large increases in tariffs that had been levied on European timber during the Napoleonic Wars, Canadian timber had a consider-able cost advantage and the trade with Ireland soared.[14] Now, as news filtered back to Ireland of the good farming opportunities to be had in mid-Canada, the Irish made their way to the fledgling communities that had been established by their family and friends. They arrived in the timber ships that regularly plied between Ireland and Quebec. Ships that had collected timber at Quebec returned to Ireland and often came back to Quebec with immigrants on board. The timber trade was the driving force behind local economies in Canada, and for the poor it provided the means to earn money to purchase land. It offered diverse employment opportunities and was often a vital component of an immigrant's livelihood.

With its thriving timber trade and shipbuilding industry, Quebec expanded rapidly in the early nineteenth century. Having arrived at the port, many Irish people went no farther. Greatly outnumbering the English and Scots, there were said to be 1,000 English-speaking Roman Catholics in Quebec City in 1819, most of whom would have been Irish. In 1830 they accounted for 7,000 people out of a total population of 32,000. They settled near the port in the Lower Town and usually found work in the nearby shipyards and on the wharves.[15]

Alexander Buchanan was struck by "the well-dressed appearance of the vast body of Irish servants and labouring classes that attended the Reverend Mr. McMahon's church on Sunday, some of whom, perhaps only a few months previous, landed with scarcely a shoe to their foot."[16]

Despite encountering sustained opposition from the city's French inhabitants, who tried to stop the Irish from building their own church, Saint Patrick's appeared in 1833 with a remit to serve all English-speaking Catholics in the city, regardless of where they lived.[17] In 1861 the Irish numbered more than 13,000, representing nearly a quarter of the entire urban population.[18] By this time, fears were being expressed that Quebec was fast becoming "an Irish colony."[19] However, with the decline in shipbuilding and the downturn in the port's economic

St. Patrick's Catholic Church, McMahon Street, Quebec City, circa 1910. The church was built in 1832 on a street named after Father Patrick McMahon, the parish's first pastor. Lying within the walls of the old city, it was replaced in 1914 by a larger church built on Grande Allée. This was demolished in 1988 and replaced by the current smaller church on De Salaberry Avenue.

activities in the mid-nineteenth century, Irish immigration slowed to a trickle and many of the Irish already living in the city left in pursuit of better jobs elsewhere.

The Irish influx to the region north of Quebec City owes much to John Neilson's colonizing zeal. Initially, he sought to entice settlers to take up farming in places where, through neglect, cultivation had not commenced. Acquiring Stoneham Township and possibly also Valcartier Township, which had both been earmarked for British and Irish ex-soldiers, he sought settlers, since much of the land was unoccupied.[20] Valcartier's land had been granted to disbanded soldiers in 1816 and Stoneham's in 1824. It was hoped that ex-soldiers would establish communities, but, as often happened, few had accepted the challenge. This meant that both places had a great deal of vacant land.[21]

In 1828, John Neilson was able to report that Valcartier had acquired 100 Presbyterians "in communion with the Church of Scotland" and five years later it had enough Church of England adherents to build an Anglican Church.[22] While this suggests that it had a substantial number of Scottish and English settlers at this time, Valcartier was principally Irish in 1851. St. Gabriel seigneury, which incorporated Valcartier by then, had 387 Irish-born and only 67 Scottish-born residents. Most of its 825 Canadian-born, non-French residents were likely to have been of Irish descent. In other words, St. Gabriel's population of 1,397 must have had a considerable Irish component. Nearby Stoneham, then known as St. Edmond, was fundamentally Irish and French, with the Irish greatly outnumbering the French.[23] St. Gabriel had roughly equal numbers of Protestants and Catholics, while Stoneham's population was predominately Catholic.[24]

While Neilson succeeded in attracting many Irish and some Scottish people to both townships, his influence went far beyond this. His primary achievement was in encouraging colonizers to settle in the vast stretch of wilderness land located behind the French-Canadian communities on the north side of the St. Lawrence. The area encompassed Portneuf, Quebec, and Montmorency counties, but to begin with Neilson concentrated on Quebec County. Having signed up mainly Irish settlers for this county, he encouraged a seigneur in Portneuf County to do the same. What resulted was a large but thinly spread Irish enclave that initially had both Catholics and Protestants but later was entirely Catholic. In 1879 Quebec's Irish Catholics would complain that because their forefathers had found it necessary to spread themselves across three counties, they were effectively a minority group in each of them, thus being denied adequate representation in the Legislative Assembly of Quebec.[25]

When John Neilson and his business partners offered land to settlers in the St. Gabriel seigneury in Quebec County in 1819, they had an immediate response from Irish farmers, many of whom were probably from Ulster.[26] In most cases the petitioners were fully aware of the background.[27] Bernard McKanty's request made that year was typical: "That your petitioner is informed that there is a considerable tract of good land which is ungranted in the seigneury of St. Gabriel on the north eastern side up the river Jacques Cartier in the rear of the lands of John Neilson and Andrew Stewart Esquires."[28] Describing themselves as farmers, men such as John O'Neil and his brother James, Edward Kearney, Patrick O'Hara, Joseph Pierce, John Malone, and William Corrigan each requested ninety to 200 acres, often specifying a preferred location.[29]

That same year Richard Angus Newman and Peter Guinan requested lots that were close together, while Peter asked for "an adjacent plot" for his brother-in-law. A year later, M. Macnamara, having been granted land in St. Gabriel, "asks to have lots granted to his sons close to the lot he was granted in his initial petition." Some, like Thomas McMillan, requested a second parcel of land five years after first arriving "as he understands that the lands in these concessions are not all granted as yet. He has a wife and six children and has been in Valcartier upward of six years."[30] George Reynar requested two lots of 180 acres each, adding that he is "approved of by the present settlers and is acting a schoolmaster in the settlement."[31]

Arriving in 1822, Jeremiah Rickaby described himself as a member of a family that emigrated from Ireland in 1817, "bringing with them ... testimonials for character and conduct from the most highly respected sources in their own country which documents may be produced if required." In the light of these documents, and his good behaviour since coming to Quebec, he requested land in St. Gabriel.

In 1828, Edward Glover, from County Meath, wrote that he wished "to settle on a portion of the Jesuit's land near Valcartier. He has a wife and eight children, some of whom are boys and have the means to enable him to improve the land and he seeks a grant of two hundred acres." Three years later, John Stewart provided a testimonial as to his good conduct "signed by Mr. Harding, Minister of St. Andrew's Church," while Thomas Wright appended a note of recommendation, stating "that he had worked for eight years as a farmer and was a sober and industrious worker."[32]

Some petitioners, like Thomas Anderson and Michael Collins, requested lots on the west side of the Jacques Cartier River along the nearby River aux Pins. "Hearing that there are some lots of unceded land between the river Jacques Cartier and the River aux Pins," Thomas Lander requested "three or four plots of good land at the nearest place," adding that he had six children, "five of whom are able to assist with the cultivation of land." Joseph Kinwell, who resided in River aux Pins, asked for a more favourable plot that was less swampy than the one he had. Michael Collins, who described himself as "a poor man with a large family," said that he was disappointed with the land he had been granted in River aux Pins and hoped for a better lot.[33] And so it went on. The petitioners were well organized and well informed and knew exactly what to expect and how to further their interests.

Meanwhile, as the Irish settlements in St. Gabriel were taking shape, English immigrants founded the Waterloo settlement in nearby Beauport seigneury in 1816. Clearly feeling bullish about Britain's victory over Napoleon at the Battle of Waterloo the previous year, their settlement attracted "with few exceptions, English, Scotch and Irish" people. They included merchants, tradesmen, and labourers and, those "who could not handle the axe" found work in Quebec City.[34] It was a largely Irish community in 1851, by which time it was known more appropriately as St. Dunstan de Lac Beauport.

John Neilson was also the driving force behind another Irish settlement which was located to the west of St. Gabriel in Gaudarville seigneury (Portneuf County). His report to the Select Committee in 1828 referred to "a large Irish settlement called St. Patrick's to the north of Quebec [City] that is contiguous to the one that we made [in St. Gabriel], the lands belonging to a Canadian seigneur. It rose in consequence of our settlement; we were the first that penetrated the swamps at the back of the seigneuries and opened the settlement; that gave them an idea that the thing could go on, because our people seemed prosperous."[35]

Joseph Bouchette sheds more light on these "new settlements" by quoting from a report given by Lieutenant Colonel Duchesnay, the proprietor, to the House of Assembly in 1823:

> These settlements mostly of Irish emigrants were commenced in October, 1820." A total of 232 grants were made, there are about 225 residents (about 80 children) and about 70 or 80 people are employed as labourers. "Very few of the settlers had any capital to begin with, most of them had hardly anything; they were therefore obliged to overcome the difficulties incident to new settlements and

the want of capital by great privation, extreme economy,
occasionally labouring for money to provide provisions,
working industriously while provided and when unpro-
vided repeating the same means — During the summer
many of the settlers obtained employment as tradesmen
or labourers in the king's [public] works in Quebec.[36]

Irish settlers were assisted by Duchesnay and charitable societies in
Quebec City, which helped them by advancing provisions, building roads,
and providing employment. Another bonus was that no rents were payable
for four years.[37] Duchesnay's apparent benevolence helps to explain the
appeal of seigneurial tenure to newly-arrived immigrants. Many would
have welcomed the prospect of living under the stewardship of a proprietor with capital who could build houses, barns, roads, mills, and public
buildings. Although they could not purchase their own land, settlers at
least had a secure base and better living conditions than would be available in some isolated clearing in a wilderness. Thus, for all of its faults, the
seigneurial system, in the right circumstances, was a spur to settlement.

St. Patrick's was part of Ste. Catherine-de-la-Jacques-Cartier parish
by 1832.[38] Twenty years later just over 60 percent of its population was
Irish-born or had Irish ancestry and virtually all were Roman Catholics.[39]
It was renamed Shannon in 1948. Fifty years later just under half of
Shannon's 1,850 residents could still trace their Irish ancestry back to the
early settlers who were said to have originated from counties Kilkenny,
Wexford, and Carlow. Reports lingered of difficult times when many of
the men had worked in lumber camps during the winter to supplement
their farming income.[40]

In addition to building up the numbers in their St. Patrick's settlement,
the Irish also colonized areas to the west of it. Alexander Buchanan, the
Quebec immigration agent reported in 1831 that Irish immigrants were
heading for Deschambault (Portneuf County); but it is clear from the 1851
Census that they had not remained.[41] Judging from the fact that there were
157 Irish, 54 Scots, and 31 English living in nearby Cap Santé at this time,
the likelihood is that the early settlers had merely relocated themselves
a short distance away to the east.[42] Nevertheless, they only represented a

Wolfe's Cove at Anse au Foulon near Sillery, Quebec City. Watercolour, painted in the nineteenth century by an unknown artist. It shows cargoes of timber being assembled for export and shipbuilding. Many of those employed in loading timber into the ships that were bound for the British Isles were Irish.

tiny proportion of the population in 1851, suggesting that their presence had been fleeting.

Years later, when Reverend E.M.W. Templeman wrote in 1908 about "the rising settlement of Irish Protestants" in his Anglican congregation at Bourg Louis, about ten miles west of St. Catherine, he was referring to a minority of the total population. "This is a place of magnificent distances with only a few English-speaking people here and there and I try to reach them once a month — "12 miles there and back."[43] However, he could not halt the declining numbers. "Soon the Englishman will become as distinct as the dove in the province of Quebec. Everything is French, I even find myself thinking in French — let alone having to speak it at every shop and office ... the poor old English Church is merely an exotic here."[44] The fact was that most of the Reverend Templeman's congregation had long since left for either the United States or Ontario.

John Neilson's influence could also be felt in the Beaupré seigneury in Montmorency County (Map 6). The Quebec Seminary,[45] its proprietor, sought Irish immigrants to settle its land in 1830 but having failed to provide an adequate road system or gristmill, progress was very slow. A later resident remembered that "when my grandfather Willie Jennings came to Laval [in 1840], it was as if you went into a bush. There was only a footpath from Beauport. He had to clear [trees] to build a camp and a log house twenty two by twenty two [feet]."[46]

John O'Shea arrived from Ireland in 1830, and Thomas Fleming, Thomas Dunn, Michael Hanley, Philip Quinn, James Britton, Patrick Dooley, and James Gillany came in the following year.[47] A further nine Irish families arrived each year between 1834 and 1836. At this stage, the Lac Beauport priest was able to report that Ste. Brigitte de Laval (Beaupré seigneury) was inhabited by Catholics "de la langue anglaise."[48] Small numbers of families continued to arrive until the 1850s, with the most prominent being the Dawson family whose chosen area of settlement produced a "Dawsontown."[49] These developments occurred despite the apparent unwillingness of the Quebec Seminary to provide even the most basic facilities such as a road and a mill.

The first Irish settlers found that little or no preparation had been made for them by their seigneur. The Quebec government was petitioned in 1831 for a grant of £700 to construct a road, on the basis that it would enable 400 lots to be granted out to poor Irish immigrants. The money was provided, and after the completion of the road that year the Irish moved in, followed by a few French Canadians who came from Quebec City.[50] However, the community lacked a gristmill, and this was still the case ten years later when forty five Irish families made this request:

We are experiencing many and severe hardships, for want of having a Grist Mill in our district: in all cases without exception we are necessitated to bring our grain to the Quebec Market and, for its produce, purchase oatmeal.

We are suffering for want of a consecrated cemetery, being at all times under the necessity of bringing our Dead to repose in the cemetery at Beauport, being sometimes a distance of eighteen miles.[51]

Later on, a resident would recall "my aunt telling me that they had to carry their market [produce] to the city. There were no horses. She said they finally got one horse. The neighbours took turns using it. On market-day they would load the horse and they walked to the city."[52] Life was a never-ending struggle and only the toughest and bravest of people could have endured this immigrants' nightmare.

The Irish pioneers of Ste. Brigitte suffered appalling conditions. That Quebec priests should treat their fellow human beings so badly seems hard to explain. The likelihood is that the Quebec Seminary had been pressurized into accepting Irish immigrants to settle on its seigneurial lands by the Quebec government, which, at the time, was anxious to expand the province's economy and farming output. Even though they were Roman Catholic, the Irish may not have been welcome. A hint of the tensions which may have been felt between Ste. Brigitte's French and Irish inhabitants can be seen in the recollection of a later resident: "There were very few French people when I was young and the Irish just wouldn't have them." Another Irish resident remembered that a French inhabitant recalled the poverty the Irish suffered, the fact that they were "good Catholics" and that they "reached for the sky" but they should not be "shown the bottle."[53]

Having experienced a large increase in its Irish population during the 1850's, Ste. Brigitte lost many of its Irish in the following decade and as it did, the French moved in.[54] While its population had been 60 percent Irish in 1851, ten years later the Irish only accounted for 30 percent of the population. A decline in the fortunes of the timber trade and shipbuilding was the last straw and the Irish left *en masse* to find better opportunities elsewhere, particularly in the United States.[55] Thus, despite sharing the same religion as their French neighbours, many of the Irish moved on and those who remained were assimilated into French communities.

The Irish immigrant story north of Quebec City had been nothing less than a virtual takeover of three adjoining counties. The influx to areas south of the city was more tightly focused. The catalyst was the completion of the Craig's Road in 1810 allowing access to the fertile farmlands south of the St. Lawrence (Map 6).[56] Being within striking distance of Quebec City, settlers could benefit from its rapidly expanding timber trade and shipbuilding enterprises. This was yet another prime site for enterprising immigrants. From the 1820s Irish immigrants had Frampton and St. Malachie (Dorchester County) and nearby St. Sylvestre (Lotbinière County) within their sights (Map 6).

Alexander Buchanan, the Quebec immigration agent, first reported happenings in Frampton in 1831. The lands, he said, "are nearly occupied and considerable settlement has extended into Cranbourne [south of Frampton] the seigneury of St. Mary's [Ste. Marie de Beauce] and along the Kennebec [colonization] Road" which linked Beauce with Maine.[57] His handbook, produced in the following year indicated that "the population is principally Irish."[58] To reach Frampton, settlers had to travel along the Craig's Road to Ste. Marie de Beauce and then make use of newly constructed roads to reach the Etchemin River area. Meanwhile, the influx of Irish settlers to nearby St. Sylvestre in Lotbinière County also caught Buchanan's eye. He noted that its proprietor was "offering encouragement."[59]

Having had its land granted to disbanded soldiers by the government after the War of 1812, Frampton Township was yet another example of an area near Quebec City that had vacant farming land waiting to be grabbed by immigrants looking for a prime location. Gilbert Henderson, a former officer, owned land on the east side of the Etchemin River and by acquiring lots from his brother and other demobilized soldiers, who were not interested in settling, he took control of what became known as East Frampton, better known later as St. Malachie. And Pierre-Edouard Desbarats, who purchased soldiers' lots on the west side of the river, assumed control of what would become known as West Frampton.[60] St. Malachie mainly attracted Irish Catholics while West Frampton's Irish settlers included a substantial number of Protestants.

Having become seigneur of St. Malachie in 1814, Henderson recruited Irish Catholics to settle on his lands but, according to Joseph Bouchette, they only arrived in substantial numbers in 1823.[61] Among the early arrivals were Timothy Connell, James Sheehey, Patrick Cahill, Peter Lyons, Magnus Murphy, Patrick Curtain, John Wilson, Thomas Fitzgerald, and James Kennedy, who were followed in around 1830 by Patrick Doyle, Michael Quigley, George Smith, John Rutherford, James Scott, James Corrigan, Patrick Hayes, Charles Harper, John Dillon, and M. Kilcullen. According to Father Jules-Adrien Kirouac, who was the parish priest of St. Malachie in 1908, the later arrivals had originated from counties Armagh, Limerick, Tipperary, and Antrim.[62] The Irish lots were named Ballyporreen and, given that this was the name of a village in County Tipperary, it is reasonable to assume that many settlers had originated from Tipperary.[63]

St. Malachie's population was just over 100 in 1832, while West Frampton had a smaller population at this time, having "sixty houses but no village." In other words, the houses were scattered widely. St. Malachie had "many tradesmen particularly masons, bricklayers and joiners who in most instances work all summer in Quebec while their families look after their farms." Both St. Malachie and West Frampton had populations with former "shoemakers, weavers, cattle doctors, wheelwrights, blacksmiths and other mechanics." Joseph Bouchette noted approvingly that "the House of Assembly has wisely contributed sums of money for the purposes of opening new roads and the erection of a bridge over the Etchemin [River]."[64]

The settlers' first houses were little more than flimsy log cabins dotted across tree-covered landscapes in a higgledy-piggledy fashion. In a journey through Frampton in the early 1830s, George Jehoshaphat Mountain, Archdeacon of Lower Canada, caught a glimpse of the really primitive housing conditions that were the norm at this time. One settler "had built his house not upon, but against a rock, a huge mass of stone forming one end of his dwelling, against which he makes his fire, which, when the whole face of the mass is heated, protects him against the most intense cold."[65] In a second visit, made in 1837, he described the first shanty, then the later, better-built, house of the Reverend Knight:

> The walls of the principal room were formed of upright trunks of trees, smoothed off in front, but with the left bark adhering to them at the edge. The floor was composed of rough boards laid loosely together, and the ceiling was in the same unfinished condition … close by the side of it is a hovel in the form of a shed, of which the elevation at the highest side of it is seven feet and a half, built of round logs with the bark on, with the rough edges projecting where they cross each other at the corners. Here the pastor dwelt before the erection of his present house.[66]

The roads were no better. Where they existed, they were often dreadful. Travelling through Frampton in 1833, Father O'Grady found it almost impossible to get to people's houses "due to the bad state of the roads. The roads in these townships surpass any description. I really do not know if they should be called roads or rather paths, very badly marked out, many of which a horse never passed through or very seldom a man on foot."[67]

As happened elsewhere in Lower Canada, the Irish presence in Frampton was short-lived. As they began to leave in the mid-nineteenth century in search of better locations, the French arrived in increasing numbers. Once again, Irish settlements became French settlements. In 1911, the French outnumbered the Irish in Frampton by a factor of three.[68] Looking back, Frampton's Irish population in 1851 had included Protestants but they were in the minority. Yet, before this, Frampton once had a substantial proportion of Protestants. According to John Neilson it had 100 Presbyterians in 1828.[69] Given that Frampton's Irish inhabitants had petitioned for funds three years earlier claiming to have thirty-three households, the total population was probably no more than 200 at this time.[70] Be that as it may, it was the Irish Anglicans who became the dominant Protestant group. Building Christ Church Anglican Church in 1836–37 at Springbrook Village in West Frampton, they made their services available to other Protestant

Christ Church at Springbrook Village near Frampton, which was built by Irish Anglicans in 1836–37. The remaining Irish families, who left Frampton in 1952, planted forget-me-nots around the church to symbolize their devotedness to this community.

denominations, including Presbyterians and Lutherans. In 1825, ten Irish Anglican families were said to be living in Springbrook, and in 1865 it had thirty-nine Anglican households.[71]

The last word in the Frampton story must surely go to Martin Murphy, who led his extended family together with thirty-nine other Irish families from Frampton to Missouri in the 1840s. After an arduous and dangerous journey of 2,500 miles, they reached their new location, re-established themselves, and flourished.[72] Described by John Maguire as "the gallant leader" who died "at a grand old age, the founder of a prosperous race," he epitomizes the Irish story.[73] The Irish never gave up and kept trying to find somewhere better to settle, irrespective of the hurdles and hardships.

This now familiar pattern of Irish immigrants establishing communities near Quebec City, only to up sticks and leave thirty or forty years later, was repeated once again in the Beaurivage seigneury in Lotbinière County. The Irish first arrived there in the mid-1820s, following encouragement from an agent acting on behalf of its seigneur, David Ross, a Montreal lawyer of Scottish descent. Continuing to arrive throughout the 1820s and 1830s, they founded St. Sylvestre.[74] Their community was three quarters Catholic and one-quarter Protestant.[75] Although Ross was assiduous in organizing this new intake of settlers and in arranging for roads and mills to be built, he took only a passing interest in their welfare, since his primary home was in Montreal.[76]

Ross acquired Beaurivage in 1825 through his wife's connections with its previous owner, Walter Davidson. Walter was her brother and after he died she inherited the seigneury along with her sister. Ross assumed control of the seigneury at this point and employed an agent who advised him that the settlers were poor and unable to pay their rents. He came to a similar conclusion himself after speaking to them: "I have done everything I could to frighten them into paying. They tell me they cannot pay without selling their last cow or their seed grain or potatoes." To his credit, Ross wrote in his journal in 1829 that he could not ask them to do this. Nevertheless, Ross clearly believed that the intake of immigrants had benefited his seigneury's economic performance: "The name of the seigneury is very good and far from being 'le pauvre St. Giles [de Beaurivage],' we have come, with the exception of some of the old inhabitants around the Manor House, to be at least as well off as those of the seigneuries around us."[77]

Judging from the references to "Rang Fermanagh," "Rang Monaghan," and "Rang Killarney" in Ross's journal, St. Sylvestre's Irish settlers had clearly given Irish names to their lots which must have commemorated the part of Ireland from which they had originated. For example, in 1836–37, Charles Murray, John Gallagher, and John Martin rented lots in the Fermanagh Concession; Mary Kerr, William Monahan, and Michael Martin had lots in the Monaghan Concession; and Patrick Green, Francis Travers, and Michael Slevin had lots in the Killarney Concession.[78] Remarkably "Rang Killarney" and "Rang Fermanagh" still appear in the present-day road atlas, with both being located at prime sites close to the Beaurivage River. In the early 1830s Irish immigrants were said to have founded settlements in this area named Fermanagh and Monaghan, but they no longer exist.[79]

In 1839 the Beaurivage seigneury passed to Arthur Ross, David Ross's oldest son. Like his father before him Arthur lived in Montreal and paid regular visits to his seigneury. Investing in timber felling and constructing sawmills, he benefited from Quebec City's flourishing timber trade and shipbuilding operations and consequently boosted his income. In the following year, he was asked by the immigration authorities in Quebec to accept 400 to 500 immigrant families, but in the end he took 200 families from southern Ireland.[80] In 1851, St. Sylvestre had 1,059 Irish-born; 1,569 non-French Canadians, who must have been of Irish descent; and only 1,048 French inhabitants.[81] In other words, 70 percent of its population was Irish.[82] This Irish dominance in matters concerned with the local church proved to be disconcerting to the French who resented having to share their religion with foreigners.

St. Sylvestre's Irish Catholic population was sufficiently large in 1836 to warrant an Irish priest. The Irish-born Father Nelligan duly replaced the French priest despite objections raised by the French residents. Father John O'Grady took over from Father James Nelligan in the 1850s, and by this stage the situation was becoming increasingly unstable. The large and sudden intake of 200 Irish families into this small community strained feelings to the breaking point. Irish Catholics fell out with French Catholics and Irish Catholics also rowed with the Irish Protestants who were living in nearby Leeds Township. When violence erupted between Irish Catholics and Protestants, the Roman Catholic Bishop intervened. Tempers calmed, although savage reprisals followed and normality only returned slowly. However, as happened elsewhere, the Irish population left and the problem solved itself.[83] In 1901 only 232 Irish families remained in St. Sylvestre, representing less than half of the French population, which amounted to 526 French families.

James Godfrey Hanna, a Quebec City silversmith of Irish descent, also attempted to live the life of a seigneur, encouraging immigrants to settle on his land from around 1820.[84] Having acquired the seigneury of St. Charles de la Belle Alliance in the Beauce region,[85] which his wife had inherited from her father, he went on to purchase an additional 3,000 acres in the area, but his farming venture was expensive and showed little profit. Nevertheless, in around 1825 he is said to have brought twenty-five families from the north of Ireland to settle on his land. Not only did they do this, but they also produced high-quality linen, which they sold in the

Quebec City market. As ever, few remained and by 1851 there were only fifty-two Irish-born left in the settlement.

However, this saga should not simply be remembered for outbreaks of religious turmoil or for the Irish tendency to use the Quebec region as a stepping stone to the United States. Edward Parks's letter home in 1871 to his brother in the north of Ireland acts as a reminder that some Irish remained and prospered. Boasting about his good crops and productive land in St. Sylvestre and the fact that the community was building a new church costing $1,000, he was brimming with confidence about his future:

> Our eldest son William ... bought a farm about seven miles from here for £150 and we have to help him pay for it. He has £100 paid on it; we also bought ninety acres of land convenient to our own place [which] is situated near a river and is well adapted for hay. We paid £116 for it and have it all paid.[86]

Irish settlements in and around St. Sylvestre marked the northern edge of the vast Eastern Townships. St. Sylvestre was just a taste of what was to come. Rather than being bound by the feudal constraints of the seigneuries, a new world opened up in the 1820s offering freehold tenure. Megantic County's townships would attract Irish settlers more or less immediately. Having crossed the St. Lawrence from Quebec City, they could simply walk along the newly opened Craig's Road to reach them (Map 6). Successive waves of Irish settlers would establish many communities across this great region. As ever, difficult challenges awaited them.

CHAPTER 4

꧂

The Eastern Townships

Gabriel Kerr, born in the north of Ireland in 1787, came to Canada in 1828 and obtained employment in a liquor store in Quebec City, where he remained for four years. At the age of 45 he was married to Ann Ferguson of Glasgow, Scotland; the same year (1832) he came to Megantic [County] and settled in the 11th Range of Halifax [Township], Lot No. 5. Mr. Kerr was a progressive farmer, a sterling citizen and even in his later years, a man of remarkable vigour. He died Aug. 17, 1882 at the advanced age of 95.[1]

Originating from County Fermanagh in the north of Ireland, Gabriel Kerr, joined by his brother and other family members, was one of the Eastern Townships' early Irish settlers.[2] Despite having few of the practical skills needed to cope with the massive forests that greeted them, Kerr's family clearly made a success of its pioneering venture. Kerr was one of many Ulster Protestants who settled in Megantic County. Huge tracts of land were being made available to family groups from the late 1820s, in this northern part of the Eastern Townships, allowing whole communities to transplant themselves. By 1851 their territory stretched across three town-ships.[3] However, there is a second strand to the Irish colonization of the Eastern Townships. People of many religions and originating from many parts of Ireland also relocated themselves to townships in the south.[4] They formed communities along the St. Francis River and in the Sherbrooke area, which eventually encompassed eight townships (Map 7). While the first group was given encouragement by government officials to settle in the Eastern Townships, the second group had no patrons and were left completely to their own devices.

Immigrants from the British Isles ventured into the Eastern Townships in growing numbers from the 1820s, once colonization roads had been built and land allocation schemes were in place.[5] Some of the earliest Irish to arrive had settled in St. Sylvestre (Lotbinière County) lying just outside their northern boundary. Early birds like Robert Bridgette's Irish-born father, and Samuel Cooper's Irish-born grandparents who came to live in St. Sylvestre in the 1820s, produced offspring who clearly prospered. Robert Bridgette became a successful farmer and owner of a general store, while Samuel Cooper rose to become foreman of a large lumbering firm after first establishing himself as a farmer.[6] However, until the 1830s, when the British American Land Company arrived on the scene, the vast wilder-ness known as the Eastern Townships attracted relatively few immigrants from the British Isles. First to appear were the Loyalists.

Loyalists began arriving from the mid-1780s, settling initially near the American border, especially in what became Missisquoi County.[7] The Irish-born John Savage is a striking example.[8] Having fought in the British Army during the American War of Independence, Savage sought refuge when the war ended in Foucault seigneury, an estate that was owned by Henry Caldwell, a fellow-Irishman. He then went on to persuade other Loyalists to join him.[9] But, since he wanted to remain in British-held territory, Savage left when a boundary change placed Focault seigneury in Vermont. Acquiring Shefford Township in 1801, Savage persuaded members of his extended family to join him. The significant Irish presence in Shefford and neighbouring Granby Township fifty years later indicates that Savage and his initial group probably attracted Irish followers to their settlement (Map 7).[10]

Map 7: Irish Concentrations in the Eastern Townships, 1851

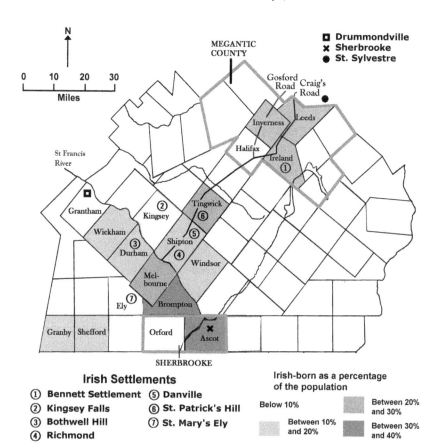

Irish Settlements

① Bennett Settlement ⑤ Danville
② Kingsey Falls ⑥ St. Patrick's Hill
③ Bothwell Hill ⑦ St. Mary's Ely
④ Richmond

Irish-born as a percentage of the population

Below 10%

Between 10% and 20%

Between 20% and 30%

Between 30% and 40%

New Englanders slipped across the border in ever greater numbers following the Loyalists influx of the 1780s, where they formed scattered communities in the southern stretches of the Eastern Townships. Some even helped themselves to seigneurial land, some of which might have been partly cleared. An early Brome Township settler noted how "a few stubborn men pitched their tents in the seigneuries, where and when there were no owners on the spot to show them off, and from thence importuning the Government for permission to settle therein, on and about Missisquoi Bay."[11] Encouraging others to follow them, they would then attempt to acquire the necessary documentation later in order to legitimize their holdings.

Small and scattered American communities were certainly not the answer to the Eastern Townships' settlement needs. With its good farmland and proximity to Quebec City, it was a prime candidate for large-scale colonization. The best land in the Maritime Provinces was being snapped up and the longer distance and higher cost involved in reaching Upper Canada did not suit everyone. There was an overwhelming case for attracting settlers from Britain and Ireland, but that was easier said than done. Alexander Buchanan, the Quebec immigration agent, told the 1826 Emigration Select Committee that many British people "dislike Lower Canada, on account of the French language and laws; the peasantry all speak French, and the emigrant is quite lost among them."[12] His remarks would have had little resonance with Irish Catholics who could see advantages in relocating to a region where their religion would be tolerated. However, the government made no effort to attract them and instead put up a large welcome sign to any Irish Protestants who might wish to settle in the Eastern Townships. Because Irish Catholics owed their religious allegiance to Rome, their loyalty to the British Crown was questioned. And since the available pool of Protestants at the time wishing to emigrate mainly originated from Ireland, they were an obvious target group.

The government's strategy of encouraging Protestants from Ulster in the north of Ireland to settle in Megantic County, while ignoring any interest there might have been from Irish Catholics, was driven by a desire to have loyal settlers in a key area of the Eastern Townships.[13] Once settled, it was hoped that that these Ulster farmers would act as a buffer between French Canadians, living along the St. Lawrence to the north and Americans based in the south. Achieving this delicate manoeuvre had required the persuasive talents of Alexander Buchanan, the Quebec immigration agent. Given that he met immigrants as they disembarked from ships, he was ideally placed to do some talent spotting. Rising to the occasion, he even compiled an alphabetized list of arrivals and destinations so that once he had persuaded someone from Ulster to go to Megantic County he could direct others known to them to follow.[14] The outcome was an Irish Protestant takeover of three Megantic County townships. Some Scots also fell into Buchanan's clutches, but they were very much a minority.

So Buchanan became a self-appointed recruiting agent for Megantic County. In striking up conversations with immigrants, he would have learned that most had intended to settle in Upper Canada. Feedback from government sources indicated that most British and Irish immigrants were reluctant to settle in Lower Canada because of the predominance of French culture. Also, its climate was less favourable. Despite these concerns, Buchanan won people over. They were influenced by his tales of "the prevalence of fevers in the Upper Province" and by his hard sell of the region's good land and its closeness to Quebec City. The prudent Archibald McKillop, leader of seventeen Isle of Arran families, said that he needed to see Megantic County with his own eyes before agreeing to any change in destination.[15] Having done so, he consented. No doubt Buchanan offered encouragement and help in smoothing over any bureaucratic hurdles that stood in their way, as he almost certainly did for the much larger Ulster group.[16]

By 1831 Buchanan was able to congratulate himself on "the great success that has attended the settlements in the townships of Inverness and Leeds which I began in 1829."[17] Some 166 families, who were mostly from the north of Ireland, had settled in Inverness Township, and beyond this a further fifty-five Irish, Scottish, and English families had settled in Leeds, Ireland, and Broughton townships (Map 7).[18] Buchanan later said that he was particularly pleased that there had been "a considerable augmentation, in the Irish population of Megantic County — "principally the friends of those who came out in 1829 and 1830."[19] In the end, nearly half of the Irish who settled in Megantic County had originated from three Ulster counties — Tyrone, Armagh, and Monaghan.[20] The families of William and Joseph Patterson, who came from County Tyrone and settled in Inverness Township, are typical of this widespread trend.[21] Reflecting local interest in events taking place in the Eastern Townships at this time, a Tyrone newspaper commented on the 355 Scottish and Irish families, who had settled "in the vicinity of Craig's Road and in other parts of this district," and reported that seventy-five of them lived in Inverness Township.[22]

However, despite its name, Ireland Township fared less well in attracting Irish settlers than did Inverness and Leeds townships. Buchanan mentioned in his 1832 *Emigrants' Handbook* that Ireland Township "is increasing much in population" and that "the inhabitants are principally Irish," but their number was probably small.[23] That same year, Joseph Bouchette referred to the "few families" in Ireland Township who were forming "what is called Lord's Settlement," a place having a sawmill, "which is found of great utility in this interior part of the country."[24] No doubt it was an Irish community. There was also Bennett Settlement, "a most important and interesting section of Upper Ireland," named after the County Wicklow–born Charles Bennett who arrived in 1821.[25] By 1851 Ireland Township had a strongly Irish but meagre population of 802, who were equally Catholic and Anglican.

Taking their religious beliefs very seriously, but not having an established church of their own, Irish Protestants did not attract missionaries to serve their needs as was the case with the English and Scots. Church of England worshippers were assisted by Anglican missionaries sent by the London-based Society for the Propagation of the Gospel,[26] a body which spent considerable funds overseas, while Presbyterian Scots were supported by the Glasgow Colonial Society, an organization which was dedicated to supporting Church of Scotland congregations across Canada.[27] Irish Protestants had no equivalent support system.[28] They usually joined either an Anglican or Presbyterian congregation or less frequently a Methodist one, but whatever their choice, they would have been regarded as outsiders, at least at the beginning. Nevertheless, the missionaries would have done their best to save souls regardless of nationality and, in the process, bring considerable comfort to countless people struggling to come to terms with pioneer life.[29] Anglican churches sprouted quickly if there was a significant English population, as was the case at Leeds Township, which managed to construct its Anglican church in the 1830s. The building still stands.

Meanwhile, although Presbyterians in Inverness Township had been receiving regular visits from Glasgow Colonial Society missionaries, they lacked financial backing and had to wait until 1862 before they could afford a well-constructed church. Before that, Inverness village had a log "Meeting House," which was built in 1832 and served both Presbyterians and Congregationalists.[30] By then, Inverness Township was reported to be "now settled ... and with every prospect of success and prosperity,"[31]

St. James Anglican Church at St. Jacques-de-Leeds, Megantic County, built in the 1830s.

having "fifty dwelling houses and barns, 129 head of cattle and a large supply of wheat for sale."[32] On a visit to the area, the Reverend John Clugston declared it to be "a most delightful and interesting part of the country ..." but the necessities of its people "till now have been over-looked and neglected. The Scotch population is great and among them are also a considerable number of Irish Presbyterians."[33] Needing to attract funds from the Glasgow Colonial Society, he stressed the sizeable Scottish population, but in truth his congregation was mainly Irish. In 1851 the Irish-born accounted for around 70 percent of the total immigrant population in both Inverness and Leeds townships.

In 1841, Buchanan had to admit that, although "most favourable accounts" had been received from the Eastern Townships extolling job opportunities and good rates of pay "very few can be induced to go to that section of the province, their prejudices are so strong against our winter."[34]Although the Ulster immigrants he had promoted succeeded in establishing viable farming communities, they had not attracted many

St. Andrews Presbyterian (now United) Church at Dublin Road, Inverness village, Megantic County, built in 1862.

followers from their native land as had been hoped. The winters were harsh and the soil was of variable quality. In his report to the Society for the Propagation of the Gospel in 1845, the Reverend John Flanagan noted that although Leeds was "a settled farming area," families were leaving and "have moved to the west."[35] Some farmers complained that they needed to work in nearby lumber camps to supplement their income while others regularly set off for New England in search of seasonal employment.[36]

Having become disgruntled by the arduous farming conditions in Megantic County, the Ulster-born John Reid moved west to take advantage of the treeless landscapes and fertile soil on offer in the prairies:

> My advice to the stalwart Megantic family is to stop your everlasting fight with stones and stumps, mud and snow, potato bugs, etc., and come out here [Saskatchewan] where there are 1000s of acres of rich black land ready for the plough. If you are as industrious and economical here as you have been in Megantic, you would soon be worth ten dollars here to one in the east.[37]

There were many more like him, and leave they did.

Robert Sellar, the outspoken Scottish radical, was convinced that Protestant farmers left because they had become disheartened not by the onerous lifestyle but by concerns over the growing dominance of the Catholic Church. He accused it of driving out Protestants.[38] A change in legislation in 1850, which allowed the Catholic Church to extend its parish system beyond the seigneuries into the townships, was proof, as far as he was concerned, of such a plot.[39] However, frustrations worked both ways. French Canadians, who were experiencing severe land shortages in their seigneuries, had greatly resented being kept out of the Eastern Townships. The simple truth was that Irish, English, and Scottish settlers were leaving the province for a whole host of reasons. Once their numbers had declined to the point where they could no longer support their Protestant schools and churches, they left in droves, and this pattern was repeated throughout the entire province.

Nevertheless, as Megantic County in the north was losing its Irish settlers to Upper Canada and the United States from the 1840s, the southern townships were experiencing the opposite trend. They were attracting immigrants from Ireland. Many were Catholics, who sought the jobs that the bustling town of Sherbrooke could offer, it being the headquarters of the London-based British American Land Company.[40] They had been coming to Sherbrooke from the 1830s, and twenty years later, when a railway line reached the town of Richmond, Irish immigrants were spurred on yet again to come to the region. The Grand Trunk Railway,[41] completed in 1853, linked Sherbrooke and Richmond with Quebec City and Montreal, thus stimulating the industrial development of both towns and the surrounding area. This boost in immigration occurred soon after the Great Irish Famine had struck in the mid-1840s, although the numbers arriving at this time were relatively small.[42] Most of the 4,000 or so Irish-born people who were living in the Lower St. Francis Valley and in the Sherbrooke area by 1851 had arrived long before the famine years.

The first great surge of Irish workers to the region had occurred in the 1830s. The establishment of the British American Land Company brought a rising demand for labouring jobs in the Sherbrooke area, which they helped to fill. Lucy Peel, the wife of a British naval officer, was amazed by the hectic scenes she observed in the mid-1830s:

The roads are now assuming the appearance of those in dear old England, thanks to the Company, which does everything in style, sparing neither labour nor money; they spend a thousand dollars a day in Sherbrooke. The town swarms with emigrants, five hundred more are coming up and buildings are raising their heads in all directions for their accommodation. Mr. Watson has full occupation, he has to visit the sheds twice a day and receives five dollars a day for his trouble; there is I hear to be a Hospital built.[43]

The sudden increase in immigrants was a response to the resettlement schemes that were being run by the land company. Modelled after the Canada Company, which had been founded eight years earlier to promote the colonization of western Upper Canada, the British American Land Company sought immigrants for its 850,000 acres of Crown land that stretched across the Eastern Townships. Many of its settlers were destitute labourers from Britain who had lost their jobs to the increasing mechanization in farming that was taking place.[44] Money to fund travel costs was raised by various benefactors while the company provided organizational backup and offered its extensive lands to settlers on easy terms. And yet, while the company helped more than 1,000 English farm labourers from Norfolk and Suffolk and a similar number of Scottish crofters from the Isle of Lewis, to settle on its lands, it did not do the same for the Irish.[45] The English had their transport costs met by parish councils and the Scots had theirs funded by landlords, but the Irish had no benefactors. The Irish had no help with their relocation costs, nor did they benefit from any land company schemes. Nevertheless, many came. Some wishing to become farmers, but lacking the resources to do so, had first to find paid employment, which they did in the rapidly expanding town of Sherbrooke and later in the town of Richmond.[46]

By 1851 Irish farming communities were principally concentrated in seven townships along both sides of the St. Francis River: Sherbrooke in Ascot, Brompton, Windsor, Melbourne, Shipton, Durham, and Wickham as well as in Tingwick Township further to the north, which was reached along Craig's Road (Map 7).[47] A memorial cross erected in the town of Richmond commemorates them and has inscribed on it the surnames of more than 170 of the early pioneers.[48] Where geographical origins in Ireland are known, they reveal that nearly half came from the north of Ireland and were of mixed religion, their arrival dates ranging from 1812 to 1923.[49]

Irish predominance in Tingwick Township indicates success in finding large amounts of vacant land in one place on which people could settle. However, Tingwick was one of the least attractive and most remote farming areas in the entire Eastern Townships.[50] When George Johnson and his wife Mary Mulderick arrived in 1824 they found that it had only one other inhabitant — Timothy Morrill, an American who had got there in the 1790s.[51] In 1832, Joseph Bouchette referred to it as "a poor and rather

The Celtic cross, erected by the St. Patrick's Society of Richmond in 2002 to commemorate principally the Irish, but also the Scots, Welsh, and Bretons who settled in the area. An inscription has been carved in English, Gaelic, and French. The cross is located at Soldiers' Park, Richmond, on the bank of the St. Francis River.

sterile tract" with "swampy ground." Not surprisingly, no one had "found sufficient inducement to attempt a settlement" even by then, despite its land in the southeastern half having been acquired by "several persons."[52] Even as late as 1852, when Thomas Neill and his wife and family from County Down arrived to establish a farm they found a township that was still sparsely populated. "The new home ... had a log house and barn and some few acres cleared. The remainder of the farm was forest, or as they would say, *standing timber.*[53] In other words, the only township which the Irish could call their own was theirs because no one else wanted it.

Although the first significant Irish influx began in the 1830s with the arrival of the British American Land Company, immigrants from Ireland had ventured into the Lower St. Francis Valley some fifteen years earlier. This happened with the founding of the Drummondville military settlement in 1815.[54] Britain's near defeat in the War of 1812–14 led the government to bring disbanded British and Irish soldiers to the western end of the St. Francis River (Map 7). The military settlement was to act as a civilian buffer capable of offering resistance in the event of an American attack at this strategic location. However, despite being granted free land, log cabins, farm implements, and food, the ex-soldiers had to accept military discipline and sites which were not necessarily well suited to farming.

The new arrivals included men such as Peter Plunkett from County Louth, who had served with the 49th "Hertfordshire" Regiment of Foot,[55] and William Mountain from County Fermanagh, who served with the 27th "Enniskillen" Regiment of Foot.[56] Seven families, who like Mountain, originated from Enniskillen, later joined him and together they settled to the east of Drummondville in Durham Township.[57] Other early residents included Joseph Griffith from County Kilkenny who arrived in 1816 and then moved on to Sherbrooke in 1826,[58] and Michael McCabe, who left County Armagh in 1816 and soon after ended up in nearby Wickham Township.[59] By 1825 the village of Drummondville was said to have twenty houses and a resident English-speaking priest from Vermont, no doubt brought in to serve Irish Catholics living in the area.[60] Yet disappointment over the poor quality of the land caused many to leave.

When he arrived at Drummondville in 1845, the Anglican minister, Reverend George Ross reported how people in his congregation, who were "ostensibly farmers," had been "drawn off by the tempting wages" they could get for cutting timber for the British market.[61] To make matters worse, British and Irish ex-servicemen, in receipt of land grants, had also left the area:

> They were accustomed from long habit to have their wants and comforts provided for without reference to themselves; it is not difficult to imagine that these early military settlers, when thrown suddenly upon their own endeavours in a scene so new to them and within circumstances so disadvantageous, should very soon have discovered a deficiency in the properties necessary for pioneers of the forest: self-reliance patience, enduring privations and hardships; and that disappointments, dissatisfaction and discontent should have paralyzed their efforts and driven them in numbers to seek out more favourable townships.... Emigrants from the Mother Country ... later take up vacant lots and then again soon become disappointed under the difficulties of first settlements and they leave for more thriving locations in the Eastern Townships.[62]

Many of the Drummondville Irish ex-soldiers and their descendents clearly moved to Wickham and Durham, both townships having a significant Irish presence in 1851.[63] A notable resident of Wickham Township was J. Ernest Leonard, who became a barrister in 1895, his grandfather having arrived from County Meath in 1832.[64]

Earlier, in 1825, Alexander Bothwell, from County Omagh, had arrived in Durham Township with his wife and nine children and settled at what became Bothwell Hill.[65] By 1861 his extended family had established seven homesteads on this site, farming just over 800 acres.[66] Having first found accommodation in Trois Rivières in 1824, for his wife and family, Joseph Haddock from County Tyrone went on his own to nearby Kingsey Falls where he "built a small cabin on his land in what was to become the town of Kingsey."[67] He chopped down trees and then returned to Trois Rivières to collect his wife and children:

> In clearing the land Joseph made a runway down which
> he could roll the gigantic logs he had chopped down. He
> burned them to make potash which he could barter for
> supplies. Later these tall trees became a source of revenue
> as they were in demand for masts of sailing vessels. The
> chopping and rolling of logs was highly dangerous for a
> man working alone …[68]

Sadly for Joseph, government surveyors ruled later that he had cleared the wrong plot, his being on the other side of a stream some distance away. Undeterred, Joseph set to work to clear the virgin forest for a second time. Having the patience of a saint, he deserves a special place in heaven!

The British American Land Company's many advertisements, some appearing in Belfast and Irish newspapers, extolling the fertile land it offered in the Eastern Townships, would have only tempted well-heeled farmers. Those of limited means had first to find labouring jobs in order to raise funds.[69] Taking up farming was stage two. Judging from where Irish farms were mainly clustered in 1851, many had remained in the region but few settled on company land. Some were to be found in Sherbrooke in Ascot Township, which was owned by the British American Land Company, but most lived in areas outside of the company's control. Because so much land in the Eastern Townships had fallen into the hands of absentee landlords, they generally had to rent land. Regarding this to be a serious disadvantage, some relocated to Upper Canada and the United States, where freehold land was more readily available.[70]

In 1851 the largest Irish concentrations were to be found in Brompton and Melbourne townships in the St. Francis Valley, in Sherbrooke in Ascot Township to the south, and in Tingwick Township lying to the north along Craig's Road (Map 7). Apart from Tingwick, which was predominately Roman Catholic, the Irish in these townships had mixed religions.[71] The Tingwick Irish community was sufficiently large in 1856 to be able to form a Roman Catholic parish, which it named St. Patrick's. Constructing a church four years later, the settlers founded a village around the church that came to be known as St. Patrick's Hill.[72]

As time went on, the town of Sherbrooke continued to grow its Irish Catholic population.[73] Twenty years earlier, the Irish had joined forces with their French-Canadian neighbours to build a chapel dedicated to St. Columban, and five years later, again working together, they built St. Michael's Church. But by 1886, as a result of the Irish influx that followed on the heels of the Great Irish Famine of the mid-1840s, they could build their own St. Patrick's Church. It became the first entirely English-speaking Catholic congregation in the Eastern Townships.[74]

The arrival of the Grand Trunk Railway in the 1850s brought economic expansion to the St. Francis Valley and also benefited the town of Richmond.[75] Before then, it was little more than a village. In 1832, Richmond had only twelve houses and eighty inhabitants who had the benefit of "three stores, two good taverns, two tanneries, a saw and gristmill and a pearlash [potash] factory."[76] But after the arrival of the railway, the population of the surrounding area grew rapidly and brought many Irish to the town's hinterland.[77] This happened especially in 1851, when some of the tenants of Mr. Charley, who owned an estate in County Donegal, arrived. He assisted them to set sail for Quebec in order to take up employment on the railway and having done so, they settled in Melbourne Township.[78] That year, Alexander Buchanan, the immigration agent at Quebec, announced that 1,000 labourers were required to work on the railway between Melbourne and Sherbrooke at a wage of a dollar an hour and men from this Irish estate had clearly responded.[79] Irish Catholic families came to the area ten years later and settled in Upper Melbourne Township, thus extending the Irish presence in the area even further.[80]

Despite the improved economic situation in Richmond, Irish settlers frequently felt the need to supplement their incomes by taking up paid employment in the New England States. Going back and forth across the border seemed to be a fact of life for many in St. Mary's Ely, this being a particularly remote place situated on the southwestern margin of the St. Francis Valley (Map 7). Edward Morrisey from County Kerry, who lived in St. Mary's Ely, was typical. Working as a sawyer and millwright in Montpellier, Vermont, from a young age, "he sent home part of his salary every year until he was aged twenty-one."[81] He then returned to St. Mary's Ely, bought land, built a house and barn, but in order to make ends meet had to work part time at a sawmill at Valcourt, just south of St. Mary's Ely, for a number of years. Finally, in 1897, at the age of thirty-two, he felt sufficiently affluent to contemplate marriage to Sarah Carroll, who was working at the time in the United States. Like Edward, Sarah had spent her younger years in New England, working in the mill towns of Vermont and New Hampshire before returning to St. Mary's Ely.

Despite the many hurdles that had to be overcome, the plight of the early Irish immigrants is remembered in a very positive way by their descendents. The St. Patrick's Society of Richmond, Danville, Windsor, and vicinity was formed in 1877, and when it held its ninety-first anniversary in 1968, "300 Irishmen and friends joined in celebrating" their Irish heritage. "A toast to the Queen" was proposed and the event was attended by "representatives from both Catholic and Anglican churches in the locality."[82] The St. Francis Valley Irish had clearly adapted well to their new surroundings and took pride in their pioneering achievements. There were no regrets. When they sought temporary work elsewhere, it was usually with the aim of returning home to their families and friends.

Members of the St. Patrick's Society in the Saint-Jean-Baptiste Day parade, held in Richmond in the early 1900s.

And, highly conscious of belonging to Richmond's Catholic community, the local St. Patrick's Society supported its events. Thus, the two patron saints, Saint Patrick and Saint John the Baptist, were commemorated together in a procession through Richmond to mark the latter's feast day.

Bonds of friendship between Richmond's French Canadians and Irish were clearly on show. Harmonious behaviour such as this can be contrasted with Robert Sellar's demonization of the Catholic Church, blaming if for the exodus of Protestants from the Eastern Townships. It is true that many Irish left and, when they did, French Canadians took their place. But there were many reasons for this.

The exodus was due primarily to the region's inability to compete with Upper Canada's better land and climate. The declining importance of the local timber trade and the rising dominance of French culture, which progressively made the Eastern Townships less attractive to some British and Irish settlers, were additional factors.

Having become a major port, the city of Montreal was proving to be a magnet for Irish immigrants. Its nearby farming regions offering fertile land and proximity to good markets also beckoned. The poor but thriving urban community of Griffintown, founded in the heart of Montreal, was rapidly becoming a home away from home for Irish labourers as major canal projects in the city guaranteed steady employment. The Montreal Irish were in a league of their own.

CHAPTER 5

Montreal and Rural Areas to the North and South

The story is that they lived there [St. Columban] the first winter. They came from Ireland and spent the winter there; it's an old, old story that I heard from the grandparents but it's true. When they came from Ireland, they had no home, no nothing, so they saw this rock, put up straight about twenty feet, and they made a roof over with logs and brush and covered it with snow and they got in there and spent their first winter.[1]

Arriving in the 1820s, Irish Catholics founded the farming community of St. Columban, located northwest of Montreal, a place that is still cherished as an Irish heritage site today. As one of the descendants of the early settlers later recalled, years of hard labour lay ahead for these people when they first arrived. However, they had not come directly from Ireland, having lived for some time beforehand in the city of Montreal. They spent their first winter in basic lean-tos and had the use of only a few primitive implements to establish their homesteads; but that was how pioneering worked for aspiring people who had no money.

Map 8: Irish Communities to the North of Montreal, 1851

Irish Settlements

① **St. Columban**
② **St. Jérôme**
③ **New Glasgow (Lacorne)**
④ **Kilkenny**
⑤ **Kilarney Lakes**
⑥ **Wexford**
⑦ **Rawdon**
⑧ **Kildare**
⑨ **Brandon (St. Gabriel)**

Located on the North River in the Two Mountains seigneury, St. Columban spawned two other Irish communities just beyond it, at St. Jérôme and at Wexford. The Irish also established more farming communities in townships north of Montreal along the Achigan and Assumption rivers, both tributaries of the St. Lawrence — places that the Quebec immigration agent had been recommending to aspiring and newly arrived immigrants (Map 8).[2] This started in around 1820, when Irish settlements began forming on the north side of the St. Lawrence, at New Glasgow (Terrebonne County), Kilkenny and Rawdon (Montcalm County), and Kildare (Joliette County). However, with their larger populations and thriving economies, Huntingdon County and Beauharnois seigneury, located near the American border on the south side of the St. Lawrence, proved to be more popular (Map 9). Between them they had 6,100 Irish-born residents in 1851, compared with only 3,900 who were living on the north side.[3]

A limiting factor for many of the Irish had been their ability to fund their relocation costs. This was especially the case for people living in Ireland, but even for those poor people who had moved to Montreal, the amount of money needed to begin farming was prohibitively expensive. Fortunately, the new Lachine Canal being built between Lachine and the port of Montreal offered them a way out since it had an insatiable need for labourers. With construction work beginning in 1821, Irish labourers had steady employment over the next four years, and after that they were the principal diggers of the Beauharnois Canal that followed. As a result of this pre-labouring phase, men were brought together at canal sites, and if they shared the hope of becoming farmers, they often decided to settle together. Identifying a sufficient amount of vacant land to do this, they would then send for their wives and families to join them. Thus, it was a shared work experience rather than the geographical origins of people in

Map 9: Irish Communities to the South of Montreal, 1851

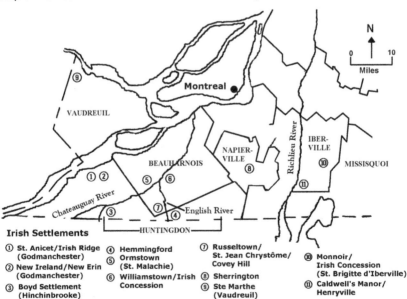

Irish Settlements

① St. Anicet/Irish Ridge (Godmanchester)
② New Ireland/New Erin (Godmanchester)
③ Boyd Settlement (Hinchinbrooke)
④ Hemmingford
⑤ Ormstown (St. Malachie)
⑥ Williamstown/Irish Concession
⑦ Russeltown/ St. Jean Chrystôme/ Covey Hill
⑧ Sherrington
⑨ Ste Marthe (Vaudreuil)
⑩ Monnoir/ Irish Concession (St. Brigitte d'Iberville)
⑪ Caldwell's Manor/ Henryville

Ireland that sometimes determined the composition of the groups that formed farming communities in Montreal's hinterland.

Raoul Blanchard described the rapid growth in Montreal's English-speaking population between 1821 and 1851 as "an Irish invasion," and with good reason.[4] Numbering 1,000 in 1821, Irish numbers trebled over the next four years. In 1851 around 12,000 Irish-born were living in Montreal, making them the largest immigrant group by far. They exceeded the combined Scottish and English-born population by a factor of two, and while religious denomination totals cannot be given with certainty, census figures show that Montreal's Irish were overwhelmingly Catholic.[5] John Maguire, the Cork-born journalist and politician, was struck by the large number of Irish Catholics he met when he visited Montreal in the 1860s.[6] An Irish businessman told him that "there is no city in the [United] States in which we [Catholics] occupy a more favourable position than we do here. We feel ourselves at home here; we are not foreigners."[7] Maguire concluded that in Montreal, an Irishman "is in a Catholic city, where his religion is respected and his church is surrounded with dignity and splendour."[8]

The Irish were Montreal's principal labourers and were renowned for their physical strength, endurance, and willingness to take on dangerous and unpleasant jobs. Although the jobs were frequently poorly paid, they earned considerably more than what would have been the case in Ireland. However, their presence sometimes caused dissension. Montreal's economy was expanding rapidly, and due to the sudden rise in their numbers and the willingness to accept lower wage rates than their French-Canadian counterparts, industrial conflicts erupted from time to time.[9] As W.F. Adams put it, "In Canada, Irish peasants, reproducing the conditions and standards of life in the old country, undersold habitants in the market of Montreal."[10] Be that as it may, they were the city's principal canal diggers, railway builders, and factory workers, and without them the large-scale construction work needed to develop Montreal's economy could not have happened as quickly as it did.

Many Irish lived near the city's port in a place called Griffintown, a working-class slum that was known for its poverty and wretchedness.[11] This shantytown was bordered by Notre-Dame Street on the north, the Lachine Canal on the south, McGill Street on the east, and Guy Street on the west (later St. Anne's Ward). It is the only part of Montreal where the Irish owned much property and the only Irish area to have been studied in detail.[12] It owed its name to Robert Griffin, a soap manufacturer who owned one of the many factories in the area.[13] Located close to the St. Lawrence River, it was prone to flooding and outbreaks of typhoid and diphtheria occurred regularly. As the water rose during spring floods, people left and came back in boats as best they could. It was "a growing jumble of wooden houses set amid soap factories, brickyards, foundries, tanneries and other noxious industries clustered near the mouth of the Lachine Canal."[14] Stephen Leacock described it as "a wretched area whose tumbled, shabby houses mock at the wealth of Montreal."[15]

However bad Griffintown was, it was not a dead end. When he visited it in the 1860s, John Maguire talked to many people who had lifted

Dilapidated housing in Griffintown, photographed in 1903. One half of Griffintown's buildings had gone by 1940 and little remained by 1970, when St. Ann's Catholic Church was demolished. Parts of the church's foundation remain visible in a local park where benches have been positioned to mark the site of the former church pews.

themselves out of poverty: "Men who could scarcely write their names when they landed on the wharf of Montreal" were now prosperous "thanks to their native energy and resolute good conduct" and, "although most Irish Catholic merchants and tradesmen arrived later than their Protestant counterparts, and under less favourable circumstances, they were now doing very well."[16] Marianne Gurd from County Longford, who was married to a Montreal factory worker, was certainly pleased with her lot. She told her sister how much she was enjoying her "nice cottage a little [away] from the bustle of the city with a very nice garden at the back," which was "about ten minutes walk from the factory for Joseph." Her "old lodger" in her previous dwelling told her that "old Ned Murray of [County] Longford is here and turned Protestant.... I never see him but he works and drinks by turn."[17] Clearly, some fell by the wayside, but relative prosperity was attainable.

With its many Irish Catholics, Griffintown was able to build the main shell of St. Ann's Church, located at the corner of McCord (now Mountain Street) and Basin Street, by 1851. The finished church was opened to the faithful for the first time three years later. It was, in fact, Montreal's second Irish Catholic church, the first being St. Patrick's, which was built seven years earlier on the slopes of Mount Royal.

St. Ann's could seat 3,000 worshippers, half as many as St. Patrick's. It was one of the few Griffintown buildings still standing in the 1950s by which time it was attracting both Catholics and Protestants from across the city to its services. "The city ran special buses for the thousands of Montrealers — many of them non-Catholics — who made the regular pilgrimages to St. Ann's, where they placed their petitions on the alter and lined up to light a float in front of the miraculous icon of Our Mother of Perpetual Help, after the service."[18]

Religion also played a prominent part in the formation of St. Columban, an Irish farming community which was established, north of Montreal under the guidance of a Montreal priest. Concerned about the squalid conditions being endured by Irish families who were living in Griffintown, their parish priest, the Kilkenny-born Father Patrick Phelan organized a major colonization scheme. It would be their chance to lift themselves out of poverty, and with his help they found a large unsettled tract of land in

St. Patrick's Basilica, René-Lévesque Boulevard, Montreal, built in a gothic revival style and completed in 1847. Photograph taken in 2007 by Diego Delso. The interior is decorated with motifs that combine the *fleurs-de-lys* with shamrocks.

the Two Mountains seigneury that had been owned by a group of priests known as the Gentlemen of St. Sulpice.[19] Arriving in the 1820s, they built their shanties and log houses and with government-supplied farm implements such as ploughs, scythes, picks, and spades, and household items, including blankets and cooking utensils, they launched their settlement. In 1832, Joseph Bouchette referred to the "new settlement "in the north of the [Two Mountains] seigneury peopled by Irish emigrants."[20] Although it eventually came to be known as St. Columban, the settlement's name in 1838 was St. Patrice.[21]

Fifty-four families were living in St. Columban in 1825, and ten years later there were 100 families.[22] In 1850 it had 200 families and at least three schools. All had made the move from Griffintown and many could trace their geographical origins back to counties Carlow, Kildare,

Kilkenny, Offaly, Laois, and Tipperary. As ever, gruelling tasks were being sustained by a deeply felt religious faith. On Sundays the Irish settlers walked nine miles through the woods to attend mass at St. Scholastique, the nearest village. "In bad weather they gathered at a wayside cross to pray together. In 1831 they built a small, rough-hewn chapel and a priest from St. Scholastique came to conduct services."[23]

The settlers benefited materially when the Limerick-born Father John Falvey took over as parish priest in 1840. He presided over the construction of new houses and barns and oversaw the introduction of sawmills. Revenue from the local timber trade greatly stimulated the economy, leading to the construction of a larger church and improved living conditions for the St. Columban settlers.[24] Meanwhile, John and Mary Phelan who had settled in St. Columban in 1830 had a daughter who became the resident nun. Teaching catechism to the children, Sister Mary St. Patrick "contributed her talents and her energy to the cause of the beloved people of St. Columban."[25]

Later, St. Columban went on to develop a potash industry and a cut-stone business but they were not sufficient. Dissatisfaction with farming yields and living conditions led many young people to move to Montreal, where they could get well-paid jobs or to go to Upper Canada or the United States where conditions were far better. Those who remained often "went to Gatineau and Grenville on the Ottawa River to work in the logging industry" during the winter.[26] In the end, many of the St. Columban farms were sold and only a small number remained in Irish hands by the middle of the twentieth century.

The Irish settlements that formed at St. Jérôme (Terrebonne County) and Wexford (Montcalm County)[27] probably represent an overspill from St. Columban, since they, too, are located along the North River and attracted Catholics. St. Jérôme acquired its Irish Catholics between 1820 and 1830, while Irish Protestants began to arrive in Shawbridge, north of St. Jérôme, from 1826.[28] St. Jérôme had around 350 Irish-born residents in 1851 of mixed religion. A significant number of Irish, who were probably Catholics, are reported to have settled in Wexford in around 1840, but only nineteen Irish-born lived there in 1851, all of whom were Presbyterians.[29] Its appearance as a place name in an 1838 map indicates that some of its Irish had arrived before 1840.[30]

Photograph of the St. Columban Cemetery, north of Montreal. The commemorative plaques refer to many of St. Columban's early Irish settlers. They include Michael Mullin, County Tyrone, died 1885; John Kenny, died 1874, and his wife Margaret Jacob, died 1844, County Queens; Michael Healey, County Antrim, died 1887; and Bridget McCara, wife of Hugh Madden, County Tipperary, died 1876.

Despite its name, New Glasgow, on the Achigan River, was settled first by Irish immigrants who arrived by at least 1820. When Joseph Bouchette visited in 1832, he described it as a "new settlement ... and considering the numerous impediments, deficiency of mills, the want of practicable roads ... much progress has been made by the industry and perseverance of this little colony."[31] Scots did come to the settlement also, but they were outnumbered by the Irish-born. In 1851 New Glasgow had around 300 Irish-born, a substantial number being Anglicans, compared with only 100 Scottish-born.[32] Around eighty Irish Presbyterians were to be found upriver at Kilkenny Township (Montcalm County) by this time, while Kilarney Lakes, just above it, probably acquired Irish settlers, but no settlement evidence survives.[33]

In addition, two Irish communities were established along the Assumption River at Rawdon (Montcalm County) and Kildare (Joliette County),[34] both having early beginnings. Irish Protestants arrived in 1816 and after only six years had sufficient people and resources to build an Anglican log church.[35] According to Joseph Bouchette, they had squatted on land that had been intended for the "officers and privates of the late Embodied Militia."[36] Presumably, in an effort to encourage Protestant Irish settlers to come to the area, the Reverend James Burton, an Anglican missionary who had been sent out by the Society of the Propagation of the

Gospel, acted as the local land agent. In 1825, Rawdon had 475 Irish-born inhabitants who were of mixed religions. And fifteen years later immigrants from Ireland were still heading for Rawdon. The Quebec immigration agent noted that "a few families [from Sligo] of about thirty persons have gone to their friends," while that same year he noted that there were twenty families who "are gone to settle in Kildare."[37] Rawdon had 570 Irish-born residents in 1851 who were predominately Protestants. As ever, the Irish were on the move by this time, looking for greener pastures, with many of them relocating to Wellington County in Upper Canada.[38]

Kildare Township's initial Irish were ex-soldiers of the 103rd Infantry Regiment who had fought in the War of 1812–14 under Major Beauchamp Colclough. In 1832, Bouchette noted that "the new emigrant settlement placed under the care of Major Colclough in 1821 has made much progress and contains a neat village."[39] However, the settlement struggled for a period after Colclough went bankrupt fourteen years later.[40] Nevertheless, Anglicans went on to build a log church in 1843 at "Rang Kildare," which was located between St. Ambroise, Ste Marcelline, and Ste Mélanie de Kildare, and eight years later Kildare had 127 Irish-born residents.[41] The Irish also settled at nearby Brandon (later St. Gabriel de Brandon), which had been founded by Bernard Monday, an Irishman who arrived in 1824.[42] It was located on the Maskinongé River, described by Bouchette as having 40,000 acres of excellent land, some of which had been granted to the Canadian militia who had served in the American War of 1812–14.[43] However, despite this positive assessment, St. Gabriel de Brandon only had eight Irish-born residents in 1851.

Unlike the north side of the St. Lawrence, where the Irish were spread across four counties, Irish enclaves on the south side were more compact. Here, they were concentrated in Huntingdon County and Beauharnois seigneury, the latter being the more popular despite its apparent drawback in only offering leaseholds to settlers.[44] According to Joseph Bouchette, they would be won over by "the general goodness of the land, the variety of timber of every description, among which oak, elm, pine, and beech are in great quantities," the extensive waterways through which felled timber could be brought to the St. Lawrence, and the "easy access by main roads" to the United States.[45]

In 1851 just over 2,000 Irish-born were to be found in Huntingdon County, while another 4,100 were living in Beauharnois seigneury (Map 9). Huntingdon tended to attract more Protestants, while the seigneury's Irish were largely Catholics, apart from St. Malachie, whose Irish were of mixed religion.

Unlike the Irish on the north side of the St. Lawrence, who generally came directly from Ireland, a significant proportion of those living on the south side had begun their stay in Lower Canada by taking up labouring work in or near Montreal. The construction jobs made available by the building of the Lachine Canal in the early 1820s, the Chambly Canal in the early 1830s, and the Beauharnois Canal ten years later were a godsend. The wages earned gave poor people the springboard they needed to finance their farming endeavours. Alexander Buchanan actually used these jobs as a selling point in his *1832 Emigrants' Handbook.* "Labourers may get employment at the canal now making at Chambly" he wrote, and ten years later he mentioned the "several hundred [labourers] now employed at the Beauharnois Canal at 3s. per day," in his immigration report.[46] In all, more than 2,000 mainly Irish labourers worked on the Beauharnois Canal between 1842 and 1845. And thousands more construction jobs were made available beginning in 1826, with the building of the Rideau Canal in the Ottawa Valley.[47]

The Irish founded an "Irish Ridge" at St. Anicet and a "New Ireland" near to it in Godmanchester Township, located on the west side of Huntingdon County. And yet, they were present in far greater numbers in Hemmingford Township on the east side of the county (Map 9). The Irish Ridge was on the La Guerre River, a tributary of the Châteauguay, while New Ireland, also known as New Erin, developed along another of its tributaries. According to Robert Sellar, editor of the *Huntingdon Gleaner* and author of an early settlement history of Huntingdon County, the Irish settlers on the west side of St. Anicet lived "in a state of harmony and mutual helpfulness" with the Highland Scots who occupied the east side.[48] The Kilkenny-born Patrick Curran, who arrived in the early 1820s, was one of Irish Ridge's first Irish inhabitants:

The Irish came in strong every summer, especially between 1832 and 1836, filling up the back ranges, the French keeping near the lake. The first Irish settlers, besides myself and [John] Smyth, were Edward Walsh, Edward Smyth, William and James Higgins, James and Michael Finnigan, Cornelius Daly, and the McGintys. They were from all parts of Ireland and most of them worked on the Rideau Canal. There was nothing else but Irish on what is known as the Irish Ridge. They did not know then of the stones, but looked at the fine timber for ashes and the dry soil.... The great want of the country was roads, and for many years we had no other way of drawing anything than in woodshed sleds or jumpers, dragged by oxen.[49]

Life was similarly very basic for the early inhabitants of New Ireland/ New Erin. It "filled up" with Irish people during the 1820s, with Protestants being more numerous than Catholics. Settlers recalled that "they had no road fit for a wagon.... It was a common sight for the villagers to see a string of New Ireland men file across Prince Arthur Square [in Montreal] each bearing on his head a bag of wheat to be ground at the mill."[50] And yet, according to Robert Sellar, their tough beginnings "evoked a spirit of clannishness which made New Ireland the brightest spot in the world to them."[51]

The Irish were also well represented at the Boyd Settlement in Hinchinbrooke Township, south of New Ireland, outnumbering the Scots by two to one in 1851. They were mostly Protestants, many having originated from the north of Ireland.[52] William Morris, the Anglican minister of Huntingdon village, would have preferred to have had more English settlers in his congregation,[53] while his successor complained bitterly about the roads being "frightful ten weeks each year," and about being surrounded by too many Irish people — "both Romanist and Protestant."[54] Hemmingford Township's Anglican missionary, the Reverend Henry Hazard, was also disapproving of Irish Catholics. According to him they were "poor settlers" who could only survive winters by working in lumber camps and selling firewood.[55] Anti-Catholic sentiments were to be expected in an Irish Protestant stronghold, but as Robert Sellar pointed out, "the settlers of Hemingford were peculiar in that few of them came directly into it from Montreal. The majority lived one or more years in Sherrington (Napierville County),[56] which they crowded into under the belief that it was ungranted Crown land." However, when their entitlement to it was later challenged by the local seigneur, they left for Hemmingford saying that they would not pay rent.[57]

Meanwhile, the Irish who opted for Beauharnois seigneury were mainly to be found at Ormstown, Williamstown, and Russeltown (Map 9). Ormstown was a prime site on the Châteauguay River, while Williamstown and Russeltown were both situated on English River tributaries that flowed into the Châteauguay. According to Robert Sellar, the cut timber and potash produced in this region provided sufficient revenue to tide people over "until the clearing yielded enough to maintain the settler's family."[58] In addition, the seigneur, Edward Ellice,[59] a London merchant and land dealer provided settlers with a basic infrastructure of buildings and roads. Thus, although conditions were still very primitive and people were saddled with various feudal taxes and duties, new arrivals could still aspire to becoming prosperous farmers.[60]

Scots outnumbered the Irish in Ormstown in 1832, but twenty years later the opposite was true.[61] Most arrivals were Protestants who originated from the north of Ireland, while a substantial number of Irish Catholics also came to the area, settling on both sides of the Châteauguay River.[62] Ormstown's St. Malachie Church, dating from the late 1820s, was the first ever Catholic Church to be built in the Upper Châteauguay Valley, its founders including Michael Furlong and James Finn, who came from County Wexford.[63] And after acquiring lots at Jamestown, south of Ormstown, men from the north of Ireland "placed their families upon them while they worked on the Lachine Canal."[64] Ormstown had a sufficiently large and affluent Anglican congregation by the mid-nineteenth century to erect its second church, "built of cut stone in the English style" and "lighted with lancet windows."[65] Costing £1,112, local residents found £480 while the rest was raised in other parts of Lower Canada and in New York and Boston.[66] Irish interests were strengthened in 1836 when the Society for the Propagation of the

St. James Anglican Church, Ormstown, built in 1852. The first church was completed in 1834 near the present church.

Gospel sent the Reverend William Brethour, an Irishman, to serve the Ormstown community.[67]

The "Irish Concession" at Williamstown, to the east of Ormstown along Norton Creek, was yet another Irish stronghold. Catholics settled along the south side of Norton Creek while Protestants were located on the north side.[68] Mrs. David McClenaghan, who sailed from Londonderry to Quebec in 1824 with her husband, recalled its beginnings:

> We had a calm passage of 6 weeks. My husband, who was a gardener, got work about Montreal, where I remained until July 1826. Before that he had been up the Châteauguay with his brother George and taken up lots in the concession, built a shanty and made a clearance. There were several before them. The first to move in was Samuel McKillen and his son David, three brothers, William,

John and Charles Abbott, and Nathanial Lannan and
I think an American, George Beach. The Abbotts and
Lannans were related and came from County Cork and
like some of the others who took up land, had worked in
making the Lachine Canal. All the first settlers, except
Beach and William Thompson, who was English, were
Irish Protestants, which gave the concession its name.[69]

Because of the extremely swampy state of the land, the timber was
unfit for making potash. As a result, the settlers had a difficult time initially
making ends meet. Their first priority was to drain the land. "It was five
years before we were able to raise wheat, but before that we had splendid
crops of potatoes and corn."[70] A school was built in 1834 and ministers
came occasionally to preach, but by around 1850 most of the original settlers had sold their lots to French Canadians and headed west. The much
repeated coming and going cycle happened yet again here.

Yet another Irish community formed between 1826 and 1830 at
Russeltown, and nearby St. Jean Chrystôme, along a tributary of the English
River. However, like the Williamstown residents, they faced draining a
swamp and were unable to produce potash. This meant that they were
denied a revenue source to tide them over until they were able to grow crops,
thus requiring them to find jobs in Montreal. To the south of Russeltown at
Covey Hill was a third Irish community that had been established by Irish
Protestants, many of whom had earlier links with Sherrington Township.[71]
According to Robert Sellar, the Covey Hill settlers "were a hard-working,
thrifty, self-denying and persevering people. Land which the Americans
thought could never be reclaimed, they transformed into good farms and
in few years wrought a marvellous change in this aspect of the country."[72]

Additional Irish communities formed just to the east of Sherrington,
although their origins date back to the Loyalist influx of the late 1780s. Many
Loyalists, such as Wexford-born Captain Garret Barron, who had served
in the army during the American War, were granted land in Major Henry
Caldwell's Foucault seigneury near Missisquoi Bay (Map 9).[73] An Irish
aristocrat, Caldwell had tried to attract affluent Ulster farmers to his land
in what became Caldwell's Manor during the early stages of the American

War.[74] Its relatively large Irish Protestant population in 1851 suggests that Caldwell had many takers whose descendants clearly remained. Nearby Henryville, in Sabrevois seigneury, and Ste Athanase in Bleury seigneury also had sizeable Irish Protestant populations by this time — further evidence of the area's pulling power for the Irish. In all, around 900 Irish-born settlers were living along the Upper Richelieu Valley at this time.[75]

The Irish Catholic influx in the 1820s to Monnoir seigneury (Iberville County)[76] on the east side of the Richelieu River may also have had its roots in the movement of Loyalists to the area (Map 9). One of many seigneuries owned by Sir John Johnson, commander of the King's Royal Regiment in the American War of Independence, it attracted Scottish Highlanders in the early 1800s.[77] Their presence was the likely a catalyst that created "a considerable settlement consisting chiefly of Irish Catholics," which was visible to Joseph Bouchette in 1832.[78] The Quebec immigration agent had referred at the time to the many respectable families heading for this area.[79] By then, Irish Catholics were well-settled along the South West River, a tributary of the Yamaska River, and their designated holdings became known as the "Rang des Irlandais."[80] Changing its name to Ste Brigitte d'Iberville in 1846, what was once the Monnoir seigneury still had around 200 Irish-born settlers in 1851.

In the early 1830s, Vaudreuil County acquired small groups of Irish, who mainly settled at Ste. Marthe in the former Rigaud seigneury lying just west of Montreal (Map 9). Some of these Irish had relocated from St. Columban (Two Mountains County). By 1851 there were nearly 200 Irish-born settlers living in or near Ste. Marthe, mainly Protestants from the north of Ireland. By the end of the century most of these families had moved on to eastern Ontario or the United States.[81]

Having cultivated vast stretches of Lower Canada, the Irish zeal for emigration grew. The rapid growth in the St. Lawrence timber trade not only brought regular and affordable Atlantic sea crossings, it also gave the Irish access to a wide range of jobs and the farming opportunities to be had in the Ottawa Valley. Thanks to the region's enormously successful timber trade, the greatest Irish concentrations formed here. While the conditions were harsh and unforgiving and would have defeated all but the hardiest, the Irish once again demonstrated their resilience and pioneering zeal.

CHAPTER 6

 ❧

The Ottawa Valley

It was only in the 1830s that Irish Catholics on the Ottawa [River] began to go into the timber trade in a big way as hewers of wood. These were not settlers, but navvies brought in to dig the Rideau Canal, and when that was completed in 1832 they sought logging jobs traditionally held by French Canadians. Since the Irish had little experience in the woods, their method of seeking employment was to try to scare the French Canadians off, and this involved fighting. Bytown [Ottawa], once a canal construction camp and now a glorified timber depot, gained a reputation as the roughest community in the country.[1]

Donald MacKay's account of the Irish Catholics who worked as lumberjacks and labourers in the Ottawa Valley's timber trade and, before that, as canal diggers, is a fitting reminder of why some of the Irish came to this region. The jobs on offer brought rates of pay that were far higher than comparable work in Ireland. Of course, the Irish, irrespective of their religion, were not just hewers of wood and navvies. Some were also accomplished farmers. Although they received less government assistance

Map 10: Irish Concentrations in the Ottawa, Gatineau, and Rideau Valleys, 1881

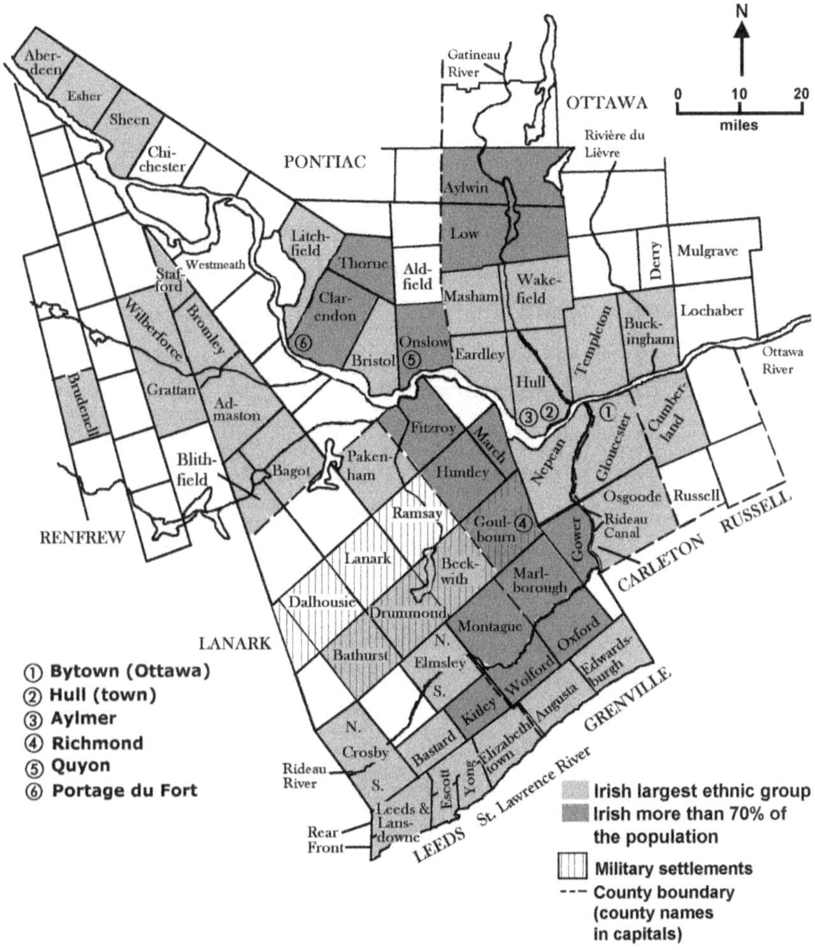

① Bytown (Ottawa)
② Hull (town)
③ Aylmer
④ Richmond
⑤ Quyon
⑥ Portage du Fort

Irish largest ethnic group
Irish more than 70% of the population
Military settlements
County boundary (county names in capitals)

to emigrate than their Scottish counterparts, they greatly outnumbered them. Quite simply, the Irish were the principal colonizers of the Ottawa Valley (Map 10).

The region's timber trade jobs and farming opportunities had been important magnets for the Irish, but there were other factors as well, the most important being the British government's determination to hang on to Upper Canada. Having won the War of 1812–14 by a close shave, it feared that the Americans might attack again and seize control over the

St. Lawrence River. To offset these fears, it sanctioned the building of the Rideau Canal, linking the St. Lawrence with the Ottawa River to provide a vital supply route in the event of an invasion. And to safeguard this militarily sensitive area it offered subsidies and free land to immigrants from the British Isles in the hope that they would farm the land while acting as civilian defenders. This policy, enacted between 1815 and 1825, brought many hundreds of Scottish but fewer Irish farmers to the so-called military settlements that were established in Lanark and Carleton counties. In addition, many of the thousands of Irish labourers who dug the Rideau Canal, completed in 1832, remained in the area, thus extending the Irish population even more.

The Irish had been quick to grab what land they could, and by 1826, when the construction of the Rideau Canal began, they were already present in substantial numbers. They had jumped the gun in the sense of having come to the region before the military settlements in the Rideau townships had even been contemplated. A small number of families from Wexford and Wicklow had settled in 1809 in Elizabethtown, one of the St. Lawrence townships to the south, and two years later another group moved in to nearby Leeds and Lansdowne Township. When the Napoleonic Wars ended in 1815, many more Irish arrived in these and the less developed townships behind them, following in the footsteps of the families and friends who had arrived earlier. Like them, they originated from Wexford, Wicklow, or the adjoining counties in the southeast of Ireland.[2]

When Wexford-born Thomas Graham arrived in Brockville (Elizabethtown Township) in 1827 he found a home away from home. He told his mother that he decided on impulse to join his "sister and friends and all my old neighbours" already living there, rather than "stop in Quebec as I intended." Working as a joiner's apprentice, he was already doing "a great deal better than in Ireland.... Men must labour very hard here; but they are well fed and well paid and what a man has is his own: there is no landlord or tyrant to reign over them.... With a little money and my industry, I could possess more property here in three or four years than I could ever have in Ireland, and I could call it my own."[3] The 1881 Census reveals the extent of the Irish takeover. They were the largest ethnic group in much of Leeds and Grenville counties and in Kitley,

Wolford, and Oxford townships they represented more than 70 percent of the population (Map 10).

The relocation of people from the southeast of Ireland to eastern Upper Canada was achieved without any government assistance. In time, they and their offspring extended their territory northward to take advantage of the free land on offer in the military settlements.

But why had the early Wexford and Wicklow families chosen to settle in Leeds and Grenville in the first place? The most likely explanation stems yet again from the British government's defence concerns. Irish ex-soldiers who had served in the Jessop's Corps, one of the Loyalist units to fight in the American War of Independence, had been allocated their land in the St. Lawrence townships in Leeds and Grenville counties, this having been designated as a crucially important defensive site. In other words, the Irish influx to the region probably dates back to the mid-1780s. It is noticeable that later Irish requests to the government for funds to relocate to Upper Canada tended to specify locations near the St. Lawrence. For instance, Thomas Lipsett from Donegal, in the north of Ireland, asked for help on behalf of fifteen householders (118 individuals), all of whom were Anglicans, stating they wished to settle "in the vicinity of Kingston,"[4] where they would be close to the St. Lawrence River. Such requests were always rejected. In any case, irrespective of the sites chosen, the region's development and economic growth could not have happened without the timber trade.

Relying on French and Irish lumberjacks and labourers for its workforce, the timber trade greatly stimulated local economies and led to a rapid population growth within many parts of the Ottawa Valley, especially the Rideau region. Ottawa, Pontiac, and Argenteuil counties, on the north side of the Ottawa River, also attracted a growing number of settlers beginning in 1817, and many of them were Irish. By 1881 the Irish dominated fifty-three townships in an almost continuous line of settlements that straddled eight counties on both sides of the Ottawa River (Map 10).[5] They accounted for 72 percent of Carleton County's population, over 50 percent of Leeds and Grenville counties, 49 percent of Lanark County, and 44 percent of Renfrew County (Map 10). This was a migration of epic proportions!

The timber trade was the lynchpin of this saga. With its sawmills and forestry clearance activities, it generated a vast number of labouring jobs and it also acted as a conduit for settlement. The Irish hacked out their first communities from vast wildernesses, choosing suitable sites from which they could easily sell their timber, thus creating the distinctive settlement pockets that stretched along both sides of the Ottawa, Gatineau, and Rideau rivers. Family was extremely important to these new arrivals, and they often sought to settle close to a relative, no matter how distant, thus creating communities in which people from particular parts of Ireland banded together. In other words, many Irish families, both Protestant and Catholic, simply decided to settle in certain townships because they knew people there. Distinctive immigrant streams were thus created and the chain of people following each other from Ireland to mid-Canada often persisted over many years.

Although the timber industry was regularly plunged into boom and bust conditions, according to the fluctuations of business cycles in Britain, it offered diverse employment opportunities and was a vital component

The Rideau Falls from the river, almost two kilometres from Bytown (Ottawa), 1851. Watercolour by James D. Duncan, W.H. Coverdale Collection.

of a settler's livelihood. For the very poor, it provided the means to earn money to purchase land, although there were plenty of lumbermen who never became farmers. The logging town of Hull, founded by the New England–born Philemon Wright,[6] was the nucleus of the Ottawa Valley's timber trade; located close to the confluence of the Ottawa and Gatineau rivers, it was a prime site.[7] Wright seized the opportunity provided by the sudden increase in tariffs on European timber, introduced in 1811 following Napoleon's blockade of the Baltic five years earlier. This effectively allowed North American timber to be sold more cheaply in Britain despite the much greater shipping distances involved.[8] However, to sell into this market, Wright had to work out how to convey the Ottawa Valley's vast timber reserves to the port of Quebec. This was no easy matter given that logs had to float through a series of rapids during their 150-mile river journey to Quebec. By trying various river routes himself, Wright established that logs could be floated using large timber rafts manned by crews:

> For 100 years timber rafts scudded down the St. Lawrence to Quebec City from Lake Ontario, the Richelieu, the Ottawa and the St. Maurice [rivers], sails billowing, banners streaming and smoke swirling from their cooking fires. Some were like floating villages a quarter of a mile long with crews of 50 men and perhaps another 100 homeward-bound from the woods.[9]

John Egan, an Irish immigrant from Galway, went on to succeed Wright as "King of the Ottawa" in the mid-1840s, every year hiring 3,800 men to cut wood and sending around fifty-five timber rafts to Quebec City. However, this being a high-risk business, he went bankrupt in 1854.[10]

All the while, the Irish raftsmen, who called themselves "Shiners," had become a law unto themselves and their fights with French Canadians were legendary. They were particularly notorious for ousting French crews and taking their rafts as their own.[11] Peter Aylen, one of the region's leading timber barons, engineered widespread conflict during the 1830s by setting the Irish and French against each other in an attempt to seize control of timber operations in Bytown (Ottawa). After much bloodshed,

Timber slide with raft at Bytown (Ottawa). Timber slides enabled floating timber to bypass falls. Watercolour, circa 1851, by Alice Mary Fulford.

the violence was quelled by government troops and afterward Bytown's riots were mostly fights between traditional foes — Irish Catholics and Irish Protestants.[12]

Although the timber trade was progressing well, the British government had still to provide funds to ensure that the region could meet its security needs. Establishing the military settlements in the Rideau Valley was the first step.[13] First of all, disbanded soldiers from the 99th and 100th Regiments, mostly Irish, who had fought in the American War of 1812–14, were granted land in Goulbourn Township, thus laying the foundations of the Richmond military settlement. Then, in 1815 the government assisted a large contingent of Scots to relocate to the newly surveyed townships of Bathurst, Drummond, and Beckwith,[14] and in 1818 it helped a much smaller Irish group consisting of fifteen families (seventy-two individuals), who were predominately Anglicans from Tipperary, to relocate to Goulbourn, Beckwith, and Drummond townships. Unfortunately, because their leader, Richard Talbot,[15] an Irish military officer, lacked the necessary skills to manage the group, many hardships were to plague him and his group.[16] However, if Frederick William Richardson's progress is anything to go by, those in the Talbot group who settled in the Rideau Valley prospered.

A shoemaker from Limerick, Richardson arrived with his wife Anne Haskett and their two daughters in 1819, joining his brothers, sisters, and parents, who had come with the Talbot group the previous year. Seventeen years later he had acquired 900 acres of land in March Township (adjoining Goulbourn) and was farming it together with his six sons and their families.[17] With its many retired half-pay officers from the 99th and 100th Regiments having substantial army pensions, March Township would become a relatively affluent district.[18] Commenting on his small and scattered congregation, the Anglican minister based in Richmond village remarked on the very good farmland that they owned and predicted that "before many years the people will be wealthy."[19]

In addition to helping the seventy or so Talbot settlers in 1818, the government also assisted 450 Scottish Highlanders to go to the military settlements that same year, but it rejected requests for similar aid from a very large group from counties Wexford and Carlow. Despite this rejection, many clearly relocated themselves to the military settlements anyway.[20] Their petition to the government, issued in 1817,[21] listed the 710 Protestant families (4,027 people) and 281 Catholic families (1,475 people) wishing to emigrate, revealing a huge expression of interest from the southeast of Ireland.[22] Given that many Irish Anglicans and Methodists from counties Wexford, Carlow, and Kilkenny are known to have been granted land in Beckwith and Drummond townships at around this time, it would seem that at least some of these people voted with their feet.[23] In view of the high cost of getting to Upper Canada, it seems quite remarkable that they were able to raise the necessary funds.

When it came to funding their sea crossings, the Irish had a card up their sleeves that was unique to them. They used a remittance system whereby family and friends already settled in Canada forwarded their loved ones the required funds to set sail. Acting collectively in this way they could fund their own assistance schemes.[24] A shipping advertisement in the June 6, 1822, edition of the *Quebec Gazette* reveals how merchants acted as middlemen in this process:

> For Belfast to return to Quebec, the brig *Ann*, Captain
> John Redpath, will be dispatched for the above port ...
> this vessel will return from Belfast to this port [Quebec]
> ... persons here [in Quebec] wishing to procure a passage
> for their friends to this country should not omit this most
> favourable opportunity.[25]

In fact, most of the nineteenth-century Irish emigration to North America was financed by remittances.[26]

However, a group of impoverished Irish Catholics from County Cork found an open door when they requested help. In 1823, some 182 families (568 immigrants) originating mostly from the north of Cork but some also from Tipperary, Limerick, and Clare were assisted by the government to move to the Rideau townships.[27] They were recruited and led by Peter Robinson, M.P., brother of the Upper Canada attorney general, John Beverley Robinson. Sailing in the *Hebe* and *Stakesby*,[28] they settled in Ramsay, Huntley, Goulbourn, Beckwith, Lanark, Bathurst, and Pakenham townships.[29]

While a few single men like Cornelius Ryan, William Gubbins, Patrick Rourke, and William Horan worked on the Rideau Canal and had little to show as far as clearing their land, most took up farming with great vigour.[30] The reports they sent home were invariably cheerful, with Michael Corkery's account of life in Ramsay Township being typical:

> I came to this country in 1823 from Ireland, under the
> charge of Mr. Robinson, and received rations for one year.
> I have now, with the exertions of myself and son, cleared
> upwards of twenty acres of land and have a yoke of steers,
> five milk cows, two yearlings, besides pigs, poultry, etc.,
> and I consider my lot and crop worth at best £200. Add
> to this, I am happy and contented.[31]

A great many prospered. Writing from Bathurst Township, John Tatlock boasted that "with the assistance of the government in serving me with rations, implements, etc., I contrived, with industry, to live so that at the termination of five years, I had thirty acres of land under cultivation, a great deal of livestock, and a property worth £300." And his family was "likewise increased to twelve children, with my father and mother in the house."[32] Michael Cronin, based in Huntley Township, advised his family in Ireland to join him: "This is as good and as free a country as any in the world and each man is paid twelve dollars a month ... and to each woman six dollars."[33] The Cork-born Charles Carrol O'Sullivan, writing from Ramsay Township, remarked on the frosty conditions that prevented people from working outdoors but said this was better to put up with than "the rebuke of a landlord and the frown of a Proctor [supervisor] at home."[34]

Having the best land, Ramsay Township attracted around half of the Robinson group. Patrick Lynch wrote approvingly from Ramsay that anyone coming under Peter Robinson's superintendence would be "as happy as gentlemen at home" provided that "they stick to their land and abstain from liquor, for that is the inclination of men in this country."[35] On a similar note, Catherine O'Brien told her brother that her husband Thomas had cleared four acres and urged him to join them, but warned about the demon drink. "Rum is very cheap ... and a great many of our settlers likes it too well, which may prove their ruin, for a drunkard will not do well here, any more than at home."[36] And John O'Mara told his brother that "our superintendent, Mr. Robinson, is behaving as humane and gentlemanly as any man in the world" and thought that his land grant "is as good as any land in the country."[37]

Yet, despite the obvious success of the 1823 Peter Robinson group, critics in Britain concerned about the drain on the public purse argued against assisting a second group of paupers, believing that Upper Canada's interests would be better served by attracting more self-sufficient farmers. However, there were far more paupers than affluent farmers wishing to emigrate, and, desirous of increasing the Ottawa Valley population, the government found the necessary funds. Another scheme materialized two years later. Setting aside £30,000 for the venture, the government assisted 2,069 Irish Catholics to relocate to the region.[38] Once again they were supervised by Peter Robinson. However, by then conditions in the Rideau townships were far worse than in 1823. Most of the best farmland had already been allocated, and the mounting tension between the area's Protestants and Catholics bred civil disorder, some of it violent.[39] In light of this, the authorities looked beyond the Ottawa Valley and granted land to this second group in a separate range of townships in the Peterborough region.[40]

A major turning point occurred in the Ottawa Valley in 1826 when work began in the building of the Rideau Canal. Linking the St. Lawrence and Ottawa rivers, it was a major undertaking, employing 1,500 to 2,500 labourers each year, many of whom were Irish. The June 11, 1829, edition of the *Montreal Gazette* reported that, in that month alone,[41] 1,000 labourers were being sought to help in the building of the canal, while two years later it was claimed that 2,000 labourers were being employed along one stretch of the Ottawa River to further the needs of the timber trade.[42] Such jobs were being filled by the French and Irish immigrants. Some Irish canal workers hoped to use their wages to set themselves up in farming once the canal was completed in 1832, but their future was far from certain. Of the 9,000 or so Irish labourers who worked on both

Hartwell's Locks, painted circa 1835, by John Burrows (1789–1848). The Rideau Canal, which linked Kingston with Bytown (Ottawa), was completed in 1832. There are forty-five locks along the main route of the canal.

the Rideau and Welland canals between 1826 and 1832, at least 1,000 lost their lives after contracting malaria-like diseases.[43]

With the completion of the Rideau Canal, many Irish labourers hired themselves out as lumbermen, but their inexperience initially put them at a disadvantage. French workers were far more proficient. The visiting commentator, John MacTaggert, observed that "it takes an Irishman a long time to learn the art of the hatchet [small axe], if he has been used chiefly to spade and shovel work, which is quite a different kind of occupation." And the French mocked them for wearing "breeches that bind at the knee and stockings," instead of trousers.[44] However, the Irish soon muscled into this labour force, leading to ongoing disputes with the French over wage rates and employment practices. Hiring and managing the lumbermen were the timber contractors, who organized the felling and transport operations, and financing their operations were the merchants. After being cut, lumber was carried on rafts down the Ottawa River to the St. Lawrence and on to the port of Quebec, where it was loaded onto ocean-going ships to be sold in Britain. And once a merchant received his money, the various contractors and lumberjacks involved in the complex felling and transport operations received their payments.[45]

The Rideau Canal was built at a time when areas of Scotland and Ireland were experiencing catastrophic economic conditions. An 1826–27 Parliamentary Select Committee advised the government to assist impoverished people who wished to immigrate to Canada, but the government rejected its advice because of the high cost of such schemes and landowner objections. However, the committee's very existence had boosted the emigration fever even further. The Colonial Office had been deluged with petitions asking for government help.[46] The 967 petitioners from County Kilkenny who were from Lord Clifden's estate in Callan were ready to emigrate, but their landlord was clearly not ready to offer financial support.[47] He would only do so when the Great Famine struck some twenty years later. Also, with the demise of the weaving trade, householders from Newry, employed as "linen manufacturers," were desperate to emigrate, as were 200 distressed families from Belfast who had formed themselves into the Belfast Canadian Emigration Society.[48] And so it went on. Very little government help was ever given.

In the meantime, the Irish presence in the Rideau townships continued to grow. With the completion of the Rideau Canal in 1832, townships
along its route suddenly acquired large numbers of redundant Irish canal
workers who mainly settled in March, Fitzroy, Huntley, Goulbourn, and
Marlborough townships (Carleton County).[49] The roots put down by the
canal workers greatly increased Irish numbers, and by 1881 they represented 70 percent of the population in each of these townships (Map 10).[50]

Montague's population also rose with its intake of Irish labourers, but
it had an additional source. Because it and the other townships along the
Rideau Canal and River route were seen by immigrants on their way to
Lake Ontario, they attracted passerby travellers who were impressed by
their attractive-looking farmland. Impulse got the better of some, and many
Irish families are known to have hopped off their steamers and remained in
Montague Township.[51] Before that time, the Irish who arrived in Montague
in the 1820s and 1830s had squatted on or rented land owned by absentee
Loyalists before purchasing their property.[52]

Photograph of St. James Anglican Church near Smiths Falls in Montague Township. The
church is one of the oldest surviving Protestant churches in eastern Ontario.

While immigrants with farming experience would have prospered in most cases, life was an uphill struggle for the humble labourer.[53] The South Elmsley Census enumerator of 1851 judged the Irish labourers who had settled in his township to be floundering: "They are settled on the poorest land in the township. Most of these persons have large families and are emigrants from Ireland and perhaps it would be a libel upon their character to say they were idle, but their Capital (that is their Labour) is not economically expended; in other words, however capable they may be to labour profitably for others, a number of them are not qualified to labour profitably for themselves."[54] It was tough making the transition. The Montague Census enumerator's assessment was much the same: "The people in general is very poor. The most part of them gets their living by working out in the winter and raising a little crop in the summer. Few could support themselves by the crops they grow."[55] And Gloucester and Osgoode townships (Russell County), on the east side of the Rideau Canal, attracted their Irish settlers relatively late, only beginning in the 1830s, either directly from Ireland or when Irish people who had already settled in the region sought better sites (Map 10).

While the building of the Rideau Canal and the establishment of the military settlements encouraged many Irish to try their luck on the Upper Canada side of the Ottawa River, conditions on the north side, in Lower Canada, were also favourable. The area's important timber processing centres were especially attractive. Government-sponsored projects were few and far between, but nevertheless, with their buoyant timber industry and good farming land, Ottawa and Pontiac counties offered incentive enough for many. The Irish began arriving soon after the end of the Napoleonic Wars in 1815. Most came directly from Ireland but after 1830 they often came as internal migrants, having lived previously in or close to the Rideau Valley settlements in Upper Canada where there was considerable competition for good land.

Hull's logging and sawmill jobs were major magnets as were the employment and farming opportunities to be found in the nearby village of Aylmer and the adjoining countryside. Having turned the area into a major stronghold, the Irish moved north up the Gatineau River, colonizing both sides. Hull and Eardley townships (Ottawa County) acquired their

Irish settlers by 1819, while later census evidence reveals that the townships to the north of them — Masham, Wakefield, Low, and Aylwin — also acquired a significant number of Irish at a fairly early stage (Map 10).[56] The first settler in Masham was said to be Dan (or John) Nichol, "a young man who came with his wife Sally and built a log cabin on the hillside about the spring near Lascelles." Another of the early settlers was "an old soldier from Tyrone" who had fought in the War of 1812–14.[57] And even though Low Township was still regarded as "a forest with few patches cleared," by as late as 1856 it was an Irish stronghold.[58] In 1881 both its population and that of the adjoining Aylwin Township was 70 percent Irish.

The large sawmills in Buckingham Township, to the east of the Gatineau River, drew many Irish people during the 1830s. They settled among the French and Americans, some of the latter having arrived as Loyalists much earlier.[59] Hoping to benefit from its lumber industry, the Irish founded a community between five and ten miles from Buckingham village.[60] Although the English were few in number, an Anglican Church prospered due to the support given to it by local Irish residents. In his 1854 report to the Society for the Propagation of the Gospel, the Anglican minister Reverend William Morris commented on the fact that the area's population was mainly Irish and French. He stated that the inhabitants of Buckingham village were chiefly employed as lumberjacks and in the sawmills and spent almost no time in farming: "Upwards of 400 men are employed in local [saw] mills and in the shanties and log houses in the woods."[61]

The Irish were said to have been well established across the entire region by 1831, most being Protestants who originated from the north of Ireland.[62] However, a sizeable number of Protestants were also coming from the southern counties of Tipperary, Wexford, and Wicklow, where sectarian concerns had long been the cause of insecurity and strife.[63]

The Irish influx into Buckingham spread westward to Templeton, while Lochaber Township, to the east, also acquired a substantial Irish population, having 248 Irish-born residents in 1851. In fact, they would have been among the inhabitants of St. Malachie de Mayo, founded by County Mayo people in 1827 in the northern part of the township. A good many more Mayo immigrants followed during the Irish Famine of the 1840s and the St. Malachie community was able to build its first Catholic chapel ten years later. Overall, the Irish dominated this region when compared with the Scots and English. The Irish population on the north side of the Ottawa River in 1851 was six times that of the Scottish population and twenty times that of the English.[64]

Bytown (Ottawa) on the Upper Canada side of the Ottawa River was an important commercial centre that thrived on the timber trade. James Moncrieff Wilson, general manager of the Queen Insurance Company in Liverpool, visited Ottawa in 1865 to witness for himself how the trade functioned:

> I was struck with the number of Inns and found they had sprung up out of the necessities of the timber trade. Most of the lumberers are furnished, that is provided with the means of carrying on operations in the woods by people in Quebec and this furnishing is advanced by instalments, the first being used to buy provisions, clothes and other necessaries, and thus the lumberers are immediately out of money. But they must have men to do the work. At certain seasons thousands of men flock to Ottawa in search of employment in the woods. As a rule they arrive penniless but are hospitably received by the Tavern keepers who follow this line of business.[65]

Thus, at certain times of the year such was the demand for labour that Ottawa innkeepers were hiring out their lodgers, who were invariably Irish, to work for local contractors as lumberjacks. The area was also a launching pad for those wishing to become farmers. John Heney, a retired soldier from the north of Ireland who had served in the British Army, settled in Bytown in 1832. His two sons went on to establish farms in nearby Gloucester and Cumberland townships (Map 10).[66]

Argenteuil County, at the east end of the Ottawa River near Montreal, had also acquired Irish settlers and, as was the case with the Rideau Canal in Upper Canada, canal building had acted as a spur to settlement. The digging of the Grenville Canal,[67] begun in 1818, brought large numbers of

Irish labourers to the area, many of whom clearly remained. In 1881 they were Grenville Township's largest ethnic group (Map 11). During his visit to the area in 1820, Lord Dalhousie, governor-in-chief of Canada, had actually observed the large number of Irish immigrants who were hard at work.[68]

In addition to the canal diggers who were probably mainly Catholics, Argenteuil also attracted Protestants from the north of Ireland, many arriving in the 1820s. James Orr, a farmer from County Down who came in 1817 but died soon after, left a widow and four sons who settled in the Gore near Lachute, an area that acquired many Irish.[69] Jean McQuat, writing to her brother in Glasgow in 1826 from what was then the Argenteuil seigneury, noted their presence:

Map **11**: Irish Concentrations in Argenteuil County, Lower Canada, **1881**

Areas where the Irish were mainly concentrated

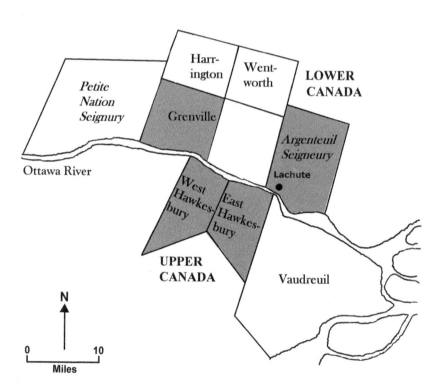

> This country is settling very fast — there were only five
> families in the East Settlement when we came here, now
> there are as many as forty, the most part of them are Irish
> folks; they are very civil people, and good neighbours
> in general.[70]

Jean was paying an annual rent of £20 for her farm: "The landlord finds a horse fit to work all of the farm, and half of the seed and half of the horse's oats and hay, and we find the other half of all." The landlord also provided her with a house, barn, and stables, as well as farming utensils: "We do all the work, reaping and threshing" and receive "half of all the produce."[71]

And Edward McClusky's arrival in 1830 in Wentworth Township, located to the northwest of Lachute, was the first step in the founding of Argenteuil's New Ireland.[72] His sons, who arrived thirty years later and cleared around 300 acres of land, had created the nucleus of this settlement.[73]

Meanwhile, George Hamilton, a local timber baron who came from County Meath, had established a great sawmilling establishment in Hawkesbury (Prescott County) in the early 1800s, opposite Argenteuil on the Upper Canada side of the Ottawa River (Map 11). The relatively large number of Irish and Scots living in Hawkesbury in 1851 probably reflect the pulling power of the jobs on offer, Hamilton having been one of the regions' major timber producers.[74] Irish Protestant mill workers were certainly very much in evidence in Vankleek Hill (West Hawkesbury) ten years later.[75] However, employment in the timber trade was not the only factor that drew the Irish to Hawkesbury. In around 1829 two prospective farmers came to the area with their families — Cork-born John Harkin and Dublin-born John Keough. Settling in Fournier near Vankleek Hill, the two families supported each other.[76] The Harkins "took their pork and other farm produce to market in Montreal," and when they did, "they stayed [overnight] at the Keogh's family [home] in Lachine." Later on, the Harkins and Keoghs settled near to each other in Fournier.[77] By way of contrast, Irish-born Thomas Dick, who arrived in Vankleek Hill in 1856, seems to have had a much easier time establishing himself in the community. Almost certainly classed as a gentleman farmer on arrival, he later became a director of the Prescott Agricultural Society.[78]

Between the 1820s and 1850s, County Antrim people established the "Irish Settlement" (later known as Centerfield) in Plantagenet Township (Prescott County) to the west of Hawkesbury. Cyrus Thomas, who visited the area in the 1890s, found that "as in many other localities along the Ottawa [River], the early settlers depended far more for their livelihood on the lumber business than they did upon stock-raising or what they could make from the produce of the soil, for which reason their land was neglected."[79] Nevertheless, in 1881 the Irish greatly outnumbered the Scots and English in Plantagenet Township.

The Irish progress west of the Gatineau Valley along the Lower Canada side of the Ottawa River only began in earnest after 1830, when the area was opened up for colonization. Onslow, Clarendon, and Thorne townships (Pontiac County) proved to be particularly popular, becoming mainly Irish by 1881, although in the case of Thorne most of the Irish arrived during the famine years of the mid-1840s.[80] Bristol and Litchfield also had a high proportion of Irish.[81] By 1881 the population of Pontiac County was nearly half Irish.

Galway-born John Egan, an Ottawa Valley timber baron of Irish descent, had given the area a boost when he founded the village of Quyon in Onslow Township in 1848.[82] Ten years later the Anglican minister, the Reverend Henry Hazard, who was based at Quyon, described the "hardy pioneers from the north of Ireland" who formed his congregation.[83] Some had arrived during the famine period of the 1840s. Quyon village itself then had ten houses, its chief industry being "the collecting of all logs which were floated down the Ottawa River from the many lumber camps in the vicinity of its banks."[84] It was a similar story in Clarendon Township to the west of Onslow, although the Irish arrived there much earlier.

Among the first settlers to come to Clarendon Township were John Dale, his wife Elizabeth, and Thomas Hodgins, all Irish Protestants from Tipperary who appeared just after 1815, having previously settled in Upper Canada. Possibly they and the other Tipperary settlers had been recruited by Lieutenant James Prendergast, an energetic land agent who had fought in the War of 1812–14. Having first become ensconced in the Richmond military settlement in Lanark County (Upper Canada) with other Irish ex-soldiers, Prendergast obtained a very large land grant in Clarendon, and soon after tried to persuade others in Richmond to join him.[85] His big selling point was that he had been made the land agent for Clarendon. Unfortunately, his anti-Catholic tendencies got the better of him and he tried to bar Catholics from settling in the area. Undeterred, Irish Catholics eventually obtained land in Portage du Fort and were well settled by the 1850s.[86]

Protestant colonists from Tipperary and other parts of southeast Ireland arrived in Clarendon Township in the 1830s and "for fifteen to twenty years this famous county [Tipperary] contributed largely to the settlement and development of Clarendon."[87] Arriving in 1842, Clarendon's first Anglican minister, the Reverend Francis Falloon, witnessed this large influx.[88] Later, it was said that the Clarendon Irish had been more successful in economic terms than in other parts of Lower Canada, thus enabling their Anglican Church to be particularly well funded.

Methodist ministers had also arrived in Onslow and Clarendon townships starting in the 1830s, although their support was strongest on the Upper Canada side of the Ottawa River, where Methodist preaching circuits had been established thirty years earlier.[89] Having been founded by Irish squatters, possibly from Upper Canada, in around 1820, the village of Shawville, just to the east of Portage du Fort, went on to acquire many more Irish from the north of Ireland between 1845 and 1855.[90] However, Shawville's prospects were far less promising. The Ebenezer Church at Radford, near Shawville, was built in the second half of the nineteenth century by "old Methodist people" who had previously held their Sunday worship in the bush.[91]

The Irish began colonizing land west of Clarendon in Pontiac County and in Renfrew County, on the opposite side of the Ottawa River in Upper Canada, much later, this region being far less accessible and less developed (Map 10). Some areas could not easily support farming, and timber was often cut not as a by-product of land clearance but as a product in its own right. The main Irish influx to these more remote areas began in the mid-1840s when the Great Famine struck in Ireland. The Ottawa Valley became a prime destination for people who had family and friends already settled in the region and who were fleeing the famine.

Sailing mainly from ports in the south and west of Ireland, those arriving between 1845 and 1855 settled primarily in Sheen, Esher, and

Aberdeen townships (Pontiac County) in Lower Canada, and in Brudenell, Stafford, Bromley, Wilberforce, Grattan, Admaston, Blithfield, and Bagot townships (Renfrew County) in Upper Canada.[92] These townships had been opened up for settlement in the 1840s and received a good part of the Catholic famine immigration of the time. However, some of the famine arrivals managed to find prime locations in long-settled areas." For instance, John Taylor wrote to his parents in County Tyrone in 1847 saying that he was enclosing £18 (£14 8s. in Ireland) for them to spend in sailing to Quebec. The implication was that they would join him in South Gower Township (Grenville County), a strongly Irish area that had been colonized since the 1820s.[93] As ever, some of the Irish influx to the new areas being made available to colonizers was due to internal migration, as Irish people who had previously settled in the Rideau Valley sought better locations.[94]

With its burgeoning timber trade, the Ottawa Valley had attracted many Irish, but more were yet to come. Their thriving settlements showed them to be industrious, highly adaptable, and self-reliant pioneers. Now, as the second Peter Robinson group made its way to Peterborough in 1825, they and others would transform yet more great wildernesses into farms and integrate themselves into the new communities being formed in eastern Ontario.

CHAPTER 7

⚜

The Rest of Eastern Ontario and the Peter Robinson Settlers

> Not a few of those who sailed form Cork in 1825 have passed away after a life of hard and ceaseless toil, and others now stand, as it were, at the brink of the grave; but their sons and their grandsons, their daughters and their granddaughters flourish in the midst of prosperity and comfort.... The shanty and the wigwam and the log hut have long since given [way] to the mansion of brick and stone; and the hand-sleigh and the rude cart to the strong wagon and well-appointed carriage.[1]

As ever, John Maguire gives the best possible gloss on an immigration success story. Under the British government's assistance scheme, supervised by Peter Robinson, 2,500 Irish people, who mainly came from County Cork, were enabled to relocate to the Peterborough area in 1825. When he visited the site in the mid-1860s, Maguire met the descendants of these early settlers forty years after the land had first been cleared. The scheme had been controversial in the beginning, and many hardships had to be endured, including deaths from ague, a type of malarial fever. In order to reach the land that had been allocated to them, the first arrivals had to traverse a trackless wilderness lying some forty miles inland from the frontier — "there was not even the semblance of a track through the wooded country." In the end, Robinson's group founded Peterborough, "one of the most beautiful and prosperous towns in Canada,"[2] which they named after him, and they also founded many successful farming communities stretching across Peterborough and Victoria counties.

While the Robinson venture was the largest and best known of the government-assisted schemes, it was not the only one. In 1817, James Buchanan, the British consul in New York, offered Irish farmers and labourers living there, who were mainly from Ulster, the chance to relocate to Upper Canada, offering them free transportation and land on which to settle.[3] More than 1,600 took up the offer and established communities in Durham County just to the west of where the Peter Robinson group would settle (Map 12).[4] Then there were one or two landlord-assisted

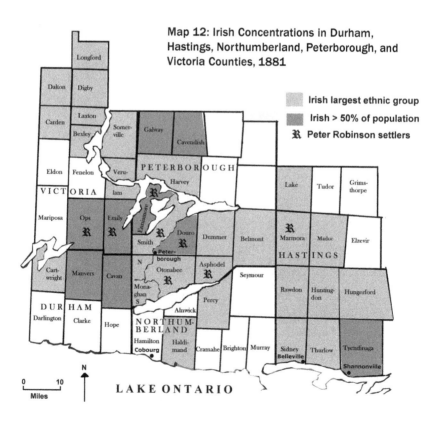

Map 12: Irish Concentrations in Durham, Hastings, Northumberland, Peterborough, and Victoria Counties, 1881

schemes. Lord Mountcashel (Stephen Moore), an Irish nobleman and one of Peter Robinson's advisers, having purchased the Amherst Island estate near Kingston in the 1820s, sought out Irish tenants to occupy his land (Map 13).[5] While normally such a prime site on Lake Ontario would have been long settled by Loyalists and their followers, on this occasion, due to the Earl of Mountcashel's initiative, an opportunity beckoned for people in Ireland. He found his prospective settlers in Ulster's Ards Peninsula (County Down). Although their numbers were relatively small — Amherst Island had 450 Irish-born residents in 1851 — it was a successful venture. Colonel George Wyndham, another landlord, assisted his County Clare tenants to relocate to the Peterborough area in 1839, but because the land was poor, many left for the United States.

Map 13: Irish Concentrations in Addington and Frontenac Counties, 1881

However, such schemes do not tell the whole story. Most of the Irish who settled in these and other regions of eastern Ontario were unassisted. They chose where they settled and financed and planned their relocation themselves. They slipped into Upper Canada unnoticed and largely undocumented, but census data indicates that they were there.[6] By 1881, people with Irish ancestry were predominant throughout much of eastern Ontario. In addition to major enclaves in the Ottawa Valley, they were particularly well concentrated in the Kingston and Belleville areas near Lake Ontario and in groups of connecting townships in Peterborough, Victoria, Durham, and Hastings counties, where they principally occupied the back townships (Map 12).

The Irish demonstrated an exceptional ability to uncover prime sites. In the 1820s a large group of Irish Catholics found an attractive site in Tyendinaga Township in the Bay of Quinte region to the west of Kingston. The land, having formerly been part of a reserve set aside for the Mohawk people, had become available and the Irish had been quick off the mark. And, even during the distressing period of the Great Irish Famine of the mid-1840s, when the number of Irish arrivals suddenly rocketed, the issue of where to settle had salience. Many found prime sites in long-settled sites near Kingston and in the Marmora region, where newly surveyed land was on offer. Far from being helpless exiles, lacking in ambition, as is sometimes alleged, the Irish grabbed their opportunities and showed themselves to be skillful planners and organizers.

The major starting point for the Irish conquest of the region was the Peter Robinson venture of 1825.[7] Having already established a smaller group of Irish Catholics in the government-sponsored military settlements in the Ottawa Valley in 1823, he proceeded with the Peterborough phase.[8] Out of 50,000 applications received from farmers, labourers, and tradesmen, Robinson selected 307 families (or 2,024 people) who came mainly from County Cork, although some also originated from counties Limerick, Tipperary, Waterford, and Kerry.[9] They mostly came from the same ninety parishes, and usually there were small numbers from each one. They were selected principally by eight landlords whose estates occupied five contiguous Irish counties, while thirty-seven other landowners chose the remaining families.[10] They had to be paupers, under the age of forty-five, and Roman Catholic.

Most of those selected were farmers, but around eighty combined farming with a trade, such as being a shoemaker, blacksmith, mason, or weaver.[11] Carefully selected families with plenty of teenagers and healthy single men were sought, thus helping to ensure the success of the venture. Landlords did not use the schemes as an opportunity to get rid of the elderly, infirm, or layabouts, as might have happened, since it was obvious that such people would fail. Well-motivated immigrants with a farming background had the best chance of success, and their favourable reports home would stimulate follow-on emigration. This clearly happened with the Robinson group.

Robinson's Irish immigrants created several settlement clusters spread over a large area, with extended families grouping together. He offered them 403 locations/lots in eight townships: the largest numbers were in Emily (142), Ennismore (67), Douro (60), and Otonabee (51) townships, while smaller numbers were in Asphodel (36), Smith (34), and Ops and Marmora (13 between them). Irish Protestants, who had come to live in neighbouring Cavan Township (Durham County) as a consequence of James Buchanan's scheme, were hired to assist in the felling of trees and the initial land clearance. Although there was some rivalry initially between Irish Protestants and Catholics living in the area, there was never any hint of trouble. In any case, in places like Douro and Emily, where the Robinson group lived in dense bush well away from already-settled areas, the issue of compatibility did not initially arise.

While Robinson's immigrants went on to create successful pioneer communities, there were some at the time who predicted that the scheme would be a disaster. Governor General Lord Dalhousie was certain it would fail "as the Irish would abandon the land and become wandering beggars," and he did all in his power to undermine the scheme.[12] There were disagreements in high places over the procedures for selecting immigrants, concerns over the scheme's heavy cost, and a belief in some quarters that once in Upper Canada the immigrants would slip across to the United States. Misinformation was rife. Writing from the Land Register Office at Port Hope in 1825, Thomas Orton publicly refuted allegations

A silhouette portrait of the Honourable Peter Robinson (1785–1838), who masterminded the relocation of many Irish Catholics to the Ottawa Valley and Peterborough region in the 1820s.

that the Peter Robinson settlers "were rapidly deserting to the United States." Writing from Cobourg that same year, Dr. A. Morton reinforced this message, stating that "he never heard of one [settler] express a wish to go to the United States."[13] Robinson's people rolled up their sleeves and within a year of arriving cleared 1,311 acres of land, and reports from them and about them were mainly positive.

The Robinson scheme had a host of onlookers and commentators who lined up to offer their verdicts. John Richards, who was sent out by the British government in 1825 to observe them, reported back that they were doing well. However, he was surprised to see how they regarded Peter Robinson, who joined him on his visits. They greeted him "more to bless him as a benefactor than to welcome him as a visitor."[14] This reaction may help to explain their bland replies to a questionnaire sent to them by Robert John Wilmot Horton, the undersecretary of state for the colonies. A total of 137 families responded.[15] When asked "Have your comforts and happiness increased?" and "Would you advise friends in Ireland to join you?" most answered yes. This they did irrespective of their circumstances. Some families had lost loved ones to disease or had lived with hunger and yet they were universally positive and cheerful in their replies. It seems that they simply wanted to please. Peter Robinson gave them their big break in life. Whatever difficulties they had to face in the future, they would always be grateful to him.

Also waiting to size them up were two affluent Ulstermen, Thomas Stewart and his brother-in-law Robert Reid, both from County Antrim, who had arrived three years earlier. Each had been awarded grants of 1,200 acres of wilderness land in Douro Township (Peterborough County) by the government, although, being a businessman and having little experience farming, Stewart made little progress. Thinking that they he would have to abandon his farm, Stewart changed his mind when he learned that 2,000 Irish were coming to live in the area.[16] No doubt he regarded them as a potential source of cheap labour. Upon learning of the new arrivals, the Stewart family's first inclination was to "put bolts and bars on our doors and windows," but Thomas Stewart quickly changed his tune after meeting them. He then became their advocate.[17] When critical and unfounded reports about the Robinson immigrants began appearing in the *Colonial Advocate*, his local newspaper, he rose to their defence, putting pen to paper:

> I am here living in the midst of them; from 20 to 30 of them pass my door almost every day. I visit the camp every week and at all times I take the opportunity of conversing with them on their affairs. I have always found them satisfied and happy. Some of them have told me with tears in their eyes that they have never known what happiness was until now.… In general they are making great exertions in clearing land and their exertions have astonished many of the old settlers.… Not one complaint has there been against them by any of the old settlers and it is the general opinion that when so large a body of people are brought together none could conduct themselves better.[18]

However, there were still some bigots who tried to cause trouble. While John MacTaggert, a Scotsman, praised the Ulster Protestants who had settled "about Rice Lake" [in Durham County], he pronounced that Robinson's "experiment … did not very well succeed; his people, all from Erin, are being so difficult to manage, so disposed to riot."[19] Even Susanna Moodie, in her *Roughing It in the Bush*, wrote how "we shrank from the rude, coarse familiarity of the uneducated people among whom we were thrown."[20] Her brother, Samuel Strickland, an English gentleman farmer who came to live in the area soon after the Robinson settlers arrived, claimed that he had been told that they included "most obnoxious and dangerous characters." Yet he, too, was won over after meeting them, proclaiming that "the labouring population of Ireland do much better abroad than at home," because they were more contented. He even went on to say, "I must do the Irish emigrants the justice to say that they are more willing to send home pecuniary assistance to their poor relations in Ireland, and so to help them to emigrate, than any other class of settlers."[21] Meanwhile, Catharine Parr Traill, another of Strickland's married sisters, described the Irish cabins in her *Backwoods of Canada* as "reeking with smoke and dirt, the common receptacle of children, pigs and fowl," but did add that the majority were being lived in "by tidy folk."[22] Clearly, affluent families like the Stricklands were apprehensive about the new arrivals and needed time to come to terms with the egalitarian ways of the New World.

By contrast, Frances Stewart, wife of Thomas, welcomed "the poor immigrants from Ireland" in her *Our Forest Home* book, and was pleased that they were going to "give us some variety.… They are encamped on the Plains, a place about two and a half miles off. Their huts look very odd, being made with poles standing up, boughs and branches of trees interwoven, and mud plastered over them. They live in these until log shanties are ready for the families in Douro.… The poor immigrants have suffered much and many died."[23] And Basil Hall, an Irish travel writer who visited in 1827, judged the scheme to have been a great success "if the object was to render a mass of destitute and miserable people independent and useful, instead of being burdens to the country."[24] Hall actually interviewed some of the settlers and in doing so came across people like Cornelius Sullivan whose sons were thriving. They had already cleared

The bridge over the Otonabee River, circa 1855. Watercolour by Edwin Whitefield (1816–1892).

a great deal of land and "liked their independence." However, Cornelius was not entirely happy with his lot:

> It is a fine country for a poor man if he be industrious, and were it not for the ague [malarial disease], a good country and a rich one, though to be sure it is rather out of the way, and the roads are bad and the winters very cold; yet there is plenty to eat, and sure employment and good pay for them that like to work.[25]

Another settler was more upbeat, stating that "we have been taken from misery and want and put into independence and happiness."[26] And yet, Hall remained unconvinced of the group's farming abilities and considered them to lack the skills and experience of their Scottish, north of Ireland, and English counterparts. He may well have been correct in this assertion, but his allegation that the Robinson immigrants were more inclined to be idle and prone to drinking too much whiskey, simply because they were Catholics who came from the south of Ireland, was malicious and smacked of bigotry. He thought that the Scots, the northern Irish Protestants, and the English could set a good example for "sobriety, regularity, morality and steadiness, not [being] fond of visiting, card playing, carousing or drinking spirits."[27] Not only were they more virtuous in Hall's eyes, but he believed that they were "much better and more independent colonists than emigrants from the south of Ireland."[28] Time would show him to be wrong in this sweeping assertion.

When John Langton, an English gentleman farmer who lived near Sturgeon Lake in Victoria County, visited the area in 1835, he noted the Irish communities in Emily Township (Victoria County) that were taking shape. What he called "another batch of Peter Robinson's Irish settlers" occupied the northern part of the township and others were ensconced in the southern part of Douro Township and "are more prosperous than in other parts." He also observed that "there are a good many Irish" in Dummer Township (Peterborough County) and that Cavan Township (Durham County) "is the oldest settled township ... occupied chiefly by northern English and Irish. Though none of the inhabitants can be called a gentleman, they are all well-off and Cavan is reckoned as the most thriving settlement in the district."[29] He was, of course, referring to James Buchanan's settlers who arrived from New York a few years before Robinson's group.

The Select Committee on Emigration, which sat in 1826–27, heard first-hand evidence from an observer that Irish immigrants "were settled at Cavan and are all doing well, and have a great deal of surplus produce. They appeared to have no money among them when they arrived, but after looking around them, they found employment and gained wages. These were chiefly Ulster Protestants."[30] James Buchanan, having provided the British government with a claim for the transportation expenses of around 3,000 Irish immigrants, had done a sterling job in coaxing these people to move to Upper Canada, reversing the usual trend of Irish defections from the Canadas to the United States.

In a bid to keep Irish Catholics and Protestants separate from each other, Buchanan's immigrants had been given land to the southwest of Peterborough, well away from the Peter Robinson group, but they soon extended their territory and by the 1830s were well ensconced in Otonabee Township (Map 12). By this time a sufficient number of Presbyterians lived in "a settlement some twelve miles from Peterborough," to attract a resident Presbyterian minister who would have served a mixed Scottish and Irish congregation.[31] Although most of Buchanan's recruits had Ulster origins some also originated from the southern counties of Dublin, Limerick, Waterford, and Wicklow. While they were granted land in Cavan and Monaghan townships,[32] another group, assisted by Buchanan, received land grants west of York (Toronto), where two local place names — Omagh and Boyne — would later immortalize their Protestant Irish origins.[33]

By 1825 large-scale land clearance throughout the Rice Lake and the Otonabee River regions was well underway. The initial cutting of trees and the provision of sawmills provided employment while the founding of individual farms was the first stage in creating what would be a dispersed pattern of settlement.[34] Although most of the Robinson people had been granted their land in Emily, Ennismore, Douro, and Otonabee townships, a solid group linked together and their territorial spread increased rapidly beyond this. By 1851 the Irish-born were the largest ethnic group in these townships, as well as in nearby Ops (Victoria County), Smith, and Asphodel (Peterborough County). In Emily and Douro they actually

St. Joseph's Catholic Church, Douro, as it appears today. Photographed by Kevin Derrick. A log church had been built on this site in 1846.

represented more than half of the total population of the township. They also made great strides in the town of Peterborough, where they greatly outnumbered the English and Scots (Map 12).

Emily Township had much good land, but because more than a third of the settlers went down with the ague during the period of the initial clearance, the physical and emotional endurance of the survivors were tested to the limit.[35] Later on, the Robinson settlers were joined by Irish Protestants from Fermanagh — led first by Humphrey Finlay and followed by James Laidley and William and Samuel Cottingham, who cleared a site at what is now Omemee in South Emily. Some 400 Protestants from Fermanagh were reported to have settled mainly in a block in South Emily and Cavan townships. Being located so far inland, they had to travel thirty-five miles to reach their nearest mill at Port Hope. Later on, when a new mill was built at modern-day Millbrook, their situation improved slightly; they then had to travel only ten miles from the Emily boundary![36]

In 1837, Emily had a population of 2,341, with almost 36,000 acres cultivated, more than half by the Irish.[37] As with the other townships, great care was taken to ensure that the settlers were granted lots with at least thirty to forty acres of good land so that they would be able to support their families.[38] Robinson's report to the British government in 1826 reveals the diverse talents and skills that various tradesmen brought to Emily's fledgling communities: Daniel Finnegan, blacksmith; Jeremiah Driscoll, mason; Andrew and George Ormsby, both shoemakers; Tobias Switzer, wheelwright; Timothy Cronin, "keeping a school"; Jeramiah Boland, mason; Edmond O'Donnell, mason; William Fitzgerald, shoemaker; James Hurley, carpenter; Patrick Ryan, schoolmaster; Moses Begly, blacksmith; Bart Kennelly, tailor; and Richard Owens, carpenter. Large numbers of immigrants arrived in Emily in the 1830s, with most being Irish, and its population more than doubled between 1832 and 1850.[39]

Meanwhile, another group of Irish immigrants, this time from Colonel George Wyndham's estates in counties Clare and Limerick, arrived in Dummer Township (Peterborough County) in 1839.[40] A total of 181 people (thirty-four families) settled on what proved to be poor farmland. Wyndham had paid their way to Cobourg, while his agent, Lieutenant Charles Rubidge, had organized their relocation and undertook to find them jobs and arrange for their accommodation.[41] Those looking for work found very well-paid employment within a day. Rubidge reported that as soon as their arrival was known, "farmers of the country came from all directions to hire them."[42] However, being very resourceful, the Irish arrivals cast their nets more widely.[43] Under Rubidge's instructions, they complied and wrote letters home extolling Cobourg's virtues. James and Mary Davis assured their mother in County Limerick that "we are all seemingly, in a way, doing better than we could expect at home."[44] Nevertheless, many of them left for the United States, where rates of pay for jobs on the canals and railways were far higher. Wyndham went on to assist many more of his tenants.[45] In 1846, responding to "pressing applications," he paid the sea crossing fares of 160 families "at a cost of not less than £800, including £1 to each full-grown person on landing in the colony. These applications come in every day and I have no doubt of receiving many more from persons anxious to join their friends already gone and doing (according to their own letters) remarkably well."[46]

When John Maguire visited the Peterborough area in the 1860s, his attention was drawn to the "pretty" town of Lindsay lying just outside Emily in Ops Township. Yet again he met the descendents of Robinson's 1825 settlers, who were feeling nostalgic about their past. They had lovingly preserved the original "log shanty" that had once been their "old church."[47] By this time Lindsay's economy was booming, having been given a boost by the building of what would become the Midland Railway of Canada. It ran from Port Hope to Lindsay and from there to the town of Midland on Georgian Bay. Having transformed itself from being a remote mill town to a major railway hub, Lindsay's future was rosy.[48]

When James Collins wrote home to his mother in Donnegal from Peterborough in 1863, the Peter Robinson venture had probably long been forgotten. James told his mother that he had 200 acres for "two decent young men" who might wish to emigrate.[49] Times had become very different. People were getting itchy feet and looking to Manitoba. Leaving his wife Ellen behind in Peterborough, Henry Dunlop, from County Antrim, stayed with various family members in Winnipeg while he considered his options. While her husband was away, Ellen came across "a poor Irish family" who had arrived recently in Peterborough from County Tyrone and needed her help. "They were so unfitted to the approaching winter; I undertook to get things gathered for them." The man (James Brown) was ill and could not work … the mother died soon after giving birth, leaving their two other children." Ellen's emotionless reaction was simply to state that James Brown was "well suited for Canada," a reminder of the stoic way in which people in this era handled their pain and suffering.[50]

Around this time, Tom Hay wrote home to his family in Ireland exulting in Peterborough's rich Irish heritage — "a more peaceable and law-abiding people never existed," he said, but he too was moving on. He and many others in Peterborough were now heading for Manitoba where "the boundless prairie seems to swallow them out of sight" and hundreds of little villages "are growing up."[51] This immigration saga was taking a new direction.

All the while, Irish Protestants had been slipping into Northumberland County to the south of Peterborough and by 1851 were particularly prominent in Hamilton, Haldimand, and Percy townships. Having made great strides in Durham County, James Buchanan's group were especially dominant in Cavan and Manvers townships, where they represented over

Log farm house, erected circa 1870 in Smith Township, Peterborough County. Photograph taken in 1925 by C.P. Meredith.

50 percent of the total population in 1881. Many were also concentrated in Cartwright Township. Cobourg in Northumberland County was fast becoming an Irish town, and by the early 1830s it had a Presbyterian congregation of 400 looking to "have a place large enough to meet in."[52] Colborne, to the east of Cobourg, was apparently then "a thriving settlement with the people around [living] in easy circumstances."[53] Although the inhabitants were mostly of Irish and Scottish descent, many had originated from the United States. By this time the town of Peterborough was said to have "a large Scotch population" who lived near to "a considerable number of Presbyterian Irish," although the Scottish Presbyterian minister who reported this would have preferred the former to have outnumbered the latter.[54]

Bigots like John MacTaggert who regarded Irish Catholics with disdain had clearly been unaware of their stunning pioneering successes in Tyendinaga Township (Hastings County), situated in the Bay of Quinte region. Fronting onto Lake Ontario, its land would normally have been snapped up by Loyalists and their followers from the United States by the late eighteenth century, but on this occasion, Irish and British Irish immigrants were first to acquire its landholdings. Formerly part of the reserve set aside for the Mohawk people, it was being opened up to immigrants in the 1820s. The Irish Catholics who responded to this opportunity were certainly not poor and were said to be sophisticated and well-educated people.[55]

When he petitioned the Colonial Office for land on which to settle in 1820, William Portt, a farmer from Shannon (County Clare), stated that he and five of his sons (John, Robert, Thomas, George, and William) were "desirous of settling in the neighbourhood of each other, and upon the north side of the road passing through the Mohawk Tract in the Bay of Quinte."[56] He clearly knew about this highly desirable site.[57] He went on to say that he and his family "had all arrived in this Province during the last seven months" and now lived in Hamilton. Each possessed "the means … to cultivate 100 acres of wild land."[58] It seems that his request was granted, since a Richard Portt was among the first Irish settlers to arrive in Tyendinaga, doing so in around 1820. He was joined by the families of John and Michael Sweeney from County Offaly and the families of John Shaughnessey, Patrick Welch, and the Murphys, who arrived soon after.

Tyendinaga's population grew rapidly in the early 1830s, tripling from 620 to 1,792 between 1831 and 1836, a period when the government released more of the Mohawk Tract to immigrants.[59] This was when the town of Shannonville took shape. When Susanna Moodie visited it in around 1850, just after there had been a later Catholic influx following the Great Irish Famine, she described it as having "arisen as if by magic within a very few years."[60] By 1860, Tyendinaga Township had a population of more than 7,000 — even exceeding Belleville's population.

Hungerford Township was also strongly Irish at this time. Some of the Earl of Fitzwilliam's former tenants, who had lived on his estate in County Wicklow and had been assisted to emigrate in the famine period, moved to Hungerford. While there is no record of actual numbers, the presence of 979 Irish-born in the township in 1851 suggests that there had been a sizeable influx.[61]

The wilderness lands in Marmora Township to the northeast also attracted Irish immigrants, with a handful from the Robinson group having been granted their land there in 1825. At that time Marmora had an opencast iron ore mine, whose proprietor was the Irish-born Charles Hayes. The mine, in operation since 1818, spawned a village which was said to have around 400 inhabitants.[62] Later transformed by Irish and British immigrants into farming and lumbering communities, Marmora's mainly Irish population stood at just over 600 in 1851.[63]

Arriving from Fermanagh in 1823, James Bailey was one of the first farmers to take up the offer of a free land grant of fifty acres in Marmora.[64] Ten years later, another Fermanagh farmer by the name of Royal Keys boasted about his favourable circumstances and those of his extended family. He repeated many times that "we all live very well." Hugh Jones, his son-in-law, owned two lots in Marmora and another near York (Toronto). The Keys family actually lived in one of Jones's Marmora properties. A near neighbour, Andrew Gauly from Fermanagh, farmed nearby, while another neighbour named John who had his son-in-law's other property, lived about a half mile from him, it having "a good house on it and some clearance." In addition to his farming output, which exceeded expectations, Keys made £300 in that year by producing potash. Apart from having to take grain and other produce long distances to a market, this close-knit Irish community had relatively few complaints and its farmers were clearly prospering. "We must be out chopping when the snow will be four or five feet deep and there will be icicles on my whiskers, but we eat and drink well: Good beef and pork three times each day and potatoes, bread, butter, and tea."[65]

By 1881, 40 percent of Hastings County's entire population was Irish-born. The Irish were the largest ethnic group in most townships and were especially prominent in townships near Lake Ontario and in the northern part of the county (Map 12). Tyendinaga's Irish roots date back to the 1820s, while Sidney and Thurlow townships had been well settled by Loyalists. Rawdon, Huntingdon, and Hungerford townships were slower to develop their communities. Huntingdon acquired an early Irish settlement northwest of Moira Lake (formerly Hog Lake)[66] at some stage, while Hungerford had some of Fitzwilliam's County Wicklow tenants who arrived in the 1840s.[67]

Most of the Irish who settled in the North Hastings townships were single young men, mainly Roman Catholics and in many cases from County Wicklow.[68] By the 1850s they were reported to have settled in Faraday and Dungannon townships, with their earliest community being at Umfraville near present-day Bancroft, at the intersection of the two townships. Farther north, the Irish founded Doyle's Corners, later renamed Maynooth, at the intersection of McClure, Monteagle, Wicklow, and Herschal townships. At this time nearby Carlow Township attracted settlers from Renfrew County, some of whom were Irish.[69] However, because of the poor soil and inadequate colonization roads, progress was slow. Widespread crop failures in the 1860s caused many to leave and by 1870 few Irish remained. And Galway and Cavendish townships in the more remote stretches of Peterborough County and Verulam, Somerville, Bexley, Laxton, Digby, Longford, Dalton, and Carden in Victoria County were also late developers, only acquiring their immigrants from around 1858–59, and they, too, were predominately Irish (Map 12).[70]

In each case the settlers had taken up offers of free land grants and had relied on newly opened colonization roads to take them to their destinations. The man in charge of organizing their settlements was Dublin-born William Hutton, Secretary of the Bureau of Agriculture.[71]

Having established himself as a farmer in Sidney Township near Belleville, Hutton was a passionate believer in the advantages that Upper Canada offered to immigrants and produced an acclaimed immigrants' guide in 1854 that met with ready sales.[72] His advice would have carried great conviction in Ireland and no doubt encouraged people of limited means to seek free land grants in the more remote parts of Upper Canada.

Having been well represented among the early arrivals, the Irish had been able to establish extensive communities in Frontenac and Addington counties, becoming the dominant ethnic group in townships nearest Lake Ontario (Map 13). Later on, Irish Catholics settled on the relatively inferior land that Camden, Sheffield, and Hinchinbrooke townships had to offer. Arriving late, they acquired the poorest land holdings which were often a considerable distance from markets. Their Irish Protestant neighbours, who had first arrived in the 1820s, had already grabbed the best locations.[73] The farming communities that they established in Amherst Island to the west of Kingston were particularly successful.

The Irish who colonized Amherst Island came from the Ards Peninsula (County Down). They were mostly Presbyterians and arrived in large family groups. Having chosen to rent what turned out to be good farmland from an absentee Irish landlord in an area that was close to markets and long settled, they were bound to succeed.[74] Amherst Island had been acquired by Sir John Johnson, the principal Loyalist leader in the American War of Independence, and it later passed to his daughter, who was said to have lost it in a card game played in Ireland.[75] Having acquired it, Lord Mountcashel (Stephen Moore), an Irish nobleman, offered leaseholds to tenants and financed the building of a general store and provided a resident land agent.[76] Tenant numbers rose in the 1830s and during the famine period in the 1840s as friends and relatives joined the first arrivals. In 1851, Amherst Island had 450 Irish-born residents, many of whom were Roman Catholics, the latter almost certainly arriving during the famine period.

Nearby Wolfe Island was also largely Irish in 1851, and mainly Roman Catholic.[77] It, too, had been a refuge for Irish people fleeing the famine ten years earlier. A particularly splendid example was Jimmy Cuffe, from County Roscommon, who had arrived penniless in the mid 1840s. Seventeen years later he had acquired 800 acres, having "bought out the old settlers."

According to John Maguire, who visited Wolfe Island twenty years later, Cuffe was especially pleased to have outperformed "a class rather inclined to think little of what the Jimmy Cuffes can do." Now he had "a fine house, a stable full of good horses, spacious barns and cattle and livestock of every kind" and "drives his family to church in a spring wagon, drawn by a pair of good horses, as grand as the Lord Mayor of London, or any real gentleman in the old country."[78]

Kingston and its hinterland also experienced a significant influx of the famine Irish, with many settling in Pittsburgh[79] and Storrington townships (Frontenac County).[80] Some actually died from typhus and other diseases while being taken in the Rideau Canal steamers to Upper Canada. Those needing hospitalization were taken to Kingston, where at least 1,400 died and are buried.[81]

Between 1851 and 1861, both Frontenac and Addington counties experienced an increase in their Irish-origin population, suggesting that some of the later arrivals were favouring more well-developed regions. Most would have settled behind the Lake Ontario frontages.[82]

Ennismore in Peterborough County, one of the more remote Peter Robinson townships, was largely bypassed by the Irish during the famine years, probably because little of its land was available, or because these people preferred to live in areas that were closer to urban centres.[83]

Other major Irish influxes into the rest of Upper Canada were still to come. Irish colonizers would continue their takeover of eastern Ontario as they headed for the Lake Erie region and on to London. From new bases they would create extensive Irish communities and help to found the city of Toronto.

CHAPTER 8

North to Lake Simcoe and Westward to the Thames Valley

This part of the country is filling up fast. The first settler came into this township in 1820 when it was all wild woods and not one tree chopped but what was cut down by the beavers. It [Brock] is the richest township there is to be found so far back from navigation [Lake Ontario]. This part of it is 36 miles from market but they will go one day and come back the next. Some will go and come in the same day in the winter as there is no delay in selling their load when they go to market.[1]

Writing to his parents in County Antrim in 1849, Richard Breathwaite described what life was like in Cannington. "A lively place," on the southeast side of Lake Simcoe in Brock Township (Ontario County), Cannington had "a grist mill and saw mill and distillery and four merchant shops and two schoolhouses and an English Church one mile and a half from it." Although he seemed well satisfied with the place, he and his fellow settlers had to travel all the way to Whitby to sell their farm produce — a seventy-two-mile round trip!

This was one of the major drawbacks of living so far away from the lake, but land in the back townships was cheap and this suited people of limited means. In his annual report to the Society for the Propagation of the Gospel, the Reverend Richard Garrett, Brock's Anglican minister, simply reported that he presided over a population of mainly "poor Irish," but that the area "was gradually improving in worldly goods."[2] In fact, Brock Township was at the eastern extremity of a huge Irish enclave that surrounded much of Lake Simcoe (Map 14).

Ten years later, John Maguire learned about "the back townships, twenty four in number," to the north of the town of York (Toronto), which Father Edward O'Grady visited from time to time to bring the Catholic faith to the scattered communities living in these remote areas: "Irish Catholics were scattered through this vast territory, very nearly all of which was in its natural state, as it came from the hand of God; but they were few and far between, hidden in the recesses of the forest, most of them not having seen a priest for years." Father O'Grady would have brought considerable comfort to countless people struggling to come to terms with pioneer life. However, Irish Catholics were in a minority in this region. While they had sufficient numbers in Adjala and Tecumseth townships to build a church by the 1830s, Irish Protestants outnumbered them and the other ethnic groups throughout most of Simcoe County.

During his travels, Father O'Grady learned from his parishioners that many had used the money they earned while working on the Erie Canal to launch their farming pursuits. As Father O'Grady made clear, only very few had been able to bring "some little money with them" from Ireland.[3] Many worked on the canal until its completion in 1826 and either found jobs in Toronto afterward or used their wages to establish farms in Simcoe County's vast wilderness. However, these Irish Catholics were not the only ones to recognize the enabling power of a Lake Erie Canal job. In 1826, the Reverend John Strachan, Toronto's first Anglican bishop, disclosed that a large group of Irish Protestants who had been living in New York City followed a similar employment path. Having been assisted nine years earlier by James Buchanan to relocate to Upper Canada, most of them had "laboured on the Erie Canal" before moving to the country to take up farming. Strachan thought that this had been a key first step, since,

Map 14: Irish Concentrations in Simcoe, Ontario, York, Peel, Halton, and Wentworth Counties, 1881

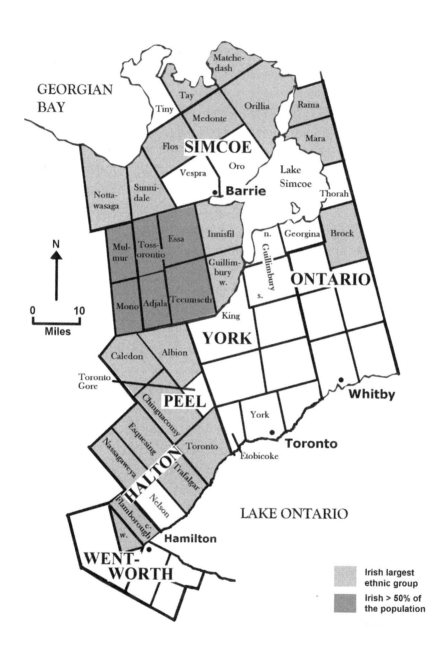

"but for that, they would have been much longer in getting forward." After acquiring their nest egg, they took up land in Peel County and established "a large settlement, west of York [Toronto]."[4] However, unlike the Simcoe County settlers, who had to cope with the severe isolation that went with living in the back townships, the Buchanan recruits could look forward to living in a relatively well-developed area. They were in the privileged position of having been allocated farmland that was much closer to Lake Ontario and to the urban centres along it.

Linking Albany with Buffalo on Lake Erie, the Erie Canal, completed in 1826, and the Welland Canal that followed shortly after, provided a navigable route between New York City and the Great Lakes. Apart from greatly stimulating trade, the new waterways transformed Upper Canada's economy by generating industrial growth in its urban centres. As a result, Toronto became a magnet for job seekers. Some of the Erie Canal labourers, who were mostly Irish, later moved to Toronto from the United States to take advantage of its growing job opportunities. Those who appreciated Upper Canada's great farming potential headed for the countryside. With its vast stretches of vacant land, the Simcoe region was an obvious destination choice.

Once the first Irish groups became established in the wilds of Simcoe County, their extended families and friends followed. Sharing a common identity and culture, they settled as one community wherever possible. This process was repeated many times, leaving Simcoe County's southern half with a population that was 60 percent Irish by 1881. The county had the highest proportion of Irish (at 42 percent) in the whole of Ontario.[5]

The movement of Irish settlers into Peel County, west of Toronto, was more measured. The first Irish arrivals would have found that the lakefront townships had been long colonized by Loyalists and Americans and what land was left behind had to be shared with the Scots and English who were also flocking to these prime locations.

By choosing to settle in Brock Township (Ontario County) on the east side of Lake Simcoe, Richard Breathwaite had set himself apart from the large stretch of townships on the north and west sides of the lake, which had predominately Irish populations. His closest Irish neighbours would have been located in Mara and Rama townships, lying to the north of

Brock, with many of them being Roman Catholics.[6] Irrespective of their religion, many of the Irish would have helped themselves to land initially by squatting and then only much later acquired documentation entitling them to the holdings. In 1881, people of Irish ancestry represented more than 50 percent of the population in Mulmur, Tossorontio, Essa, Tecumseth, Adjala, and Mono townships and were the largest ethnic group in nine other Simcoe townships (Map 14).

Irish Catholics began arriving in Simcoe County in the 1820s, settling in Adjala and Tecumseth townships in the south, and Vespra, Flos, Medonte, and Nottawasaga townships in the north. Although they did not settle in a consolidated block, some effort had clearly been made to enable them to form small township groups of which the Adjala/Tecumseth communities were the earliest to develop. According to John Maguire, Adjala and Tecumseth were "amongst the most Irish and Catholic of any [townships] in Upper Canada." When he spoke to Father Edward Gordon in the 1860s he was told that they each had forty or fifty Irish Catholic families who were widely scattered across the county.[7] Adjala's pioneers included men like Owen Keogh who died aged ninety-six and James Duross who died aged 113, their longevity demonstrating "the great strength of nerve and constitution on the part of these Irish pioneers."[8]

In 1833, the Adjala Catholics built a log church dedicated to Saint James, while the Tecumseth Catholics also built a church that same year at Colgan, named after its first Irish-born inhabitant, John C. Colgan, who had arrived ten years earlier.

Most of the Irish who had arrived in the region since the 1820s were Protestants from Ulster. They established major settlements in West Gwillimbury, Innisfil, Essa, Tecumseth, Tossorontio, Mono, and Mulmur townships. Arriving in 1831, ten Irish Protestant families having German ancestry (Palatine Irish)[9] settled in West Gwillimbury. Irish families like the Scroggies, who had previously settled in Rawdon Township north of Montreal, relocated to Innisfil and Essa townships starting in the 1840s.[10] Some, like James D. Stephens, who arrived from Ireland in 1845, looked for business opportunities. After managing the "Green Bush Tavern" in Glen Huron (Nottawasaga Township), "a famous hostelry in the pioneer days," and a store, he went on to run a sawmill in the area.[11] And a group from

Ulster who sailed from Londonderry in 1850 settled together in Innisfil Township.[12] Thus the Irish either came directly from their homeland or migrated from other parts of Canada in the belief that they would benefit economically in the Simcoe region.

In 1841, the Reverend Richard Garrett, West Gwillimbury's Anglican minister, said that his parish "consisted entirely of Irish emigrants."[13] The 1851 Census certainly provides proof of this statement, only it would be more accurate to state that Irish Protestants dominated much of Simcoe County! Their principal enclave appears to have been centred on the southwest end of Lake Simcoe. Here, their communities were spread across four townships. They occupied much of West Gwillimbury, the northeast of Tecumseth, the southeast of Essa, and the southwest of Innisfil. Writing in 1948, Andrew Hunter referred to it as "a large settlement of Protestant Orangemen from the North of Ireland," having Cookstown as its centre.[14]

From his base at Shanty Bay near Barrie, the Irish-born Anglican missionary Samuel B. Ardagh presided over a congregation between 1842 and 1867 that encompassed much of Simcoe County. While his English parishioners were mainly concentrated in Oro and Vespra townships, the

Log house, Nottawasaga Township, Simcoe County, 1850. Photograph taken in 1925.

Irish Protestant members were widely scattered. He regularly travelled distances of up to 100 miles to bring the word of God to his flock, his circuit stretching to Nottawasaga, Sunnidale, Flos, Medonte, Vespra, and Oro in the north and Innisfil, West Gwillimbury, Essa, and Mono in the south.[15]

Much of this immigration saga has its roots in the rapid economic growth of Toronto, which was still a wilderness in 1800. When Irish-born William Watson visited it in 1822, it consisted of "one street" with one or two handsome buildings, such as the Assembly House and Gaol. "Almost all the houses are built of wood and roofed with shingles or tin and its streets are not much paved; nor is it a place of much mercantile trade."[16] However, the situation changed dramatically with the arrival of the Great Lakes waterways. Between 1826 and 1834, Toronto's population soared from 1,700 to just over 9,000, and by 1851, when it reached 31,000, it was

St. Michael's Cathedral Basilica, Toronto, located on Church Street, photographed in 2011. One of the oldest churches in the city, it was constructed in 1848, having been primarily financed by Irish immigrants. It has a seating capacity of 1,600.

very much an Irish town.[17] The Irish had built St. Paul's Roman Catholic Church by 1834[18] and this had been followed by St. Michael's Cathedral, which was completed in 1848.[19]

Irish labourers, many of them Catholics, began arriving in Toronto in appreciable numbers beginning in 1820.[20] Establishing Corktown, a slum close to the wharves, warehouses, mills, and factories that were springing up along the lakefront, where Toronto's growing industrial life was concentrated, the Irish congregated together near their places of work.[21] Predictably, Corktown's reputation for poverty and sleaze attracted controversy. In 1834, William Lyon Mackenzie, the Scottish-Canadian journalist and politician and Toronto's first mayor, thought that the "huts and shanties … on the [Don River] bank and on the beach in front of the City" offered scope for "gambling and vice in its blackest shapes."[22] And commenting on it much later, the Canadian author and clergyman Henry Scadding dismissed Corktown as "a row of dilapidated wooden buildings inhabited for the most part by a thriftless and noisy set of people."[23]

The rising demand for manual labour stemming from Toronto's increasing industrialization fuelled a growing influx of labourers. As this happened, yet another shantytown, whose inhabitants were predominately Irish, sprouted up in the 1840s.[24] Called Cabbagetown and situated just to the north of Corktown, it housed the labourers who worked in the factories near the Don River end of the harbour and along the lakefront. In fact, Corktown and Cabbagetown were contemporaneous shantytowns. However, with the rapid growth in Toronto's population, Irish dominance in both communities dwindled.[25] By 1891 less than a quarter of Corktown's inhabitants were Roman Catholic.[26] While Corktown still had a sizeable Irish Catholic population at this time, "Cabbagetown, the alleged home of the Irish, was more of a ghetto for working class Irish and English Protestants than for Catholics."[27] This inevitably provoked the religious clashes that broke out from time to time during the late nineteenth century.

Although Toronto's industrial centre attracted a great many Irish, there were some Irishmen, like James Humphrey, who found work in Highland Creek (Scarborough Township), just outside of town. His upbeat report home to his father in County Tyrone, written in 1824, suggests that he may have landed a weaving job. It was a good place apart from the roads:

> This is a better place than at home, labouring men get
> 12$ per month.... A girl will get $5 per month. I would
> not advise any person to come here for the road is very
> dangerous and if anything would happen to them they
> would blame me. But I don't rue it. Weaving is doing
> very well. You will get 7 ½ d. per yard and plenty of it to
> do.... The land is better here than at home.[28]

Arriving in Toronto in 1826, William Hanavan from County Cavan took up a labouring job and in just over ten years was able to acquire a 100-acre farm in Chinguacousy Township (Peel County).[29] Moses Staunton, a wallpaper hanger from Ulster who came thirty years later, also prospered. He found Toronto to his liking, although he and his family had to work very hard to build up their business. He thought it to be a splendid place "for the carpenter or blacksmith," but "clerks and gentlemen, with kid gloves on, need not come here."[30] Hugh Kennedy, who arrived from Belfast in 1912, was struck by Toronto's plentiful job opportunities and greatly admired the city:

> There are a hundred vacancies for women workers to
> every one for men here. There is also a great demand for
> carriage and wagon builders, house carpenters, cabinet
> makers, in fact all kinds of wood workers and building
> trades generally. This is a splendid, well laid city all built,
> so far as I can see, in squares, a good tram service — for
> five cents you can go all over the city, changing from one
> car to another if desired or necessary.[31]

Meanwhile, farming areas west of Toronto experienced an Irish influx in around 1804 when a small number of relatively affluent Irish Catholics came to live in present-day Mississauga (Toronto and Etobicoke townships), many having previously resided in the United States. Thomas Carroll, who arrived in Toronto Township that year from County Wexford, acquired considerable landholdings in Chinguacousy Township to the north.[32] Others like him came to the area, leading to the clustering of

Irish Catholic communities in Toronto and Chinguacousy townships (Peel County) and Etobicoke Township (York County). From his base at St. Paul's Catholic Church in Toronto, Father Edward Gordon regularly visited his scattered flock and, during the 1830s, his circuit comprised most of Peel County (Toronto, Chinguacousy, Albion, and Caledon), Trafalgar in Halton County, and Mono, Adjala, Tecumseth, and West Gwillimbury in Simcoe County.[33]

The area west of Toronto in Toronto Township also attracted Irish Protestants, who founded Erindale. The settlement's Anglican minister, the Reverend James Magrath, arrived in Upper Canada from Dublin in 1827 at the age of sixty and acquired considerable land in Toronto Township. The name of "Erindale," that he gave to his property was adopted later by the residents of the community whose farms were established along the Credit River.[34] Many of Erindale's early settlers had been Loyalists and Americans, and they in turn had been followed to the area by people who came from Atlantic Canada, especially from New Brunswick. Erindale was also reported to have acquired "a large group of Irish immigrants who came from New York City."[35]

It is certainly the case that Toronto Township did acquire a large group of Irish farmers, tradesmen, craftsmen, and labourers from New York City just before 1820. These were mainly Protestants originally from Ulster, but also included people from the southern counties of Ireland.[36] They arrived in very favourable circumstances, having been assisted by James Buchanan, the British consul in New York, who provided them with free transportation and land in Toronto Township on which to settle. By 1826 their communities were reported to be "as prosperous and satisfied as those in the township of Cavan" in the Peterborough region,[37] which Buchanan had also organized.[38] Given that Buchanan had assisted 1,600 Irish people to relocate from New York to the Peterborough area, the Peel County settlements must have been substantial, as well.[39]

Buchanan's group immediately established footholds across much of Toronto Township, arrangements having been made beforehand with the Upper Canada government to have the requisite land set aside for them.[40] Barney Doherty only learned about the Buchanan scheme on his return to New York City in 1818, after having been abroad. Realizing that the British consul was making land available in Upper Canada to Irish colonizers, Doherty "hastily travelled up the Hudson route and was rewarded upon his arrival with a grant in Toronto Township."[41] He sent for the rest of his family in Ireland and within a few years most had joined him.

Having already taken up a labouring job in Lower Canada by 1813, Cork-born Francis Kennedy headed for York County after learning that land was being made available on good terms. He then sent for his brother Patrick, who moved to "the wilds of Caledon [Township]."[42] And the availability of good land in Upper Canada was also being advertised in Irish newspapers, further stimulating the influx of immigrants to the region west of Toronto. Eventually, the Irish extended their territory to Chinguacousy, Caledon, Albion, and Toronto Gore townships, thereby becoming the dominant ethnic group in Peel County. As ever, a major

The Road Between Kingston and York, (Toronto), circa 1830. Watercolour by James Pattison Cockburn (1779–1847).

drawback for settlers in the back townships was the poor state of the roads and the large distances that people had to travel to take their produce to market towns, some living "thirty miles more or less from these public roads."[43]

The Irish were soon well ensconced in the neighbouring county of Halton, where Esquesing, Nassagaweya, and Trafalgar townships became major strongholds, with many of Nassagaweya's early residents having originated from County Antrim (Map 14).[44] The Barber family from County Antrim, who arrived in 1822, took possession of a small woollen mill along the Credit River at Georgetown (Esquesing Township) in 1837. Six years later they founded a woollen mill at Streetsville,[45] located farther down the Credit River in what was then Toronto Township. In 1853 they built even larger mills at Streetsville, which became known as the Toronto Woollen Mills.[46] During the famine period of the mid-1840s, many Irish immigrants came to the area and settled in the Port Credit area.[47]

All the while, canal building and other public works taking place near Hamilton in the late 1820s and 1830s created jobs that were snapped up by Irish workers who flocked to the area.[48] Most were Irish Catholics who originated from the south of Ireland. Hamilton's *Western Mercury* announced on June 17, 1832, that "upwards of 700 [immigrants], including those in the cabin and infants," had arrived at Toronto in the steamer *Great Britain*. The newspaper went on to report that some were Irish labourers who intended to work on the Welland Canal, a waterway that would link Lake Erie with Lake Ontario. In fact, a good many had been recruited at ports in Montreal and New York soon after disembarking from the ships that they had sailed in from Ireland.[49]

As was the case in Toronto, Catholic Irish workers later took up jobs in Hamilton, congregating together near their work sites, thus creating yet another Corktown, which sprouted up on the southeast side of the town. It was founded in 1832.[50] By then, 12 percent of Hamilton's population was Irish-born and Catholic. Four years later, Irish Catholics were present in sufficient numbers to be able to build a church, dedicating it to St. Mary. Corktown remained a downtrodden place, largely occupied by labourers, although its population did include Irish merchants, artisans, shopkeepers, tavern owners, and politicians.[51]

The good farmland near Hamilton attracted many Irish.[52] Some, like Henry Johnson from County Antrim, had another reason for relocating to the area. He was fleeing from his debtors back in Ireland. After a difficult journey, he arrived in Hamilton in 1848, deeply regretting that he had not brought his wife, Jane, with him. Hamilton was not for him and he noted that "after wandering through the principal towns of Upper Canada and trying every means in my power to obtain a situation of any kind, I have at last lighted into a farmer's house near the far famed falls of Niagara where I am doing a little work for my board and washing."[53] Johnson had difficulty in finding his way, probably because of a drinking problem, and he died two years later,[54] just as Jane was making her way to Quebec. In his last letter to Jane, Johnson reveals that he has joined a temperance society:

> Drinking is the curse of this country, as well as our own — many a dreadful case and consequence of it I have seen since I came here. In order to save myself from temptation I went to the Presbyterian minister in this place [Niagara] and took the temperance pledge so that as far as that is concerned I am safe, and if I had you out here I think I would be happy. Persons coming out here at first are very much annoyed and discontent until they are settled down and then they like this country better than the old.[55]

Others clearly prospered. Martha Cranston, who was living in Tapleytown, to the south of Hamilton, wrote to an uncle in Donegal in 1886 stating that she and her husband "have a good market for all of our produce." They had 112 acres of land for which they paid $5,000: "We live very comfortable; we keep from fifteen to eighteen head of cattle, six head of horses, fifteen head of sheep." Her father and brother also lived nearby.[56]

Although Irish immigrants settled in substantial numbers in southwestern Upper Canada, they rarely registered as the dominant ethnic group. Middlesex County had nearly 22,000 residents of Irish descent in 1881; but they only represented 30 percent of the population. However, the Irish were able to use their early pioneering efforts in London Township in Middlesex County to launch large communities to the north of it (Map 15). While London had filled up with settlers relatively early, the townships to the north of it, having large amounts of vacant land, were ripe for the picking as future Irish enclaves.

London Township's Irish communities were kick-started by Richard Talbot, an Irish military officer who assisted thirty Irishmen from County Tipperary to relocate to the area.[57] The group comprised fifteen men with families and fifteen who were single, the latter including Talbot's two sons.[58] In his *The Irishman in Canada*, published in 1887, Nicholas Flood Davin, the Limerick-born journalist, lawyer, and politician who lived in Toronto, sang the praises of London's early Irish pioneers, although his list mostly consisted of families who had not been recruited by Talbot:

> The Hodgins, and O'Neals, the Deacons and Shoebottoms, the Talbots and Fitzgeralds, the Waldens, the Langfords, the Gowens, the Stanleys ... then we have the Eadys and Jermyns from Cork and the Weirs from the North of Ireland; the Westmans, the Ardills, the Gusets, the Hobbs. All these have done good work in clearing the wilderness and making comfortable homes for themselves. The Irish are preeminent as merchants, lawyers, teachers and preachers in London. I have not mentioned the Densmores, the Willises, the Ryans, the Dickeys, the Dickensons.... Forty years ago those men have carried a bag of wheat on their backs forty miles to get it ground. Dr. Evans was on the London circuit thirty-two years ago and often slept in a log cabin in which he could not stand upright.[59]

The Hardy family, who sailed in the *Brunswick* in 1818, had been among Talbot's recruits and they are known to have settled in Nissouri and London townships.[60] John Fitzgerald, who came from Ireland in 1820, settled in London Township with his wife, Rebecca, and various others followed, no doubt as word spread among families and friends that good farming opportunities were available.[61] It would seem that Alexander McEwen, a Presbyterian minister from County Down, had his ear close to the ground. In 1826 he petitioned on behalf of labourers and small farmers [holding two to five acres] who, because they were unable to support their families, wished to emigrate, preferably to Canada: "Their forefathers were from Scotland on the soil of Ulster," and as such preferred to live in British North America. Asking for "a grant of land of good quality on some healthful situation on the borders of Lake Erie, or as near the projected site of New London[62] as possible," the Reverend McEwen was clearly well informed. He added that the petitioners wished to settle "on the banks of some stream or river where there is a site for a Mill, and where their exertions might be more available for themselves and their families, and useful, if need be, in defence of their adopted country."[63]

William Radcliff, who originated from Dublin, settled in Adelaide, a township to the west of London: "Never was there a township so quickly filled up with respectable people.... A vast number of those who came out this year have congregated in this township, proof that the land is good. It is considered the best in Upper Canada, the settlement it is thought will be one of the most flourishing." However, he still pined for his family and

A view of London from the bank of the Thames River, circa 1842, showing the London District Courthouse in the distance. Watercolour by George R. Dartnell (1798–1878).

his old way of life in Ireland: "Sometimes, not withstanding the outrages and the murders, the politics and the poverty of that unhappy country, I would give all that I am worth to be walking beside you, shooting the Enfield bottoms, as in those happy days we have spent together."[64]

Some of these newcomers were urban dwellers. Having previously settled in Quebec City, Patrick and Margaret McDonagh from County Limerick relocated to the town of London in 1832, where they ran a grocery store. The Reverend Benjamin Cronyn, an Anglican minister who hailed from County Longford, appeared soon after this with his wife, Margaret, and two children and began ministering to a congregation of about 1,200 who were located in the town and surrounding area.[65]

Having come to live in Westminster Township at this time, Nathaniel Carrothers, from County Fermanagh, could later boast about his 187-acre farm to his brother:

> This is a fine country for a man to live in; an industrious man that cannot make out a good living here need not go to the gold mines of California or Australia. There never was a better time for emigration here, wages of all kinds is good; mechanics get from a dollar to one and a half [dollars] a day; they are giving a dollar a day to all the labourers on the great western railroad which is making [its way] through this part of the country, it runs through London. London has become a large and fine place since we came to this country; there is a great many fine churches and merchant shops and wholesale warehouses all of brick; the land in this part of the country is very good and I can raise as many potatoes as I wish without any dung.[66]

Nathaniel scolded his brother for not having "plucked up courage and come to America a few years ago and got a good farm in this part of the country before the land got dear, you would have no cause to rue it and I am sure your children would ever bless the day that they came to Canada. I never was sorry for coming, but ever shall be [sorry] that I spent so many days in Ireland."[67]

The town of London, founded in 1826, also attracted many Irish. By 1842, people of Irish ancestry represented just over one third of the town's entire population. Over the next decade, when the famine struck in Ireland, Irish immigrant numbers rose more than ever, with 1,500 Irish-born arriving during this period. And yet, despite having a relatively large Irish component to its population, the town of London never acquired a Corktown or anything similar. This was because its Irish residents were scattered across the town rather than being concentrated in a particular area as had been the case in Toronto and Hamilton.

Irish immigrants were also prominent in Lambton County on the southwest extremity of Upper Canada, particularly after oil mania gripped the area. With the discovery of the first petroleum wells in 1858, land speculators had a field day in Enniskillen Township, causing its population to grow rapidly.[68] The first oil well was brought into production in 1860 and shortly afterward Petrolia became Canada's major oil-producing centre. The first "gusher" in the area was owned by Irish-born Hugh Nixon Shaw who went on to run a general store in Cooksville. John Doyle Noble, son of a clergyman from County Meath, arrived in 1862 and acquired a great deal of property in the area and became a business magnate and politician.[69] Writing home from Petrolia twenty-six years later, his wife, Helen, reported that she was happily settled among the many people in her vicinity who originated from Ireland.[70] At that time Mrs. John J. Johnston (formerly Maggie Breen) told her cousin in Michigan that she was due to get married and would be moving to Petrolia.[71] Petrolia was clearly attracting many Irish, and by 1881 they were the largest ethnic group in Enniskillen and five other Lambton County townships (Map 15).

Another factor in the strong Irish presence in Lambton County was the availability of its good farmland. Having been opened up to colonizers relatively late — in the mid-1830s, long after much of the southwest region had been cleared — Lambton County was a godsend for already-established Upper Canada farmers who wished to acquire better sites. The Caswell, Cox, and Powell families, all from Tipperary, relocated there from the Ottawa Valley in the late 1830s and 1840s, typifying a widespread population movement. Similarly, a large group from County Wexford who had previously settled in the Ottawa Valley relocated to

Map 15: Irish Concentrations in Lambton and Middlesex Counties, 1881

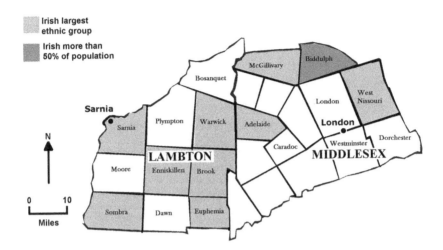

Brook Township (Lambton County) in the mid-1850s, while Irish families from Lanark County also came to Lambton during the 1840s.[72]

All the while, the building of a new colonization road in Essex County, to the west of Lambton, opened the way to immigrants from Ireland there, too. They founded their "Irish Settlement" in the 1840s at Maidstone just south of Lake St. Clair,[73] with many of their number having arrived from other parts of Canada.[74]

The Irish were clearly very knowledgeable about Upper Canada's prime farming sites and were quick to act on the intelligence they gathered from family, friends, and newspapers. Someone like Daniel Waide, living in County Antrim in the 1850s, was aware that London was the place to be, his son having settled near several Antrim families on a recently purchased fifty-acre farm. In a letter to his son, Waide asked about the distance of his farm to "New London," the nearest public road, the nearest market town, and the railway.[75] The answers would no doubt be circulated among family and friends in County Antrim, thus adding to their Upper Canada information pool.

As the Irish pushed northward from Lake Erie, they reached the vast wildernesses of the Huron Tract and the other areas in the western peninsula that were being opened up to colonizers. Having founded early communities in the north of Middlesex County, they had a springboard from which to take over large areas of Biddulph Township in Huron County and before long they were the major occupiers of nearby McGillivray and Blanshard townships. Many were attracted by the prospect of settling on the Canada Company's land. Through its capital investment in roads, bridges, and buildings, the Company attracted settlers who otherwise might have balked at the prospect of living in such a remote part of Upper Canada. The Irish would now make their way north through the Huron Tract and beyond, and would soon predominate in large swathes of Huron, Perth, Wellington, Bruce, and Grey counties.

CHAPTER 9

᎒᎒

Ontario's Western Peninsula

Nothing but forest was to be seen. To find the way to and from his shanty to the trail he had to blaze the trees. Very soon Thomas Stewart settled on the adjoining lot, and Robert Kilpatrick opposite, so that there were three tiny clearings in that immense stretch of forest.[1]

When Robert Carson established a farm south of present-day Owen Sound in Sullivan Township (Grey County) in 1840, he was being very brave, if not foolhardy. Arriving from County Donegal, he faced the daunting task of clearing a vast wilderness, initially on his own and without the requisite skills. Fortunately, the region's good farmland was attracting many people who had previously settled in other parts of Canada. Wishing to have better locations, they came to the western peninsula, but unlike newcomers from Britain and Ireland, they brought practical pioneering skills with them. W.M. Brown described Grey County's first settlers as "men of iron vigour, who underwent labour and hardship and destitution in their battle to overcome the mantle with which Nature had covered the land."[2] They did all of this, yet their heroic efforts went largely unrecorded.

Before the western peninsula could be opened up to settlers, two developments had been necessary: better inland routes allowing access to the region from other parts of Canada and the establishment of the Canada Company, a land company that enabled farmers to purchase land in the region on relatively easy terms.[3] With the founding of the Company in 1826, farming progressed in Huron, Perth, and Wellington counties initially, while the more remote areas to the north in Grey and Bruce counties were colonized some twenty years later. The Canada Company made Goderich and Guelph its company towns and constructed roads, mills, and other amenities to promote the region's economic development. Settlers welcomed the jobs that became available as a consequence of these construction projects, and those arriving with insufficient funds to purchase land benefited from the Company's credit facilities.[4]

The Irish made a considerable impression in the region, dominating the northern part of Huron, Perth, and Wellington counties and most of Grey County by 1881 (Map 16). They were given a considerable head start from their earlier and extensive colonizing efforts in the nearby area. Since the 1820s, they had been major colonists in nearby Simcoe County, to the east of Grey County, in Halton and Peel, to the east of Guelph, and in London Township (Middlesex County), which shares a boundary with Huron County on its south side. These springboards enabled them to grab good sites in these newly opened areas.

Travelling along the colonization roads that had been built by the Canada Company, they could reach their desired destinations relatively easily, although in some cases they had to share their locations with other ethnic groups.[5] The Irish were not necessarily the earliest settlers in the area, as the first arrivals had been mainly Scottish Highlanders and Pennsylvania Germans, the latter being more capable than most in coping with the extremely harsh conditions that awaited them.[6]

Acquiring 2.5 million acres of Crown land in western Upper Canada, the Canada Company's stated aim was "not to encourage or deal with speculators, but to open access to the settlement of lands by a steady, agricultural population."[7] Nearly half of its holdings fell within the Huron Tract, a vast, triangular-shaped 1.1-million-acre area fronting Lake Huron. The tract contained most of Huron and Perth counties (Map 16).[8] Having

Map 16: Irish Concentrations in Huron, Perth, Wellington, Bruce, and Grey Counties, 1881

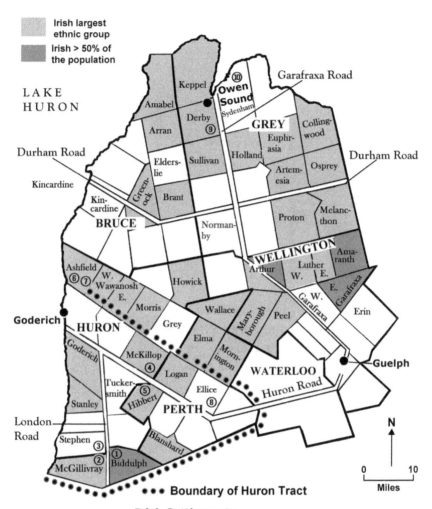

Irish Settlements

① Adare/Clandeboye/ Flanagans' Corner
② Maguire
③ Mount Carmel
④ Irish Settlement/Dublin
⑤ Irishtown/St. Columban
⑥ Kingsbridge
⑦ Belfast
⑧ Kinkora
⑨ Irish Settlement
⑩ Irish Block

Log house and clearing at Orillia, Simcoe County, 1844. Watercolour by Titus Hibbert Ware (1810–1890).

obtained these vast quantities of wilderness land, the Company sold farm lots on fairly easy terms to settlers and provided them with a basic infrastructure within which they could build their communities. The Company offered free transport to the head of Lake Ontario to anyone making a down payment on its land, although such help did not always materialize. In later years there were complaints about the Company's inflated land prices.[9] Moreover, the Company was regularly accused of exaggerating the state of development of its lands, leaving some immigrants with broken promises and little return for the money that they had paid.

Oddly enough, a Scottish-born novelist by the name of John Galt had been the Canada Company's first commissioner and superintendent, having been the driving force behind its establishment.[10] Galt's writing skills added flair to the Company's promotional activities in Britain and Ireland. Smooth publicity campaigns were run in the British Isles, whereby the Company's agents distributed pamphlets giving details of its lands and services that were careful slanted to regional factors and conditions. The Company promoted western Upper Canada with a new effectiveness, and large numbers of immigrants who would otherwise have been lost to the United States succumbed to its message.[11] However, while Galt was a superb publicist, he lacked managerial skills and after three years was sacked from his influential post.[12] Overall, the Company earned little credit for its colonizing achievements. Its shareholders expected quick profits that were never realized, while many of the farmers who settled on its lands felt dissatisfied with their treatment.[13]

Along with land, the Canada Company offered another important service to settlers that had particular resonance with the Irish. It acted as an agent for people already living in North America who wished to send funds (so-called remittances) to loved ones in their homeland.[14] Through this service they could transfer funds to named individuals back home who wished to emigrate. Their relatives and friends then used the remittances to fund their sea passages to Quebec.[15] The Canada Company's "Remittance Books" for 1843 to 1847 reveal that most of those helped in this way lived in Ireland. Most originated from the north, especially the counties of Tyrone, Fermanagh, Monaghan, Cavan, Armagh, and Antrim, while a significant number also came from Tipperary, Cork, Leitrim, Donegal, Mayo, and Kerry.[16] The majority of those able to send remittances would have arrived in North America one or two decades earlier — a period when Ulster arrivals dominated the influx. Thus the remittance scheme mainly helped people from the north of Ireland. Without remittances, impoverished Irish people generally relied on landlords and philanthropic bodies for financial aid, and this was especially the case throughout the famine period.[17]

Mr. A.B. Hawke, the Upper Canada immigration agent, pointed out in 1846 that "the sums remitted by settlers in Canada to enable their relations to emigrate are rapidly increasing in amount; a few years ago such remittances were rare, they are now becoming almost general."[18] However, Alexander Buchanan, the Quebec immigration agent, was becoming increasingly alarmed by this development. People were arriving without sufficient funds to reach their final destinations and his department had to foot the bill. Buchanan blamed a mischievous letter that was being circulated in Ireland for this state of affairs:

> Because the Government in Canada is good to the poor,
> [it] will pay their passages up the country and give them
> oatmeal or bread to eat on the road, so you may all come
> if you can pay your passages to Quebec.[19]

And come they did! "Thousands have left the United Kingdom during the last two or three years entirely depending upon the assistance of the Emigrant Department to enable them to reach their destinations in Western Canada."[20] They were mainly Irish and a good many were heading for the Canada Company's lands in the Huron Tract.

Founded in 1827 by the Canada Company, the town of Goderich soon became a focal point for early settlement in the region. Its well-paid and plentiful jobs attracted a good many Irish labourers and tradesmen, while its surrounding hinterland appealed to affluent farmers. Jane White, from a prosperous County Down family, hated Goderich. Writing in the 1850s to her friend Eleanor in Ireland, she described it as "becoming an abominably Yankiefied place, being so near the States ... strangers coming here would find this the poorest, coldest, most profitless place they could come to."[21] Sadly, from her viewpoint, the special privileges that went hand in hand with her exalted social status in Ireland were not available to her in Goderich and never would be. Ensnared by her Old World prejudices, she remained deeply unhappy with the place and died in 1867 without even beginning to understand the nature of the pioneer society that she had joined.[22] She would not be alone in suffering this fate.

Goderich Township's earliest Irish settlers arrived in the 1830s, having grabbed the best sites they could along the Huron Road, especially those closest to the town (Map 16).[23] Writing to his father in County Fermanagh, John McCullagh reported that he had made great strides in establishing a farm. "[Because of the high cost of employing labour,] I have done all my work myself.... A farmer here can make the money fast if he has help within himself."[24] Four years later he was even more upbeat about his situation:

Cabin in the Woods, circa 1838–1842. Watercolour by Millicent Mary Chaplin (1790–1858).

> I hear from everyone that leaves the country that Ireland is failing fast. You want to know do I like America better than Ireland. America is in my opinion the best by far for any man that will work. No place for walking about Gentlemen. The people altogether live better here than they can do at home. Flesh every day, tea and loaf bread, every day — great places for pies and custard and apple pies — particularly among the Dutch and English — the truth, the whole truth and nothing but the truth — no place for Lazy Folks.[25]

Guelph, about ninety miles east of Goderich, was the other Company town. According to Dr. Robert Alling, the Canada Company's Guelph immigration agent, wrote in 1827, the year it was founded, that it was "untenanted but by the wild beasts of the forest, without a tree having been felled." Twenty years later it was "a district town with four churches, numerous public buildings, possessing a large and increasing population, and is still progressing in wealth and importance."[26] Like Goderich, it grew rapidly and the plentiful jobs it had to offer were a boon to Irish labourers.

While Alling was pleased to have affluent Ulster farmers in the area, "the lower orders," by which he meant Irish labourers, were not, in his opinion, welcome. He ranked them third after the Scots and English in terms of their suitability as potential pioneer farmers. He criticized them for rashly launching into farming without having made adequate preparation or acquiring the necessary resources.[27] Then, later on, he accused them of doing the exact opposite:

> When the Canada Company was in Guelph, many of these settlers were employed for many months and even years in the cutting of roads, clearing town plots, constructing bridges, making mill dams, raising and hauling building … and thus long kept off their several lots of land; and it appears that when they did go on the land, they did not do much, having been nearly and some quite spoilt by the Company's high wages, too liberal treatments, and much too liberal overseers.[28]

Alling was certainly not alone in harbouring a deep aversion toward the lowly paid Irish, who were often Roman Catholics. When the Englishman Robert Fisher claimed that Guelph Township was "peopled with our own country people principally, and what few Irish are here are selling off their farms and moving further up the country," he was echoing similar anti-Irish prejudices.[29] That not being surrounded by Irish farmers should be a selling point to the English indicates widespread prejudice on their part. Although the Irish were second to the English in numbers, they were certainly not leaving, and were actually arriving in Guelph in ever-increasing numbers.

A humble Irish blacksmith by the name of John Eagan came to the town of Galt, south of Guelph, in around 1846, and after working in various jobs was able to finance his future life as a farmer. He was "a landowner with a home of his own" fifteen years later.[30] However, many Irish labourers and tradesmen were content with their lot and did not have Eagan's ambition to succeed in farming or in other ways. In 1861, when Irish Catholics accounted for 17 percent of Guelph's population, most were still employed in low-paid jobs. The earliest arrivals had settled near the Speed River, the site of a flour and gristmill that had been built by the Canada Company.[31] Possibly they had provided the labour for this undertaking, but unlike Toronto and Hamilton, where Irish workers were clustered together near their places of work, Guelph's Irish were more scattered and never formed their own shantytown.[32]

When the town of Guelph raised funds for its grand basilica, the Kilkenny-born Bishop John Walsh of London preached the sermon soon after its inaugural ceremony. In it, he reminded the congregation of the "generosity, sacrifice and labour of the poor immigrant settlers of Guelph, pointing out that the church had been built "by money raised from the working men who had built our canals and railways, [and by] servant girls, mechanics and other hard-working people."[33] The lowly Irish workers' contribution to the town's early development was at long last recognized and acclaimed.

Church of Our Lady Immaculate in Guelph, photographed in April 2008. When John Galt founded Guelph, he allocated the highest point in the newly founded town to his friend Alexander Macdonell, the Roman Catholic bishop of Kingston. A wooden church, the first to stand on the site, was destroyed by fire in 1844 and replaced by a small stone church two years later. The present magnificent church, completed in 1888, was designed by Joseph Connolly, a Limerick-born architect. Some two thousand people attended the opening ceremony.

With its relatively cheap and abundant land, the Huron Tract attracted Irish settlers in great numbers. By 1881, they dominated eight townships spread across Huron and Perth counties, with all but one situated along a colonization road. The strong prevalence of Orange Order lodges in the region points to a large intake of Irish Protestants.[34] The Irish were the largest ethnic group in the townships of Goderich, Stanley, and McGillivray on the west side of the London Road and Biddulph[35] on the other, and in McKillop and Logan on the north side of the Huron Road and Hibbert on the other. They also dominated Blanshard, an eastward extension of Biddulph (Map 16).[36] While some arrived directly from Ireland, many had relocated from other parts of Canada. A typical example was Adam Stewart and his wife, Ann Barkley, who left County Antrim for Upper Canada in 1833, settling in Smiths Falls in the Rideau Valley. Sometime later, their eldest son moved from Smiths Falls to Huron County and established a farm in Stanley Township.[37] The Stewarts and some of the rest of their children joined their son in the mid-1850s, all of them having moved west from their various locations in eastern Upper Canada.[38]

Having arrived in the 1830s, Stanley Township's mainly Protestant settlers were as unpleasant as they could be to their Catholic neighbours who came a decade later. Protestants established a so-called "Goshen Line" (Concession Road), along which Catholics were barred from holding land. However, it was decreed that Catholics could settle along the so-called "Babylon Line," suitably named by the Protestants to signify "an area of sin and vice."[39]

Thus, in addition to the perils and hazards of pioneer farming, Stanley's Catholics had also to contend with this sort of silliness. On the other hand, Stephen Township to the south of Stanley seemed to be devoid of religious tensions. Having previously settled in Pickering Township (Ontario County), Irish Catholics founded Mount Carmel in the 1840s, and a decade later they were able to build their first church.[40] This was one of three Irish communities to form close together in the southern tip of the Huron Tract, the most important being the one in Biddulph (Map 16).

By 1881, some 80 percent of Biddulph's population was Irish, making it the greatest Irish stronghold within the Huron Tract.[41] Its ability to attract so many Irish can be attributed to its closeness to a large, already-established

Irish population in London Township (Middlesex County) just to the south, and to the readiness of the Irish who had settled in the Ottawa Valley to pick up sticks and head west.[42] Such was the scale of the Irish influx that it created an overspill extending into McGillivray Township in the west and Blanshard Township in the east (Map 16).

The Canada Company clearly recognized that Biddulph's land allocations had to be managed carefully. Appointing Lieutenant Colonel James Hodgins, who came from Tipperary, as their land agent in 1832, the Company gave him the task of allocating lots to settlers and overseeing their work in colonizing the site.[43] Irish Protestants and Catholics were allocated land in separate parts of the township — with Catholics being mainly concentrated in the northwest end.[44] The Adare community, named by Catholics after a place in Limerick that may suggest their geographical origins, was founded in the 1840s. It was situated near to Mount Carmel, the Irish Catholic community in Stephen Township (Map 16). The Adare settlers built their first Roman Catholic Church a decade later. In addition, Patrick Flanagan gave Biddulph its Flanagan's Corner (now Clandeboye).[45] Irish Catholics further extended their territory in McGillivray Township opposite Biddulph when Maguire was founded. Lying on the opposite side of the London Road, it was named after William Maguire, a cobbler from Enniskillen (County Fermanagh).[46]

McKillop and Hibbert townships, on opposite sides of the Huron Road in the northern half of the Huron Tract, also had separate areas within which Irish Protestants and Catholics settled. First to arrive in McKillop were the families of Michael Rawley and Patrick Carlin, who founded a Protestant "Irish Settlement," also known as "Dublin," along the Huron Road, having acquired the deeds for their land in 1827–28.[47] And Hibbert's Irishtown,[48] an Irish Catholic community, was established by Dennis Downey in 1835, and it, too, was located at the junction of the two townships on the Huron Road. Some, like William Storey, who arrived in the 1840s from County Donegal with his wife, Fanny Laird, and their children, earned money locally before settling into a life of farming in McKillop Township. Various members of the Storey family took up employment with a lumber company in the town of Haysville, situated along the Huron Road southwest of Guelph, before moving to

McKillop. Purchasing a homestead from the Canada Company in 1856, the family began farming, but even then continued to work part of the year in Haysville.[49]

With its exceptionally good land and transportation links, Hibbert Township attracted Irish settlers relatively early — doing so in the 1830s. It acquired many Irish Catholics by the 1850s, who not only excelled as farmers but also had outstanding success in business. In fact, most of Hibbert's hotels, general stores, and sawmills were owned by Irish Catholics.[50] On the other hand, the Irish were less prominent in the eastern half of the Huron Tract, where they had to compete with large Scottish, English, and German populations. During the 1840s, Irish Catholics founded Kinkora in Ellice Township, to the east of Hibbert, a name that commemorated the settlers' County Clare origins. Ellice was one of the few areas having available lots that were still unsold by this time.[51]

Meanwhile, the Irish made considerable inroads in Ashfield and Wawanosh townships (Huron County), which, although they were outside the Huron Tract, were attracting settlers since the 1840s because of their proximity to the town of Goderich. People from Kerry founded an Irish community at modern-day Kingsbridge[52] in Ashfield in the 1840s, while a second Irish community called Belfast sprouted up nearby in 1855 (Map 16).[53]

Morris Township's earliest agricultural community was founded in 1849–50 by Kenneth McBean, a Scot who had previously lived in Perth County, and William McConnell, an Irishman who arrived from County Down. They were joined shortly after by John McRae, Christopher Corbett, John Brandon, and Robert Armstrong, all County Fermanagh people who had settled previously in Simcoe County.[54]

The northern townships of Howick (Huron County), Mornington, Elma, and Wallace (Perth County) were also well-colonized by the Irish, who were the dominant ethnic group in 1881. Arriving in Mornington Township with five sons and two daughters in 1849, Mr. and Mrs. Hamilton Dowd from County Monaghan settled on a 500-acre tract. Eventually "the five Irish brothers owned 100-acre farms in a row from east to west."[55]

Similarly, Samuel Boyd, who originated from County Antrim, relocated to Elma from Lanark County in 1857 and prospered. Families like these, who came on their own or in small groups, having first acquired some experience of life and farming in Canada elsewhere, were the lifeblood of the area.

The Irish territorial spread also advanced into Wellington County. Having farmed extensively in nearby Peel and Halton counties on the southeast side of the County, they were well placed to acquire land-holdings in Wellington.[56] In fact, some of Garafraxa Township's earliest settlers were Irish people who had relocated from Streetsville and Port Credit in Toronto Township (Peel County) and from Oakville in Trafalgar Township (Halton County) during the 1830s. Others had relocated from the Ottawa Valley. Garafraxa also attracted many Irish farmers who had previously settled in Lower Canada, with the Rawdon relocations being particularly well documented.[57]

By 1881, the Irish accounted for more than 50 percent of the population of Garafraxa, Amaranth, and Arthur townships. And they were

Corduroy Road, 1832. Watercolour by Sir Henry Byam Martin (1803–1865). A corduroy road was constructed of baulks of cut timber and designed to create a raised pathway for wagons driving through swampy regions. The workforce that built it would have been mainly Irish.

the largest ethnic group in Luther, Peel, and Maryborough townships. The Kells family, comprising nineteen people, who had arrived from County Cavan in 1846 and established a farm at Peel Township, exemplified those Irish who came directly from Ireland.[58] More typical were the many who simply moved locations from Lower Canada and elsewhere in Upper Canada. Also, Peel and Arthur townships, on opposite sides of the Garafraxa Road, had sizeable Irish Catholic populations by 1851.[59]

The even more remote areas between Lake Huron and Georgian Bay were the last areas in the western peninsula to be colonized. Immigrants faced enormous challenges in venturing this far north into the outback. To encourage settlers to come to the region, the government had offered fifty-acre lots as free grants on either side of the new colonization roads that extended through the region (Map 16). Both the Garafraxa Road, linking Guelph with Owen Sound (formerly Sydenham), and the Durham Road, linking Durham with Kincardine, helped to facilitate the growing influx of people.[60] As was the case in Huron, Perth, and Wellington counties, the region drew many of its settlers from Lower Canada and other parts of Upper Canada.[61]

By 1843 most of the lots along the Garafraxa and Durham roads were occupied and were therefore "no longer open for settlement on the principle of free grants." However, the government offered further grants "on the same conditions in the immediate vicinity of the roads, which will afford the means of advantageous settlement."[62] Despite these efforts by the government to encourage the take up of land, Grey and Bruce counties were still sparsely populated in the 1850s. However, Grey County's Irish numbers nearly doubled in the following decade.[63]

As was the case elsewhere, Grey County's early settlers generally came with farming expertise, having lived previously in "the older townships."[64] The Irish were the dominant ethnic group by 1881, with their heaviest concentrations being in the north and east of the county. Most of the early arrivals were Protestants from the north of Ireland.[65] Many of Grey's Irish settlers would have simply walked the short distance from the adjacent Simcoe County, yet another area that had experienced an Irish takeover. Early arrivals would have had their pick of the best locations when Grey County's good land suddenly became available. Fronting along the Garafraxa Road, Keppel, Derby, Sullivan, and Holland townships were prime sites and in each case the Irish predominated (Map 16). By the 1850s the southern half of Derby Township acquired an "Irish Settlement" and its Irish population grew further over the next decade.[66]

Large Irish communities also formed in Artemesia, Osprey, Proton, and Melancthon townships, lying on either side of the Durham Road, as well as in Euphrasia and Collingwood townships in the northeast of the county.[67] Wilson Benson, a weaver from County Armagh, who settled to the east of Markdale[68] in Artemesia Township in the early 1840s, had come without any previous experience of Canadian farming conditions but nevertheless took everything in his stride:

> The prospect was lovely; where the surface was not covered with ground-hemlock, there was an abundance of wild nettles, cow cabbage, wild onions [leeks], etc. which certainly gave the virgin forest a luxuriant appearance. The black flies and mosquitoes assailed one in myriads, coming through the Township of Melancthon, especially; but even these torments seem frivolous when you get used to it.[69]

Although Sydenham Township was primarily Scottish, it had acquired an "Irish Block" northeast of present-day Owen Sound by the 1840s.[70]

Numerically the Irish came second to the Scots in Bruce County. However, they were the dominant ethnic group in Greenock and Brant townships situated along the Durham Road, and in Amabel and Arran townships in the north of the county (Map 16).

Arriving in Brant Township in 1849–50, Joseph Walker from County Tyrone established flour mills and sawmills in Walkerton, the town named after him.[71] Before that, in the early 1820s, he and his family had settled in West Gwillimbury and Tecumseth townships in Simcoe County.

One of Amabel Township's earliest settlers was James Allen, who, having left the north of Ireland in 1832, first settled in Peterborough County, then moved with his parents in 1850 to Bruce County. Similarly, some of the Tipperary Protestants who had settled previously in London Township (Middlesex County) relocated to Kincardine Township in the early 1850s.[72] As ever, settlement patterns in the western peninsula reflect Irish willingness to relocate to better sites while preserving links with family and friends.

As economic conditions deteriorated in Ireland throughout the first half of the nineteenth century, the Irish influx to Upper Canada intensified. When the Great Irish Famine struck in the mid-1840s, unprecedented numbers arrived. Many thousands emigrated from Ireland, particularly from the west, and when they reached Quebec, local people watched in dismay as hordes of destitute and diseased people disembarked from the ships. Typhus claimed many thousands of Irish lives both during the sea crossings and later when they were placed in quarantine. It is also alleged that poor standards of shipping contributed to the high mortality rate. The causes of this tragedy and who was to blame will now be considered.

CHAPTER 10

ᘐᑭᘗ

Irish Arrivals During the
Great Famine of 1847

Our early potatoes was smitten with the Blight in the middle of July.... I do think before the month of November next there will not be any potatoes here either for seed or bread. There is a great many reasons and cures given but of no effect, but there is nothing surer that it is the breath of an Angry God. There is every appearance of famine.[1]

Writing from County Antrim in November 1846 to Adam Stewart, a relative who had settled in Smith Falls, Hugh and Elizabeth Barkley predicted the terrible famine that would soon engulf Ireland. Josiah MacDonald wrote to his relatives in Upper Canada from Belfast five months later, stating that "there are a great number of people dying in the provinces of Munster and Connaught in the west of Ireland [Map 1] — on an average thirty to forty a day" and soup kitchens had been opened for the relief of the poor.[2] Faced with famine conditions, many Irish people headed for North America, but because of the uncontrollable spread of disease in ports and onboard ships, there would be a shocking death toll. A living hell was about to unfold.

The Quebec immigration agent's report of May 1, 1847, had an air of measured calm. Alexander Buchanan thought that Irish immigrants had been coping well once they arrived in Quebec despite being generally of limited means and in some cases quite destitute. Labourers were finding ready employment in Quebec City and Montreal, while those with friends and relatives who had already settled knew of secure destinations and were going to them. He thought that the people emigrating were "more comfortably off" than before and consequently he did not expect to see an increase in destitution or sickness. The Limerick agent had informed him that he expected "an immense emigration to be realized" despite the fare to Quebec being £4 — double what it had been in the previous year — while the Sligo agent was anticipating increased emigration, mainly to Quebec, adding that "passengers emigrating have more money than usual." The Londonderry agent thought that because ships were scarce, this "in some degree will check the emigration."[3] Sounding a word of caution, Dr. George Douglas, the chief medical officer at the quarantine station on Grosse Île, predicted that many more Irish would arrive in a sickly condition, but neither he nor Alexander Buchanan had any idea of the scale of the impending crisis.[4]

The Great Famine that struck Ireland in the mid-1840s, one of the greatest human catastrophes of modern times, was caused principally by successive failures of the potato crop.[5] It claimed one million Irish lives while precipitating the relocation of a further two million people to North America.[6] A collapsing economy and scarcity of food had created a sense of panic by 1847. The desire to escape possible starvation and destitution fuelled an exceptionally large exodus. Another stimulus was the passing of the 1838 Poor Law (Ireland) Act, which, for the first time required landlords to provide financial aid to their tenants.[7] By making one-off payments to fund emigration schemes, landlords could reduce the payment of their poor rates while at the same time give their tenants an escape route to a better life. Yet another factor that inflated the Quebec passenger arrival numbers at the time was the cheaper fares on offer on the Quebec route when compared with that to New York. As a result, many of the Irish immigrants who arrived in Quebec were merely in transit to the United States, having no intention of settling in Canada. Thus Quebec bore the brunt of the huge North American influx from Ireland that took place during 1847.

Needless to say, the port of Quebec was exceptionally busy. Some 54,310 immigrants arrived there from Irish ports in 1847 — this being two and one half times the number for the previous year.[8] Around 17,500 Irish died either onboard ship or shortly after landing, mostly as a result of a typhus epidemic.[9] However, given that a large proportion of the 21,500 Liverpool immigrant arrivals that year were Irish, the actual Irish total was probably nearer to 70,000 and the death toll even greater.[10] Ships began arriving in May, and by the end of the month 12,000 mostly Irish immigrants were being accommodated either in quarantine buildings and hospitals or remained in the ships awaiting clearance.[11] Estimates indicate that by the end of that year some 20,000 Irish immigrants had died, with the bodies of around 5,000 being interred in a hastily dug mass grave in the cemetery at Grosse Île. This was a tragedy of epic proportions!

The Celtic Cross, erected at Grosse Île in 1909 to commemorate the many Irish who, in 1847, perished on the sea or shortly after arriving at Quebec. Photograph by Jules-Ernest Livernois.

Buchanan and Douglas had their first inkling of the approaching nightmare on May 23rd when the *Jane Black* arrived from Limerick with nineteen dead and dying passengers (Table 1). They included tenants of Colonel Wyndham, who had provided them with financial assistance for this crossing. Soon after, four vessels arrived with a total of 216 sick people onboard. Dr. Douglas reported that they "are still on board as I have not a bed to lay them on or a place to put them in.... I never contemplated the possibility of every vessel arriving with fever as they do now."[12] Arriving from Dublin soon after was the *Wandsworth* with 51 dead and another 53 who would die in the quarantine hospital.[13]

After a relative lull in the mortality rate in June, exceptionally high death tolls were experienced at the port throughout July and August. By September the situation had eased considerably (Table 1).[14] The worst cases were the crossings of the *Virginius* (267 deaths), the *Avon* (246 deaths), the *Larch* and the *Naomi* (each had 196 deaths), the *John Munn* (187 deaths), and the *Triton* (186 deaths). Some twenty ships reported passenger deaths totalling 100 or more and in such cases they usually represented around half of the total carried. The children caught up in this ordeal were cared for in an orphanage in Quebec City and later many were adopted by local French-Canadian and Irish families.[15] Most crossings had relatively few or no deaths. Nevertheless, some were indisputably coffin ships.

And yet, the destitute Irish continued to come in ever greater numbers. Because of the imbalance between the size of the population and the food supply, normal economic life in parts of Ireland was unsustainable. People knew from family and friends already living in North America that a better life was possible. With starvation staring them in the face, the offer of funds from a landlord would have been grabbed with both hands. Staying put was not a realistic alternative. Emigrating, however risky, was the better option.

Irish immigrants suffered an appalling and unacceptable death toll. Almost all of the deaths were due to disease and malnourishment, the two working hand in hand. The primitive state of medical knowledge at the time meant that contagious diseases could neither be prevented nor cured by outside intervention. They swept rapidly through the confines of a ship's hold, and once people fell ill the outcome depended much more on their immune system than on any preventive measures that might have been taken. Any vessel could be a potential coffin ship in the sense that a high fever and an inability to eat could be a death sentence. However, as Dr. Douglas pointed out on several occasions, most of the deaths occurred in ships that had left from Liverpool and Cork. The risk of catching deadly bacteria and viruses was ever present, but it was highest at the busiest ports.

While disease was an obvious uncontrollable peril, most immigrants had access to a decent standard of shipping. Lloyd's shipping codes, which indicate the quality of a vessel's construction and state of repair, show unequivocally that the Irish generally sailed in top-quality vessels (A1 or AE1) that had been recently built (Table 1).[16] The so-called coffin ships did claim many lives through the spread of disease — not through the wilful negligence of shipowners and captains as is sometimes alleged. For instance, in his study of immigration, Edward Guillet quoted one Grosse Île physician who claimed that "while there were plenty of seaworthy vessels, the worst only were generally used in the emigrant trade."[17] It is easy to titillate with this sort of nonsense, but the facts show otherwise.

Meanwhile, the explosive rise in the number of immigrants clearly caught officials in Quebec by surprise, despite the fact that the impending starvation faced by people in Ireland was being reported widely in the Quebec newspapers. Such were the numbers that the quarantine facilities could not cope and people were left in their ships without receiving treatment. The sheds on the island were overcrowded and filthy. Dr. Douglas spoke of forty to fifty deaths per day in the hospital:

> Every vessel bringing Irish passengers (but more especially those from Liverpool and Cork) has lost many by fever and dysentery on the voyage and has arrived here with numbers of sick ... seventeen vessels have arrived with Irish passengers, five from Cork, four from Liverpool and the others from Sligo, Limerick, Belfast, Londonderry and New Ross. The number of passengers with which these vessels left port was 5,607; out of those, the large numbers of 206 have died on the passage and

upwards of 700 have been admitted to Hospital or are being treated on board their vessels, waiting vacancies to be landed.[18]

The main culprit was typhus. Officials faced the dilemma of knowing that healthy immigrants might catch the disease from others while being kept in quarantine with them for the normal two-week period. They could be carriers of the disease in its early stages and not appear to be ill. If they were released too early, they might unwittingly become a threat to public health by spreading disease in the cities, towns, and countryside through which they travelled. Choosing to release the immigrants early from Grosse Île as the better of the two evils, Dr. Douglas went on to issue this stark warning on June 8:

Out of the 4,000 or 5,000 emigrants who have left this [island] since Sunday, at least 2,000 will fall sick somewhere before three weeks are over. They ought to have accommodation for 2,000 sick at least at Montreal and Quebec, as all the Cork and Liverpool passengers are half dead from starvation and want before embarking; and the least bowel complaint, which is sure to come with a change of food, finishes them without a struggle. I never saw people so indifferent to life; they would continue in the same berth with the dead person until the seamen or captain dragged out the corpse with boat hooks. Good God! What evils will befall the cities wherever they alight? Hot weather will increase the evil. Now, give the authorities of Quebec and Montreal fair warning from me. I have not time to write, or should feel it my duty to do so. Public safety requires it.[19]

Dr. Douglas was a tower of strength who, despite everything, kept calm and dealt with problems as they arose. The army was on hand to offer support, with one of their more heartrending tasks being to clear away the dead bodies:

A memorial service in 1849, held in the Grosse Île cemetery, commemorated the many Irish deaths with great solemnity. Around seven thousand people attended. The photograph appeared in the *Standard*, Montreal, August 28, 1909.

Dr. Douglas supervised the medical work, going from one end of the island to the other both night and day, sometimes on horseback. His office recorded the number of ships, the number of immigrants brought to hospital, occupying the "healthy" tents, the deaths and the people dismissed from the hospitals. The professional men and several nurses worked loyally and steadily.... While hospital personnel offered what care they could in medicines and bedtime attention, the clergy brought spiritual assistance to the dying and their families. Both Catholic and Protestant clergy from Quebec City and the country parishes came to the island, worked in the hospitals and went on board the ships.... Bishop George Mountain, Anglican Bishop of Montreal, twice came to the island that summer.[20]

Dr. Douglas also found time to admonish the editors of the *Quebec Mercury* and the *Quebec Gazette* for printing distorted and exaggerated reports of the misery and distress being experienced by immigrants at Grosse Île and called on them to act more responsibly.[21]

The Irish influx had been dominated initially by departures from ports in Ulster in the north. However, this situation changed dramatically during the famine period, when a far greater proportion of people left for Quebec from the ports of Cork and Limerick in the southwest, from Dublin and New Ross in the southeast, and from Sligo in the west (Table 2). Liverpool immigrant arrivals, who were probably largely Irish, also soared, especially in 1847. These trends reflect the assistance given by landlords in funding sea crossings in the sense that most of their aid was directed at people living in counties Clare, Limerick, and Kerry in the southwest, Kilkenny and Wicklow in the southeast, and Sligo in the west. And a good many of the landlord-assisted crossings sailed from Liverpool (Table 3).

The actual number of paupers who received financial aid from landlords cannot be quantified because of the inadequacy of the official figures, which fail to take a full account of the help granted.[22] The records show that Colonel George Wyndham assisted at least 700 of his County Clare

View of cholera hospital and telegraph, Grosse Île. Pencil drawing by Ralph Anderson.

tenants between 1839 and 1848, while Charles Butler Clarke did the same for around 300 of his Kilkenny tenants between 1841 and 1849. Lord Fitzwilliam assisted at least 1,000 of his Wicklow tenants between 1842 and 1851, while Lord Palmerston assisted at least 550 of his Sligo tenants in 1847 during the height of the famine. The Marquis of Lansdowne provided aid to around 800 of his Kerry tenants in 1851 while the Marquis of Bath helped around 200 of his Monaghan tenants that same year (Table 3). However, the official figures reveal only a fraction of the total number.[23]

Some landlords, like Colonel Wyndham and Colonel C.B. Wandesford were lauded for ensuring that most of their tenants landed in good health and spirits.[24] By contrast, the haggard appearance of Major Denis Mahon's Roscommon tenants, who arrived from Liverpool in the *Virginius* in August 1847, caused an outcry. Tragically, 267 of the *Virginius*'s 476 passengers died, either on the crossing or at the quarantine station at Grosse Île. Dr. George Douglas thought that they were "the worst-looking passengers he had ever seen."[25] Later that year, Lord Palmerston's tenants had to endure a difficult passage, arriving in the *Richard Watson* in early November, this crossing being the last of the season. Their deplorable state led Colonial Secretary Earl Grey to fire off this rebuke to his lordship on November 12th:

> Of the passengers, about one fourth were males and the remainder women and children; and we have been assured by the gentlemen who saw them that a more destitute and helpless set have not come out this year. They were penniless and in rags, without shoes or stockings and lying upon the bare boards — not even having straw. When the health officer visited them he saw other visible instances of destitution — three poor children — infants we might say from their age, sitting on the bare deck perfectly naked huddled together, shivering.[26]

There were many reports of the poor and destitute arriving in a dire state. However, these happenings were sometimes disputed. Figures are imprecise as to how many Irish immigrants were actually ill-treated by landlords. Nor is there reliable information on the total number of Irish who were assisted, since a great deal of help went unrecorded. For instance, although Lord Fitzwilliam provided the financing for 312 of his Wicklow tenants to sail in the *Dunbrody* to Quebec in 1847, they do not appear in the official list of assisted passengers (Table 1).[27] It is thought that the assisted Irish represented around one third of the total during the famine period between 1846 and 1850; but this is only an estimate.[28] Nevertheless, although the actual number is probably much higher than the official figures reveal, the assisted Irish were still very much in the minority. Most of the Irish were self-funded, either having raised their own money or by having received remittances from family and friends already settled in North America. In other words, however poor and bedraggled they may

Memorial at Grosse Île, erected 1898, dedicated to the doctors and their assistants who lost their lives while caring for the sick and dying Irish who were treated in the hospital.

have looked on arrival, very few had been dragooned into emigrating by heartless landlords as is frequently alleged. Most left of their own free will and paid their own way themselves.

All the while, landlords were criticized severely for seemingly depositing large numbers of their surplus tenants on Canadian shores. Canadian authorities felt that they were being left to deal with an unfolding humanitarian crisis that they attributed to the heartlessness of landlords. Shouldering the financial burden was bad enough, but the realization that a good one third of the people disembarking from ships were merely in transit to the United States added to their sense of outrage.[29] However, landlord motives have also to be considered. They funded emigration schemes to make their estates more economically viable. From their point of view, this was cheaper than maintaining their unproductive tenants in a workhouse. Landlords hoped that all of their tenants would be able to grasp the opportunities of the New World and in doing so become beneficial additions to the population. However, the Canadian authorities looked for more sinister motives. They believed that landlords simply wanted to get rid of their tenants to save money and had no interest in their future welfare or usefulness once they arrived in Canada.

Although there were undoubtedly cases of disreputable behaviour by landlords, their culpability should not be exaggerated. A good test is their choice of ships. The *Lloyd's Shipping Register* provides unequivocal proof that many paid the extra cost of selecting high-quality ships for their tenants' crossings. Many sailed in A1 or AE1 ships — the best quality shipping on offer. This helped to ensure greater comfort and safety. For instance, Francis Spaight, a shipping agent as well as a landowner, sent his Tipperary tenants to Quebec in the *Jane Black*, an A1 ship that he owned. He also provided the AE1 *Bryan Abbs*, another of his ships, to Colonel Wyndham's tenants, who sailed in it in 1842 and 1846. Similarly, the ships provided by the Marquis of Lansdowne and Lord Fitzwilliam were generally of the highest quality (Table 3).

Landlords should not have been made scapegoats for the dreadful suffering and loss of life that occurred. For a start, assisted immigrants were a minority of the total. Secondly, where assisted immigration schemes were offered, landlords generally provided help well beyond ensuring that their tenants crossed the Atlantic safely. Lord Fitzwilliam and Colonel Wyndham offered assisted schemes over a number of years in which agents helped tenants to organize their relocations. They were given help in finding jobs and obtaining land. For instance, the Fitzwilliam tenants mainly went to Irish-dominated areas in the Ottawa Valley, especially locations near present-day Ottawa, and to the Irish strongholds in Halton, Peel, and Simcoe counties, to the west of present-day Toronto.[30] They could not have done this without help from agents working on their behalf. Some of Francis Spaight's Tipperary tenants ended up in the Toronto area, as well, for the same reason.[31] Colonel Wyndham's tenants mainly went to bolt-holes in the Peterborough region, this being another area that had attracted the Irish in great numbers starting in the 1820s.[32]

In other words, assisted tenants were not usually at the mercy of an uncaring landlord, as is often suggested. No one sent them to some randomly selected lonely place on the other side of the Atlantic. Assisted tenants usually settled in areas where family and friends had previously established their communities. Had they been able to finance their fares themselves, these are the very destinations that they would have chosen. For instance, the more remote parts of Renfrew County in Upper Canada and Ottawa and Pontiac counties in Lower Canada attracted Irish people during the famine period because they were Irish-dominated areas having available land. Some came as assisted tenants while others were self-funded. The outcome was exactly the same either way. Similarly, those of Lord Fitzwilliam's tenants who came to live in Marmora Township (Hastings County) in eastern Upper Canada during the famine years chose another remote area, which had long attracted Irish settlers. They no doubt rubbed shoulders with compatriots who had paid their own way. Mr. Charley's Donegal tenants were set to take up railway jobs near Sherbrooke in the Eastern Townships of Lower Canada.[33] Other mainly self-funded Irish were also arriving in this region at this time, having been attracted by the employment opportunities arising from the industrial development of the region.

Tragically, the hastily constructed immigration sheds in Montreal, Toronto, and Kingston, which offered quarantine facilities, also became mortuary sites for the many Irish who died from disease. Montreal's Griffintown had long been a holding bay for newly arrived Irish immigrants, who stayed with family and friends while they planned their final destinations, but during the famine it witnessed a death toll that rose dramatically.[34] Between 3,500 and 6,000 Irish people died of typhus while being accommodated in the immigration sheds at Windmill Point, located across the canal from Griffintown. Workers constructing the Victoria Bridge in 1859 would later discover the mass grave which had been dug. Many of the workers, being of Irish descent, were unsettled by the discovery and established a "Black Rock" memorial to ensure that their gravesite would never be forgotten.[35] Similarly, some 1,400 Irish died in Kingston in 1847, despite the efforts of charitable and religious groups to save them.[36] They were buried near the present-day Kingston General Hospital and later moved to St. Mary's cemetery in Kingston. By June 1847, some 5,784 mainly Irish immigrants reached Toronto.[37] That summer, 863 died of typhus while being treated in the Toronto "fever hospital," a building on King Street having been converted for that purpose.[38]

Despite having a rural background, many of the Irish who arrived during the famine period headed for the towns and cities in Lower and Upper Canada.[39] Whereas, in the past, some immigrant farm labourers would seek agricultural employment in the hope of accumulating capital and owning their own farm one day, now, a higher proportion of the new arrivals preferred to be urban dwellers. Times had changed. The prospect of finding a job in the city near where the ships and steamers had left them carried considerable appeal. They had come to Canada to escape the famine and had few plans beyond this. Most were penniless and many would have been recovering from the rigours of their Atlantic crossing. Also, some Canadian farmers were reluctant to employ men who might be carriers of disease and, in any case, few of the Irish arrivals had the requisite skills. Coming as they did from the south and west of Ireland, they knew how to till a tiny plot with a spade and plant a few potatoes but did not know how to hitch a horse or use an axe. As the Catholic politician Thomas D'Arcy McGee observed, "never in the world's history, were so purely an agricultural population so suddenly and unpreparedly converted into mere town labourers."[40]

High concentrations of the Irish-born formed in the major towns and cities by 1871, thus revealing where many of the famine arrivals had settled.[41] The search for jobs had led them to the ports and the factories near Quebec City, Montreal, Toronto, and Hamilton, while the urban centres in the vicinity of Kingston and Belleville in the east and St. Catharines, Brantford, Guelph, and London in the west also attracted them. Railway jobs on offer in Sherbrooke and Richmond in the Eastern Townships were another magnet. The mining districts north of Lake Simcoe also experienced a substantial Irish influx during the famine years and beyond. Meanwhile, many Irish women and girls clearly found jobs as domestic servants in the major cities. As might be expected, the mainly Catholic Irish arrivals settled near to one another wherever possible. They lived in their shantytowns in Montreal, Toronto, and Hamilton — places that would later become battle zones in the ongoing religious disputes between Protestants and Catholics.[42]

The famine lasted three to four years. It is well to remember that this immigration saga had been running for 100 years before it struck. Despite the scale of their suffering, the Irish who arrived during the famine were a small part of the story. The catastrophic events of the famine years must not be allowed to divert attention from their pioneering achievements. The simple fact is that before the arrival of the steam engine, all immigrants had to rely on sailing ships. They were basic, uncomfortable, and could be breeding grounds for disease. That was how it was at the time. There was no other mode of transport for people who could not afford the greater comforts of a cabin. Judged by the living conditions of the time, though, most immigrants were well treated onboard ship and they normally sailed in well-constructed vessels.

Table 1:
Irish Immigrant Ship Arrivals at Quebec in 1847

Date	Vessels (type, tonnage)	Captain	Place and Year Built	Lloyd's Code	Departure Port	Passenger Numbers	Deaths*
May							
20	*Syria* (bk, 543)	Cox, M.B.	Q.C., 1842	A1	Liverpool	242	49
23	*Celeste* (bk, 284)	Mulcahy, D.	N.B., 1846	A1	Limerick	199	1
23	*Jane* (bk)	Dunn, R.	n/k, 1845	A1	Limerick	200	0
23	*Jane Black* (s)	Gorman, T.	Dundee, 1840	A1	Limerick	426	19
23	*Perseverance* (bk)	Seeds, H.	N.B., 1839	AE1	Dublin	311	19
25	*Dunbrody* (bk)	Baldwin, J.	N.B., 1840	AE1	New Ross	312	8
25	*Helen Thompson* (bg, 299) п	Gray	n/k	n/k	Londonderry	371	4
25	*Jessie* (bk, 304)	McGee, H.	P.E., 1845	AE1	Sligo	243	10
25	*Wallace* (s, 762)	Morton	N.B., 1840	AE1	Liverpool	417	5
25	*Wandsworth* (s)	Dunlop, G.	n/k	n/k	Dublin	527	104
26	*Aquamarine* (bk)	Connolly, S.	n/k	n/k	Liverpool	27	0
26	*Fame* (bk, 325)	Miller, W.	Q.C., 1845	A1	Limerick	207	1
26	*Ganges* (bk, 430)	Dron, T.	Greenock, 1816	AE1	Cork	411	5
26	*Tottenham* (bk, 308)	Evans, E.	Q.C., 1825	n/k	Youghall	228	3
27	*Chieftain* (bk, 325)	McGowan, W.	Montreal, 1826	AE1	Belfast	248	2
27	*Concord* (bg, 299)	Burden, H.	Sunderland, 1846	A1	Dublin	182	3
27	*Sir Colin Campbell* (s)	Campbell, J.	n/k	n/k	Belfast	379	3
28	*Annie* (s, 553)	Mearns, W.	Q.C., 1843	A1	Belfast	429	1
28	*Industry* (bk)	Stevens, J.	Sunderland, 1839	A1	Dublin	301	6
28	*Souvenir* (bg)	Lancaster, J.	n/k	n/k	Limerick	124	1
29	*Albion* (bk)	Daly, C.	n/k	n/k	Galway	211	4

Date	Vessels (type, tonnage)	Captain	Place and Year Built	Lloyd's Code	Departure Port	Passenger Numbers	Deaths*
June							
1	Constitution (bg)	Wilson, J.	n/k	n/k	Sligo	152	12
2	Ann (sr, 174)	McFee, A.	P.E., 1839	AE1	Limerick	119	4
2	Argent (bg, 228)	Allison, J.	N.B., 1841	n/k	Limerick	127	0
2	Bryan Abbs (bg, 256)	Wood, W.	Jarrow, 1834	AE1	Limerick	194	6
3	Nerio (sr, 199)	Gibson, W.	P.E., 1840	n/k	Limerick	132	6
3	Transit (bg)	Ferguson, C.	n/k	n/k	Sligo	158	6
5	Dew Drop (bg)	Burke, J.	n/k	n/k	Westport	32	0
5	Phoenix (bg, 384)	Kerr, D.	Miramichi, 1826	AE1	Liverpool	286	7
7	Erin (bg, 187)	McDonald	N. S., 1840	AE1	New Ross	120	3
7	Henry (bg)	McFell, H.	n/k	n/k	Donegal	169	16
7	Hope (bg, 243)	Lester	Whitehaven, 1808	E1	Maryport	24	0
7	Leveret (bg, 200)	Robinson, W.	Sunderland, 1839	A1	Limerick	125	0
7	Royalist (bk, 560)	Beveridge	N.B., 1844	A1	Liverpool	437	36
7	Tryagain (bk, 291)	Barry, J.	Q.C., 1826	n/k	Cork	182	16
8	Achilles (bk)	Taylor, W.	n/k	n/k	Liverpool	411	51
8	Blonde (bk, 604)	Crawford, A.	Montreal, 1841	A1	Liverpool	424	19
8	British Queen (bg)	Errington, R.	n/k	n/k	Limerick	190	1
8	Clarendon (bk,450)	McFarlane, J.	London, 1827	AE1	Liverpool	281	54
8	Constitution (s, 502)	Neil, R.	Q.C., 1840	n/k	Belfast	394	19
8	Mary (bk, 338)	Ellis, R.	N. S., 1828	n/k	Liverpool	37	1
8	Orlando (bk, 297)	Cockerill, W.	Sunderland, 1836	A1	Newry	209	8
8	Scotland (s)	Thompson, W.	n/k	n/k	Cork	564	166
9	Tay (bk)	Brennan, H.	n/k	n/k	Sligo	303	12
9	Wave (bk, 570)	Smallman, R.	N.B., 1838	AE1	Dublin	396	5
10	Agnes (s, 690)[Π]	McCawley, T.	Miramichi, 1845	A1	Cork	430	160

Date	Vessels (type, tonnage)	Captain	Place and Year Built	Lloyd's Code	Departure Port	Passenger Numbers	Deaths*
10	*Christina* (bk, 640)	Kenyon, D.	Lower Canada, 1838	AE1	Londonderry	479	33
10	*Columbia* (bk)	Aim, J.	n/k	n/k	Sligo	246	34
10	*Congress* (bg, 299)	Carwin, W.	Maryport, 1818	AE1	Sligo	217	54
10	*Dykes* (bg)	Sewell, J.	n/k	n/k	Sligo	170	25
10	*John Bolton* (s)	Samson	n/k	n/k	Liverpool	578	141
10	*John Francis* (s, 362)	Deaves, H.	Montreal, 1827	AE1	Cork	260	69
10	*Lord Seaton* (bk)	Talbot, W.	n/k	n/k	Belfast	289	51
10	*Springhill* (bk)	Gunn, W.	n/k	n/k	Sligo	227	9
10	*Thistle* (bg, 265)	Thomas, P.	N.B., 1835	n/k	Waterford	172	0
10	*Urania* (286)	Mills, R.	Whitby, 1825	AE1	Cork	179	36
10	*Wolfville* (bk, 415)	Ritchie, D.	N. S., 1841	AE1	Sligo	311	85
10	*Yorkshire* (bg, 310)	Lynas, J.	N.B., 1839	AE1	Donegal	233	2
12	*Argo* (s)	Mitchell, A.	n/k	n/k	Liverpool	590	69
12	*Bee* (bk)	Muir, T.	n/k	n/k	Cork	352	165
12	*Caithness-shire* (bk, 319)	Leggate, T.	Richibucto, 1842	AE1	Belfast	234	30
12	*George* (s)	Simpson	n/k	n/k	Liverpool	397	150
12	*Mary Brack* (bg, 305)	Smith, B.	Sunderland, 1838	A1	Limerick	184	9
12	*Ninian* (bk,299)	Fittock, D.	P.E., 1840	AE1	Limerick	261	31
13	*Aberdeen* (bk, 560)	McGrath	N.B., 1840	n/k	Liverpool	392	61
14	*Dominica* (bk, 381)	Slorah, G.	Whitby, 1808	AE1	Cork	254	11
14	*Eliza Caroline* (s)	Briggs, J.	Maryport, 1785	AE1	Liverpool	540	79
14	*Pasha* (bk, 291)	Allen, W.	Sunderland, 1846	A1	Cork	217	15
14	*Rankin* (bk)	Lawson	n/k	n/k	Liverpool	573	51
14	*Thompson* (bg, 210)	Burton, W.	n/k	AE1	Sligo	159	12
16	*Princess Royal* (s)	Duguid, J.	n/k	n/k	Liverpool	599	30
18	*Albion* (bg)	Bowman, H.	n/k	n/k	Limerick	189	19
18	*Despatch* (bk)	Walsh, R.	n/k	n/k	Waterford	255	6
18	*Gilmour* (bk)	Parkeham, J. J.	n/k	n/k	Cork	368	72
18	*Josepha* (s)	Leitch, H.	n/k	n/k	Belfast	298	2

Date	Vessels (type, tonnage)	Captain	Place and Year Built	Lloyd's Code	Departure Port	Passenger Numbers	Deaths*
18	Pacific (bk, 361)	Walsh, W.	Sunderland, 1846	A1	Waterford	197	1
18	Primrose (s, 477)	Irvine, C.	N.B., 1841	AE1	Limerick	337	15
18	Thomas Handford (bg, 228)	Herbert, A.	N.B., 1824	AE1	Limerick	155	1
19	Cape Breton (bk, 242)	Murray, J.	London, 1833	A1	Dublin	176	8
19	Lord Glenelg (bk)	Martin, A.	n/k	n/k	Limerick	264	8
19	Mail (bk, 371)	Gordon, W.	Q.C., 1842	A1	Cork	289	36
19	Standard (bk)	Ritchie, R.	n/k	n/k	New Ross	369	11
20	Araminta (s, 511)	Rogers, J.	Q.C., 1842	A1	Liverpool	412	50
20	Elizabeth (s)	Thompson, W.	n/k	n/k	Liverpool	341	26
20	Lady Gordon (s, 283)	Scurr, T.	Whitehaven, 1817	AE1	Belfast	204	19
20	Sisters (s, 744)	Christian, T.	N.B., 1841	n/k	Liverpool	507	119
20	Thetis (bk, 251)	Richmond, W.	Whitby, 1811	AE1	Limerick	161	3
20	Wilhelmina (bk)	Leslie, J.	n/k	n/k	Belfast	276	4
20	William Pirrie (s, 499)	Agnew, A.	Q.C., 1839	AE1	Belfast	414	14
21	Abbotsford (s)	Gibson, W.	n/k	n/k	Dublin	382	21
21	Tay (bk)	Longwill, J.	n/k	n/k	Liverpool	371	13
22	Mary & Harriett (bg, 284)	Saxton, J.	Sunderland, 1838	A1	Limerick	178	9
22	Ross-shire (bg, 297)	Teaster, J.	Pictou, 1843	A1	Limerick	212	0
23	Achsah (bg, 255)	Monet, J.	Sunderland, 1845	A1	Limerick	174	2
23	Ajax (bk, 466)	Scott, R.	P.E., 1846	A1	Liverpool	359	87
23	Pursuit (s)	Spence, W.	n/k	n/k	Liverpool	472	73
24	Lotus (s)	Watson, J.	n/k	n/k	Liverpool	546	99
24	Maria & Elizabeth (bg, 279)	Wood, W.	Sunderland, 1834	AE1	Liverpool	81	4
24	Sesostris (s, 561)	Dano, W.	N.S., 1841	AE1	Londonderry	428	17
25	Eagle (bg)	Catterson, W.	n/k	n/k	Dublin	211	6
25	Juverna (bk, 311)	Sedgewick, J.	Waterford, 1838	A1	Waterford	182	1

Date	Vessels (type, tonnage)	Captain	Place and Year Built	Lloyd's Code	Departure Port	Passenger Numbers	Deaths*
25	*Lawrence Forristal* (s)	Toole, J.	n/k	n/k	Waterford	143	3
25	*Louisa* (bk)	McKinley	n/k	n/k	Limerick	213	4
25	*Swallow* (bg)	Wright, C.	n/k	n/k	Limerick	147	1
26	*Agnes King* (bk, 278)	Gaunson, J.	Sunderland, 1846	A1	Limerick	183	9
26	*Herald* (s, 801)	Auld, H.	N.B., 1840	AE1	Dublin	559	17
26	*Jane Blain* (s, 305)	Kelley, P.	Greenock, 1836	A1	Sligo	225	7
26	*Jessie* (s)	Gorman, D.	P.E., 1845	AE1	Limerick	489	58
26	*Lady Flora Hastings* (bk)	Wetherall, G.	n/k	n/k	Cork	454	76
26	*Lady Milton* (s)	Hayes, J.	n/k	n/k	Liverpool	432	56
26	*Lord Sandon* (bk, 404)	Feneran, A.	Richibucto, 1839	AE1	Cork	246	27
26	*Nelson Village* (bk, 384)	McBerrine, J.	Miramichi, 1826	AE1	Belfast	263	18
26	*Trade* (bg, 204)	Plewes, J.	Hull, 1817	AE1	Waterford	134	5
28	*Jane Avery* (bg, 267)	Tate, C.	Jarrow, 1839	AE1	Dublin	183	24
28	*Sarah Maria* (bg, 169)	Faucett, E.	Q.C., 1827	AE1	Sligo	116	14
29	*Elizabeth* (s)	Duddet, T.	n/k	n/k	Liverpool	434	36
29	*Georgiana* (bk, 256)	Wilson, J.	Ipswich, 1816	AE1	Dublin	184	2
29	*John Bell* (bk, 454)	Carroll, J.	Q.C., 1834	AE1	New Ross	254	4
29	*New York Packet* (bk, 642)	Kemp	N.B., 1839	AE1	Liverpool	470	9
29	*Panope* (bg, 205)	Lelly, H.	Yarmouth, 1839	A1	Dublin	112	2
29	*Sobraon* (s, 342)	Wilson, J.	Dumbarton, 1846	A1	Liverpool	606	67
30	*Ann* (bk, 539)	Johnston, W.	Miramichi, 1838	AE1	Liverpool	348	50
30	*Elliotts* (bg, 280)	Gascoigne, P.	Sunderland, 1839	A1	Dublin	197	15
30	*Solway* (bk, 594)	McLelland, J.	N.B., 1843	A1	New Ross	361	4

Date	Vessels (type, tonnage)	Captain	Place and Year Built	Lloyd's Code	Departure Port	Passenger Numbers	Deaths*
July							
1	*Rose* (bk)	McKinlay, D.	n/k	n/k	Liverpool	384	139
2	*Agent* (s)	Mills, J.	n/k	n/k	New Ross	387	13
2	*Agnes & Ann* (bk, 413)	Bowle	Q.C., 1826	AE1	Newry	297	7
2	*Charles* (bg)	Skinner, G.	n/k	n/k	Limerick	122	1
2	*Coromandel* (s)	Hubback, M.	n/k	n/k	Dublin	446	27
2	*Ellen* (bg)	Forristal	n/k	n/k	Limerick	130	1
2	*Linden* (bg)	Caithness, H.	n/k	n/k	Limerick	179	2
2	*Margaret* (s)	Black, J.	n/k	n/k	New Ross	531	26
2	*Woodbine* (bk, 425)	Skeoch, R.	Newcastle, 1843	AE1	Londonderry	243	1
3	*Junior* (bk, 566)	Gillis, J.	Q.C., 1845	A1	Liverpool	356	34
3	*New Zealand* (s)	Wilson, J.	n/k	n/k	Newry	473	7
4	*Aberfoyle* (bk)	William, J.	N.S., 1845	AE1	Waterford	328	7
4	*Durham* (bk, 358)	Davidson, J.	Sunderland, 1843	A1	Liverpool	269	8
4	*Eliza Morrison* (s, 671)	Leitch, J.	Q.C., 1845	A1	Belfast	471	17
4	*Elizabeth* (bk)	Richards	n/k	n/k	Limerick	112	0
4	*Kate Robertson* (sr, 146)	Watt, J.	N. S., 1845	A1	Youghall	25	0
4	*Triumph* (bk)	O'Brien, P.	n/k	n/k	Donegal	115	0
5	*Energy* (bg)	Warren, M.	n/k	n/k	Limerick	209	5
6	*Emily* (bg)	Coombs, J.	n/k	n/k	Cork	157	15
6	*Yorkshire Lass* (bk, 345)	Price, J.	Q.C., 1845	A1	Killala	282	45
7	*Admiral* (bk, 722)	Buchanan, R.	Q.C., 1845	A1	Waterford	480	6
7	*Bolton* (bg, 290)	Stove, J.	Newcastle, 1836	AE1	Dublin	208	4
7	*Camilla* (bg)	Laughton	n/k	n/k	Sligo	138	4
7	*Independence* (s, 584)	Harper, J.	Q.C., 1839	AE1	Belfast	432	19
7	*Rodeng* (bg)	Ashton, J.H.	n/k	n/k	Cork	94	2
7	*Wm. S. Hamilton* (bk)	Joyce, W.	n/k	n/k	New Ross	206	24

Date	Vessels (type, tonnage)	Captain	Place and Year Built	Lloyd's Code	Departure Port	Passenger Numbers	Deaths*
8	*Margaret* (bk)	Hardcastle	n/k	n/k	New Ross	399	25
9	*Unicorn* (bg)	Boyd	n/k	n/k	Londonderry	178	11
10	*Ellen* (bk, 397)	Hood, T.	N.B., 1834	AE1	Sligo	247	8
10	*Free Briton* (bg, 290)	Sanderson, W.	Sunderland, 1845	A1	Cork	185	9
11	*Huron* (s)	Evans, H.	n/k	n/k	Belfast	329	20
11	*James Moran* (s, 538)	Morrison, G.	N.B., 1837	AE1	Liverpool	353	56
11	*Tamarac* (bk)	Cooper	n/k	n/k	Liverpool	497	40
11	*Venelia* (s)	Marshell, P.	n/k	n/k	Limerick	391	14
12	*Tom* (bg, 165)	Coulthard, W.	Chester, 1815	AE1	Dublin	115	4
12	*Wakefield* (s)	Broomhead, J.	n/k	n/k	Cork	398	72
13	*Collingwood* (bg)	McLintock, W.	n/k	n/k	Londonderry	202	4
14	*Lively* (bg, 271)	Checkley, W.	Sunderland, 1838	A1	Cork	189	45
14	*Progress* (s)	Abel, E.	n/k	n/k	New Ross	555	62
14	*Royal Adelaide* (bk, 453)	Smith, A.	Q.C., 1831	AE1	Waterford	198	10
15	*Alert* (bk, 405)	Laughlin, J.	N. S., 1843	A1	Waterford	247	6
15	*Wonder* (bg, 265)	Hunter, T.	Stockton, 1843	A1	Sligo	176	3
16	*Charles Richards* (bk, 258)	Angus, S.	Sunderland, 1845	A1	Sligo	174	16
16	*John Jardine* (bg, 508)	Sampson, J.	Richibucto, 1842	A1	Liverpool	389	18
16	*Medusa* (bg, 294)	Woodworth, J.	Sunderland, 1845	A1	Cork	205	3
17	*Manchester* (s, 740)	Browne, P.	Q.C., 1845	A1	Liverpool	512	28
18	*Goliah* (s, 900)	Slater, C.	Q.C., 1840	AE1	Liverpool	600	89
18	*Roseanna* (bk)	Wilkinson, W.	n/k	n/k	Cork	272	7
18	*Thistle* (bk, 558)	Turner, J.	Q.C., 1830	AE1	Liverpool	381	13
19	*Sarah* (bk)	Fletcher, G.	n/k	n/k	Liverpool	255	70
23	*Erin's Queen* (s, 681)	Davidson, J.	Q.C., 1846	A1	Liverpool	493	136

Date	Vessels (type, tonnage)	Captain	Place and Year Built	Lloyd's Code	Departure Port	Passenger Numbers	Deaths*
24	*Friendship* (bk)	Allan	n/k	n/k	Dublin	202	1
24	*Jessie* (s)	Oliver, W.	P.E., 1845	AE1	Cork	409	83
24	*Triton* (s, 676)	Smith, J.	N. S., 1839	AE1	Liverpool	462	186
26	*Ann* (bk)	Nicholson, J.	n/k	n/k	Donegal	109	1
26	*Avon* (s)	Johnston, M.	n/k	n/k	Cork	550	246
26	*Rega* (bk, 207)	Patrick	Dundee, 1846	A1	Cork	119	3
27	*Asia* (bk)	Hannah, J.	n/k	n/k	Cork	409	36
27	*Mary* (bg)	Copton, W.	n/k	n/k	Sligo	154	11
27	*Numa* (bk, 323)	Miller, T.	Sunderland, 1811	E1	Sligo	257	37
28	*Alexander Stewart* (bg, 172)	William, D.	N. S., 1837	AE1	Limerick	103	8
29	*Blenheim* (s, 689)	Morrison, A.	S. Shields, 1845	A1	Cork	355	16
29	*Greenock* (bk)	Walker, A.	n/k	n/k	Liverpool	816	80
31	*Abbeylands* (bk)	Arken, C.	n/k	n/k	Liverpool	398	5
31	*Agamemnon* (s)	McKenly, J.	n/k	n/k	Liverpool	646	45
31	*Argo* (bg, 177)	Fearson, P.	Workington, 1808	AE1	Sligo	127	3
31	*Leander* (s)	Sheridan, B.	n/k	n/k	Londonderry	427	6
31	*Marchioness of Bute* (s, 850)	Renning, J.	N.B., 1838	AE1	Belfast	496	25

August

Date	Vessels (type, tonnage)	Captain	Place and Year Built	Lloyd's Code	Departure Port	Passenger Numbers	Deaths*
1	*Cygnet* (s)	Thompson, W.	n/k	n/k	Londonderry	210	0
1	*Eliza Ann* (sr)	Ferguson, J.	n/k	n/k	Limerick	112	0
1	*X.L.* (bg, 176)	Owen, W.	Anglesey, 1842	A1	Galway	130	4
2	*Edward Kenny* (bg, 315)	Cook, D.	P.E., 1843	A1	Belfast	241	0
2	*Oregon* (bk)	Robertson, T.	n/k	n/k	Killala	231	11
2	*Union* (bg, 105)	Francis, D.	Appledore, 1810	AE1	Limerick	54	16
3	*Curraghmore* (bk, 343)	Ball, W.	Waterford, 1841	A1	Waterford	214	1
3	*George* (bg, 179)	Sheridan, W.	N. S., 1840	AE1	Dublin	104	11
3	*Maria* (bg, 192)	Omalley, M.	P.E., 1842	AE1	Limerick	132	0

Date	Vessels (type, tonnage)	Captain	Place and Year Built	Lloyd's Code	Departure Port	Passenger Numbers	Deaths*
3	Ocean Queen (s)	McBride, J.	n/k	n/k	Cork	498	6
3	Rockshire (bg)	McLeury, P.	n/k	n/k	Liverpool	44	0
4	Allan Kerr (bk, 493)	Gily, W.	Miramichi, 1836	AE1	Sligo	416	15
4	Pandora (bk, 561)	White, W.	Miramichi, 1839	AE1	New Ross	401	24
5	Ann Kenny (bk, 434)	Baldwin, W.	P.E., 1842	AE1	Waterford	360	10
5	Charles Walton	Baker, J.	n/k	n/k	Killala	272	16
5	Helen (bk)	Hasson, W.	n/k	n/k	Belfast	212	0
5	Lady Campbell (bk, 308)	Hodge, J.	N.B., 1832	AE1	Dublin	241	41
5	Marchioness of Abercorn (bk)	Hegarty, J.	n/k	n/k	Londonderry	414	17
6	Broom (bk)	White	n/k	n/k	Liverpool	513	63
6	Grace (bg, 157)	Bell, T.	Workington, 1824	AE1	Westport	41	1
6	John & Robert (bk, 501)	McKechney, A.	N.B., 1834	AE1	Liverpool	346	33
7	Rosalinda (s)	Hay, D.	n/k	n/k	Belfast	508	19
7	Sir Henry Pottinger (bk, 543)	Crowel, M.	Miramichi, 1844	A1	Cork	400	127
9	Covenanter (bk)	Patterson, J.	n/k	n/k	Cork	400	130
9	Frankfield (s, 750)	Robinson, J.	N.B., 1840	n/k	Liverpool	528	13
9	Jessie (s)	McAllister, H.	n/k	n/k	Limerick	108	2
9	Odessa (bk, 324)	Laverty, C.	N.B., 1839	AE1	Dublin	242	75
9	Royal Adelaide (bk, 417)	Potts, T.	Miramichi, 1830	AE1	Killala	328	21
9	Vesta (bg, 209)	Bagg, A.	Sunderland, 1827	E1	Limerick	118	2
10	Countess of Arran (bk, 316)	Henderson	Q.C., 1840	AE1	Donegal	201	2
10	Henry Volante (bg)	Collins, J.	n/k	n/k	Ballyshannon	66	0
10	Naomi (bk)	Wilson, J.	n/k	n/k	Liverpool	421	196
10	Westmorland (bg)	Walker	n/k	n/k	Sligo	207	15
10	Yorkshire (s, 658)	Tripp, T.	Richibucto, 1842	AE1	Liverpool	416	80
11	Anna Maria (bg)	Dillon, T.	n/k	n/k	Limerick	118	2

Date	Vessels (type, tonnage)	Captain	Place and Year Built	Lloyd's Code	Departure Port	Passenger Numbers	Deaths*
11	Trinity (bg)	Boler, T.	n/k	n/k	Limerick	89	0
12	Marchioness of Breadalbane (bk, 217)	Reid, J.	Perth, 1840	A1	Sligo	187	27
12	Virginius (s)	Austin, W.	n/k	n/k	Liverpool	476	267
13	John Munn (bk, 585)	Watt, J.	Q.C., 1840	A1	Liverpool	452	187
13	Marinus (bg, 293)	Maypee, H.	Sunderland, 1832	AE1	Dublin	202	38
14	Cores (s)	Finlay	n/k	n/k	Liverpool	495	25
14	Ellen Simpson (bk, 290)	Newman, W.	Sunderland, 1847	A1	Limerick	192	6
14	Free Trader (s, 668)	Thompson, J.	Q.C., 1846	A1	Liverpool	481	138
14	Minerva (bg, 183)	Cubbitt, G.	N.B., 1840	AE1	Galway	138	22
15	Brothers (bk)	Craig, J.	n/k	n/k	Dublin	321	15
16	Lillias (bk, 315)	Harrison, T.	Drogheda, 1843	A1	Dublin	214	11
19	Ayrshire (bk, 625)	Neil, N.G.	Q.C., 1845	A1	Newry	434	11
20	Larch (bk)	Dove, A.	n/k	n/k	Sligo	440	196
21	Ganges (s, 614)	Smith, G.	Q.C., 1843	A1	Liverpool	393	98
22	Saguenay (bk)	Trannack, R.	n/k	n/k	Cork	476	167
23	Naparina (bk, 290)	Birley, J.	Q.C., 1826	AE1	Dublin	229	41
24	Emma (sr, 170)	Head	P.E., 1839	AE1	Limerick	118	2
26	Mecca (bg, 251)	Hale	Miramichi, 1841	AE1	Dublin	74	1
26	Washington (s, 474)	Wilkie, J.	Virginia, 1833	AE1	Liverpool	308	47
28	Champion (bk, 673)	Cochrane, J.	Canada, 1838	AE1	Liverpool	422	94
29	Bridgetown (bk, 599)	Wilson, J.	N. S., 1836	AE1	Liverpool	471	161
29	Colonist (s)	Sinott, J.	n/k	n/k	New Ross	453	25
29	Minerva (bg, 264)	Parker, A.	N.B., 1840	AE1	Waterford	126	0
29	Robert Newton (bg)	Mosely, W.	Sunderland, 1837	A1	Limerick	205	1
29	Royalist (bg, 250)	Campbell, J.	Maryport, 1812	AE1	Limerick	168	1
29	Sir Henry Pottinger (bk, 543)	Loss, A.	Miramichi, 1844	A1	Belfast	253	34

Date	Vessels (type, tonnage)	Captain	Place and Year Built	Lloyd's Code	Departure Port	Passenger Numbers	Deaths*
30	*Industry* (bk, 258)	Vincent, E.	Sunderland, 1839	A1	Sligo	178	9

September

Date	Vessels (type, tonnage)	Captain	Place and Year Built	Lloyd's Code	Departure Port	Passenger Numbers	Deaths*
3	*Horatio* (bk, 403)	Smyson	Hull, 1815	AE1	Limerick	277	11
4	*Provincialist* (s)	Williams, D.	n/k	n/k	Londonderry	205	0
5	*Julius Caesar* (s, 610)	Flemming, M.	N.B., 1838	AE1	Liverpool	460	53
9	*Highland Mary* (s)	Crosby, D.	n/k	n/k	Cork	100	7
10	*Maria Somes* (bk, 600)	Taylor, H.	Yarmouth, 1841	A1	Cork	329	49
12	*Atlanta* (bk, 286)	Moore, J.	N.B., 1846	A1	Dublin	226	5
14	*George Ramsay* (bg, 249)	Flavin, W.	Sunderland, 1833	A1	New Ross	26	0
17	*Charles* (bg)	Hanlon, S.	n/k	n/k	Youghall	65	0
17	*Emerald* (bg)	Montgomery, A.	n/k	n/k	Newry	85	1
17	*Isabella* (bk, 337)	Robson, G.	P.E., 1841	AE1	Killala	236	12
17	*Jane Black* (s)	Gorman, T.	n/k	n/k	Limerick	395	4
17	*Superior* (s, 491)	Mason, J.	P.E., 1845	A1	Londonderry	366	39
19	*Sir Robert Peel* (s, 740)	Murray, J.	N.B., 1845	A1	Liverpool	480	49
20	*Virgilia* (bk, 309)	Bane, S.	Sunderland, 1846	A1	Liverpool	208	17
20	*Wellington* (bk)	Press	n/k	n/k	Liverpool	438	31
25	*Anne* (bg, 174)	McFee, A.	P.E., 1839	AE1	Limerick	116	0
25	*Ariel* (sr)	Stewart, J.	n/k	n/k	Kilrush (Clare)	119	0
25	*Chieftain* (bk, 325)	McEwan, W.	Montreal, 1826	AE1	Belfast	96	0
25	*Sophia* (bg, 192)	Bellord, J.	Q.C., 1840	AE1	Waterford	23	0
27	*Nerio* (bg, 199)	Gibson, W.	P.E., 1840	AE1	Limerick	134	3
29	*Albion* (bk)	Daly, C.	n/k	n/k	Cork	184	6
29	*Henrietta Mary* (s)	Reid, J.	n/k	n/k	Cork	267	19
30	*Douce Davie* (bk, 371)	Kinney, T.J.	Q.C., 1842	A1	Sligo	281	7

Date	Vessels (type, tonnage)	Captain	Place and Year Built	Lloyd's Code	Departure Port	Passenger Numbers	Deaths*
October							
3	*Emigrant* (bk)	Price, J.	n/k	n/k	Liverpool	529	85
7	*Sir John Campbell* (s)	Campbell, J.	n/k	n/k	Belfast	385	2
9	*Sarah Milledge* (bk)	McDonough	n/k	n/k	Galway	270	8
12	*John Hawkes* (bg)	Richards, J.	n/k	n/k	Limerick	114	5
13	*Bryan Abbs* (bg, 256)	Donald	Jarrow, 1834	AE1	Limerick	179	5
14	*Messenger* (bk)	Shields	n/k	n/k	Liverpool	227	13
15	*Ninian* (bk, 299)	Elliot, T.J.	P.E., 1840	AE	Limerick	109	1
November							
1	*Lord Ashburton* (s)	Bell, E.	n/k	n/k	Liverpool	483	65
8	*Richard Watson* (bg, 255)	Henney	Sunderland, 1832	AE1	Sligo	170	4

Source: BPP 1847–48(50)XLVII, *Lloyds Shipping Register, Quebec Mercury,* Charbonneau, André, and André Sévigny, *Grosse Île: A Record of Daily Events*

*   Includes deaths while in port as well as during the crossing.
Π   Passenger list available on Ships List website.

Table 2:
Immigrant Arrivals at Quebec from Irish Ports During the Famine Years

Year	Londonderry, Belfast, and Other Ulster Ports	Dublin, New Ross, Waterford, and Other South-eastern Ports	Cork, Limerick, and Other South-western Ports	Sligo and Other Western Ports	Total from Irish Ports	Liverpool
1846	4,339	7,196	7,091	4,543	23,169	5,701
1847	11,526	12,579	16,642	6,724	47,471	21,428
1848	3,120	2,249	7,834	2,260	15,463	1,612
1849	3,962	7,289	9,591	2,512	23,354	4,251
1850	2,430	5,542	8,122	1,375	17,469	5,061
1851	2,233	6,266	12,035	1,771	22,305	4,202
Totals	27,610	41,121	61,315	19,185	149,231	42,255

Source: BPP 1847–48(964) XLVII; 1849(1025) XXXVIIII; 1850(734) XL; 1851(348) XL; 1852(1474) XXXIII

Table3:
Vessels Used by Landlords Who Assisted Their Irish Tenants to Emigrate to Upper Canada, 1841–51

Year	Vessel	Place and Year built	Lloyd's Code	Departure Port	Number Assisted
1. Bath, Marquis of (Monaghan)					
1851	*Alcyone* (bk, 392 tns)	Hull, 1810	AE1	Dublin	88
1851	*Die Seelust*	n/k	n/k	Dublin	57
1851	*Safeguard* (sw, 269 tns)	Sunderland, 1841	AE1	Dublin	59
2. Butler-Clarke, Charles (Kilkenny)					
1841	*Perseverance* (bk, 597 tns)	N.B., 1839	AE1	Dublin	106
1843	*Henry* (bg)	n/k	n/k	Dublin	113
1843	*Perseverance* (bk, 597 tns)	N.B, 1839	AE1	Dublin	131
1849	*Perseverance* (bk, 597 tns)	N. B., 1839	AE1	Dublin	91
1850	*Perseverance* (bk, 597 tns)	N.B., 1839	AE1	Dublin	130
3. Charley, Mr. (Donegal)					
1851	*Countess of Arran* (bk, 316 tns)	Q.C., 1840	n/k	Donegal	220
4. Fitzwilliam, Lord (Wicklow)					
1841	*Catherine*	n/k	n/k	Liverpool	286
1842	*Ayrshire* (bk, 625 tns)	Q.C., 1840	A1	Dublin	62
1843	*Industry* (bk, 258 tns)	Sunderland, 1839	A1	Dublin	83
1848	*Aberfoyle* (bk, 496 tns)	N.S., 1845	AE1	New Ross	192
(The vessel carried 120 tenants of Lord Fitzwilliam together with 72 tenants of Lord Clifton.)					
1849	*Aberfoyle* (bk, 496 tns)	N.S., 1845	AE1	New Ross	277
1850	*Juno*	n/k	n/k	New Ross	40
1850	*Lord Ashburton*	n/k	n/k	New Ross	60
1851	*Confiance*	n/k	n/k	New Ross	250
1851	*Mary & Ellen* (s, 303 tns)	Sunderland, 1836	AE1	Dublin	260
5. Kildare, Marquis of & William Fitzpatrick (Kildare)					
1847	*Odessa* (bk, 324 tns)	N.B., 1839	AE1	Dublin	111
1848	*Odessa* (bk, 324 tns)	N.B., 1839	AE1	Dublin	74
6. Lansdowne, Marquis of (Kerry)					
1851	*Brilliant*	n/k	n/k	Cork	147
1851	*Clio*	n/k	n/k	Cork	59
1851	*Die Seelust*	n/k	n/k	Dublin	38
1851	*Dominion* (bk, 291 tns)	Whitby, 1808	AE1	Cork	100
1851	*Industry* (bk, 258 tns)	Sunderland, 1839	A1	Cork	229

Year	Vessel	Place and Year built	Lloyd's Code	Departure Port	Number Assisted
1851	*Pallas* (bk, 316 tns)	N.B., 1826	AE1	Valentia (Co. Kerry)	136
1851	*Prompt* (bk, 354 tns)	Q.C., 1838	AE1	Cork	102

7. Mahon, Major Dennis (Roscommon)

Year	Vessel	Place and Year built	Lloyd's Code	Departure Port	Number Assisted
1847	*Virginius*	n/k	n/k	Liverpool	476 (267 deaths on voyage)

8. Ormande, Lord (Kilkenny)

Year	Vessel	Place and Year built	Lloyd's Code	Departure Port	Number Assisted
1846	*Despatch*	n/k	n/k	Waterford	60

9. Palmerston, Lord (Sligo)

Year	Vessel	Place and Year built	Lloyd's Code	Departure Port	Number Assisted
1847	*Richard Watson* (bg, 255tns)	Sunderland, 1832	AE1	Sligo	161
1847	*Springhill*	n/k	n/k	Sligo	227
1847	*Transit*	n/k	n/k	Sligo	156

10. Spaight, Sir Francis (Tipperary)

Year	Vessel	Place and Year built	Lloyd's Code	Departure Port	Number Assisted
1848	*Jane Black* (s, 240 tns)	Dundee, 1840	A1	Limerick	96

(Col. Wyndham's tenants also travelled on this vessel.)

11. Wandesford, Col. C.B. (Kilkenny)

Year	Vessel	Place and Year built	Lloyd's Code	Departure Port	Number Assisted
1846	*Naparina* (bk, 290 tns)	Q.C., 1826	AE1	Dublin	120
1847	*Naparina* (bk, 290 tns)	Q.C., 1826	AE1	Dublin	82

12. Wyndham, Colonel George (Clare)

Year	Vessel	Place and Year built	Lloyd's Code	Departure Port	Number Assisted
1840	*James Cook* (201 tns)	n/k	n/k	Limerick	48
1842	*Bryan Abbs* (bg, 256 tns)	Jarrow, 1834	AE1	Limerick	104
1842	*Sapphire*	n/k	n/k	Limerick	43
1846	*Bryan Abbs* (bg, 256 tns)	Jarrow, 1834	AE1	Limerick	148
1846	*Jane Black*	Dundee, 1840	A1	Limerick	96
1848	*Jane Black*	Dundee, 1840	A1	Limerick	51
1848	*Governor*	n/k	n/k	Limerick	130
1849	*Governor*	n/k	n/k	Limerick	44

Sources: BPP: 1840(613) XXXIII; 1841(298) XV; 1842(373) XXI; 1843(109) XXXIV; 1844(181) XXV; 1844(777) XXXIX; 1847–48(964) XLVII; 1849(1025) XXXVIII; 1850(173) XL; 1851(348) XL; 1852(1474) XXXIII, Gerard Moran, *Sending Out Ireland's Poor*

CHAPTER 11

◈

Sea Crossings

We left Belfast on the 25th of May, 1847, in an emigrant ship called "the Independence," father, mother, and seven of us children.… Six weeks and three days afterwards we arrived at quarantine [Grosse Île] and were delayed for inspection. Considering the times, we had fair accommodation for the six hundred passengers, but there were seven deaths during the voyage, one of them my brother Thomas, aged three years, who died with measles and was buried at sea. Our accommodation was worse afterwards in emigrant sheds and canal boats.[1]

After reaching the port of Quebec, David McCloy and his family proceeded west to Waterloo County in Upper Canada, having friends already settled there. Even though they had sailed across the Atlantic during the height of the Great Irish Famine and suffered the loss of three-year-old Thomas, the worst part of their journey was still to come. Taking what proved to be an overcrowded Rideau Canal steamer to Kingston, where male passengers were required to remain on deck at all times, David's father and younger brother suffered "congestion of the lungs." They had travelled through the night without shelter in incessant rain and died soon after reaching their destination.[2] Nevertheless, despite this appalling beginning, David McCloy went on to establish himself in farming, having married Annie Byrens, "who was willing to risk with me the hardships of pioneer life in the woods."[3]

Disease was a constant concern, whether contracted on an Atlantic crossing or the onward journey westward, but it was only one of many perils that had to be endured. Travelling in the hold of a sailing ship as a steerage passenger was dangerous, unpleasant, and uncomfortable at the best of times. The fact that there were any ocean-going ships at all was due entirely to the explosive growth of the timber trade. The higher tariffs imposed on European timber from 1811 effectively priced it out of the British market, making North American timber the cheaper alternative. Ever-increasing numbers of vessels plied between ports in the British Isles and Quebec to collect timber, and as they did, some carried immigrants on their westward journeys. However, although immigrants were a much-valued source of extra revenue, little attention was paid to their creature comforts. Vessels were selected primarily for their suitability in meeting the stowage requirements of the timber trade and robustness in withstanding North Atlantic gales. Passenger needs were a low priority.

Accommodation below deck in the steerage was basic to say the least. Timber, loaded into the ship's hold one-way, replaced the passengers who had been accommodated in the same hold going the other. Wooden planking was hammered over cross beams and temporary sleeping berths were constructed along each side. The only means of ventilation was through the hatches, and in stormy seas they could be kept battened down for days. People had to face the discomforts of being cooped up for several weeks and the misery of being blown about in stormy seas. It was not that shipowners were being deliberately cruel. This was how shipping services operated until the advent of steamships. For people who could not afford the greater privacy and comforts of a cabin, a berth in the steerage was their only practical means of crossing the Atlantic.

Storms at sea were a constant threat. When James Wilson, a Methodist preacher and one of 121 passengers sailing in the *Mary and Bell* from Dublin in 1817, experienced a heavy storm, he expected "to be swallowed

The old city of Quebec from Prescott Gate. Watercolour by Thomas Mower Martin, 1838–1934.

up in the great deep." It caused the vessel to roll from side to side "and overturned the passengers' boxes, pans, kettles and vessels of water, in such a manner as that no tongue can express or mind conceive."[4] Throughout the voyage he admired Captain Cunningham's skill in dealing with such occurrences, this incident being typical:

> This morning we had a view of a large mountain of ice, a considerable distance off, which caused the captain to ascend to the top mast of the vessel, to get a better view of it, when suddenly he perceived a huge body of ice right ahead, about a gun shot from the ship; it caused him to hasten down and alter the course of sailing, otherwise the consequence would have been awful, as the force of the vessel coming against the ice would have rent [ripped] it to pieces.[5]

William Graves, travelling in the *Maria* from New Ross two years later owed his life to another quick-thinking captain. The 163 passengers froze with terror as a gale drove their vessel ever closer to a rocky shore off Newfoundland; but they were saved by a sudden change in wind direction. Captain Robert Key, who was later commended by the passengers, said that "no human skill could have kept us from it [the shore] had the wind continued to blow from the south a little longer — I trust no heart was so hardened on board as not to feel grateful to that Great Being that, in the hour of such danger, protected us."[6] The 119 passengers who transferred to the *Tom*, after sailing from Westport in the *Emerald* many years later, had also suffered "great distress on the Banks of Newfoundland" and thanked Captain Coulthard "for his kindness and gentlemanly conduct."[7] So much depended on the captain's navigational skills and his attitude to his passengers.

As his ship left Belfast in 1824, James Humphrey, one of 117 passengers in what was probably the *Diadem*,[8] described how dreadful storms kept causing it to topple over:

> On the 16th June we lost our mast and got up another. On the 18th our brig fell on her side and it was wonderful to hear the shouts from passengers for about five minutes. On the 24th June we had high winds and snow and on the 27th June we lost our mast again and did not get it

FOR QUEBEC,
To Sail the first Week in April,
THE SUPERIOR FIRST CLASS SNOW
PATIENCE,
500 Tons Burthen,
T. D. BOWMAN, Master.

This Vessel is daily expected to arrive here, and has most excellent accommodations for Passengers, being high and roomy between decks; abundance of Water and Fuel will be provided for the voyage, and every attention and kindness will be shown by Captain BOWMAN. As a number of Passengers are engaged, those who intend emigrating should come forward to make early engagements.

For Freight or Passage, apply to
T. G. FOLINGSBY,
Belfast, March 4, 1822.   7, Hanover-Quay.
82)

Advertisement for the crossing of the *Patience* from Belfast to Quebec in the *Belfast Commercial Chronicle*, March 18, 1822. The *Patience* arrived in July with 212 passengers.

mended until we landed. On the 5th of July we passed mountains of ice as high as the mast of our ship.[9]

James Coulter, travelling as a cabin passenger, described the pandemonium that ensued during the worst of the storms:

> Owing to the severe gale the light was blown out in the binnacle, the fire was out in the Cabin and the Tinder Box and matches could not be found. Fortunately, however, the Cook got a candle lighted for the Captain to go to the steerage, where we found the passengers in a deplorable state. The occupants of the berths that had broken (nearly sixty souls) [together] with their bedding and most of their luggage, were all lying in a confused mess totally unable to assist themselves ... most providentially, not a person [was] hurt.[10]

William Campbell, a medical doctor on his way to Peterborough in 1832, described how an approaching storm drove the captain to curse "so that he might have been heard distinctly on the coast of Waterford ... our cordage and canvass [stet] was torn to tatters, aye to baby rags ... and most of the passengers assisted.... We lay there repairing our sails for three days.... I would advise everyone in coming out to be particularly careful what ship and captain they come with."[11]

That same year the *Symmetry* from Londonderry, carrying 260 passengers, became trapped in the ice and sprang a leak. John and Eliza Anderson described how "it had to be pumped day and night from the 6th of May until we landed in Quebec [in June]." Throughout their ordeal the passengers had also to "let down logs of timber with chains and ropes about the vessel to keep her from being wrecked in the ice ... but we had reason to bless God for his mercies unto us ... we had as good a Captain [in Captain Dale] as ever sailed the sea; he was never intoxicated."[12]

In his crossing from Liverpool, Henry Johnson, who came from County Antrim, was awakened in the night by people screaming "the ship's lost, the ship's sinking." But much to Johnson's displeasure, the mainly Catholic passengers were down on their knees seeking Divine intervention — they "would do nothing but sprinkle holy water, cry, pray and cross themselves … instead of giving a hand to pump the ship."[13]

George Pashley, an Englishman who sailed in the *Reward* from Liverpool, was equally uncharitable to the Irish, blaming them for the "abominable smell" in the ship. In his view, they were all "filthy."[14]

Despite the fact that the 233 Irish passengers who sailed in the *Macoa* from Londonderry ten years later had to turn back to Belfast in distress and were detained for nearly a month, they expressed their gratitude to Captain Milligan, "who was most kind and attentive to their wants during the voyage."[15] However, the 240 passengers who sailed in the *Exmouth* of Newcastle from Londonderry in May 1847 were not so fortunate. They, together with their captain, Isaac Booth, perished in a gale off the island of Islay in the west of Scotland.[16] Tragedy also struck a few years earlier when the *Minstrel*, sailing from Limerick to Quebec with 141 passengers aboard struck Red Island Reef in the St. Lawrence. As passengers were loaded into the lifeboats, the vessel suddenly capsized, taking everyone down. "Captain Outerbridge behaved most gallantly during the awful scene and perished with the rest," declaring that he would not leave the vessel until his passengers were rescued.[17] Travelling in a sailing vessel at this time was extremely perilous!

In addition to overseeing the safety of their passengers, captains had also to make sure that adequate provisions were on board. The 1803 Passenger Act, the first attempt to legally enforce conditions for travellers, stipulated the daily minimum of beef, bread, biscuit or oatmeal, molasses, and water that had to be provided to each passenger.[18] This ruling was introduced even though it was widely recognized that many immigrants declined meat. Irish passengers generally preferred potatoes and oatmeal and found hard biscuits unpalatable. As a result, they often supplied their own food, and in doing so paid lower fares. For instance, David McCloy and his family left Belfast with their own food, not wishing to eat "the hard-tack" (dried biscuits) that the ship provided.[19] During the 1820s, fares averaged £3.10s for steerage passengers who supplied their own food, and in the following two decades they fell to between £2 and £3.[20] But conditions remained far from perfect and regulations continued to be flouted.[21]

On his crossing from Belfast in 1839, William Campbell thought that "it was well [the Captain] was not tossed overboard by the passengers.... I saw a shilling offered for one pound of meal and a penny for a noggin [1/4 pint] of dirty water say ten weeks old."[22] Because it was stored in crude wooden casks, water quickly became contaminated. It was smelly and had a foul odour. Adding vinegar helped a little, but the water was still obnoxious unless it was boiled. Passengers sailing in the *Constitution* from Belfast in 1843 had a more serious problem in not having been provided with a sufficient amount of water, no matter how smelly! The captain was fined £25 twice — for this misdemeanour and for misinforming the passengers about the ship's provisions. He had claimed that oatmeal and bread would be provided on the voyage, but this had not been the case.[23] Another concern was the failure of some captains to provide passengers with a clean and safe storage area for their potatoes. Alexander Buchanan, the Quebec immigration agent, reported several instances "where potatoes are brought on board in sacks and thrown into the hold or on the water casks ... and in the course of a few days (owing to the thoroughfare made over them by the crew and passengers going for water and other provisions or baggage) they soon become so trampled and bruised as to be unfit for use."[24]

Overcrowding was another contentious issue since space in the hold of a vessel was always at a premium. The Passenger Act of 1817 specified a space allocation of one and one half tons per person in the steerage, while the 1828 Act required a passenger to tonnage ratio of three passengers for every four tons. These regulations were meant to limit overcrowding, but the setting of a minimum height of only five feet six inches between decks reveals that, despite these safeguards, people still had to tolerate very cramped conditions. It would not be until the passing of the 1842 Act that six feet would become the minimum height requirement between decks, and it would rise again to seven feet in 1855.[25] However, the raising of the height in 1842 met with fierce opposition from Irish shippers who complained that the new ruling would bar around half of the vessels that they had been using to carry immigrants overseas.[26] Nevertheless, the government stood firm against all protests.

Instances of overcrowding were few and far between until the 1840s when, with the great surge in immigration that took place, more captains disobeyed the passenger legislation. However, while Alexander Buchanan uncovered several instances where captains had exceeded their vessel's passenger number allowance, most were relatively minor infringements. A typical example was the *Grace*, sailing in 1841 from Liverpool with 303 passengers, all Irish, which exceeded its passenger limit by twenty-nine, with the captain being fined £20. Although the sleeping berths in the *Grace* had been "put up in so slight a manner that they fell down several times during the voyage in heavy weather," no fine was payable for that transgression.[27] While Captain Hutchison, in charge of the *Pomona*, sailing with 250 passengers from Sligo, paid the same fine of £20 for exceeding his ship's limit by twenty, the captain of the *Lord Cochrane*, sailing from Tralee, paid exactly the same amount despite exceeding his passenger limit by sixty. According to Buchanan, "these people, notwithstanding their crowded state, landed in good health," but he was still unhappy that over-crowding fines were not being set higher to deter excesses such as this.[28]

Overcrowding was more common in the vessels that left from west coast ports, particularly Limerick — and with good reason. According to the Limerick emigration officer, people could easily "obtain a passage by stealth." Since the port of Limerick was some sixty miles from the sea, there were considerable chances for them to hop on a vessel from either side of the River Shannon after the official passenger count had been taken. In this way they and the ship's captain could easily evade the Passenger Act regulations.[29] For obvious practical reasons, the Limerick emigration officer and his staff were powerless to stop them. People faced a harsh reality. They desperately wanted to escape from their worsening economic situation and, being very poor, opted for the cheapest and most basic form of sea transport they could find. Desperate times called for desperate actions and a compliant ship's captain.

One of the worst ship crossings ever to be reported involved the *Elizabeth and Sarah*,[30] sailing from Killala in 1845. When the 259 passengers arrived at Quebec, Alexander Buchanan found them to be "in a most wretched state of filth and misery, brought on by the crowded state of the vessel, want of cleanliness, bad water and starvation."[31] The captain and seventeen passengers died on the crossing and a further seven passengers died at the quarantine hospital. When Dr. George Douglas came on board to inspect the ship, he described the scene as "fully realizing the worst state of a slaver." The berths along one side had fallen down after a few days at sea and in all respects living conditions were slovenly and chaotic. The passengers had insufficient space in which to sleep and "no issue of provisions whatever was made to the passengers, and never more than two quarts of water per day was served out ... the captain, from all accounts was a man unfit morally and physically to take charge of a passenger vessel; he was of ill health and intemperate habits."[32] To add to their misery, the captain's body had been kept in the ship's hold for two to three weeks after his death.

The survivors of the *Elizabeth and Sarah* crossing eventually cleaned themselves up at Grosse Île. Lacking any bedding or much in the way of belongings, they went on their way, with most being "destitute of a second change of clothes."[33] Their wretched situation can be contrasted with the contented and comfortable state of the 315 passengers who sailed in "the fine barque" *Josephine* from Belfast in 1840. Having completed "a quick passage," duly noted in the *Quebec Mercury*, they expressed their gratitude to Captain McIntyre for his care and attention, presenting him with "a valuable snuff box of elegant workmanship and bearing an appropriate inscription."[34] The staggering divide between rich and poor

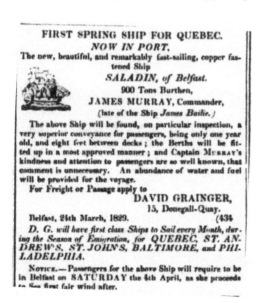

The *Saladin*'s spacious accommodation for passengers wishing to travel from Belfast to Quebec is highlighted in this advertisement from the *Belfast Commercial Chronicle*, March 25, 1829.

at this time is symbolized by these two arrival scenes — one pitiful and the other joyous.

The *Elizabeth and Sarah's* cruel and incompetent captain is an extreme case of a rotten apple. He is not typical and his behaviour should not be allowed to distort the largely good reputation of ship's captains. Immigrant diaries and the letters columns of the *Quebec Gazette* and other newspapers often contain eulogies to captains who were remembered most for their kindness, skill, and humanity. Most of all, passengers relied on them to keep order on the ship and to keep them safe. To do that, captains had to ensure that their vessels were clean and well-ventilated. Good hygiene was paramount, since infectious diseases like typhus and cholera could flare up at any time.

The port of Quebec witnessed its first serious cholera outbreak in 1832, prompting the authorities to build a quarantine station at Grosse Île, its cost being met through the passing of the Quarantine Act requiring passengers to pay an immigrant tax of five shillings.[35] Predictably, the new tax was bitterly opposed by shipowners, who feared that it would deter people from emigrating, but this did not happen. Because the initial quarantine inspections were very haphazard and rudimentary, arriving immigrants unwittingly carried cholera to Quebec City and Montreal that year, and thousands of people died.[36] Despite the imposition of better quarantine regulations, a second cholera outbreak ran its course in 1834. When the *William Herdman* arrived that year with 283 passengers, 151 had to be admitted to the quarantine hospital, where nearly one third of them later died.[37] However, nothing can compare with the typhus outbreak of 1847 when Grosse Île witnessed the gravest of Irish immigrant tragedies.

When the *Argo* arrived from Liverpool in June 1847 with several cases of typhus on board, it queued up with the other ships while the captain waited to hear when his passengers could disembark. Because of the unavailability of space in the quarantine station and hospital, they could not be removed straight away and were forced to wait in the vessels. This meant that the sick could not be treated in hospital, nor could any of the others be admitted to the quarantine station. Alexander Mitchell, captain of the *Argo*, understandably feared that the disease would spread to his other passengers and wrote a letter to the *Quebec Morning Chronicle* saying so.[38] Other captains faced a similar dilemma. They fretted about the spread of disease and some were said to have confided to the priests stationed at Grosse Île that many more of their passengers were dying on board ship after arriving at Grosse Île than during the sea crossing.[39] This was certainly the case with the *Argo*. Of its 590 passengers, ten died on the passage, but considerably more — fifty-nine — died either at the quarantine station or at the quarantine hospital. Meanwhile, despite the great suffering and turmoil at this time, Richard Henderson, a passenger who had sailed in the *Achilles*, thanked Captain Taylor in a letter that he sent to the *Quebec Gazette*. Although there had been forty-two deaths on the passage and another nine in the quarantine hospital (out of 411 passengers who embarked from Liverpool) he pronounced that Captain Taylor's "zeal and generosity toward the passengers had saved several lives."[40] He had done his best in trying circumstances. As this nightmare unfolded, the authorities slowly improved their facilities and hastened the onward journey of immigrants fit to travel.[41]

The Archbishop of Quebec's solution to the problem was to try to stop the influx in its tracks. Writing to Ireland's archbishops and bishops, he implored them to discourage their congregations from leaving for North America, claiming that even those arriving in good health would be disappointed with the work opportunities, which he believed had been oversold. However, his message fell on deaf ears and the Irish kept coming.[42] Later in 1847, the Canadian government beseeched Queen Victoria to intervene: "Under the affliction with which this land has been visited and is still further threatened, not to permit the helpless, the starving, the sick and diseased, unequal and unfit as they are to face the hardships of a settler's life, to embark for these shores, which if they reach, they reach in too many instances only to find a grave."[43] This, too, went unheeded. However, the number of Irish arrivals did drop in the following year, but increased sharply in 1849 to just over 23,000 and remained high until the mid-1850s (Table 4).

Undoubtedly the highest death toll occurred on ships that left from Liverpool. As a major seaport, it could offer immigrants cheaper sea crossings even with the additional travel to get there and the cost of staying in boarding houses once they arrived. Sadly, although Dr. Douglas had warned that Liverpool's overcrowded and filthy boarding houses were likely to be seed beds of typhus and cholera, his proposals for ensuring

CHEAP PASSAGE TO NORTH AMERICA.
FOR QUEBEC.

TO Sail on Sunday, 7th June, the Beautiful Fine Brig BRILLIANT, Captain SIMKINS.

This fine Vessel will be elegantly fitted up for the accommodation of Passengers. She will be well supplied with Water and Fuel, and the Captain and Crew will pay every attention during the Voyage.

Four or Five can be comfortably accommodated in the Cabin.   Apply to

JOHN M'AULIFFE,
Ship Agent, 4, Warren's Place.

The *Brilliant's* sailing from Cork to Quebec in 1830 announced in the *Cork Constitution*, June 1, 1830. It is advertised as a "cheap passage." One hundred and twenty people sailed from Cork in this crossing.

safer accommodation had not been acted upon. That was probably a major factor in the high death tolls experienced on Liverpool ships. To make matters worse, Irish immigrants had also been targeted by Liverpool's unscrupulous shipping agents before they sailed. The agents often charged them extortionate prices and sold them passage on ships that did not exist or were not scheduled to depart for weeks.[44] Liverpool must have seemed like a living hell to many Irish people at this time.

The arrival of over 54,000 Irish immigrants to Quebec in 1847 represented a major upturn compared with previous years (Table 4).[45] However, they were not all planning to remain in Canada. A substantial number were on their way to the United States, having used the Quebec route as a cheaper alternative to going directly to New York. Thus many were merely in transit.[46] While many of the 1847 arrivals came from Liverpool, thus obscuring the geographical origins of passengers, the large turnout from Cork and Limerick indicates that a goodly proportion of the immigrants came from the south and west of Ireland. This had not been the case at the beginning. Between 1817 and 1830 around half of all immigrant arrivals had departed from Ulster ports in the north (Table 5). However, after 1830, an increasing proportion of immigrants came from ports in the south and west. Between 1830 and 1840, immigrant arrivals from the south and west ports equalled those from the Ulster ports, accounting for 80 percent of the total.

While considerable attention has been focused on the human misery associated with the famine years, little notice has been taken of the shipping services that were offered to immigrants. Remarkably, evidence taken from the *Lloyd's Shipping Register* indicates that they mostly sailed on the best quality ships that were available at the time. A source dating back to the late eighteenth century, the register provides records of a vessel's age, quality of construction, and state of repair.[47] As major insurers, Lloyd's of London needed reliable shipping intelligence, which it procured through the use of paid agents in the principal ports. Vessels were inspected by Lloyd's surveyors and assigned a code according to the quality of their construction and maintenance.[48] An honest and open inspection was vital to the insurer's risk assessment, and the shipowner's ability to attract profitable trade depended on the classification given to his vessels. Shipowners actually complained that the codes were too stringent, particularly in the way a ship's age and place of construction could affect its classification.[49]

Shipping codes have been identified for around 60 percent of the vessels that arrived at Quebec with Irish immigrants during the height of the famine in 1847.[50] They show that the vessels were of outstanding quality (Table 1). They were nearly always ranked at "A1" or "AE1" — the best quality available. Most had been built in the 1830s and 1840s, but those constructed earlier still had top rankings. The *Argo*, built in 1808, had been sailing to Quebec from Sligo with Irish immigrants since 1835; the *Thetis*, built in 1811, had been doing the same from Limerick; and the *Tom*, built in 1815, had been taking immigrants from Dublin since 1831, always under the charge of Captain Coulthard. And the same Captain Coulthard steered the *Tom* to Quebec in July 1847 with 115 passengers aboard, four having died on the passage.[51]

Again, where it has been possible to identify shipping codes, they show that the vessels used by the landlords who provided assisted passages to their tenants also had top ratings (Tables 3 and 6). The *Bryan Abbs* and the *Jane Black* sailing from Limerick, the *Aberfoyle* from New Ross, the *Odessa* and *Industry* from Dublin, all having A1 or AE1 rankings, arrived with immigrants in 1847; in addition, they sailed in other years with landlord-assisted immigrants. Thus, there is indisputable evidence that in most cases the Irish, even the very poor, had access to the best quality shipping available at this time. Conditions twenty years earlier, however, would have been far worse.

View of the St. Lawrence River from the Citadel, Quebec City, circa 1842. Watercolour by Sir Harry James Warre (1819–1898).

Vessels were generally smaller and had longer journey times in the 1820s, when the passenger trade first developed. The trade was built around the so-called regular traders, which marked a new era in passenger travel.[52] They left Ireland with steerage and cabin passengers and, upon reaching Quebec, immediately returned to their home ports with timber. They would complete the voyage two, sometimes three times a year, often with the same captain. A particular star among the Quebec merchants was Captain Thomas Grandy, who commanded the *City of Waterford* as it plied between Waterford and Quebec between 1826 and 1837 (Table 7). They awarded him a silver cup "as testimony to the high sense they entertain of his industry and seamanship in having during the season ... performed three voyages out and home between Quebec and ports of the United Kingdom."[53]

Regular traders dominated the passenger trade, both in the frequency with which they sailed and the number of passengers carried. They varied in size from the 155-ton *Sally* of Belfast, the 203-ton *Agnes* of Limerick, the 367-ton *Ocean* of Waterford, the 394-ton *Dominica* of Cork, and the

425-ton *Quintin Leitch* of Newry (Table 7). Their rankings were often E1, rather than the A1 and AE1 designations that were more common in the 1840s. This meant that, although they were unfit for carrying dry cargoes, they were suitable for long-distance sea voyages.

Regular traders usually had the same captain. Captain Daniel Mearns took charge of the *Earl of Aberdeen* from 1828 to 1832 and the *Helen of Aberdeen* between 1834 and 1840, both sailing from Belfast. Captain Gorman's career in the Limerick passenger trade extended from at least 1827, when he was in charge of the *Agnes* of Limerick until 1831, the *Breeze* from 1831 to 1834, the *Byran Abbs* from 1835 to 1837, the *Borneo* from 1837 to 1839, and the *Barnes* from 1837 to 1839.[54] Similarly, Captain Cringle commanded passenger crossings from Belfast in the *Andrew Nugent* between 1828 and 1836 and Captain Richardson did the same with the *Belsay Castle*, which sailed from Sligo between 1831 and 1837.

The historian Arthur Lower once claimed that "the Canadian timber trade became the last refuge of all battered hulks on the Atlantic."[55] Because the passenger trade developed on the coat tails of the timber trade, the implication is that immigrants sailed in sub-standard ships. This assumption is widely made, but without justification. Travelling as a steerage passenger in a ship's hold was very unpleasant. Yes, there were perils and discomforts, and there were infamous voyages, particularly when storms struck. However, what was on offer was the best available shipping at the time.

In 1847, Stephen de Vere, a Limerick landowner, social reformer, and nephew of Lord Monteagle, wanted to gain first-hand experience of what it was like travelling in the hold of a sailing ship. Booking himself as a steerage passenger in an unnamed vessel to Quebec, he hoped to be "a witness to the suffering of emigrants" and intended that his findings would bring pressure on the authorities to improve their travel conditions.[56] It was an appalling crossing. "Hundreds of people — men, women and children of all ages … were packed together like sardines in a tin without light, without air, wallowing in filth and breathing a fetid atmosphere, sick in body, dispirited in heart," all the while being denied adequate amounts of water, food, and medicine.[57] Armed with his dossier, De Vere went on to make recommendations to the British government about how the provisioning of food, ventilation on the passenger decks, and care of the sick might be improved; the changes had minimal impact.[58] Accommodation in the steerage was always going to be smelly and cramped. While the aristocratic Stephen de Vere found life in the hold unbearable, his fellow passengers would have been much more resigned to their plight. Most had to live with overcrowded and poor sanitary conditions in their own homes. That was the way it was.

Unfortunately, the miseries of steerage travel have become the focus for much of the doom-laden storytelling that is associated with the famine period. Some of what has been written is pure fiction. For instance, Gerald Keegan's diary, describing an Irish schoolteacher's woeful voyage in 1847 from Ireland to Quebec was fabricated by Robert Sellar, editor of the *Huntingdon Gleaner*.[59] It first appeared in 1895[60] and made another appearance in 1982 when it was rebranded as *The Voyage of the* Naparima: *A Story of Canada's Island Graveyard*.[61] This was a fabricated tale of a crossing that never happened. Of course grisly and morbid tales of death and suffering sell books, but they (in this case) have nothing whatever to do with the truth.

A diary written by Robert Whyte describing a voyage to Quebec taken in 1847 may be genuine, although it is difficult to authenticate. Published in the following year as *The Ocean Plague, or A Voyage to Quebec in an Irish Emigrant Vessel*, it describes the suffering experienced in a harrowing transatlantic voyage. Whyte claimed that he had been a cabin passenger and that many of his fellow passengers in the steerage were the former tenants of a County Meath landlord, but he does not name the vessel. The details that he gives indicate that Whyte must have sailed in the *George*, which arrived at Quebec from Dublin on August 3 with 107 passengers aboard.[62] However, it had no cabin passengers, nor did it carry any land-lord-assisted passengers. His diary is therefore highly suspect.

The lacing of fact with fiction is certainly one way of seeking redress for suffering and past grievances. Highly emotive accounts of disease and death arouse feelings over the many injustices suffered by immigrants and are sometimes used to underscore the cause of Irish nationalism. Yet this has little to do with the facts. Most of the Irish travelled in good quality ships. Their owners sought good and experienced captains to attract them. This was a highly competitive market, since the available passenger accommodation far exceeded the number of potential passengers. Shipping advertisements appeared in newspapers extolling the merits of the ships and captains. For instance, one stated that Captain Daniel Mearns "was well known to be of the highest character and passengers who go out from Belfast in the *Earl of Aberdeen* [to Quebec] may expect the usual comfort and accommodation."[63] There were many more like this that appeared over the years.

Where criticism might be warranted is in the disregard given to Dr. George Douglas's timely warning over the dangers that lurked in Liverpool boarding houses. Had the British authorities taken up his recommendations and ensured that they ceased to be breeding grounds for the spread of disease, countless lives would have saved. Dr. Douglas was the hero of this tragic story. But for his vigilance, skill, and courage in managing the medical facilities at Grosse Île, many more immigrants would have died. The loss of life must never be forgotten, but the gallantry and goodness of the doctors, nurses, priests, and people of Quebec who sought to help should remain in our thoughts as well.

Table 4:
Immigrant Arrivals at Quebec, 1829–55 (Annual Reports of the
Immigration Agent at Quebec)

Year	England	Ireland	Scotland	Europe	Maritime Provinces	Total
1829	3,565	9,614	2,634	--	123	15,936
1830	6,799	18,300	2,450	--	451	28,000
1831	10,343	34,133	5,354	--	424	50,254
1832	17,481	28,204	5,500	15	546	51,746
1833	5,198	12,013	4,196	--	345	21,752
1834	6,799	19,206	4,591	--	339	30,935
1835	3,067	7,108	2,127	--	225	12,527
1836	12,188	12,590	2,224	485	235	27,722
1837	5,580	14538	1,509	--	274	21,901
1838	990	1,456	547	--	273	3,266
1839	1,586	5,113	485	--	255	7,439
1840	4,567	16,291	1,144	--	232	22,234
1841	5,970	18,317	3,559	--	240	28,086
1842	12,191	25,532	6,095	--	556	44,374
1843	6,499	9,728	5,006	--	494	21,727
1844	7,698	9,993	2,234	--	217	20,142
1845	8,883	14,208	2,174	--	160	25,425
1846	9,163	21,049	1,645	896	--	32,753
1847	31,505	54,310	3,747	--	--	89,562
1848	6,034	16,582	3,086	1,395	842	27,939
1849	8,980	23,126	4,984	436	968	38,494
1850	9,887	17,979	2,879	849	701	32,295
1851	9,677	22,381	7,042	870	1,106	41,076
1852	9,276	15,983	5,477	7,256	1,184	39,176
1853	9,585	14,417	4,745	7,456	496	36,699
1854	18,175	16,156	6,446	11,537	857	53,171
1855	6,754	4,106	4,859	4,864	691	21,274

Table 5:
Immigrant Arrivals at Quebec from Irish Ports by Region, 1817–40
(British Parliamentary Papers, Quebec Mercury)

Years	Londonderry, Belfast, and Other Ulster Ports	Dublin, New Ross, Wexford, Waterford, and Other South-Eastern Ports	Cork, Limerick Tralee, and Other South-Western Ports	Sligo, Galway, Westport, and Other Western Ports	Totals
1817–20	8,752	6,466	1,177	433	16,828
1821–29	30,120	22,098	12,672	3,421	68,311
1830–40	45,437	33,164	27,479	19,001	125,081
Totals	84,309	61,728	41,328	22,855	210,220

Table 6:
Vessels Taking Landlord-Assisted Irish Immigrants to Quebec, 1842–51

Vessel (type, tonnage)	Captain	Place and Year Built	Lloyd's Code	Departure Year	Departure Port	Numbers Assisted
Agnes & Ann (bk, 413 tns)	Anderson	Q.C., 1826	AE1	1849	Newry	64
Argo	n/k	n/k	n/k	1849	Liverpool	72
Atlanta (bk, 286 tns)	n/k	St. John, N.B. 1846	A1	1847	Dublin	175
Belle (bg)	Bouchier	n/k	n/k	1850	Waterford	68
Blenheim (s, 689 tns)	Morrison	S. Shields, 1845	A1	1847	Cork	351
Bridgetown (bk, 599 tns)	Mills	N.S., 1836	AE1	1849	New Ross	180
Brothers (bk)	Craig	n/k	n/k	1847	Dublin	204
California (s, 600 tns)	Lawson, E.	St. John, 1846	A1	1849	Dublin	60
Cashmere	n/k	n/k	n/k	1848	Sligo	60
City of Lincoln (s, 740 tns)	Rigby	Q.C., 1847	A1	1849	Liverpool	100
Dauntless (bg)	Hudson	n/k	n/k	1849	Limerick	117
Dykes (bg, 226 tns)	Peters	Maryport, 1809	AE1	1849	Newry	90
Emerald (bg, 285 tns)	Smith	Sunderland, 1837	AE1	1849	Limerick	146
Empire (s)	Findlater	n/k	n/k	1849	New Ross	200
Energy (bg)	Warren	n/k	n/k	1849	Limerick	52
Erin (bg, 187)	Walsh	N. S., 1840	AE1	1849	New Ross	75
Florentia (bg)	McLennon	n/k	n/k	1848	Cork	249
Friendship (bk)	Harrison	n/k	n/k	1849	Dublin	59
Gazelle	n/k	n/k	n/k	1843	Donegal	97

Vessel (type, tonnage)	Captain	Place and Year Built	Lloyd's Code	Departure Year	Departure Port	Numbers Assisted
Hugh (bg)	Smith	n/k	n/k	1849	Newry	79
Independence (s, 584 tns) (An Emigration Society)	McCappin	Q.C., 1839	AE1	1842	Belfast	158
India (s, 475 tns)	Willis	Greenock, 1844	A1	1850	New Ross	150
Jane (s)	Plaugh	n/k	n/k	1849	New Ross	170
Jane Black (s, 24 tns)	Gorman	Dundee, 1840	A1	1849	Limerick	59
Jane Lockhart (bk)	Brown	n/k	n/k	1849	Limerick	100
Jessie (bk, 304 tns)	n/k Oliver Gorman	P.E., 1845 P.E., 1845 P.E., 1845	AE1 AE1 AE1	1848 1848 1849	Sligo New Ross Limerick	120 300 128
John Francis (s, 362 tns)	Deaves, H	Montreal, 1827	AE1	1849	Waterford	70
Lady Bagot (bk)	Williams	n/k	n/k	1846	New Ross	53
Lady Peel (s)	Jones	n/k	n/k	1849	Limerick	60
Marinus (bg, 293 tns)	Maypee, H.	Sunderland, 1832	AE1	1847	Dublin	170
Northumberland (bk, 499 tns)	Moore	N.B., 1848	A1	1849	Galway	188
Numa (bk, 323 tns)	Miller, T.	Sunderland, 1811	E1	1847	Sligo	244
Primrose (s, 477 tns)	Irvine	N.B., 1841	AE1	1848	Limerick	130
Prince Albert (bk 350 tns)	Hedwith	Newcastle, 1840	AE1	1849	Limerick	70
Princess Alice (bk 142 tns)	Stone	Christchurch, 1843	n/k	1849	Dublin	200
Robert Newton (bg 285 tns)	Mosely, W.	Sunderland, 1837	A1	1847	Limerick	71

Vessel (type, tonnage)	Captain	Place and Year Built	Lloyd's Code	Departure Year	Departure Port	Numbers Assisted
Sea-Bird (s, 492 tns)	McDonough	N.B., 1846	AE1	1848	Galway	253
Stadacona (bk, 619 tns)	Irons	Q.C., 1844	AE1	1846	Limerick	63
Strang (bk, 393 tns)	Harrison	St. Andrews, 1848	A1	1848	Liverpool	66
Superior (s, 491 tns) (39 deaths among 366 passengers)	Mason, J.	P.E., 1845	A1	1847	Londonderry	159
Swan (s)	Taylor	n/k	n/k	1848	New Ross	80
Swan (s)	Wylie	n/k	n/k	1849	New Ross	110
The Duke (s, 609 tns)	Dady	Liverpool, 1843	A1	1849	Dublin	150
Tom (bg, 165 tns)	Coulthard, W.	Chester, 1815	AE1	1847	Dublin	112
Traveller	n/k	n/k	n/k	1842	Dublin	51
Triton (s, 676 tns)	Smith	N.S., 1839	AE1	1850	New Ross	59
Vesta (bg, 209 tns)	Bagg, A.	Sunderland, 1827	E1	1847	Limerick	88
Viceroy (s, 667 tns)	McMahon	N.S., 1849	A1	1850	Liverpool	85
Wave (bk, 570 tns)	n/k	N.B., 1838	AE1	1850	Limerick	74

Ship wrecked on Cape Rosier. All 166 passengers saved.

Source: British Parliamentary Papers; *Elgin-Grey Papers, 1846–1852*; *Lloyd's Shipping Register*; *Quebec Mercury, Belfast Mercury*; Gerard Moran, *Sending Out Ireland's Poor*

Table 7:
Frequently Used Passenger Ships: Numbers Carried and Ship Quality

Vessel	Captain(s)	Year Built	Place Built	Lloyd's Code	Departure Years	Departure Port	Crossings/ Passengers
Agnes of Limerick (bg, 203 tns)	Outerbridge	n/k	Dunbarton	A1	1827–37	Limerick	6/877
Argo of Whitehaven (bg, 177 tns)	Greig	1808	Workington	AE1	1831–39	Sligo	7/1012
Barbados of Cork (bg, 322 tns)	Lee	1811	Cork	E1	1829–37	Cork	8/1257
Belsay Castle of Sunderland (bg, 204 tns)	Richardson	1820	Sunderland	AE1	1831–37	Sligo	5/837
Bolivar of Waterford (bk, 385 tns)	Crosby/ Ballard	1826	P.E.	E1	1826–31	Waterford/ Belfast	10/1704
Breeze of Glasgow (bg, 322 tns)	Gorman/ Patterson/ O'Donnell	1830	Q.C.	A1	1831–40	Limerick	8/1247
City of Waterford of Waterford (s, 375 tns)	Thomas/ Grandy	1825	Q.C.	AE1	1826–37	Waterford	11/1317
Dominica of Cork (bk, 394 tns)	Bowman	1808	Whitby	E1	1828–40	Cork	7/781
Earl of Aberdeen of Newry (bg, 278 tns)	Mearns, D.	1820	Newbury	AE1	1828–34	Belfast	8/1235
Eleanor of Leith (bg, 184 tns)	Potts, Robert	1814	Whitehaven	E1	1826–35	Dublin/ Sligo	9/660
Friends of Dublin (bk, 324 tn)	Duncan	1797	Selby	AE1	1834–37	Dublin	4/822

Vessel	Captain(s)	Year Built	Place Built	Lloyd's Code	Departure Years	Departure Port	Crossings/ Passengers
Greenhow of Newry (bk, 291 tns)	McKay	1812	Whit-haven	AE1	1819–40	Newry	13/1211
Helen of Aberdeen (bk, 305 tns)	Mearns	1826	N.S.	E1	1830–40	Belfast	11/1563
Maria of Liverpool (bg, 195 tns)	Key/ Nicholson	1811	Q.C.	E1	1818–23	Waterford/ New Ross	7//1038
Mary Ann of Limerick (bg, 156 tns)	several	1811	Q.C.	E1	1821–26	Limerick	6/660
Ocean of Waterford (bk, 367 tns)	Hearn	1826	Q.C.	AE1	1829–37	Waterford	8/996
Pomona of Dublin (bg, 306 tns)	Brown/ Stevens	1824	N.B.	E1	1831–35	Dublin	7/1143
Prince of Asturias of Dublin (bg, 203 tns)	Morris/ Donald	1810	Plymouth	E1	1819–27	Dublin	7/605
Princess Charlotte of Newry (s, 322 tns)	Reid/ Roach	1826	Pictou	E1	1829–35	Newry	6/659
Quintin Leitch of Newry (s, 425 tns)	McKay/ Hunter/ Robinsom	1829	Q.C.	A	1831–40	Newry	6/1458
Robert Kerr of Belfast (s, 358 tns)	Boyd/ Agnew	1824	N.B.	AE	1825–40	Belfast	5/1085
Rose Macroon of Waterford (bg, 175 tns)	Thomas/ Jacobs	1805	Q.C.	A2	1816–30	Waterford, New Ross	7/806
Rosebank of Belfast (bg, 308 tns)	Boyd	1825	N.S.	AE2	1828–39	Belfast	6/862

Vessel	Captain(s)	Year Built	Place Built	Lloyd's Code	Departure Years	Departure Port	Crossings/ Passengers
Sally of Belfast (bg, 155 tns)	Ball	1826	Pictou	E	1818–22	Belfast/ Newry	5/797
Thomas Gelston of Belfast (s, 442 tns)	Laurie	1812	Saint Andrews, N.B.	E	1824–35	Belfast	8/2210
Tom of Whitehaven (bg, 165 tns)	Coulthard	1815	Chester	E	1831–40	Dublin	5/636
Tottenham of New Ross (bk, 308 tns)	Cornforth/ Jeffries	1825	Q.C.	E1	1826–40	New Ross	12/1204
Town of Ross (bk, 268 tns)	Key/Evans	n/k	Q.C.	A1	1827–32	Waterford	8/842

CHAPTER 12

The Irish in Ontario and Quebec

The Irishman has played so large a part in Canada that his history could not be written without, to some extent, writing the history of Canada.[1]

Nicholas Flood Davin, himself an Irishman, peppered his book, *The Irishman in Canada*, published in 1877, with example after example of Irishmen who prospered in Canada. Men who started with nothing were upwardly mobile in no time, giving Canada many of its doctors, lawyers, clergy, businessmen, farmers, and other people of note. When John Maguire visited Ontario and Quebec ten years earlier, he focused on the more lowly Irish — the labourers who built Canada's canals and railways. He observed then that Canada's workforce was almost entirely Irish and being paid much higher wages than could be expected in Ireland.

By 1871 the Irish outnumbered their combined English and Scottish counterparts in Quebec and were the largest immigrant group in Ontario. They arrived much earlier than the English and were therefore assimilated into the general population earlier. Around half of Canada's Irish population lived in Ontario, with Protestants outnumbering Catholics by two to one. Without a doubt, their *pièce de résistance* was Montreal.

There they had the largest concentration of Irish, not only in Quebec but in the whole of British North America.[2]

However, their stunning progress as settlers had its ups and downs, never more so than in the mid-1860s when Canada came under armed attack by an Irish Republican group known as the Fenians.[3]

The threat posed by the Fenians was minimal, but their presence indicated that a troubling political undercurrent was bubbling away under the surface. The organization, based in the United States, had no quarrels with Canadians and simply hoped that, by attacking British army forts and other military targets, they could somehow make Britain relinquish its political control over Ireland. Predictably, this half-baked nonsense came to nothing. The armed raids that took place in New Brunswick and Ontario between 1866 and 1871 were rebuffed very easily and, needless to say, British rule over Ireland continued unchanged. Moreover, not only did their armed action end in failure, but the Fenians also had very little success in enlisting Canadian Irish Catholics to join their cause. Nevertheless, there were a good many Irish people in Canada who supported their aims and principles.

Matters came to a head when Thomas D'Arcy McGee, Canada's leading Irish Catholic politician at the time, called on Irish Canadians to champion the cause of Canadian nationalism. Although he had supported Irish independence as a young man, McGee, a journalist, politician, and gifted orator, now sought to guide Canada's progress to nationhood.[4] He told Irish Catholics living in Canada that however much they might want to see the end of British rule in Ireland, they must stop wasting their time on Irish politics and instead concentrate on Canada's future. He spoke of the need for there to be "a Canadian nationality, not French Canadian, nor British Canadian, nor Irish Canadian."[5]

McGee railed against the Fenian movement and the cause of Irish Republicanism, believing that the best solution for Ireland was to adopt the Canadian model of being a self-governing country within the British Empire. Clearly underestimating the extent of the seething resentment felt by many Irish Catholics toward Britain, McGee's pronouncements suddenly made him a hated figure and he was expelled from government office and the St. Patrick's Society. Sadly, in April 1868, his bold stand cost him

Hon. Thomas D'Arcy McGee, Irish-born politician, photographed circa 1863 in Montreal by William Notman (1826–1891).

his life. While walking down a street in Ottawa after a late-night session in Parliament, he was shot in cold blood by a Fenian sympathizer. Suddenly McGee became a martyr to his cause and he regained his popularity. His funeral in Montreal had the appearance of a state occasion — "six grey horses pulled his glass-panelled bier, which was draped with a black cloth embellished with the likeness of a silver harp and shamrock. And a poet compared his death with that of Abraham Lincoln."[6]

When speaking in the House of Commons on the day before his death as the member of Parliament for Griffintown in Montreal, McGee described himself as "thoroughly and emphatically a Canadian."[7] Decades would pass before many of the Irish Catholics in his constituency and throughout the rest of Canada would share these ardent sentiments. In the meantime, they

D'Arcy McGee's funeral procession in Montreal, April 13, 1868. Photograph by James Inglis (1835–1904).

would have split loyalties to Ireland and Canada. They could not let go of the past. Their desire to see Ireland freed from British rule was unabated. And while not necessarily approving of the methods used by the Fenians, they agreed passionately with the group's aims. Thus McGee had misjudged the situation. Nevertheless, thousands of people mourned his death:

> One hundred thousand people lined the streets for McGee's funeral procession, the largest in the history of Canada. Father Michael O'Farrell, a close friend and the former pastor of St. Ann's Church in Griffintown,

delivered one of the eulogies at the funeral at St. Patrick's Church on Monday, April 13 ... the entire Canadian cabinet was present.

In death, McGee had become a hero. But the Fenian threat did not disappear, although government forces easily quelled their small abortive risings in 1870 and 1871. Nor did the acrimony between Montreal's Catholics and Protestants soon fade.[8]

The thorny issue of Irish self-government under the British Crown had been promoted thirty years earlier by a peaceful, grassroots organization known as the "repealer movement,"[9] which formed branches in Canada. Later, St. Patrick's Societies took up this cause.[10] In a speech delivered during the 1875 St. Patrick's Day Concert, the County Meath–born Michael Thomas Stenson, a farmer, member of Parliament for Richmond in the Eastern Townships, and a supporter of the repeal movement, made an emotional appeal for all Irishmen to "seek by all constitutional means to restore their noble island [Ireland] to its rightful position among the nations of the earth." To do so, he argued, would simply give Ireland what Canada had achieved: "Why should not the Irish at home enjoy the same privileges that we enjoy? Why not have a parliament of their own in which the affairs of their country could not fail to be managed to better advantage than by being ministered to by others"[11] Irish politics mattered greatly to Canada's Irish Catholics. The feeling that something had to be done to help Dear Old Ireland would simply not go away.

Meanwhile, Irish Catholics living in Griffintown found the perfect replacement for their ancient sport of hurling. They played lacrosse.[12] The Shamrock team's lacrosse matches drew immense crowds — as many as 9,000, "most of whom, like the players, hailed from Griffintown." Their boisterous enthusiasm provided a stark contrast to the gentlemanly restraint displayed by Montreal's Protestant fans."[13] While events like this kept the Irish sense of community alive, their culture and traditions soon became subsumed in a melting pot having many ingredients. However, a desire to celebrate their Irishness, especially through music and dance, lingers on into modern times.

A 1985 St. Patrick's Day celebration in St. Gabriel de Valcartier, to the northwest of Quebec City, evoked the time when, over 150 years earlier, Ulster farmers and their families came to settle along the Jacques Cartier River on land formerly owned by the Jesuits. A roast beef dinner was enjoyed by 450 people in the community centre, which was decorated with shamrocks, green streamers, and other items with Irish themes. "The dinner attracted people from Quebec, Shannon and Ste. Foy.... Even though not all were Irish, everyone was Irish for the occasion."[14] A violin concert took place in the church before Mass on the following day, while in his sermon, the parish priest traced St. Gabriel's beginnings as an Irish community:

> The server was Danny Johnston, a member of an Irish family who had been in Valcartier for five generations. At the end of the service, the singing of "God Save Ireland" accompanied by the musicians, with the addition of Roger Lamont on the guitar, almost lifted the roof right off.[15]

Another aspect of the Irish was their apparent predilection for the demon drink, although their problems with alcoholism were probably no worse than those of their Scottish and English counterparts. Father Patrick Phelan, who served the Irish Catholic congregation in Griffintown, became so alarmed by the extent of poverty and excessive drinking among the Irish that he helped them to found a farming community north of Montreal, dubbed St. Columban, which, by 1835, had 100 Irish families. Possibly they were put under pressure to become teetotallers, since five years later Father Phelan founded the St. Patrick's Total Abstinence Society, the first North American branch of Father Theobald Mathew's temperance crusade that began in Cork in 1838. Its membership eventually grew to 3,000.[16] The relative cheapness of alcohol and the hardships of day to day life were a lethal combination for many and becoming teetotallers was one obvious way of dealing with these perils.

Father Phelan clearly saw it as his duty to direct his parishioners away from taverns and to help them when they went astray. When feuding

The Irish Lacrosse Team, Montreal, 1887.

broke out between rival gangs of Irish workers who were employed in digging the Beauharnois Canal in 1843, he stepped into the breach and convinced them to end their dispute. Holding a special Mass during which a collection was taken for those injured in the riots, the charismatic Father Phelan addressed 2,000 Irish workers after the service. "Not only did he convince them to end their dispute, he also enrolled ninety Irishmen in the temperance society."[17]

In a similar troubleshooting vein, the Irish-born William Beatty encouraged the first settlers in the company town that he founded in Parry Sound in the early 1870s to become teetotal, having witnessed the ravages caused by alcohol in other lumbering centres.[18] Similarly, as colonizers were also being attracted to the vast wildernesses of northern Ontario by the government's offer of 100-acre free land grants, they, too, were considered at risk for alcoholism.[19] To this end, Thomas McMurray, the son of a County Armagh weaver, used the *Northern Advocate*, the newspaper that he founded covering the Muskoka-Parry Sound area, to

Seal of St. Patrick's Total Abstinence Society, Montreal. Designed by John Henry Walker (1831–1899).

promote support for the temperance movement. He also campaigned actively for prohibition, reflecting the rising concerns over alcohol abuse in Canada at the time.[20]

A public display of temperance was also apparent in Ottawa during its 1862 St. Patrick's Day Parade:

> In the St. Patrick's procession was the St. Patrick's Temperance Society, each [member] displaying on the breast of his coat a badge of green and white silk having impressed thereon in gold bronze the Harp of Erin and

the title of the association. At their head was raised the temperance banner showing a life-sized portrait of Father Mathew, the world-renowned temperance advocate. They were led by the St. Patrick's band who presented quite an imposing figure being uniformly attired in black cloth pants and coats with scarlet bands round the cuffs and collars…. Their caps were of fine cloth with bands of gold lace surmounted in front by a silver shamrock.[21]

The Orange Order made a deep impression in Ontario, especially when it flaunted its colours on the "Glorious Twelfth" of July. When Orangemen celebrated King William of Orange's victory in 1690 over the Catholic King James at the Battle of the Boyne, they extolled Protestant supremacy. Predictably, disturbances sometimes followed. Believing that Catholic loyalty to the Pope and Church of Rome was incompatible with loyalty to the Protestant British Crown and Empire, Orangemen viewed Catholics with suspicion. They paraded to express such feelings. And their behaviour often became more vexatious when large numbers of Irish Catholics came to live in places that had formerly been Protestant strongholds. Nevertheless, the Orange Order always stressed its role as a mutual benefit society.

Expanding beyond its Irish origins in Canada, the Orange Order eventually embraced all Protestants, transforming itself into a British men's social club, whose principal role was to proclaim British values and provide mutual support to its members. Membership was a Protestant's guarantee of landing a job. The order grew rapidly, and by 1835 there were more than 150 Orange Lodges in Canada, most being located in Ontario and New Brunswick. Toronto, having seventeen lodges thirty years later, was fittingly described by John Maguire as the "Belfast of Canada." Orange Order lodges were particularly prevalent in Irish Protestant strongholds, and were often formed to counter a perceived threat from Catholic influences.[22] In 1861, the largest numbers were located in Simcoe, York, Huron, Grey, and Middlesex counties in western Ontario, and in Durham, Carleton, Lanark, Frontenac, and Hastings counties in the eastern region of the provinceo.[23] By comparison, the lodges in Quebec were few and

Loyal Orange Lodge, Arnprior, Ontario, circa 1906.

far between, mainly being confined to Montreal, Quebec City, and the Eastern Townships.

The 400 to 500 Irish Catholics who sailed from Liverpool to Quebec in 1824 had a taste of what to expect in Ontario when twenty-six Orangemen suddenly appeared on their ship's deck. This notable group celebrated the 12th of July by walking "three times around the deck and giving three cheers for Old Ireland." Afterward, they were said to have "bought four gallons of rum and parted in peace."[24] These Irishmen definitely brought their politics and religion with them to Canada!

Although punch-ups occurred from time to time, particularly after Orangemen's parades or St. Patrick's Day parades, serious encounters were relatively rare. Some of the worst clashes occurred during the famine migration period, when large numbers of Irish suddenly arrived, creating rundown shantytowns in the cities. In a confrontation in 1849, between Irish Catholics and Orangemen in Hamilton's Slabtown slums, four men died and six were wounded. Later, as Toronto acquired many

St. Patrick's Day greeting
postcard circa 1914.

more Irish Catholics, it became a major hotbed of sectarian violence. The worst incident was the bloody battle that broke out in 1875 involving 6,000 to 8,000 people and put the entire city out of control for a number of hours.[25]

Irish Catholics had to struggle with Protestant intolerance and organized bigotry at every turn, but they did not let this stand in their way. John Maguire described the prejudice that they encountered as "neither latent nor slumbering — it was open and active: it met the Catholic Irishman in every rank of life and in every branch of Industry."[26] He may have had Walter O'Hara in mind. On his tour of Ontario in 1827, he complained about the unsuitability of the Irish, not as people, but as servants:

The country is rendered disgusting by the plague of bad servants; the most of them are Irish. They come out to this country quite helpless as to any of the arts of making life comfortable: they know literally how to do nothing as servants; their habits are often vicious, almost always disorderly and irregular.[27]

Thus the Irish came with a bad reputation, justified or not, which they had to circumvent as best they could. Irish Catholics had a harder road to climb than their Scottish and English counterparts, but despite these obstacles, they prospered. John Maguire noticed a marked contrast between the Irishmen he met during his travels in Canada and those who remained in Ireland:

Crossing the Atlantic ... one is enabled, almost at a glance, to recognise the marked difference between the position of the Irish race in the old country and in the new.... In the old country stagnation and retrogression, if not actual decay — in the new, life, movement, progress; in the one, depression, want of confidence, dark apprehension of the future — in the other energy, self-reliance, and a perpetual looking forward to a grander development and a more glorious destiny.[28]

The Irish immigrants very often arrived with little means, many having had to rely on money sent to them by family and friends who had already settled in Canada to fund their passage. Although they suffered many disadvantages, particularly because of prejudice, they at least had prospects. The Irish had a partially open door to push at in Canada, whereas in Ireland there was a brick wall. In Ireland they were bound by anti-Catholic discrimination, rigidly enforced by legislation; but in Canada the sky was the limit. Irish Catholics needed time to feel that they belonged to a Canada, which had a British (and Protestant monarchy). In the end, the Irish of all denominations contributed greatly to Ontario and Quebec's early pioneering communities.

This saga is dominated by ordinary people who brought their brawn, skills, and wide work experience to Canada and put them to good use. Although the Irish contribution to Canada's infrastructure through canal and railway building was immense, it has largely gone unrecorded. This is because they frequently resorted to violence to resolve pay disputes and seek decent working conditions and as a result were dismissed as worthless troublemakers.[29] The fact that they had no other way of obtaining a fair deal from their unscrupulous employers is ignored.

The majority of Irish had put down roots in Ontario and Quebec long before the Great Famine struck and should be remembered more for their pioneering achievements rather than the suffering and loss of life that occurred during that period. Their memories and love of old Ireland ran deep and never left them; but they also became staunch Canadians. Because they were in at the beginning, the Irish played a major role in shaping Ontario's future and in influencing Quebec's economic and cultural development.

ACKNOWLEDGEMENTS

I am indebted to a great many people. First, I wish to thank the Quebec Government Office in London for the Prix du Québec award, which I have put toward my research and travel costs in writing this book.

I am grateful for the many kindnesses of archivists and librarians on both sides of the Atlantic. In particular, I wish to offer special thanks to Jody Robinson at the Eastern Townships Resource Centre in Lennoxville, to Marc St-Jacques at the Archives Nationales du Québec Gatineau Centre in Hull, and to Michael Simard at the Archives Nationales du Québec Centre in the University of Laval. I was also well served by the staff at the Ontario Archives and I thank them for their help. In addition, I wish to acknowledge my debt to the staff at the Public Record Office for Northern Ireland for helping me to make my way through the vast body of material that they hold relating to Irish settlers in early Canada.

I thank the many people who helped me to locate and obtain illustrations. In particular, I am grateful to Kevin Derrick for his photograph of St. Joseph's Church in Douro (Peterborough) and permission to use it as an illustration in this book. The present-day church gives us a visual reminder of the pioneering achievements of the Peter Robinson settlers and I was very grateful to have this photograph.

As ever, I am indebted to my long-suffering husband, Geoff, who helped me with every aspect of both the research and writing. We are a team, and I could not have written this book without his help. I am greatly indebted to Allison Hirst for her meticulous work in turning my manuscript into a book. I also thank my dear friend Jean Lucas who, once again, has done the proofreading and offered welcome guidance. Finally, I wish to express my appreciation to Jane Gibson for her dedication and hard work in producing the index to this book.

APPENDIX

IMMIGRANT SHIP CROSSINGS FROM IRELAND TO QUEBEC, 1817–1840

Explanatory Notes

Vessel Name

The name sometimes includes the name of the port where the vessel is registered. The vessel type and tonnage, where known, appear after the vessel name.

Tonnage

This was a standard measure used to determine customs dues and navigation fees. Because it was a calculated figure tonnage, did not necessarily convey actual carrying capacity.

Vessel type

Brig (bg) is a two-masted vessel with square rigging on both masts.

Barque (bk) is a three-masted vessel, square-rigged on the fore and main masts and for-and-aft rigged on the third aftermost mast.

Ship (s) is a three-masted vessel, squared rigged on all three masts.

Schooner (sr) has fore-and-aft sails on two or more masts. They were largely used in the coasting trade and for fishing, their advantage being the smaller crew than that required by square-rigged vessels of a comparable size.

Month

Unless otherwise stated the month shown is the vessel's arrival month.

Documentary Sources

Details of the number of passengers carried by ships, crossing from Ireland to Quebec, have been obtained from a variety of documentary sources, the most important being the *Quebec Mercury,* together with the Quebec immigration agent's annual reports and the colonial land and emigration commissioners' annual reports, the latter two being taken from the British Parliamentary Papers. In addition, some entries have been taken from theshipslist.com. Some passenger figures are approximate. Uncertainties arise as to whether passenger numbers include all adults (not just heads of households) and children and infants.

Passenger Lists

No official passenger lists were kept for ships crossing from Britain to the port of Quebec until 1865. Consequently, few passenger lists survive before then. Where a passenger list has been identified in this study, the documentary reference is given with the crossing information.

Year	Month	Vessel	Master	Departure Port	Passenger Numbers
1817	06	*Alexander* (s)	Reid	Belfast	131
1817	06	*James Bailey* (s)	Sullivan	Belfast	50

Had damaged her rudder in the ice and put into Halifax for repair.

Year	Month	Vessel	Master	Departure Port	Passenger Numbers
1817	06	*Victoria* (bk)	McKenna	Dublin	52
1817	07	*Mary & Bell* (nk)	Cunningham	Dublin	121
1817	07	*Ocean* (bg)	Blake, H.	Dublin	91
1817	07	*Thomas* (bg)	Bouch	Belfast	151
1817	08	*Active* (bg)	Whitley	Wexford	75
1817	08	*Atlantic* (bg)	Harper, Richard	Dublin	140
1817	08	*Belvoir Castle* (bg)	Proudfoot, D.	Sligo	86
1817	08	*Eclipse* (bg)	Moore	Belfast	121
1817	08	*General Moore* (bg)	Horne	Wexford	96
1817	08	*Lord Wellington* (bg)	Henderson, Chas.	Cork	69
1817	08	*Loyal Sam* (s)	Middleton	Sligo	80
1817	08	*Mary Ann* (bg)	Barey	Wexford	120
1817	08	*Saltoun* (bg)	Henderson	Waterford	70
1817	09	*Anne* (bg)	Wood, J.	Coleraine	81
1817	09	*Joseph* (bg)	Bell	Dublin	71
1818	05	*Briton* (bg)	Evans	Dublin	50
1818	05	*Ceres* (s)	Raitt, David	Belfast	150
1818	06	*Ann* (bg)	Shaw, George	Sligo	129
1818	06	*Atlantic* (bg)	Harper, Richard	Dublin	158
1818	06	*Cleopatra* (bg)	Broderick	Belfast	25
1818	06	*Comet* (bg)	Thompson	Dublin	75
1818	06	*Expedition* (bg)	Watson	Belfast	140
1818	06	*Francis* (bg)	Danson	Waterford	66
1818	06	*Lady Hamilton* (s)	Young, A.	Cork	12
1818	06	*Maria* (bg)	Key, Robert	Waterford	138
1818	06	*Prince of Asturias* (bg)	Donald, A.	Dublin	138
1818	06	*Sally* (bg)	Ball, Samuel	Belfast	176
1818	06	*Sarah and Marianne* (bg)	Christian, J.	Belfast	128
1818	07	*Alexander* (s)	Reid	Belfast	220
1818	07	*Brunswick* (s)	Blake	Cork	230

Richard Talbot's settlers sailed in this vessel.

Year	Month	Vessel	Master	Departure Port	Passenger Numbers
1818	07	George Ponsonby (bg)	Hull	Dublin	63
1818	07	Grace (sr)	Inglis	Coleraine	52
1818	07	Pomona (bg)	Wilson	Dublin	103
1818	07	Royal Edward (bk)	Madelton, Thos.	Belfast	250
1818	07	Union (s)	Stewart	Limerick	64
1818	08	Economy (bg)	Owen	Dublin	122
1818	08	Henry (bg)	Newport	Dublin	137
1818	08	Marinlow (bg)	Burns	Dublin	115
1818	08	Mary (bg)	Breen	Dublin	116
1818	08	Nelson (bg)	Donaghue	Cork	39
1818	08	North Star (bg)	Crowly	Cork	15
1818	08	Perseverance (s)	Fisher	Belfast	144
1818	08	Pitt (s)	Hamilton	Belfast	211
1818	08	Robert (s)	Garnip	Belfast	229
1818	08	Sarah (bg)	Clement, James	Belfast	170
1818	08	Sir John Cameron (bg)	Selby	Newry	200
1818	08	Speculator (bg)	Organ	Dublin	135
1818	08	Suffolk (s)	Bean	Belfast	186
1818	09	Kate (bg)	McKenna	Dublin	49
1818	09	Neptune (bg)	Wilson	Dublin	70
1819	05	Alexander (s)	Drummond, George	Belfast	235
1819	05	Perfect (bg)	Sullivan, Owen	Belfast	164
1819	05	Prince of Asturias (bg)	Donald	Dublin	124
1819	05	Sarah (bg)	Clement, James	Belfast	150
1819	06	Aeolius (s)	Thomas, Robert	Waterford	202
1819	06	Ann (bg)	Shaw, George	Sligo	50
1819	06	Atlantic (bg)	Harper, Richard	Dublin	151
1819	06	Economy (bg)	Harper	Dublin	76
1819	06	Greenhow (bg, 291 tns)	Hossack, J.	Belfast	n/k
1819	06	Industry (bg)	Armstrong	Belfast	215
1819	06	Integrity (bg)	Wilson, J.	Strangford	60
1819	06	Janet (bg)	Devereux, James	Wexford	63

Year	Month	Vessel	Master	Departure Port	Passenger Numbers
1819	06	*Maria* (bg)	Key, Robert	New Ross	163
1819	06	*Mary & Betsey* (sr)	Lambert	Waterford	50
1819	06	*Pitt* (s)	Hamilton	Belfast	288
1819	06	*Resolution* (bg)	Brown, Robert	Waterford	32
1819	06	*Sally* (bg)	Ball, Samuel	Belfast	173
1819	06	*Spartan* (s)	Craig	Londonderry	223
1819	07	*Ajax* (bg)	Watson, George	Dublin	248
1819	07	*Anglim* (bg)	Grayson, Thomas	Baltimore	113
1819	07	*Columbia* (bg)	Hamilton, John	Dublin	154
1819	07	*Isabella* (bg)	n/k	Dublin	113
1819	07	*Martha* (bg)	Thomas	Cork	69
1819	07	*Ocean* (bg)	Blake, H.	Belfast	139
1819	07	*Pheasant* (bg)	Barnes, J.C.	Waterford	37
1819	07	*Quaker* (bk)	Anderson	Baltimore	35
1819	07	*Thomas* (bg)	Drury, John	Waterford	137
1819	07	*Vittoria* (bg)	Bowness, William	Belfast	273
1819	08	*Agnes* (bg)	Beveridge, William	Belfast	210
1819	08	*Constantia* (bg)	Moyne, William	Waterford	90
1819	08	*Grace* (sr)	Dotle, Peter	Ballycastle	47
1819	08	*James* (bg)	Jack, William	Dublin	161
1819	08	*Jane* (bg)	Bernie, Alex	Newry	163
1819	08	*Margaret* (bg)	Crookes, J.	Dublin	108
1819	08	*Richard and John* (bk)	Henlon, George	Belfast	126
1819	09	*Argo* (s)	Lorriman, William	Londonderry	240
1819	09	*Blucher* (bg)	Grayson, John	Belfast	154
1819	09	*Catherine* (bg)	Wilkie, D.	Belfast	70
1819	09	*Emily* (bg)	Thompson, B.	Shannon	82
1819	09	*General Brock* (bg)	Giddesom, James	Londonderry	198
1819	09	*Mania* (bg)	Davies, Edward	Dublin	82
1819	09	*Margaret* (bg)	McGill, D.	Waterford	87

Vessel left from Ross near Waterford.

Year	Month	Vessel	Master	Departure Port	Passenger Numbers
1819	09	*Margaret* (bg)	McGill, D.	New Ross	87
1819	09	*Marshland* (bg)	Ditchburn, John	Cork	52
1819	09	*Martha* (bg)	Simpson, George	Belfast	137

Year	Month	Vessel	Master	Departure Port	Passenger Numbers
1819	09	*Shannon* (bg)	Hale, John	Dublin	131
1819	11	*Kate* (bg)	McKenna	Dublin	47
1820	05	*Ann* (bg)	Moore	Sligo	41
1820	05	*Eliza* (s)	Purdy, J.	Dublin	101

Two cabin passengers plus ninety-nine settlers.

Year	Month	Vessel	Master	Departure Port	Passenger Numbers
1820	05	*Nassau* (s)	Gaspard	Waterford	40
1820	05	*Prince of Asturias* (bg)	Donald, A.	Dublin	110
1820	05	*Sally* (bg)	Ball, Samuel	Belfast	100
1820	06	*Active* (s)	Baird, Thomas	Belfast	154
1820	06	*Ajax* (bg)	Watson	Dublin	183
1820	06	*Ann* (bg)	Whitley	Wexford	63
1820	06	*Britannia* (bg)	Clary	Dublin	42
1820	06	*Dominica Packet* (bg)	Clarke, J.	Londonderry	180
1820	06	*Duke of Wellington* (bg)	Wilson, J.	Londonderry	173
1820	06	*Halifax Packet* (s)	Craig	Londonderry	170
1820	06	*Isabella* (bg)	Robinson, J.	Dublin	195
1820	06	*Maria* (bg)	Key, Robert	New Ross	150

Master was commended by passengers who were on their way to the Perth region of Lanark County.

Year	Month	Vessel	Master	Departure Port	Passenger Numbers
1820	06	*Martha* (bg)	Moore, M.	Dublin	115

Captain died.

Year	Month	Vessel	Master	Departure Port	Passenger Numbers
1820	06	*Neptune* (bg)	Wright, J.	Belfast	240
1820	06	*Rodie* (s)	Read	Belfast	165
1820	06	*Sarah* (bg)	Frank, E.H.	Cork	98
1820	06	*Suffolk* (s)	Kenn	Belfast	173
1820	06	*Thomas* (bg)	Harris	Limerick	89
1820	07	*Albion* (bg)	Harper, Edward	Dublin	133
1820	07	*Catherine* (bg)	Drysdale	Belfast	200
1820	07	*Effort* (bg)	Farrent, W.	Cork	108
1820	07	*James* (bg)	Atkinson	Belfast	277
1820	07	*Maria* (bg)	Thormthwaite	Dublin	188
1820	07	*Mary and Betty* (sr)	Lanbert, Thos.	Wexford	55
1820	07	*Pitt* (s)	Hamilton, J.	Belfast	285
1820	07	*Santon* (bg)	Gaitskill	Newry	75
1820	08	*Amphion* (bg)	Little	Dublin	76

Year	Month	Vessel	Master	Departure Port	Passenger Numbers
1820	08	*Dwina* (bg)	Thompson	Belfast	133
1820	08	*Hannah* (bg)	Sevin	Dublin	120
1820	08	*Jemima* (bg)	Doyle, Edward	Dublin	77
1820	08	*Lansteffan Castle* (bg)	Thomas, J.	New Ross	42
1820	08	*Mary* (bg)	Inglis, W.	Coleraine	67
1820	08	*Thomas and Mary* (s)	Dysart, J.	Cork	93
1820	09	*Felicity* (bg)	Mickle, James	Belfast	63
1820	09	*John Howard* (bk)	Smith	Cork	9
1820	10	*Hope* (bg, 157 tns)	Simpson, George	Belfast	143
1820	10	*Prince of Asturias* (bg)	Donald, A.	Dublin	43
1821	05	*Aeolius* (s)	Thomas	Waterford	75
1821	05	*Greenhowe* (bg)	Hossack, J.	Belfast	288
1821	05	*Mariane* (bg)	Christian, J.	Belfast	170
1821	05	*Prince of Asturias* (bg)	Donald, A.	Dublin	101

Two cabin passengers.

Year	Month	Vessel	Master	Departure Port	Passenger Numbers
1821	06	*Eliza* (s)	Lawson	Dublin	77
1821	06	*Grace* (bg)	Fishley	Cork	120

Vessel started voyage at Ilfracombe.

Year	Month	Vessel	Master	Departure Port	Passenger Numbers
1821	06	*Maria* (bg)	Key, Robert	New Ross	41
1821	06	*Mary* (bg)	Carr	Coleraine	32
1821	06	*Mary & Betty* (bg)	Hall	Wexford	130
1821	06	*Nestor* (s)	Thorn	Belfast	300
1821	06	*Sally* (bg)	Ball, Samuel	Newry	180
1821	06	*Sisters* (bg)	Miller	Londonderry	161
1821	07	*Brilliant* (bg)	Scott	Dublin	175
1821	07	*Douglas* (bg)	Pevis	Newry	52
1821	07	*Effort* (bg)	Farrent, W.	Cork	67

Passengers were troops, not settlers.

Year	Month	Vessel	Master	Departure Port	Passenger Numbers
1821	07	*General Brock* (bg)	Whitton	Belfast	250
1821	07	*Isla* (bg)	Watlake, R.	Waterford	6
1821	07	*John* (bg)	Hutchinson	Ballycastle	15
1821	07	*Mary Ann* (bg)	Gorman	Limerick	97
1821	07	*Ocean* (bg)	Blake, H.	Belfast	137
1821	07	*Pilgrim* (bg)	Masterton	Belfast	138
1821	07	*Robert Nelson* (bg)	Shaw	Cork	140

Year	Month	Vessel	Master	Departure Port	Passenger Numbers
1821	07	*Samuel Ponsonby* (bg)	Parkinson	Sligo	55
1821	07	*Sarah* (bg)	Rodgers, D.	Belfast	55
1821	07	*Westmorland* (s)	Smith	Belfast	200
1821	08	*Indian Trader* (s)	n/k	Belfast	200
1821	08	*Lavinia* (bg)	Baily, Thomas S.	Dublin	28
1821	08	*Perseverance* (bg)	Wills	Belfast	101
1821	08	*Robert* (bg)	Jones, John	Dublin	123
1821	09	*Ann* (bg)	Shaw, George	Sligo	15
1821	09	*Columbia* (bg)	Hamilton, John	Dublin	56
1821	09	*Maria* (bg) One cabin passenger.	Nicholson	Dublin	21
1821	09	*Monarch* (bg)	Martin	Belfast	22
1821	09	*Sir James Spring* (bk)	Stewart	Cork	20
1821	09	*William McGillivray* (bg)	Poag, John	Belfast	23
1822	05	*Fidelity* (bg)	Lelbourne	Cork	190
1822	05	*Maria* (bg)	Key, Robert	New Ross	113
1822	05	*Rob Roy* (bg)	Kenn	Belfast	136
1822	05	*Sarah* (bg)	Rodgers, D.	Belfast	114
1822	05	*Stanton* (bg)	Harris	Cork	55
1822	06	*Aeolius* (s)	Thomas	Waterford	202
1822	06	*Albion* (bg)	Harper, Edward	Dublin	131
1822	06	*Ann* (bg)	Hearn	Sligo	140
1822	06	*Ann* (s)	Cuthbert	Newry	191
1822	06	*Brilliant* (bg)	Scott	Dublin	168
1822	06	*David Shaw* (s)	Harrison	Westport	231
1822	06	*Greenhow* (bg)	n/k	Newry	181
1822	06	*Hercules* (s)	Cochran	Belfast	160
1822	06	*Jane & Margaret* (bg)	Harper	Galway	52
1822	06	*Pacific* (bg)	Potts, Robert	Limerick	146
1822	06	*Sally* (bg)	Ball, Samuel	Newry	168
1822	06	*Sarah and Marianne* (bg, 194 tns)	Christian, J.	Strangford	170
1822	06	*Sir James Kempt* (bk)	Stewart	Cork	255

Year	Month	Vessel	Master	Departure Port	Passenger Numbers
1822	07	*Alexander* (bg)	Bodle, W.B.	Belfast	141
1822	07	*Amphitrite*	Chaplin	Newry	188
1822	07	*Ann* (bg)	Quigley	Ballycastle	125
1822	07	*Atlas* (bg)	Jones	Belfast	117
1822	07	*Betsy* (bg)	Cowan	Londonderry	162
1822	07	*Cossack* (s)	Thompson	Londonderry	275
1822	07	*Doris* (bk)	Cairns	Belfast	309
1822	07	*Earl Talbot* (bg)	Battens	Cork	104
1822	07	*George* (bg)	Thompson	Belfast	118
1822	07	*George & Elizabeth* (bg)	Rennison	Cork	82
1822	07	*James* (bg)	Johnson	Sligo	130
1822	07	*Jane* (bg)	McGrath	Waterford	56
1822	07	*Kent* (bg)	Sterling	Londonderry	157
1822	07	*Lavinia* (bg)	Baily, Thomas S.	Dublin	171
1822	07	*Liberty* (bg)	Storey	Dublin	190
1822	07	*Lord Wellington* (s)	n/k	Newry	230
1822	07	*Martha* (bg)	Thomas	Limerick	120
1822	07	*Mary Ann* (bg)	Dureck	Limerick	109
1822	07	*Matthews* (bg)	Steele	Sligo	110
1822	07	*Nautilus* (bg)	Watson, John	Belfast	119
1822	07	*Patience* (bg)	Bowman	Belfast	212
1822	07	*Rose* (bg)	Lee	Belfast	110
1822	07	*Sarah & Eliza* (bg)	Mortimer	Limerick	83
1822	07	*William* (sr)	Norris	Dublin	65
1822	08	*Eliza* (bg)	Glowstone	Limerick	71
1822	08	*Hercules* (s)	Power	Londonderry	130
1822	08	*Jane* (bg)	Williams	Dublin	140
1822	08	*Janet Dunlop*	Snowdon	Londonderry	63
1822	08	*True Blue* (bg)	Hodson	Cork	63
1822	08	*Union* (bg)	Nicholson	Belfast	138
1822	09	*Columbia* (bg)	Hamilton	Dublin	110
1822	09	*Hope* (bg)	Sanders	Dublin	120
1822	09	*Margaret* (bg)	Fox	Cork	25

Year	Month	Vessel	Master	Departure Port	Passenger Numbers
1822	10	*Ann* (bg)	Redpath	Belfast	52
1822	06	*Aid* (bg)	Leslie	Belfast	130
1823	05	*Alexander* (bg)	Booth	Dublin	142
1823	05	*Canada* (s)	Lamb	Belfast	191
1823	05	*Ceres* (s)	Walker	Cork	67
1823	05	*Diadem* (s)	Archer	Belfast	316
1823	05	*Endeavour* (bg)	Levy	Dublin	112
1823	05	*George IV* (bg)	Thomas	Waterford	111
1823	05	*Jane* (bg, 147 tns)	McGrath	Waterford	88
1823	05	*Maria* (bg)	Key, Robert	New Ross	121
1823	05	*Prince of Asturias* (bg)	Dennon	Dublin	127
1823	05	*Sarah* (bg)	Rodgers, D.	Belfast	136
1823	05	*Sarah and Marianne* (bg)	Christian, J.	Belfast	201
1823	05	*Sir James Kempt* (bk)	Stewart	Cork	118
1823	06	*Alexander* (bg)	Bodle, W.B.	Belfast	103
1823	06	*Canada* (bg)	Potts	Newry	153
1823	06	*Cossack* (s)	Thompson	Londonderry	313
1823	06	*Dorcas Savage* (bg)	Bailie	Portaferry	51
1823	06	*Eliza* (bk)	Boswell	Dublin	159
1823	06	*General Elliott* (bk) Vessel had called at P.E.I.	Frank	Cork	30
1823	06	*John & Mary* (bg)	Grant	Dublin	164
1823	06	*Resolution* (bg)	Neil	Belfast	130
1823	06	*Sally* (bg)	Little	Sligo	130
1823	06	*William Tell* (bg)	Barnes	Newry	210
1823	07	*Active* (bg)	Johnson	Newry	136
1823	07	*Amphion* (bg)	Little	Dublin	98
1823	07	*Cygnet* (bg)	Maxwell	Newry	104
1823	07	*Fanny* (s)	Blair	Belfast	326
1823	07	*Fortitude* (bg)	Nelson	Limerick	123
1823	07	*Hamilton* (bk)	Williams	Belfast	245
1823	07	*Harrison* (s, 296 tns)	Wales	Londonderry	401
1823	07	*James* (bg)	Coleman, John	Ballycastle	85
1823	07	*Jane* (bg)	Johnson	Sligo	139

Year	Month	Vessel	Master	Departure Port	Passenger Numbers
1823	07	*Mary* (bk)	Clark	Belfast	202
1823	07	*Mary Ann* (bg)	Kendall	Limerick	142
1823	07	*Prince of Wales* (s)	Gray	Belfast	235
1823	07	*Trafalgar* (bg)	Christopherson	Belfast	170
1823	07	*Williams* (bg)	Norris, William	Dublin	82

Vessel had carried fifty more passengers than was allowed. Norris was fined £25. Eleven children died on the crossing.

Year	Month	Vessel	Master	Departure Port	Passenger Numbers
1823	08	*British Tar* (bg)	Colbick	Belfast	110
1823	08	*Harriet* (bg)	Carr	Belfast	212
1823	08	*Hebe* (s)	Hare	Cork	288

One cabin passenger and 287 settlers. The first of two vessels carrying the Peter Robinson settlers.

Year	Month	Vessel	Master	Departure Port	Passenger Numbers
1823	08	*Liddle* (bg)	Wheatley	Belfast	257

Two cabin passengers plus 255 settlers.

Year	Month	Vessel	Master	Departure Port	Passenger Numbers
1823	08	*Margaret* (sr)	Hearn	New Ross	52
1823	08	*Mary* (bg)	Yeoward	Dublin	120
1823	08	*Orient* (bg)	Galilee	Dublin	185
1823	08	*Sprightly* (bg)	Johnson	Belfast	178
1823	09	*Aeolius* (s)	Thomas	Waterford	8

One cabin passenger plus seven settlers.

Year	Month	Vessel	Master	Departure Port	Passenger Numbers
1823	09	*Alchymist* (bg)	Stevens	Cork	134
1823	09	*Donald* (bk)	Donald	Dublin	72
1823	09	*Endeavour* (bg)	Levy	Dublin	19
1823	09	*Fortune* (bg)	West	Belfast	76
1823	09	*Mayflower* (bg)	David	Dublin	42
1823	09	*Sir James Kempt* (bk)	Stewart	Cork	13
1823	09	*Stakesby* (s)	Johnson	Cork	293

This was the second vessel carrying the Peter Robinson settlers. Peter Robinson was one of the two cabin passengers.

Year	Month	Vessel	Master	Departure Port	Passenger Numbers
1823	09	*William Harris* (s)	Beercroft	Cork	143

Nine officers and 134 men of the Royal Artillery.

Year	Month	Vessel	Master	Departure Port	Passenger Numbers
1823	10	*Canada* (s)	Lamb	Belfast	55
1823	10	*George IV* (bg)	Thomas, R.	Waterford	69
1823	10	*St. Charles* (bk)	Leslie	Cork	10
1824	05	*Rob Roy* (bg)	Kenn	Belfast	25

Departed Belfast 2 April, had a "boisterous" passage. Delayed by ice.

Year	Month	Vessel	Master	Departure Port	Passenger Numbers
1824	06	*Caledonian* (bk)	McComb	Belfast	214
1824	06	*Canada* (s)	Lamb	Belfast	186

Year	Month	Vessel	Master	Departure Port	Passenger Numbers
1824	06	*Ceres* (s)	Doeg	Waterford	30
1824	06	*Diadem* (bk)	Currie	Belfast	117

James Coulter was a passenger (LAC MG24 H11).

Year	Month	Vessel	Master	Departure Port	Passenger Numbers
1824	06	*Dublin* (bk)	Donald	Dublin	181
1824	06	*Gales* (bg)	Dawson	Cork	37
1824	06	*Gilbert Henderson* (bk)	Creigson	Dublin	146
1824	06	*Greenfield* (bg)	Wyley	Belfast	15
1824	06	*James* (bg)	Dixon	Dublin	61
1824	06	*James Bailey* (s)	Gowan	Belfast	28
1824	06	*Jane* (bg)	Hossack	Belfast	148
1824	06	*John & Thomas* (s)	Hamilton	Newry	261
1824	06	*Lord Wellington* (s)	Maxwell	Newry	152
1824	06	*Marquis of Anglesey* (bg)	William	Limerick	60
1824	06	*Mary Ann* (bg)	Connell	Limerick	95
1824	06	*Nassau* (s)	Grossard	Waterford	11
1824	06	*New Draper* (bg)	Barwise	Dublin	80
1824	06	*Resolution* (bg)	Neil	Belfast	19
1824	06	*Richard* (bg)	Cox	Limerick	54
1824	06	*Thomas Gibson* (s)	Strachan	Belfast	235
1824	06	*Vine* (bg)	Hunter	Dublin	74
1824	06	*Wellington* (bg)	Leppington	Cork	40
1824	06	*William* (bg)	Thomas	New Ross	62
1824	07	*Fame* (bg)	Malcolm	Belfast	113
1824	07	*Harrison* (s, 720 tns)	Buchanan	Londonderry	409
1824	07	*Janus* (bg)	Johnson	Sligo	75
1824	07	*Prosperous* (bg)	Peniment	Dublin	77
1824	08	*Albion* (bg)	Hall	Dublin	102
1824	08	*Alchymist* (bg)	Mills	Cork	37

One cabin passenger, Rev. Crawly.

Year	Month	Vessel	Master	Departure Port	Passenger Numbers
1824	08	*British Tar* (bg)	Newby	Belfast	187
1824	08	*Friends* (bg)	Norris	Dublin	126
1824	08	*Glory* (bg)	Morgan	Belfast	153
1824	08	*Mary* (bg)	Anderson	Dublin	33
1824	08	*Providence* (bk)	Wenlock	Belfast	181

Year	Month	Vessel	Master	Departure Port	Passenger Numbers
1824	08	*Stentor* (s)	Harris	Limerick	241
1824	08	*Union* (bg)	Hunslow	Cork	16
1824	08	*Wesley* (bg)	Anderson	Limerick	46
1824	09	*Albion* (bg)	Halm	Dublin	74
1824	09	*Isabella* (bg)	Robinson	Sligo	41
1824	09	*John & William* (bg)	Lister	Dublin	39
1824	09	*New Astley* (bg)	Bartlett	Dublin	63
1824	09	*Sir William Ashton* (s)	Guy	Belfast	176
1824	09	*William* (bg)	Jackson	Dublin	43
1824	10	*Albion* (bg)	Stewart	Cork	12
1824	10	*John Howard* (bk)	Tisdall	Cork	8
1824	10	*William* (bg)	Thomas	New Ross	1
1825	05	*Aeolius* (s)	Thomas	Waterford	121
1825	05	*Albion* (bg)	Dunn	Dublin	84
1825	05	*Argyle* (bk)	Grossard	Waterford	21
1825	05	*Canada* (s)	Lamb	Belfast	151
1825	05	*Dublin* (bk)	Donald	Dublin	178
1825	05	*Favourite* (bg)	Gray	Cork	21
1825	05	*John & William* (bg)	Dickinson	Dublin	73
1825	05	*John Howard* (bk)	Bruce	Cork	123
1825	05	*Maria* (bg)	Sewell	Dublin	95
1825	05	*Maria* (bk)	Elsworthy	Waterford	223
1825	05	*Richard Pope* (bk)	Maloney	Belfast	176
1825	05	*Rob Roy* (bg)	Kenn	Belfast	18

Two cabin passengers.

Year	Month	Vessel	Master	Departure Port	Passenger Numbers
1825	05	*Robert Kerr* (s, 358 tns)	Boyd	Belfast	103
1825	05	*Sir James Kempt* (bk)	Patterson	New Ross	201
1825	05	*Veronica* (bg)	Euston	Belfast	148

Six cabin passengers.

Year	Month	Vessel	Master	Departure Port	Passenger Numbers
1825	06	*Albion* (bg)	Mills	Cork	187

Peter Robinson settlers. They took the steam boat *New Swiftsure* to Montreal.

| 1825 | 06 | *Amity* (bk) | Arrowsmith | Cork | 149 |

Peter Robinson settlers. They took the steam boat *New Swiftsure* to Montreal.

| 1825 | 06 | *Brunswick* (s) | Blake | Cork | 343 |

Peter Robinson settlers. They took the steam boat *Lady Sherbrooke* to Montreal.

Year	Month	Vessel	Master	Departure Port	Passenger Numbers
1825	06	*Fortitude* (s)	Lewis	Cork	287

Peter Robinson settlers. They took the steam boat *New Swiftsure* to Montreal.

1825	06	*Greenhow* (bg)	Jones	Newry	34
1825	06	*Harrison* (s)	Young	Londonderry	450
1825	06	*Henry* (bg)	Trance	Dublin	81
1825	06	*James* (sr)	n/k	Dublin	80
1825	06	*Peggy* (bk)	Stephens	Belfast	194
1825	06	*Regulus* (s)	Dixon	Cork	157

Peter Robinson settlers. They took the steam boat *Lady Sherbrooke* to Montreal.

1825	06	*Request* (bg)	Davidson	Belfast	146
1825	06	*Resolution* (bg)	Neil	Dublin	80
1825	06	*Resolution* (bk)	Ward	Cork	227

Peter Robinson settlers. They took the steam boat *Lady Sherbrooke* to Montreal.

1825	06	*Sarah* (bg)	Rodgers, D.	Belfast	22
1825	06	*Star*	Becket, Joseph	Cork	214

Peter Robinson settlers. They took the steam boat *Lady Sherbrooke* to Montreal.

1825	06	*Wellington* (bg)	Maxwell	Newry	147
1825	07	*Broughton* (bg)	Love	Belfast	117
1825	07	*Cheviot* (bg)	Stephenson	Belfast	143
1825	07	*Comet* (s)	Hylton	Belfast	204
1825	07	*Edward* (bg)	Edmundson	Belfast	6
1825	07	*Elizabeth* (s)	Morrison	Cork	209

Peter Robinson settlers. They took the steam boat *Quebec* to Montreal.

1825	07	*Gateshead* (bg)	Palmer	Dublin	151
1825	07	*Greenfield* (bg)	Wyley	Dublin	36
1825	07	*Hope* (bg)	Tomlinson	Limerick	97
1825	07	*Hopewell* (bg)	Patterson	Sligo	12
1825	07	*Jane* (bg)	Morris	Dublin	111
1825	07	*John* (bg)	Warden	Belfast	157
1825	07	*John Barry* (s)	Roach	Cork	253

Peter Robinson settlers. They took the steam boat *New Swiftsure* to Montreal.

1825	07	*Mary* (bg)	Young	Newry	94
1825	07	*Mary & Betty* (bg)	Porteous	Dublin	91
1825	07	*Mary Ann* (bg)	Forrest	Limerick	126
1825	07	*Seham* (bg)	Stewart	Waterford	18
1825	07	*Sprightly* (bg)	Johnson	Belfast	97

Year	Month	Vessel	Master	Departure Port	Passenger Numbers
1825	08	*Anachron* (s)	Stonehouse	Sligo	195
1825	08	*Brisk* (bg)	McDewall	Newry	26
1825	08	*Fame* (bg)	Malcolm	Belfast	92
1825	08	*Grace* (bg)	Little	Limerick	93
1825	08	*Hannah* (s)	Graham	Belfast	173
1825	08	*Isabella* (bg)	Booth	Dublin	121
1825	08	*Joseph & Jane* (bg)	Baird	Belfast	150
1825	08	*Kelton* (bk)	Brocklebank	Dublin	149
1825	08	*Mary* (bg)	Wilson	Dublin	22
1825	08	*Mary* (bg)	Ainsley	Londonderry	121

In addition, one cabin passenger.

Year	Month	Vessel	Master	Departure Port	Passenger Numbers
1825	08	*New Draper* (bg)	Wilkinson	Dublin	40
1825	08	*Nottingham* (s)	Sharp	Londonderry	140
1825	08	*Rambler* (bg)	Baxter	Dublin	31
1825	08	*Vine* (bg)	Hunter	Dublin	57

Also two cabin passengers.

Year	Month	Vessel	Master	Departure Port	Passenger Numbers
1825	09	*Dublin* (bk)	Donald	Dublin	43
1825	09	*Jane* (bg)	Johnson	Sligo	43
1825	09	*John Howard* (bk)	Bruce	Cork	29
1825	09	*Spencer* (bg)	Huggup	Limerick	7
1825	09	*Trio* (bg)	Leslie	Cork	31
1825	09	*William* (bg)	Lamour	Belfast	15
1825	10	*Richard Pope* (bk)	Maloney	Belfast	17
1825	10	*Sisters* (bk)	Kerr	Dublin	17
1826	04	*Trio* (bg)	Leslie	Waterford	28
1826	05	*Aeolius* (s)	Thomas	Waterford	160
1826	05	*Amazon* (bg)	Blews	Belfast	117
1826	05	*Argyle* (bk)	Anderson	Waterford	141
1826	05	*Bolivar* (s, 385 tns)	Crosby	Belfast	270
1826	05	*City of Waterford* (s, 375 tns)	Thomas	Waterford	207
1826	05	*Dorcas Savage* (bg)	Warnock	Belfast	43
1826	05	*George IV* (bg)	Morgan	New Ross	116
1826	05	*Greenhow* (bg)	Anderson	Newry	120
1826	05	*John Howard* (bk)	Bruce	Cork	169

Year	Month	Vessel	Master	Departure Port	Passenger Numbers
1826	05	*Lord Wellington* (bk)	Freer	Newry	81
1826	05	*Mary* (bg)	Duncan	Dublin	81
1826	05	*Ocean* (bg)	Thompson	Belfast	126
Also one cabin passenger.					
1826	05	*Pacific* (bg)	Driscoll	Cork	117
1826	05	*Prince of Asturias* (bg)	Morris	Dublin	75
1826	05	*Rob Roy* (bg)	Kenn	Belfast	150
1826	05	*Royal George* (bk)	Grant	Dublin	158
1826	05	*Tottenham* (bk, 308 tns)	Keys	New Ross	172
1826	05	*Trafalgar* (bg)	Christopherson	Waterford	107
1826	05	*Volunteer* (bk)	Bell	Cork	26
Also two cabin passengers.					
1826	05	*William* (bg)	Potts	Dublin	147
1826	06	*Commerce* (bg)	Robinson	Limerick	106
1826	06	*George Bentinck* (bg)	McKenny	Limerick	91
1826	06	*Grace* (bg)	Ismay	Dublin	98
1826	06	*Green* (bg)	Mairs	Cork	41
1826	06	*Hayle* (bg)	Ramsay	Limerick	124
1826	06	*Kelton* (bk)	Brocklebank	Dublin	121
1826	06	*Letitia* (bk)	Simons	Dublin	89
1826	06	*Mary Ann* (bg)	Brown	Limerick	91
1826	06	*Rival* (bg)	Leslie	Londonderry	74
1826	06	*Rose Macroon* (bg, 175 tns)	Thomas	New Ross	91
1826	06	*Thomas* (bg)	Coffey	Dublin	113
1826	06	*Thomas* (bk)	Barfill	Cork	241
1826	06	*Thomas Farrell* (bg)	Barry	Wexford	28
1826	07	*Blossom* (bg)	Williamson	Londonderry	80
Also one cabin passenger.					
1826	07	*Combatant* (s)	Barnes	Sligo	205
1826	07	*Dublin* (s)	McClaren	Dublin	144
1826	07	*Duncan Gibb* (bk)	Evans	Dublin	197
1826	07	*Eleanor* (bg, 109 tns)	Russell	Limerick	23
Three cabin passengers also.					

Year	Month	Vessel	Master	Departure Port	Passenger Numbers
1826	07	*Eudora* (bg)	Garrick	New Ross	140
1826	07	*Fanny* (s)	Alexander	Belfast	238
1826	07	*Harrington* (bg)	Halliday	Dublin	92

Also one cabin passenger.

Year	Month	Vessel	Master	Departure Port	Passenger Numbers
1826	07	*Harrison* (s)	Carling	Londonderry	32
1826	07	*Hope* (bg)	Tomlinson	Limerick	106
1826	07	*Janes* (bg)	Johnson	Sligo	49
1826	07	*Mars* (bg)	Brown	Sligo	130
1826	07	*Mary* (s)	Wyley	Newry	29
1826	07	*Pacific* (bg)	Taylor	Belfast	109
1826	07	*Rosebank* (bg, 308 tns)	Boyd, J.	Belfast	176
1826	07	*Sarah* (bg)	Hamilton	Dublin	89
1826	07	*Tennis* (bg)	Newry	Sligo	196
1826	07	*Triton* (bg)	Douglas	Dublin	67
1826	07	*Welcome* (bg)	Kirk	Dublin	108
1826	08	*Anachron* (s)	Stonehouse	Sligo	189
1826	08	*Aurora* (bg)	Carr	Dublin	76
1826	08	*Betsy* (bg)	Bacon	Sligo	42
1826	08	*Brisk* (bg)	Hodson	Sligo	58
1826	08	*British Tar* (bg)	Merritt	Belfast	115
1826	08	*Constantia* (bg)	Richardson	Waterford	14
1826	08	*David* (bg)	Bartleman	Limerick	45
1826	08	*Eclair* (bg)	Griffith	Limerick	89
1826	08	*Friendship* (bg)	Smith	Tralee	23
1826	08	*Gales* (bg)	Lawson	Belfast	16
1826	08	*George & William* (bg)	Nicholson	Dublin	149
1826	08	*Good Intent* (bg)	Connelly	Youghall	9
1826	08	*Hero* (s)	Hart	Cork	95
1826	08	*Hibernia* (bg)	Barry	Cork	49
1826	08	*Hibernia* (bg)	Plane	Belfast	25

One cabin passenger, Rev. Smart.

Year	Month	Vessel	Master	Departure Port	Passenger Numbers
1826	08	*Hope* (bg)	Hall	Belfast	15
1826	08	*John* (bg)	Warden	Dublin	7
1826	08	*John Twizell* (bg)	Grant	Dublin	156

Year	Month	Vessel	Master	Departure Port	Passenger Numbers
1826	08	*Liberty* (bk)	Cooper	Waterford	45

Also carried Mr. Gregory and son and Miss Kingwell.

Year	Month	Vessel	Master	Departure Port	Passenger Numbers
1826	08	*Marcus Hill* (s)	Mathewson	Londonderry	48
1826	08	*Martha* (bg)	Basson	Dublin	39
1826	08	*Newcastle* (bg)	Clay	Limerick	10
1826	08	*Orion* (bg)	White	Dublin	114
1826	08	*Phillips* (bg)	Jackson	Limerick	19
1826	08	*Robert Kerr* (s)	Boyd	Belfast	155
1826	08	*Three Brothers* (bg)	Hall	Cork	139
1826	08	*Union* (bg)	Burton	Limerick	48
1826	08	*Wilson* (bg)	Simson	Belfast	119
1826	09	*Fortune* (bg)	Vaughan	Cork	21
1826	09	*Grace* (bg)	Little	Cork	52
1826	09	*John & James* (bg)	Nixon	Dublin	120
1826	09	*Peace* (bk)	Ballany	Limerick	25
1826	10	*Argyle* (bk)	Anderson	Waterford	10
1826	10	*City of Waterford* (s)	Thomas	Waterford	5
1826	10	*Greenhow* (bg)	Anderson	Newry	16
1826	10	*Mary* (bg)	Brocklebank	Dublin	23
1826	10	*Prince of Asturias* (bg)	Morris	Dublin	13
1826	10	*Rob Roy* (bg)	Kenn	Belfast	29

Also carried Mr. Sparrowhawk.

Year	Month	Vessel	Master	Departure Port	Passenger Numbers
1826	10	*Sir Watkin* (bk)	Sanderson	Belfast	43
1826	10	*Volunteer* (bk)	Thompson	Cork	19
1827	04	*Bolivar* (s)	Crosby	Belfast	229
1827	05	*Aeolius* (s)	Williams	Waterford	146
1827	05	*Albuera* (bg)	Holmes	Belfast	95
1827	05	*Champlain* (bk)	Hughes	Cork	106
1827	05	*City of Waterford* (s)	Thomas	Waterford	192
1827	05	*David* (bg)	Scotland	Cork	33
1827	05	*Duncan Gibb* (bk)	Evans	Dublin	239
1827	05	*Fidelity* (bg)	England	Cork	40
1827	05	*General Hewitt* (s)	Williams	Waterford	458
1827	05	*George IV* (bg)	Morgan	Waterford	144
1827	05	*Granicus* (bk)	Wilkie	Cork	25

Year	Month	Vessel	Master	Departure Port	Passenger Numbers
1827	05	*Greenhow* (bg)	McKie	Newry	103
1827	05	*Helena* (bk)	Currie	Dublin	153
1827	05	*Henry Brougham* (bg)	Reigh	Waterford	29
1827	05	*Heroine* (bg)	Hall	Cork	102
1827	05	*Isabella* (bg)	Morris	Limerick	130
1827	05	*John Howard* (bk)	Bruce	Cork	44
1827	05	*John Twizell* (bg)	Galley	Dublin	150
1827	05	*Lady Ridley* (s)	Scott	Dublin	200
1827	05	*Phoebe* (bg)	Finn	Youghall	39
1827	05	*Portaferry* (bg)	Donnan	Portaferry	19
1827	05	*Quebec Trader* (bk)	Halm	Dublin	147
1827	05	*Sir Watkin* (bk)	Sanderson	Belfast	117
1827	05	*Thomas Farrell* (bg)	Barry	Wexford	60
1827	05	*Tottenham* (bk)	Thomas	New Ross	150
1827	05	*Town of Ross*	Key (bk, 308 tns)	New Ross	158
1827	05	*Volunteer* (bk)	Thompson	Cork	28
1827	05	*Young Samuel* (bg)	Horsley	Dublin	116
1827	06	*Agnes* (bg, 203 tns)	Gorman	Limerick	205
1827	06	*Anglum* (bg)	Bell	Limerick	220
1827	06	*Aurora* (bg)	Carr	Sligo	132
1827	06	*Collins* (bg)	McCubbin	Limerick	205
1827	06	*Commerce* (bg)	Rees	Limerick	110
1827	06	*Dale* (bg)	McNeil	Londonderry	90
1827	06	*Earl Moira* (bg)	Allison	Belfast	249
1827	06	*Economy* (bg)	Atkinson	Dublin	121
1827	06	*Favourite* (bg)	Grey	Cork	26
1827	06	*Gilbert Henderson* (bk)	Pithy	Dublin	209

Also carried Lieut. Brown with thirty recruits for the 79th Highlanders.

Year	Month	Vessel	Master	Departure Port	Passenger Numbers
1827	06	*Harrison* (s)	Carling	Londonderry	320
1827	06	*Isabella* (bk)	Thirbeck	Dublin	227
1827	06	*John & James* (bg)	Nixon	Dublin	140
1827	06	*Martha* (bg)	Sewell	Dublin	160
1827	06	*Mary* (bg)	Ditchburn	Dublin	120
1827	06	*Mary* (bg)	Dunlop	Westport	86

Year	Month	Vessel	Master	Departure Port	Passenger Numbers
1827	06	*Nicholson* (bg)	Carr	Belfast	129
1827	06	*Peace* (bk)	Bellamy	Cork	181
1827	06	*Prince of Asturias* (bg)	Morris	Dublin	122
1827	06	*Rambler* (bg)	March	Dublin	140
1827	06	*Robert Kerr* (s)	Boyd	Belfast	250
1827	06	*Rosebank* (bg)	Boyd, J.	Belfast	300
1827	06	*Royalist* (bg)	Ashbridge	Newry	218
1827	06	*Sarah* (bg)	Witherington	Newry	112
1827	06	*Tinley* (bg)	Hall	Belfast	240
1827	06	*Ulster* (s)	Shannon	Londonderry	305
1827	06	*Veronica* (bg)	Eustace	Belfast	300
1827	06	*William Tell* (bg)	Fraser	Newry	150
1827	07	*Alcyone* (bk)	Muir	Newry	304
1827	07	*Brisk* (bg)	Coulthard	Dublin	120
1827	07	*Britannia* (bg)	Connor	Sligo	100
1827	07	*British Tar* (bg)	Bouch	Limerick	208
1827	07	*Caledonian* (bk)	Colburn	Sligo	219
1827	07	*Cyclops* (bg)	Spencer	New Ross	220
1827	07	*Diana* (bg)	McLean	Belfast	181
1827	07	*Dowson* (bk)	Tickle	Belfast	170
1827	07	*England* (bg)	Stephenson	Dublin	260
1827	07	*Enterprise* (bg)	Gordon	Drogheda	79
1827	07	*Fisher* (bg)	Wilson	Dublin	170
1827	07	*Frances Mary* (bk)	Grandy	Waterford	150
1827	07	*Grace* (bg)	Mairs	Cork	58
1827	07	*Harbinger* (bk)	Harland	Belfast	209
1827	07	*Harrington* (bg)	Halliday	Dublin	140
1827	07	*Henderson* (bg)	Steele	Sligo	90
1827	07	*Henry* (bg)	France	Dublin	121
1827	07	*Louisa* (bg)	McAdam	Dublin	180
1827	07	*Nelson Village* (bg)	Jackson	Belfast	361
1827	07	*Newcastle* (bg)	Clay	Limerick	160
1827	07	*Sarah and Marianne* (bg)	Christian, J.	Londonderry	100

Year	Month	Vessel	Master	Departure Port	Passenger Numbers
1827	07	*Thomas* (bk)	Barfill	Cork	219
1827	07	*Maria* (bg)	Lowry	Dublin	186
1827	08	*Agenoria* (bg)	Evans	Cork	36
1827	08	*Mary* (bk)	n/k	Newry	281
1827	08	*Mary Ellen* (bg)	Benn	Dublin	7
1827	08	*Volunteer* (bk)	Thompson	Cork	91
1827	08	*Wave* (bk)	Richardson	Cork	49
1827	09	*Albion* (bg)	Isaacs	Cork	20
1827	09	*Baltic Merchant* (bk)	Parry	Dublin	56
1827	09	*Betsey* (bg)	Carroll	Dublin	60
1827	09	*Brothers* (bg)	Fulton	Dublin	93
1827	09	*Canada* (bg)	Patterson	Dublin	20
1827	09	*City of Waterford* (s)	Thomas	Waterford	25
1827	09	*Dunlop* (s)	Gowan	Belfast	82
1827	09	*Fidelity* (bg)	English	Cork	16
1827	09	*Good Intent* (bg)	Edwards	Youghall	13
1827	09	*Greenhow* (bg)	McKay	Newry	49
1827	09	*Hope* (bg)	Hall	Belfast	185
1827	09	*Margaret* (bg)	Attridge	Cork	100
1827	09	*Maria* (bk)	Boyes	Waterford	66
1827	09	*Orwell* (s)	Halwell	Dublin	60
1827	09	*Queen* (bk)	Heath	Limerick	74
1827	09	*Rose Macroon* (bg)	Thomas	New Ross	76
1827	09	*Sir Watkin* (bk)	Sanderson	Belfast	20
1827	09	*Town of Ross* (bk)	Key	New Ross	15
1827	09	*Two Brothers* (bk)	McCracken	Dublin	10
1827	10	*William & George* (bk)	Brydon	Londonderry	35
1828	05	*Acadia* (bg)	Hutchinson	Dublin	74
1828	05	*Bolivar* (bk, 355 tns)	Hearn	Waterford	10
1828	05	*City of Waterford* (s)	Thomas	Waterford	30
1828	05	*Corsair* (bg)	McAlpine	Dublin	130
1828	05	*Dawson* (bk)	Boyes	Belfast	13
1828	05	*Dominica* (bk, 381 tns)	Bowman	Cork	18
1828	05	*Henry Brougham* (bg)	Wright	New Ross	110

Year	Month	Vessel	Master	Departure Port	Passenger Numbers
1828	05	*Maria* (bg)	Lowry	Cork	40
1828	05	*Newry* (bk)	Gibson	Newry	200
1828	05	*Percival* (bg)	Johnson	Dublin	80
1828	05	*Portaferry* (bg)	Donnan	Belfast	41
1828	05	*Quebec Trader* (bk)	Baker	Dublin	180
1828	05	*Rose Macroon* (bg)	Jacob	New Ross	160
1828	05	*Sir Watkin* (bk)	Sanderson	Newry	69
1828	05	*Thomas* (bg)	Coffey	Newry	44
1828	05	*Tottenham* (bk)	Spencer	New Ross	180
1828	05	*Trafalgar* (bg)	Christopherson	Limerick	17
1828	06	*Agnes* (bg)	Gorman	Limerick	216
1828	06	*Argo* (bk)	Murphy	Dundalk	40
1828	06	*Canada* (bg)	Blair	Dublin	110
1828	06	*Ceres* (bg)	Miller	Portrush	140
1828	06	*Donegal* (bg)	Heyton	Belfast	125
1828	06	*Europe* (bk)	Willis	Belfast	176
1828	06	*Favesar* (bk)	Robertson	Dublin	77
1828	06	*General Hewitt* (s)	Lee	Waterford	100
1828	06	*James* (bg)	Johnson	Sligo	140
1828	06	*John & Thomas* (s)	Gowan	Belfast	272
1828	06	*Mary* (bg)	Ditchburn	Dublin	50
1828	06	*Nicholson* (bg)	Carr	Dublin	33
1828	06	*Phillis* (bg)	Penrice	Belfast	15
1828	06	*Sally* (bg, 155 tns)	Ditchburn	Dublin	23
1828	06	*Waterloo* (s)	Rayne	Belfast	330
1828	06	*William Tell* (bg)	Farren	Newry	60
1828	07	*Baltic Merchant* (bk)	Crow	Dublin	170
1828	07	*Britannia* (bg)	Connell	Sligo	103
1828	07	*Brothers* (bk)	Robinson	Dublin	240

Also carried in the cabin Col. Forster, lady, and family.

Year	Month	Vessel	Master	Departure Port	Passenger Numbers
1828	07	*Commerce* (bg)	Rees	Limerick	120
1828	07	*Eliza Ann* (bg, 324 tns)	Burton	Belfast	196
1828	07	*Gilbert Henderson* (bk)	Pethey	Dublin	230
1828	07	*Grecian* (bg)	Atkinson	Cork	91

Year	Month	Vessel	Master	Departure Port	Passenger Numbers
1828	07	*Harrington* (bg)	Halliday	Dublin	95
1828	07	*Henry* (bg)	Fance	Newry	86
1828	07	*Lady Francis* (bg)	Barry	Newry	58
1828	07	*Latona* (bg)	Patterson	Cork	58
1828	07	*Mary* (bg)	Duncan	Dublin	158
1828	07	*Ocean* (bg)	Hall	Belfast	316
1828	07	*Ross* (bk)	Evans	Belfast	285
1828	07	*Thomas* (bk)	Carling	Cork	124
1828	07	*Ythan* (bg)	Cairns	Dublin	178

Also two cabin passengers.

Year	Month	Vessel	Master	Departure Port	Passenger Numbers
1828	08	*Andrew Nugent* (bg)	Cringle	Sligo	80
1828	08	*Brothers* (bg, 297 tns)	Young	Cork	44
1828	08	*Catherine McDonald* (bg)	Williamson	Sligo	160
1828	08	*Earl of Aberdeen* (bg, 278 tns)	Mearns, D.	Belfast	114
1828	08	*Jane* (bg)	McLean	Belfast	90
1828	08	*New Draper* (bg)	Barwise	Dublin	90

Vessel had called at St. John's, N.L., and landed forty-five settlers.

Year	Month	Vessel	Master	Departure Port	Passenger Numbers
1828	08	*Rose Macroon* (bg)	Jacob	New Ross	160
1828	08	*Thomas Warham* (bg)	Smith	Dublin	101
1828	08	*Union* (bg)	Wallace	Dublin	72
1828	09	*Fenwick* (bg)	Irvison	Limerick	15
1828	09	*Greenhow* (bg)	McKay	Newry	21
1828	09	*Hope* (bg)	Ramsden	Limerick	60
1828	09	*Priscilla* (bk)	Mitchell	Cork	8
1828	09	*Rosebank* (bg)	Boyd, J.	Belfast	115
1828	09	*Thetis* (bg)	Gorman	Limerick	26
1828	09	*Town of Ross* (bk)	Key	New Ross	15
1828	09	*Two Brothers* (bk)	McCracken	Dublin	90
1828	09	*Volunteer* (bk)	Thompson	Cork	12
1828	10	*Donegal* (bg)	Gordon	Belfast	26
1828	10	*George Canning* (bk)	Bryham	Cork	7
1828	10	*Granicus* (bk)	Martin	Cork	7
1828	10	*Hannah* (bg)	Smith	Dublin	45
1828	10	*Hugh* (bg)	Crosby	Dublin	7

Year	Month	Vessel	Master	Departure Port	Passenger Numbers
1828	10	*Sir Watkin* (bk)	Sanderson	Belfast	93
1829	05	*Albion* (bg)	Isaac	Cork	18
1829	05	*Argyle* (bk)	Dunn	New Ross	22
1829	05	*Champlain* (bk)	Hughes	Cork	85
1829	05	*Dorcas Savage* (bg)	Fitzsimmonds	Belfast	5
1829	05	*Ellen* (bk)	Henderson	Belfast	280
1829	05	*George IV* (s)	Morgan	Waterford	34
1829	05	*Good Intent* (bg)	Edwards	Youghall	83
1829	05	*Greenhow* (bg)	McKie	Newry	27
1829	05	*Henry Brougham* (bg)	Reigh	Waterford	145
1829	05	*Heroine* (bg)	Hall	Cork	172
1829	05	*Newry* (bk)	Crosby	Newry	110
1829	05	*Ocean* (bk, 367 tns)	Hearn, Joseph	Waterford	96
1829	05	*Perseus* (bk)	Jackson	Dublin	58
1829	05	*Princess Charlotte* (s, 322 tns)	Reid	Newry	44
1829	05	*Sir Watkin* (bk)	Sanderson	Belfast	164
1829	05	*Thetis* (bg)	Gorman	Limerick	130
1829	05	*Thomas Gelston* (s, 442 tns)	Laurie	Belfast	206
1829	05	*Tottenham* (bk)	Evans	New Ross	84
1829	05	*Town of Ross* (bk)	Key	New Ross	193
1829	05	*Volunteer* (bk)	Patterson	Cork	18
1829	05	*William Tell* (bg)	Farren	Newry	114
1829	05	*Ythan* (bg)	Cairns	Dublin	84
1829	06	*Aisthorpe* (bg)	Renny	Dublin	116
1829	06	*Baltic Merchant* (bk)	Crow	Dublin	55
1829	06	*Jane* (bg)	Thompson	Cork	103
1829	06	*Lady Ridley* (s)	Scott	Dublin	196
1829	06	*Triton* (bg)	Quin	Wexford	40
1829	07	*Bolivar* (s)	Cochran	Belfast	270
1829	07	*Hope* (bg)	Middleton	Dublin	184
1829	07	*Hope* (bk)	Brown	Londonderry	250
1829	07	*Majestic* (bg)	McLean	Belfast	350
1829	07	*Barbados* (bk)	Lee	Cork	200

Year	Month	Vessel	Master	Departure Port	Passenger Numbers
1829	07	*Ross* (bk)	Brown	Waterford	40
1829	07	*Sally* (bg)	Ditchburn	Dublin	32
1829	07	*Triton* (bg)	Douglas	Dublin	120
1829	08	*Alexander* (bg)	Wetherington	Dublin	75
1829	08	*Beltona* (s)	Hutchinson	Sligo	26
1829	08	*Douglas* (bg)	Malcolm	Coleraine	78
1829	08	*Hibernia* (bg)	Mahoney	Cork	65
1829	08	*James* (bg)	Johnson	Sligo	140
1829	08	*Jane* (bg)	Burke	Waterford	5
1829	08	*Jane* (s)	McLean	Belfast	304
1829	08	*John Porter* (s)	Maxwell	Dublin	41
1829	08	*Magnificent* (bg)	Tooker	Cork	102
1829	08	*Matilda* (bg)	Mitchell, Alexander	Newry	134
1829	08	*Medway* (bg)	Searchwell	Dublin	25

Mr. P. Roe and family in the cabin.

Year	Month	Vessel	Master	Departure Port	Passenger Numbers
1829	08	*Nimrod* (bk)	Agnew	Belfast	80
1829	08	*Ranger* (bk)	Harper	Belfast	290
1829	08	*Reliance* (bg)	Maguire	Belfast	32
1829	08	*Two Brothers* (bk)	McCracken	Dublin	217
1829	08	*Vista* (bg)	Mickle	Belfast	50
1829	09	*Agnes* (bg)	Gorman	Cork	9
1829	09	*City of Waterford* (s)	Thomas	Waterford	19
1829	09	*Friends* (bg)	Smith	Belfast	17
1829	09	*Good Intent* (bg)	Edwards	Youghall	17
1829	09	*Percival* (bg)	Johnson	Dublin	30
1829	09	*Princess Charlotte* (s)	Roach	Newry	10

One cabin passenger.

Year	Month	Vessel	Master	Departure Port	Passenger Numbers
1829	09	*Resolution* (bg)	Todd	Waterford	143

Departure port uncertain.

Year	Month	Vessel	Master	Departure Port	Passenger Numbers
1829	09	*Rosebank* (bg)	Boyd, J.	Belfast	56
1829	09	*Sir Watkin* (bk)	Sanderson	Belfast	52
1829	09	*Smales* (bg)	Tyres	Londonderry	13
1829	09	*Thetis* (bg)	Gorman	Limerick	42
1829	09	*Town of Ross* (bk)	Key	New Ross	23
1829	10	*Acadia* (bg)	Dervent	Dublin	4

Year	Month	Vessel	Master	Departure Port	Passenger Numbers
1829	10	*Hannah* (bg)	Campbell	Limerick	45
1829	10	*Henry Brougham* (bg)	Reigh	New Ross	18
1829	10	*Newry* (bk)	Crosby	Newry	35
1829	10	*Saladin* (bk)	Murray	Belfast	13
1829	11	*John Porter* (s)	Maxwell	Dublin	5
1830	05	*Universe* (bk)	Alexander	Belfast	40
1830	06	*Acadia* (bg)	Dervent	Dublin	250
1830	06	*Ann* (s)	Key	New Ross	177
1830	06	*Bolivar* (bk, 355 tns)	Ballard	Waterford	74
1830	06	*Canada* (bg)	Coxon	Belfast	258
1830	06	*Canada* (bg)	Wood	Dublin	140
1830	06	*Carricks* (bg)	Johnson	Londonderry	170
1830	06	*Castor* (bg)	McGilton	Youghall	139
1830	06	*Champlain* (bk)	Hughes	Cork	62
1830	06	*Dale* (bg)	McNeil	Belfast	130
1830	06	*Dorcas Savage* (bg)	Fitzsimmonds	Portaferry	44
1830	06	*Duncan Gibb* (bk)	Donnell	Dublin	200
1830	06	*Dunlop* (s)	Gowan	Belfast	297
1830	06	*Earl of Aberdeen* (bg)	Mearns, D.	Belfast	192
1830	06	*Elizabeth & Ann* (bg)	Wright	Londonderry	110
1830	06	*Enterprise* (bg)	Terry	Sligo	178
1830	06	*Fame* (bg)	Brown	Limerick	36
1830	06	*Gilbert Henderson* (bk)	Smith	Dublin	177
1830	06	*Good Intent* (bg)	Edwards	Youghall	150
1830	06	*Helen* (bk, 305 tns)	Henderson	Belfast	300
1830	06	*Henry Brougham* (bg)	Reigh	New Ross	80
1830	06	*Isabella* (bk)	Dunlop	Dublin	171
1830	06	*James* (bg)	Johnson	Sligo	150
1830	06	*Janet* (bg)	Brown	Limerick	101
1830	06	*Jessie* (bg, 339 tns)	Wilford	Belfast	200
1830	06	*John Porter* (s)	Maxwell	Dublin	142
1830	06	*Laburnum* (bg)	Brown	Dublin	180
1830	06	*Mary* (bg)	Taggart	Dublin	112
1830	06	*Mayflower* (bg)	Moore	Ballyshannon	63

Year	Month	Vessel	Master	Departure Port	Passenger Numbers
1830	06	*Memnon* (bg)	Mather	Dublin	38
1830	06	*Percival* (bg)	Johnston	Dublin	90
1830	06	*Rose Macroon* (bg)	Jacob	Waterford	232
1830	06	*Saladin* (bk)	Murray	Cork	5
1830	06	*Scotia* (bg)	Miller	Limerick	94
1830	06	*Sophia* (bk)	Blake	Londonderry	289
1830	06	*Thomas Gelston* (s)	Laurie	Belfast	350
1830	06	*Transit* (bg)	Potts	Dublin	41
1830	06	*Volunteer* (bk)	Thompson	Cork	88
1830	06	*Wexford* (bk)	Barry	Wexford	131
1830	06	*William Pitt* (s)	Ogilvy	Sligo	300
1830	06	*William Tell* (bg)	Farren	Newry	228
1830	07	*Aisthorpe* (bg)	Kenny	Sligo	142
1830	07	*Brothers* (bk)	Hynes	Dublin	228
1830	07	*Cleopatra* (bg)	Hewitt	Dublin	117
1830	07	*Frances Peabody* (bk)	Mock	Newry	241
1830	07	*Itinerant* (bg)	Nicholson	Belfast	120
1830	07	*Jane* (s)	Warnock	Belfast	100

Vessel had called at Miramichi with passengers in poor condition.

Year	Month	Vessel	Master	Departure Port	Passenger Numbers
1830	07	*Mary* (bg)	Brown	Sligo	110
1830	07	*Sally* (bg)	Ditchburn	Dublin	156
1830	07	*Tarbolton* (bg)	O'Hagan	Newry	170
1830	08	*Albion* (bg)	Isaacs	Cork	129
1830	08	*Brilliant* (bg)	Simpkins	Cork	120
1830	08	*Britannia* (bg)	Kelk	Youghall	24
1830	08	*Cyclops* (bg)	Cochran	Sligo	182
1830	08	*Hebron* (bk)	Wray	Dublin	176
1830	08	*Hope* (bg)	Turner	Dublin	89
1830	08	*James Hamilton* (bg)	Wilson	Dublin	76
1830	08	*John* (bg)	Gray	Belfast	150
1830	08	*Prince Leopold* (bg)	Richardson	Dublin	180
1830	08	*Rosebank* (bg)	Boyd, J.	Belfast	268
1830	08	*Scipio* (bg)	Cowan	Dublin	110
1830	08	*Two Brothers* (bk)	Evans	Dublin	280

Passengers were poor emigrants who were found work by Buchanan.

Year	Month	Vessel	Master	Departure Port	Passenger Numbers
1830	08	*Wilkinson* (bg)	Roper	Belfast	130
1830	09	*Atlantic* (bg)	McFarlane	Belfast	314
1830	09	*Hibernia* (bg)	Sullivan	Cork	25
1830	09	*Ross* (bk)	Hunter	Londonderry	70
1830	10	*Castlereagh* (bk)	Coates	Dublin	26
1830	10	*Earl of Aberdeen* (bg)	Mearns, D.	Belfast	48
1830	10	*Hope* (bg)	Middleton	Dublin	10
1831	05	*Agenoria* (bg)	Hardcastle	New Ross	243
1831	05	*Ajax* (bk)	Sims	Cork	209
1831	05	*Ann* (bk)	Key	New Ross	200
1831	05	*Argo* (bg)	Potts	Sligo	162
1831	05	*Barbados* (bk)	Evans	Dublin	229
1831	05	*Blakiston* (bg, 204 tns)	Molloy	Galway	112
1831	05	*Bolivar* (bk)	Ballard	Waterford	170
1831	05	*Bolivar* (s)	Dorman	Belfast	353
1831	05	*Bowes* (bg)	Johnson	Londonderry	228
1831	05	*Breeze* (bg)	Gorman	Limerick	252
1831	05	*Briton* (bk)	Baxter	Dublin	249
1831	05	*Cambrian* (bg)	Grayson	Ballina	177
1831	05	*Carricks* (bg)	Potts	Dublin	170
1831	05	*Castlereagh* (bk)	Coates	Dublin	216
1831	05	*Castor* (bg)	McGelton	Youghall	139
1831	05	*City of Waterford* (s)	Morgan, John	Waterford	150
1831	05	*Dale* (bg)	McNichol	Sligo	114
1831	05	*Earl of Aberdeen* (bg)	Mearns, D.	Belfast	217
1831	05	*Elizabeth Robertson* (s)	Gudd	Belfast	260
1831	05	*Fletcher* (bk)	Gregg	Belfast	288
1831	05	*Good Intent* (bg)	Davies	Youghall	63
1831	05	*Grace* (bg)	Martin	Limerick	120
1831	05	*Greenhow* (bg)	Aiken	Newry	172
1831	05	*Helen* (bk)	Henderson	Belfast	250
1831	05	*Hero* (bg)	Wilson	Strangford	100
1831	05	*Hibernia* (s)	Lamb	Dublin	256
1831	05	*Industry* (bk)	Lodge	Limerick	258

Year	Month	Vessel	Master	Departure Port	Passenger Numbers
1831	05	*James* (bg)	Johnson	Sligo	150
1831	05	*Jane* (s)	Warnock	Belfast	326
1831	05	*Jessie* (bg)	Wilford	Belfast	320
1831	05	*John Campbell* (bk)	Patterson	Cork	230
1831	05	*John Porter* (s)	Gadin	Dublin	269

Also Mr. Hamilton and Mr. Dunford as cabin passengers.

Year	Month	Vessel	Master	Departure Port	Passenger Numbers
1831	05	*Mars* (bg)	Watt	Belfast	240
1831	05	*Nicholson* (bg)	n/k	Belfast	147
1831	05	*Ocean* (bk)	Hearn, Joseph	Waterford	77
1831	05	*Pallas* (bk)	Campion	Cork	210
1831	05	*Pilgrim* (bg)	Small	Newry	150
1831	05	*Pons Aeli* (bk, 315 tns)	Calender	Cork	233
1831	05	*Princess Charlotte* (s)	Roach	Newry	266
1831	05	*Quintin Leitch* (s, 485 tns)	McKay, Adam	Newry	382
1831	05	*Sisters* (bg)	Pitt	Dublin	163
1831	05	*Thetis* (bg)	Outerbridge	Limerick	216
1831	05	*Thomas* (bg)	Coffey	Sligo	110
1831	05	*Tottenham* (bk)	Cornforth	New Ross	256
1831	05	*Town of Ross* (bk)	Evans	New Ross	250
1831	05	*Transit* (bg)	Potts	Dublin	117
1831	05	*Volunteer* (bk)	Thompson	Cork	200
1831	05	*William Tell* (bg)	Farren	Newry	191
1831	05	*Wilton* (bg)	Purdy	Sligo	130
1831	05	*Zetes* (bk)	Briton	Belfast	253
1831	06	*Agnes* (bg)	Gorman	Limerick	180
1831	06	*Aisthorpe* (bg)	Renny	Killala	161
1831	06	*Andrew Nugent* (bg)	Cringle	Sligo	130
1831	06	*Brown* (bg)	Jackson	Westport	153
1831	06	*Canada* (bg)	Wood	Sligo	163
1831	06	*Chance* (bg)	Horgrave	Belfast	159
1831	06	*Chillas* (bg)	Fearon	Dublin	132
1831	06	*Derwent* (bg)	Golded	Sligo	190
1831	06	*Dorothy* (s)	Deerness, John	Londonderry	379

Plus at least six cabin passengers.

Year	Month	Vessel	Master	Departure Port	Passenger Numbers
1831	06	Eleanor (bg)	Reid	Dublin	266
1831	06	Eleanor (bg)	Potts	Sligo	145
1831	06	Elizabeth (bg)	Windsor	Dublin	180
1831	06	Felicity (bg)	Miller	Limerick	130
1831	06	Fisher (bg)	Kay	Belfast	129
1831	06	George Wilkinson (s)	Yeoman	Belfast	367
1831	06	Granger (bg)	Blenkinsop	Belfast	268
1831	06	Henry Brougham (bg)	Connelly	New Ross	180
1831	06	Hope (bg)	Grey	Dublin	188
1831	06	Hope (bg)	Colgin	Belfast	110
1831	06	Huntley (s)	Hess	Londonderry	297
1831	06	Iphigenia (bg)	Bird	Dublin	222
1831	06	James Bailey (s)	Jackson	Belfast	245
1831	06	Jane (bg)	Barwise	Sligo	143
1831	06	John (bg)	Thomas	Belfast	250
1831	06	Kent (bg)	Stirling	Londonderry	200
1831	06	Lady Digby (bk)	Jefferson	Sligo	311
1831	06	Lady Stewart	n/k	Dublin	167
1831	06	Liza Ann	Hall	Cork	362
1831	06	Mayflower (bg)	Moore	Ballyshannon	110
1831	06	Pomona (bg, 306 tns)	Brown	Dublin	242

Mr. & Mrs. Carrol, cabin passengers.

Year	Month	Vessel	Master	Departure Port	Passenger Numbers
1831	06	Robert (bg)	Blake	Belfast	157
1831	06	Sally (bg)	Ditchburn	Dublin	160
1831	06	Samuel (bg)	McGhee	Belfast	128
1831	06	Sophia (bk)	Blake	Londonderry	267
1831	06	Speculation (bg)	Brehault	Sligo	130
1831	06	Symmetry (bg)	Dale	Londonderry	290
1831	06	Thomas Gelston (s)	Laurie	Belfast	377
1831	06	Tinley (bg)	Wright	Limerick	214
1831	06	Ulster (s)	n/k	Londonderry	505
1831	07	Belle Isle (bg)	Biglands	Belfast	142
1831	07	Belsay Castle (bg)	Richardson	Sligo	167
1831	07	Bettock (bg)	Hunter	Dublin	140

Year	Month	Vessel	Master	Departure Port	Passenger Numbers
1831	07	*Brutus* (bk)	Griffith	Cork	283
1831	07	*Catherine* (bk)	Reid	Sligo	206
1831	07	*Jamaica Packet* (bg)	n/k	Dublin	139
1831	07	*Kingston* (bk)	Fleck	Waterford	407
1831	07	*Manly* (bg)	Thompson	Sligo	159
1831	07	*Mary* (bg)	Mona	Dublin	188
1831	07	*Mary* (bg)	Hudson	Dublin	115
1831	07	*Medway* (bg)	Tomlinson	Westport	186
1831	07	*New Draper* (bg)	Barwise	Dublin	121
1831	07	*Nicholson* (bg)	Craig	Dublin	129
1831	07	*Penelope* (bg)	Anderson	Newry	346
1831	07	*Prince of Wales* (bg)	Little	Dublin	88
1831	07	*Rosebank* (bg)	Boyd, J.	Belfast	314
1831	07	*Thomas Tyson* (bg)	Stockdale	Westport	147
1831	07	*Tom* (bg, 165 tns)	Coulthard	Dublin	141
1831	07	*Union* (bg)	Tweedie	Tralee	92
1831	08	*Brunswick* (s)	Blake	Londonderry	315
1831	08	*Horsley Hill* (bg)	Hunter	New Ross	125
1831	08	*Margaret Johnson* (bk)	Sowry	Belfast	336
1831	08	*Nelson Village* (bg)	Kenn	Belfast	354
1831	08	*Priscilla* (bk)	Mitchell	Limerick	116
1831	08	*Sarah* (bg)	Plane	Belfast	200
1831	08	*Ant* (bg)	Sheridan	Dublin	117
1832	05	*Agenoria* (bg)	Hardcastle	New Ross	121
1832	05	*Albion* (bg)	Isaacs	Cork	74
1832	05	*Argus* (bg)	Potts	Sligo	122
1832	05	*Betsy Miller* (bg)	Allan	Belfast	124
1832	05	*Bolivar* (s)	Dorman	Belfast	279
1832	05	*Breeze* (bg, 322 tns)	Gorman	Limerick	274
1832	05	*Catherine* (bg)	Clarke	Newry	157
1832	05	*Clyde* (bg)	Hall	Belfast	280
1832	05	*Constitution* (bg)	Cragg	Belfast	106
1832	05	*Dale* (bg)	McNichol	Sligo	133
1832	05	*Dominica* (bk)	Bowman	Cork	60

Year	Month	Vessel	Master	Departure Port	Passenger Numbers
1832	05	*Earl of Aberdeen* (bg)	Mearns, D.	Belfast	270
1832	05	*Eleanor* (bg)	Potts	Dublin	137
1832	05	*Emma* (bg)	Loller	New Ross	256

Voyage started at Aberdeen. Vessel called at New Ross to collect passengers.

Year	Month	Vessel	Master	Departure Port	Passenger Numbers
1832	05	*Greenhow* (bg)	Hagen	Newry	179
1832	05	*Harvey* (bk)	Jordieson	Limerick	245
1832	05	*Hebron* (bk)	O'Hara	Dublin	n/k

Thirty-two deaths (men, women, and children) occurred during the crossing — not believed to have been from cholera. No sick on board at Grosse Île.

Year	Month	Vessel	Master	Departure Port	Passenger Numbers
1832	05	*Henderson* (bg)	Parke	Dublin	138
1832	05	*Lancaster* (bg)	Creighton	Dublin	202
1832	05	*Martha* (bg)	Sewell	Limerick	171
1832	05	*Mary* (bg)	Watt	Belfast	205
1832	05	*Mary Ann* (bk)	Laidler	Londonderry	252
1832	05	*Princess Charlotte* (s)	Roach	Newry	270
1832	05	*Priscilla* (bk)	Havelock	Limerick	91
1832	05	*Quintin Leitch* (s, 485 tns)	McKay, Adam	Newry	396
1832	05	*Recovery* (bg)	Murphy	Waterford	152
1832	05	*Shannon* (bg)	Thompson	Dublin	226
1832	05	*Sophia* (bk)	Blake	Londonderry	300
1832	05	*Swan* (bg)	Lamb	Belfast	57
1832	05	*Town of Ross* (bk)	Evans	New Ross	105
1832	05	*Volunteer* (bk)	Thompson	Cork	247
1832	06	*Agnes* (bg)	Outerbridge	Limerick	169
1832	06	*Aisthorpe* (bg)	Rinner	Dublin	160
1832	06	*Albion* (bg)	Dugget	Belfast	156
1832	06	*Alexis* (bg)	Vaughan	Galway	99
1832	06	*Andrew Nugent* (bg)	Cringle	Sligo	120
1832	06	*Ann* (bk)	Key	New Ross	125
1832	06	*Argus* (bg)	Kirkhough	Belfast	130
1832	06	*Astrea* (bg)	Park	Belfast	165
1832	06	*Avon* (bg)	Nicholson	Belfast	228
1832	06	*Barbados* (bk)	Lee	Cork	127
1832	06	*Bellona* (bk)	Storey	Dublin	296

Year	Month	Vessel	Master	Departure Port	Passenger Numbers
1832	06	*Betsey* (bg)	Mearn	Dublin	131
1832	06	*Blakiston* (bg, 204 tns)	Esdale	Galway	162
1832	06	*Brown* (bg)	Jackson	Westport	189
1832	06	*Canada* (bg)	Carson	Belfast	260
1832	06	*Carricks* (bg)	Hudson, James	Dublin	135
1832	06	*Dalusia* (bg)	Parnell	Dublin	167
1832	06	*Daniel O'Connell*	Rittie	Donegal	113

For the passenger list see theshipslist.com.

Year	Month	Vessel	Master	Departure Port	Passenger Numbers
1832	06	*Deveron* (bg)	Day	Londonderry	255
1832	06	*Eliza Ann* (bg)	Clark	Sligo	233
1832	06	*Europa* (bk)	Noble	Sligo	371

Several passengers were sick with small pox on their arrival.

Year	Month	Vessel	Master	Departure Port	Passenger Numbers
1832	06	*George & Thomas* (bk)	Dowling	Dublin	245

Captain was thanked by passengers for his kindness and attention. (*Quebec Mercury*, June 28, 1832).

Year	Month	Vessel	Master	Departure Port	Passenger Numbers
1832	06	*Grace* (bg)	Tennyson	Sligo	163
1832	06	*Grace* (bg)	Martin	Sligo	150
1832	06	*Herald* (bk)	Hunter	Belfast	300
1832	06	*Hero* (bg)	Wilson	Strangford	182
1832	06	*Iphigenia* (bg)	Bird	Baltimore	184
1832	06	*Isabella* (bg)	Morris	Drogheda	90
1832	06	*Jane* (bg)	Dunn	Sligo	272
1832	06	*Latona* (bg)	Patterson	Belfast	245
1832	06	*Leslie Galt* (bg)	Donaldson	Belfast	171
1832	06	*Lord Brougham* (bg)	Watt	Sligo	178
1832	06	*Mary* (bg)	Brown	Sligo	103
1832	06	*Ocean* (bk)	Hearn, Joseph	Waterford	271
1832	06	*Pomona* (bg)	Brown	Dublin	230
1832	06	*Pan Moor* (bg)	Grey	Cork	36
1832	06	*Ranger* (bk)	Day	Waterford	120
1832	06	*Robert* (bg)	Lake	Dublin	136
1832	06	*Robert McWilliams* (bg)	Jackson	Cork	250
1832	06	*Sarah* (bg)	Tweedie	Limerick	108
1832	06	*Scipio* (bg)	Cowan	Dublin	165
1832	06	*Stamper* (bg)	Seckers	Sligo	163

Year	Month	Vessel	Master	Departure Port	Passenger Numbers
1832	06	*Susan* (bk)	Crawford	Belfast	162
1832	06	*Symmetry* (bg)	Dale	Londonderry	260
1832	06	*Tarbolton* (bg)	Thompson	Newry	10
1832	06	*Thomas Gelston* (s)	Laurie	Belfast	379
1832	06	*Thomas Tyson* (bg)	Wyley	Westport	138
1832	06	*Tottenham* (bk)	Cornforth	New Ross	60
1832	06	*Wexford* (bk)	Barry	Wexford	150
1832	06	*Wilkinson* (bg)	Westray	Belfast	212
1832	06	*William Tell* (bg)	Farren	Newry	195
1832	07	*Acteon* (bg)	Grayden	Sligo	215
1832	07	*Albury* (bk)	Rodgers	Belfast	294
1832	07	*Ann & Mary* (sr)	Lloyd	Cork	150
1832	07	*Baltic Merchant* (bk)	Crow	Dublin	195
1832	07	*Belsay Castle* (bg)	Davies	Sligo	194
1832	07	*Constantine* (bg)	Barry	Galway	164
1832	07	*Duncan Gibb* (bk)	Donald	Dublin	280
1832	07	*Elizabeth* (bg)	Winder	Sligo	152
1832	07	*Emblem* (bg)	Tordy	Dublin	n/k
1832	07	*Fanny* (bg)	Bowson	Belfast	332

There were twenty-seven deaths during the passage.

Year	Month	Vessel	Master	Departure Port	Passenger Numbers
1832	07	*Fidelity* (bg)	English	Dublin	257
1832	07	*Garland* (bg)	Forbes	Sligo	214
1832	07	*Jean* (sr)	Gorman	Limerick	155
1832	07	*John* (bg)	Hall	Dublin	276
1832	07	*John & Mary* (bg)	White	Dublin	245
1832	07	*John Pedder* (bg)	Atkinson	Cork	131
1832	07	*Mary* (bg)	Morris	Dublin	134
1832	07	*Robert Kerr* (s)	Boyd	Belfast	324
1832	07	*Royalist* (bg)	McKie	Belfast	185
1832	07	*Salamis* (bg)	Royal	Limerick	256
1832	08	*Alchymist* (bg)	Smith	Dublin	197
1832	08	*Anna* (bg)	Taggart	Dublin	161
1832	08	*Brothers* (bk)	Kirk	Dublin	272
1832	08	*Dorothy* (bg)	Crosley	Belfast	190
1832	08	*Elizabeth* (s)	Miller	Dublin	105

Year	Month	Vessel	Master	Departure Port	Passenger Numbers
1832	08	*Hibernia* (s)	Smith	Dublin	349
1832	08	*Horsley Hill* (bg)	Hunter	New Ross	141
Vessel also called at Waterford.					
1832	08	*John & Thomas* (bk)	Jones	Belfast	309
1832	08	*Lord Wellington* (bk)	Collaton	New Ross	167
1832	08	*Manly* (bg)	Dobson	Sligo	109
1832	08	*Margaret Johnson* (bk)	Sowry	Belfast	215
1832	08	*Margaret Miller* (bg)	Kenn	Belfast	222
1832	08	*Mary* (bg)	Hutchinson	Dublin	161
1832	08	*Matura* (bg)	Crott	Belfast	190
Captain was commended by passengers.					
1832	08	*Pons Aeli* (bk)	n/k	Cork	92
1832	08	*Rising Sun* (bg)	Parker	Belfast	46
1832	08	*Trial* (bg)	Moore	Londonderry	116
1832	08	*Victoria* (bk)	Mitchell	Cork	118
1832	08	*William* (bg)	Phillips	Cork	28
1832	09	*Ann* (bg)	Ross	Dublin	36
1832	09	*Annandale* (bg)	Anderson	Dublin	55
1832	09	*Gilbert Henderson* (bk)	Robinson	Dublin	80
1832	09	*Granger* (bg)	Blenkinsop	Londonderry	252
1832	09	*Jessie* (bg)	Wilford	Belfast	207
1832	09	*Pallas* (bk)	Hall	Cork	87
1832	09	*William Booth* (bk)	Lindsay	Belfast	225
1832	10	*Dunlop* (s)	Gowan	Belfast	60
1832	10	*Earl of Aberdeen* (bg)	Mearns, D.	Belfast	24
1832	10	*Eliza Ann* (bg)	Dagerville	Cork	17
1832	10	*Ocean* (bk)	Hearn, Joseph	Waterford	4
1832	10	*Pomona* (bg)	Brown	Dublin	29
1832	10	*Princess Charlotte* (s)	Roach	Newry	37
1832	10	*Sarah* (bg)	Tweedie	Tralee	12
1832	10	*Thomas* (s)	Duncan	Dublin	150
1832	10	*Town of Ross* (bk)	Evans	New Ross	83
1832	10	*Volunteer* (bk)	Thompson	Cork	10
1834	05	*Aid* (bk)	Johnson	Dublin	238
1834	05	*Aisthorpe* (bg)	Renny	Dublin	156

Year	Month	Vessel	Master	Departure Port	Passenger Numbers
1834	05	*Albion* (bg)	Padden	Limerick	182
1834	05	*Ann* (bk)	Key	New Ross	63

Also thirteen cabin passengers.

Year	Month	Vessel	Master	Departure Port	Passenger Numbers
1834	05	*Argyle* (bk)	Baldwin	Waterford	15
1834	05	*Ariadne* (s)	Conn	Londonderry	260
1834	05	*Astra* (bg, 227 tns)	Fitzsimmonds	Belfast	52
1834	05	*Bolivar* (bk)	Ballard	Waterford	39
1834	05	*Bowes* (bg)	Johnson	Londonderry	28
1834	05	*Brutus* (bk)	Scott	Cork	313

There were five deaths on the *Brutus* during the voyage. Three were from typhus.

Year	Month	Vessel	Master	Departure Port	Passenger Numbers
1834	05	*Canada* (bg)	Coxon	Belfast	238
1834	05	*Champlain* (bk)	Newman	Cork	219
1834	05	*City of Waterford* (s)	Grandy	Waterford	310
1834	05	*Dominica* (bk)	Bowman	Cork	185
1834	05	*Eleanor* (bg)	Wilson	Belfast	64
1834	05	*Emerald* (bg)	Todd	Dublin	262
1834	05	*Friends* (bk)	Duncan	Dublin	279

Also six cabin passengers and their children.

Year	Month	Vessel	Master	Departure Port	Passenger Numbers
1834	05	*Governor Douglas* (bk)	Mark	Cork	174
1834	05	*Grace* (bg)	Forrest	Cork	172
1834	05	*Helen* (bk)	Mearns, D.	Belfast	95

Also ten cabin passengers.

Year	Month	Vessel	Master	Departure Port	Passenger Numbers
1834	05	*John Thomas* (bk)	Peterson	Belfast	50
1834	05	*Loyal Briton* (bg)	Watson	Dublin	235
1834	05	*Malvina* (bk)	Crocket	Newry	290
1834	05	*Maria* (bg)	Hewitt	Tralee	204

Also five cabin passengers. There was one death from typhus on the journey.

Year	Month	Vessel	Master	Departure Port	Passenger Numbers
1834	05	*Mentor* (bg)	Barlow	Wexford	6
1834	05	*Mercury* (bg)	Galgey	Waterford	65

Also carried twenty-seven settlers from the wreck of the brig *Isabella*.

Year	Month	Vessel	Master	Departure Port	Passenger Numbers
1834	05	*Ocean* (bk)	Hearn, Joseph	Waterford	171

Also three cabin passengers.

Year	Month	Vessel	Master	Departure Port	Passenger Numbers
1834	05	*Onondago* (s)	Morgan	Waterford	208
1834	05	*Penelope* (bg, 314 tns)	Edwards	Youghall	203

There were six deaths on the journey. Five from typhus.

Year	Month	Vessel	Master	Departure Port	Passenger Numbers
1834	05	*Pomona* (bg)	Stevens	Dublin	244

Year	Month	Vessel	Master	Departure Port	Passenger Numbers
1834	05	*Priscilla* (bk)	Isaac	Limerick	331
There was one death from typhus on the journey.					
1834	05	*Recovery* (bg)	Sunkins	Youghall	213
There were three deaths during the voyage.					
1834	05	*Robert McWilliam* (bg)	Williamson	Cork	190
1834	05	*Thetis* (bg)	n/k	Limerick	217
1834	05	*Triton* (s)	McLean	Newry	290
Also two cabin passengers plus children and servants.					
1834	05	*William Tell* (bg)	Farren	Newry	221
1834	06	*Active* (s)	Robson	Londonderry	281
Also four cabin passengers.					
1834	06	*Ardgown* (bg)	n/k	Belfast	160
1834	06	*Argo* (bg)	Thompson	Sligo	193
1834	06	*Brilliant* (bg)	Norton	Cork	108
1834	06	*Constantia* (bg)	n/k	Limerick	170
1834	06	*Derwent* (bg)	Purdy	Sligo	226
1834	06	*Earl of Aberdeen* (bg)	Mearns, D.	Belfast	209
1834	06	*Elizabeth & Sarah* (bk)	Patterson	Dublin	200
1834	06	*Henderson* (bg)	n/k	Dublin	110
1834	06	*Home* (bg)	Cawell	Dublin	274
1834	06	*Industry* (bg, 196 tns)	McCappin	Belfast	123
1834	06	*Lancer* (bg)	Thompson	Londonderry	222
1834	06	*Lord Goderich* (bk)	Hopper	Belfast	316
1834	06	*Mary* (bk)	Deaver, Henry	Cork	218
Eighty-one of the passengers were left at Grosse Île.					
1834	06	*New Prospect* (bk)	Knox	Dublin	334
There were five deaths from typhus on the journey.					
1834	06	*Old Maid* (bg)	n/k	Dublin	137
1834	06	*Regalia* (bg)	Box	Londonderry	306
1834	06	*Richardson* (bg)	McVennon	Sligo	218
1834	06	*Rose Macroon* (bg)	Thomas	New Ross	87
1834	06	*Scipio* (bg)	Cowan	Dublin	125
1834	06	*Tom* (bg)	Coulthard	Dublin	140
1834	06	*Union* (bg)	Taylor	Dublin	169
1834	06	*William & Anne* (bg)	Patterson	Dublin	212
There was one death of typhus on the journey.					

Year	Month	Vessel	Master	Departure Port	Passenger Numbers
1834	06	*William Tell* (bg)	Farren	Newry	221

A one-year-old child died from variola on the voyage.

Year	Month	Vessel	Master	Departure Port	Passenger Numbers
1834	07	*Andrew Nugent* (bg)	Cringle	Sligo	164
1834	07	*Avon* (bg)	Nicholson	Belfast	199
1834	07	*Bettock* (bg)	Hunter	Dublin	110
1834	07	*Dale* (bg)	McNeil	Sligo	154
1834	07	*Douglas* (bg)	Custard	Westport	221
1834	07	*Glenora* (bg)	Cousins	Cork	119
1834	07	*Hawkesbury* (bk, 410 tns)	Smith	Belfast	400
1834	07	*Hope* (bk)	White	Sligo	347
1834	07	*Jane* (bg)	Irwin	Newry	149
1834	07	*John* (bg)	Hall	Dublin	216

Also three cabin passengers.

Year	Month	Vessel	Master	Departure Port	Passenger Numbers
1834	07	*Marmaduke* (bg)	Mason	Belfast	217
1834	07	*Margaret* (bg)	Rankin	Ballyshannon	110
1834	07	*Mary* (bg)	Scott	Waterford	8
1834	07	*Shubenacadie* (bg)	Cullin	Wexford	17
1834	07	*Susan* (bk)	Crawford	Belfast	138
1834	07	*Thomas Gelston* (s)	Laurie	Londonderry	317

There were two deaths on the voyage. One caused by cholera, the other by typhus. Passengers complained that they did not receive adequate provisions and water and that there was considerable overcrowding (*Montreal Gazette*, Aug. 1, 1834).

Year	Month	Vessel	Master	Departure Port	Passenger Numbers
1834	07	*Tottenham* (bk)	Cornforth	New Ross	113
1834	07	*Trio* (bg)	Carr	Dublin	134
1834	07	*Welcome* (bg)	Davies	Dublin	5

Also three cabin passengers plus children.

Year	Month	Vessel	Master	Departure Port	Passenger Numbers
1834	07	*Weser* (bg)	Taylor	Sligo	246
1834	08	*Agnes* (bg)	Outerbridge	Limerick	61
1834	08	*Belsay Castle* (bg)	Richardson	Sligo	211
1834	08	*Bob Logic* (bg)	n/k	Cork	48
1834	08	*Breeze* (bg)	Gorman	Limerick	29

Captain was commended by passengers — "proof of this gentleman's well-earned popularity" (*Quebec Mercury*).

Year	Month	Vessel	Master	Departure Port	Passenger Numbers
1834	08	*Consbrook* (s)	Bristow	Belfast	71
1834	08	*Countryman* (bg)	Douglas	Sligo	154
1834	08	*Feronia* (bg)	Newman	Limerick	92

Year	Month	Vessel	Master	Departure Port	Passenger Numbers
1834	08	*George* (sr)	Brown	Cork	29
1834	08	*Guardiana*	Yule	Belfast	186
1834	08	*Hannah* (sr)	n/k	Cork	49
1834	08	*Hebron* (bk)	Higginson	Dublin	121
1834	08	*Mayflower* (bg)	Brunt	Ballyshannon	44
1834	08	*Naparina* (bk)	Anderson	Dublin	15
1834	08	*Sisters* (bg)	Dryden	Londonderry	22
1834	08	*Warner* (bg)	Crawford	Belfast	143

There were two deaths during the voyage.

Year	Month	Vessel	Master	Departure Port	Passenger Numbers
1834	08	*William Herdman* (s)	n/k	Belfast	283

The *William Herdman* arrived at Grosse Île July 21–23 and 155 persons were admitted to hospital, of whom about one-third died. The vessel was held in quarantine until mid-August.

Year	Month	Vessel	Master	Departure Port	Passenger Numbers
1834	09	*Ann* (bk)	Key	New Ross	16
1834	09	*Bolivar* (bk)	Ballard	Waterford	10
1834	09	*Edward Charlton* (bg)	Morrison	Dublin	174

The vessel was detained at Grosse Île for thirty-five days. Of fifty-five persons admitted to the hospital, there were more than twenty-five deaths, mostly from cholera.

Year	Month	Vessel	Master	Departure Port	Passenger Numbers
1834	09	*Helen* (bk)	Mearns, D.	Belfast	162
1834	09	*Lochiel* (bg)	Hughes	Cork	34

Also one cabin passenger.

Year	Month	Vessel	Master	Departure Port	Passenger Numbers
1834	09	*Sarah & Margaret* (bg)	Molloy	Galway	12
1834	09	*Transit* (bg)	Potts	Dublin	36
1834	09	*Tryagain* (bk, 291)	Heacock	Cork	29
1835	05	*Barbados* (bk)	Lee	Cork	200
1835	05	*Bryan Abbs* (bg)	Gorman	Limerick	70
1835	05	*Champlain* (bk)	Newman	Cork	115
1835	05	*City of Waterford* (s)	Grandy	Waterford	141
1835	05	*Dorchester* (s)	McLean	Newry	42
1835	05	*John Bell* (s)	Black	Waterford	20
1835	05	*John Esdale* (bg)	Wright	Cork	25
1835	05	*John Thomas* (bk)	Patterson	Belfast	18
1835	05	*Ocean* (bk)	Hearn, Joseph	Waterford	32
1835	05	*Onondago* (s)	Morgan	Waterford	39

Also three cabin passengers.

Year	Month	Vessel	Master	Departure Port	Passenger Numbers
1835	05	*Penelope* (bg)	Edwards	Youghall	63
1835	05	*Pomona* (bg)	Stevens	Dublin	140

Year	Month	Vessel	Master	Departure Port	Passenger Numbers
1835	05	*Princess Charlotte* (s)	Roach	Newry	28
1835	05	*Thomas Carty* (bk)	Kelly	Dublin	42
1835	05	*William Tell* (bg)	Farren	Newry	114
1835	06	*Albion* (bg)	Padden	Cork	126

Also seven cabin passengers and their six children.

Year	Month	Vessel	Master	Departure Port	Passenger Numbers
1835	06	*Andrew Nugent* (bg)	Cringle	Sligo	151
1835	06	*Betty* (bg)	Sewell	Dublin	126
1835	06	*British Heroine* (s)	Shield	Newry	169
1835	06	*Camilla* (bg)	Simpson	Belfast	55
1835	06	*Eleanor* (bg)	Donaldson	Belfast	38
1835	06	*Eliza Ann* (bg)	Hyde	Cork	33
1835	06	*Elizabeth* (bg)	Grave	Dublin	128

Also two cabin passengers.

Year	Month	Vessel	Master	Departure Port	Passenger Numbers
1835	06	*Elizabeth Clark* (bg)	Alder	Limerick	6
1835	06	*Friends* (bk)	Duncan	Dublin	97

Also one cabin passenger.

Year	Month	Vessel	Master	Departure Port	Passenger Numbers
1835	06	*Helen* (bk)	Mearns, D.	Belfast	280
1835	06	*Industry* (bg)	Lennox	Belfast	60
1835	06	*Mercury* (bg)	Doyle	Waterford	2
1835	06	*Nestor* (bk)	Clanes	Cork	5
1835	06	*Thomas Gelston* (s)	n/k	Belfast	49
1835	06	*Thomas Tyson* (bg)	Wyley	Westport	111
1835	06	*Trade* (bg)	Mosey	Dublin	24
1835	06	*Wexford* (bk)	Quin	Limerick	40
1835	07	*Argo* (bg)	George	Sligo	180
1835	07	*Astrea* (bg)	Neill	Belfast	67

Also one cabin passenger.

Year	Month	Vessel	Master	Departure Port	Passenger Numbers
1835	07	*Ceres* (bk)	Dempsey	Sligo	158
1835	07	*Confidence* (bg)	Driscoll	Baltimore	99

Also one cabin passenger.

Year	Month	Vessel	Master	Departure Port	Passenger Numbers
1835	07	*Constitution* (bg)	Brown	Sligo	217
1835	07	*Dorcas Savage* (bg)	Lightbody	Belfast	158

Also one cabin passenger.

Year	Month	Vessel	Master	Departure Port	Passenger Numbers
1835	07	*Francis Spaight* (s)	Gorman	Limerick	245
1835	07	*Hawkesbury* (bk)	Smith	Londonderry	161

Also one cabin passenger.

Year	Month	Vessel	Master	Departure Port	Passenger Numbers
1835	07	*Henderson* (bg)	Southward	Dublin	132
1835	07	*Hotspur* (bg)	Steele	Sligo	167

Also two cabin passengers.

Year	Month	Vessel	Master	Departure Port	Passenger Numbers
1835	07	*Mary* (bg)	Brere	Dublin	121
1835	07	*Ocean* (bk)	Clark	Londonderry	99
1835	07	*Quintin Leitch* (s, 485 tns)	McKay, Adam	Newry	214
1835	07	*Regalia* (bg)	Barr	Londonderry	269
1835	07	*St. George* (bg)	Robinson	Cork	31

Plus nine cabin passengers and seven children.

Year	Month	Vessel	Master	Departure Port	Passenger Numbers
1835	07	*Susannah* (bg)	Daniel	Limerick	169
1835	08	*Brothers* (bk)	Potts	Dublin	31
1835	08	*Clutha* (bg)	Thomson	Belfast	74

Vessel may have called at Iona.

Year	Month	Vessel	Master	Departure Port	Passenger Numbers
1835	08	*Mary* (bk)	Deere	Cork	121
1835	09	*Argyle* (bk)	Baldwin	Waterford	11
1835	09	*Blanche* (bg)	Hughes	Donegal	4
1835	09	*Brothers* (bg)	Bartlett	Limerick	3
1835	09	*Dominica* (bk)	Bowman	Cork	16
1835	09	*Elizabeth & Ann* (bg)	Wright	Cork	11
1835	09	*John Bell* (s)	Black	New Ross	9
1835	09	*Mercury* (bg)	Doyle	Waterford	6
1835	09	*Rosebank* (bg)	Montgomery	Belfast	7
1835	10	*Eleanor* (bg)	Donald	Belfast	23
1835	10	*Eliza Ann* (bg)	Hyde	Cork	5
1835	10	*Helen* (bk)	Mearns, D.	Belfast	8
1835	10	*Industry* (bg)	Lennox	Belfast	11
1835	10	*John Esdale* (bg)	Wright	Cork	11
1835	10	*Pallas* (bk)	Hall	Cork	12
1835	10	*Trader* (bg)	Mosey	Westport	7
1835	10	*Venture* (bk)	Wilson	Belfast	7
1835	10	*William Tell* (bg)	Farren	Newry	2
1836	05	*Argyle* (bk)	Baldwin	Waterford	73
1836	05	*Belisle* (bg)	Sutherland	Dublin	112
1836	05	*Breeze* (bg)	Patterson	Limerick	199

Year	Month	Vessel	Master	Departure Port	Passenger Numbers
1836	05	Bryan Abbs (bg)	Gorman	Limerick	164
1836	05	City of Waterford (s)	Grandy	Waterford	184

Captain Grandy was presented with a silver cup by the merchants of Quebec (*Quebec Mercury*, May 21, 1836).

Year	Month	Vessel	Master	Departure Port	Passenger Numbers
1836	05	Dominica (bk)	Bowman	Cork	254
1836	05	Elizabeth & Ann (bg)	Wright	Cork	191
1836	05	Helen (bk)	Mearns, D.	Belfast	79
1836	05	John Esdale (bg)	Wright	Kinsale	50
1836	05	Margaret Balfour (bg)	Fitzsimmonds	Belfast	43
1836	05	Ocean (bk)	Bellard	Waterford	35
1836	05	Penelope (bg)	Isaac	Youghall	114
1836	05	Recovery (bg)	Sinpkin	Youghall	133
1836	05	Springhill (bk)	Auld	Dublin	175
1836	05	Tottenham (bk)	Jeffries	Waterford	15
1836	05	Urania (bk)	Clark	Cork	193
1836	05	Voyager (bk)	Wilsons	Dublin	124
1836	05	Wexford (bk)	Quin	Wexford	18
1836	06	Abercromby (bk)	Ford	Cork	281
1836	06	Abernathy (bk)	Ford	Cork	284
1836	06	Active (bk)	Robson	Waterford	153
1836	06	Aisthorpe (bg)	Swinburne	Sligo	163
1836	06	Andrew Nugent (bg)	Cringle	Sligo	119
1836	06	Argo (bg)	Greig	Sligo	154
1836	06	Barbados (bk)	Lee	Cork	213
1836	06	Belsay Castle (bg)	Richardson	Sligo	168
1836	06	Camilla (bg)	Simpson	Belfast	96
1836	06	Ceres (bk)	Dempsey	Belfast	157
1836	06	Constitution (bg)	Brown	Sligo	162
1836	06	Cornwallis (bg)	Green	Waterford	71
1836	06	Countryman (bg)	Wilson	Dublin	131
1836	06	Eleanor (bg)	Potts	Dublin	113
1836	06	Ethelbert (bg)	Campbell	Belfast	145
1836	06	Friends (bk)	Duncan	Dublin	229
1836	06	Hope (bg)	Haddart	Dublin	131
1836	06	Jane (bg)	Ashridge	Ballyshannon	109

Year	Month	Vessel	Master	Departure Port	Passenger Numbers
1836	06	*John & Mary* (bg)	Young	Cork	148
1836	06	*Medusa* (s)	Robinson	Belfast	71
1836	06	*Pomona* (bg)	Stevens	Dublin	155
1836	06	*Priscilla* (bk)	Havelock	Cork	220
1836	06	*Robert McWilliam* (bg)	n/k	Belfast	106
1836	06	*Stamper* (bg)	Scurr	Dublin	126
1836	06	*Tarbolton* (bg)	Caldwell	Londonderry	130
1836	06	*Thetis* (bg)	Scally	Limerick	122
1836	06	*Thomas* (bg)	Coffey	Baltimore	166
1836	06	*Thomas* (s)	Worthington	Cork	335
1836	06	*Thomas Green* (bg)	Donkin	Waterford	196
1836	06	*Thompson* (bg)	Burton	Sligo	177
1836	06	*Trade* (bg)	Mosey	Dublin	135
1836	06	*Triton* (bg)	Killam	Tralee	93
1836	06	*William Tell* (bg)	Farren	Newry	144
1836	07	*Agnes* (bg)	Outerbridge	Limerick	132
1836	07	*Amphion* (bg)	Little	Dublin	27
1836	07	*Ariadne* (s)	Cone	Londonderry	215
1836	07	*Blanche* (bg)	Hughes	Donegal	66
1836	07	*Ewen* (bg)	McTaggart	Londonderry	219
1836	07	*Henderson* (bg)	Simon	Sligo	113
1836	07	*Joseph Wheeler* (bg)	Pollock	Cork	123
1836	07	*Richardson* (bg)	Park	Sligo	174
1836	07	*Sir William Wallace* (bg)	Johnston	Belfast	223
1836	07	*Tiffin* (bg)	Prest	Sligo	125
1836	07	*William* (bg)	Phillips	Sligo	147
1836	08	*Duke of Clarence* (bg)	Brown	Dublin	154
1836	08	*Edward* (bg)	Pye	Cork	178
1836	08	*Eliza* (bg)	Grieves	Dublin	99
1836	08	*Nelson Village* (bg)	Rodgers	Belfast	171
1836	08	*Rochdale* (bg)	Tucker	Belfast	69
1836	08	*Rosebank* (bg)	Montgomery	Belfast	40
1836	08	*Royalist* (bg)	Ashbridge	Killala	130
1836	08	*Unity* (bg)	Hanny	Killala	103

Year	Month	Vessel	Master	Departure Port	Passenger Numbers
1836	08	*Zier* (bg)	Toft	Tralee	157
1836	09	*Argus* (bg)	Kirkhough	Sligo	53
1836	09	*Betsy Heron* (bg)	Storey	Cork	165
1836	09	*Breeze* (bg)	Patterson	Limerick	59
1836	09	*Chieftain* (bk)	Newman	Cork	64
1836	09	*Eleanor* (bg)	Wilson	Belfast	3
1836	09	*George Barclay* (bg)	Morrison	Waterford	20
1836	09	*Industry* (bg)	McKee	Belfast	7
1836	09	*Magdalen* (bg)	Nicholson	Limerick	133
1836	09	*Nancy* (sr)	Gailey	Ballyshannon	12
1836	09	*Newton* (bg)	Cordry	Waterford	11
1836	09	*Townsend* (bg)	Ablett	Galway	53
1836	09	*Tryagain* (bk)	Heacock	Cork	17
1836	10	*Helen* (bk)	Mearns, D.	Belfast	14
1836	10	*Pallas* (bk)	Hall	Cork	15
1837	05	*Argyle* (bk)	Baldwin	Waterford	147
1837	05	*Borneo* (s)	Gorman	Limerick	263
1837	05	*Bryan Abbs* (bg)	Gorman	Limerick	196
1837	05	*City of Waterford* (s)	Bennett	Waterford	51
1837	05	*Energy* (bg)	Irwin	Limerick	46
1837	05	*Favourite* (bg)	Taylor	Belfast	147
1837	05	*Helen* (bk)	Mearns, D.	Belfast	57
1837	05	*Isabella* (s, 666 tns)	Meredith	Cork	419
1837	05	*Margaret Johnson* (s)	McAuley	Belfast	151
1837	05	*Mary* (bg)	Nicholson	Newry	49
1837	05	*Pons Aeli* (bk)	Deaves	Cork	207
1837	05	*Tottenham* (bk)	Jeffries	New Ross	63

Also one cabin passenger.

Year	Month	Vessel	Master	Departure Port	Passenger Numbers
1837	05	*Urania* (bk)	Clark	Cork	196
1837	05	*Woodman* (bk)	Murphy	Belfast	59
1837	06	*Agnes* (bg)	Binch	Limerick	130
1837	06	*Aisthorpe* (bg)	Sewell	Sligo	127
1837	06	*Amity* (bg)	Leslie	Cork	199
1837	06	*Ann* (bk)	Joyce	Cork	190

Year	Month	Vessel	Master	Departure Port	Passenger Numbers
1837	06	*Argo* (bg)	Gregg	Sligo	119
1837	06	*Ariadne* (s)	Baird	Belfast	236
1837	06	*Atlantic* (bk)	Hardesbrooke	Londonderry	420
1837	06	*Barbados* (bk)	Trevis	Cork	145
1837	06	*Beluna* (bk)	Ottagan	Newry	228
1837	06	*Canada* (bg)	Young	Cork	194
1837	06	*Ceres* (bk)	Galt	Sligo	151
1837	06	*Clinton* (bk)	Dunn	Cork	236
1837	06	*Comet* (bg)	Cashman	Cork	122
1837	06	*Constitution* (bg)	McMinn	Sligo	168
1837	06	*Cornwallis* (bg)	Davies	Waterford	33
1837	06	*Donegal* (bg)	Hudson	Dublin	147
1837	06	*Elizabeth & Ann* (bg)	Wright	Baltimore	195
1837	06	*Friends* (bk)	Duncan	Dublin	217
1837	06	*Hope* (bg)	Douglas	Dublin	163
1837	06	*Ides* (bk)	Sirbunner	Cork	189
1837	06	*Indemnity* (bg)	Campbell	Cork	164

One hundred and forty-four passengers landed at the Gut of Canso. The remaining twenty came to Quebec.

Year	Month	Vessel	Master	Departure Port	Passenger Numbers
1837	06	*Kensington Garden* (bk)	Garde	Cork	106
1837	06	*Lord John Russell* (bg)	Ritchie	Baltimore	165
1837	06	*Martha* (bg)	Cowman	Sligo	127

Also two cabin passengers.

Year	Month	Vessel	Master	Departure Port	Passenger Numbers
1837	06	*Mercury* (bg)	Hags	Waterford	45
1837	06	*Penelope* (bg)	Edwards	Youghall	245
1837	06	*Prince Lebon* (bg)	Raw	Dublin	143
1837	06	*Sapphire* (bk)	Hall	Sligo	211
1837	06	*Springhill* (bk)	Auld	Dublin	218
1837	06	*Swan* (bg)	Errington	Cork	142
1837	06	*Terry* (bg)	Sharp	Sligo	185
1837	06	*Thomas Gelston* (s)	Laurie	Belfast	233
1837	06	*Tom* (bg)	Coulthard	Dublin	123
1837	06	*Transit* (bg)	Braithwaite	Dublin	150
1837	06	*Wellington* (bg)	Gillan	Dublin	45
1837	07	*Ann* (bg)	Strong	Donegal	113

Year	Month	Vessel	Master	Departure Port	Passenger Numbers
1837	07	*Belmont* (bg)	Ford	Sligo	196
1837	07	*Betsy Heron* (bg)	Scorfield	Cork	173
1837	07	*Breeze* (bg)	Murrison	Tralee	97
1837	07	*Brown* (bg)	Lamb	Sligo	125
1837	07	*Earl Selkirk* (bg)	Clark	Sligo	121
1837	07	*Gales* (bg)	Deld	Belfast	102
Also one cabin passenger.					
1837	07	*Harriet Scott* (s)	Arnold	Belfast	243
1837	07	*Hawkesbury* (bk)	Woodward	Londonderry	238
1837	07	*John* (bg)	Hill	Tralee	92
1837	07	*John & Robert* (s)	McKenzie	Belfast	352
1837	07	*Kingston* (bk)	Rutlidge	Waterford	251
1837	07	*Regalia* (bg)	Smith	Londonderry	256
1837	07	*Royal William* (bk)	Wilson	Dublin	209
1837	07	*Seymour* (bk)	Dare	Limerick	200
1837	07	*Susan* (bk)	Neil	Londonderry	117
1837	07	*Thomas* (bg)	Coffey	Dublin	141
1837	07	*Thompson* (bg)	Burton	Sligo	157
1837	07	*Triton* (bg)	Edkin	Tralee	97
1837	08	*Eleanor* (bg)	Potts	Killala	114
1837	08	*Georgian* (bg)	March	New Ross	54
1837	08	*Minerva* (bg)	Edmondson	Sligo	96
1837	08	*Naparima* (bk)	Anderson	Dublin	163
1837	08	*Ocean* (bk)	Bellard	Dublin	233
1837	08	*Warner* (bg)	Crawford	Killala	109
1837	09	*Belsay Castle* (bg)	Richardson	Sligo	97
1837	09	*Hugh* (bg)	Crosby	Dublin	67
1837	09	*Tryagain* (bk)	Heacock	Cork	6
1837	10	*Courtney* (s)	Ellis	Cork	11
1838	05	*Agitator* (bg)	Wilson	Belfast	98
1838	05	*Dominica* (bk)	Bowman	Belfast	14
1838	05	*Eliza Ann* (bg)	Hyde	Cork	54
1838	05	*Helen* (bk)	Mearns, D.	Belfast	22
1838	05	*Ocean* (bk)	Slattery	Waterford	10

Year	Month	Vessel	Master	Departure Port	Passenger Numbers
1838	06	*Argo* (bg)	Gregg	Sligo	90
1838	06	*Caroline* (bk)	Robinson	Londonderry	170
1838	06	*Ceres* (bk)	Galt	Sligo	97
1838	06	*Quintin Leitch* (s, 485 tns)	Robinson	Newry	17
1838	06	*Waterloo* Col. Wyndham's tenants.	n/k	Limerick	181
1838	06	*Westoe* (bg)	Lowery	Cork	5
1838	07	*Comet* (bg)	Benny	Cork	37
1838	08	*Borneo* (s)	Gorman	Limerick	6
1838	08	*John* (s)	Bell	New Ross	6
1838	08	*Planter* (bg)	McMahon	Belfast	13
1838	08	*Pons Aeli* (bk)	Mills	Cork	15
1838	08	*Thetis* (bg)	Scally	Limerick	59
1838	08	*Venture* (bk)	Wilson	Belfast	15
1838	09	*Carlton* (bg)	Anderson	Dublin	12
1838	09	*Eliza Ann* (bg)	Hyde	Cork	14
1838	09	*Napoleon* (s)	McAlpine	Belfast	95
1838	09	*Robert Alexander* (bk)	Parke	Belfast	32
1838	10	*Ann* (bg)	Strong	Donegal	7
1839	05	*Borneo* (s)	Gorman	Limerick	223
1839	05	*Breeze* (bg)	O'Donnell	Limerick	136
1839	05	*Bridgewater* (bk)	Hadley	Waterford	23
1839	05	*Chieftain* (s)	Neil	Larne	36
1839	05	*Clifton* (bk)	Bisson	Cork	73
1839	05	*Despatch* (bk)	Walsh	Waterford	33
1839	05	*Hector* (bg)	Thompson	Belfast	92
1839	05	*James Bailey* (bk)	Hunter	Newry	105
1839	05	*John & Mary* (bk)	Moore	Galway	11
1839	05	*John Bell* (s)	Black	Waterford	35
1839	05	*Lady Gordon* (s)	Scurr	Dublin	12
1839	05	*Quintin Leitch* (s, 485 tns)	Hunter	Newry	105
1839	05	*Rosebank* (bg)	McKee	Belfast	69
1839	05	*Sir Robert Key* (s)	Reid	Belfast	12

Year	Month	Vessel	Master	Departure Port	Passenger Numbers
1839	05	*Tottenham* (bk)	Jeffries	New Ross	19
1839	05	*Urania* (bk)	Clark	Cork	33
1839	06	*Argo* (bg)	Greig	Sligo	114
1839	06	*Blanche* (bg)	O'Brien	Donegal	34
1839	06	*Cherub* (bg)	Duggan	Dublin	120
1839	06	*Edwin* (bg)	Shelton	Sligo	146
1839	06	*Hope* (bg)	Douglas	Sligo	158
1839	06	*Industry* (bk)	Stephens	Dublin	164
1839	06	*Jessie* (s)	Jackson	Sligo	121
1839	06	*Margaret Johnson* (s)	McAuley	Belfast	293
1839	06	*Richardson* (bg)	Forbes	Sligo	127
1839	06	*Susan Jane* (bg)	Strong	Donegal	30
1839	06	*Swan* (bg)	Elrington	Cork	123
1839	06	*Warner* (bg)	Crawford	Killala	91
1839	06	*Waterloo* (s)	Robinson	Limerick	131
Col. Wyndham's tenants.					
1839	07	*Ann* (bg)	Hamilton	Donegal	128
1839	07	*Ann* (bg)	Trotter	Tralee	100
1839	07	*Argus* (bg)	Linde	Sligo	126
1839	07	*Camona* (bg)	Coyle	Sligo	247
1839	07	*Senhouse* (bg)	Potts	Dublin	28
1839	07	*Tom* (bg)	Coulthard	Dublin	93
1839	07	*Tryagain* (bk)	Heacock	Cork	113
1839	08	*Albion* (bg)	Robinson	Londonderry	132
1839	08	*Dumfriesshire* (s)	Gowan	Belfast	367
1839	08	*Eliza Ann* (bg)	Hopper	Cork	23
1839	08	*Industry* (bk)	Barratt	Belfast	228
1839	08	*Naparima* (bg)	Donel	Dublin	50
1839	09	*Barnes* (s)	Gorman	Limerick	63
1839	09	*Chieftain* (s)	Neil	Larne	26
1839	09	*Tottenham* (bk)	Jeffries	New Ross	9
1839	10	*Napoleon* (s)	Montgomery	Belfast	58
1840	05	*Albion* (bg)	Robinson	Londonderry	117
1840	05	*Ann* (bg)	O'Brien	Donegal	115

Year	Month	Vessel	Master	Departure Port	Passenger Numbers
1840	05	*Ann* (bg)	Blair	Sligo	121
1840	05	*Barnes* (s)	Gorman	Limerick	279
1840	05	*Breeze* (bg)	O'Donnell	Limerick	201
1840	05	*Centenary* (bk)	Foster	Sligo	273
1840	05	*Champlain* (bk)	Dunn	Youghall	147
1840	05	*Consbrook* (s)	Pollock	Belfast	288
1840	05	*Despatch* (bk)	Walsh	Wexford	185
1840	05	*Dominica* (bk)	Bowman	Cork	234
1840	05	*Energy* (bg)	Irvine	Limerick	173
1840	05	*Grosvenor* (bk)	Gorman	Limerick	138
1840	05	*Helen* (bk)	Mearns, D.	Belfast	296

There were three deaths and two sick of the small pox.

Year	Month	Vessel	Master	Departure Port	Passenger Numbers
1840	05	*Iden* (bk)	Wemyss	Belfast	196
1840	05	*Isabella* (s) (s, 666tns)	Meredith	Cork	118
1840	05	*John & Mary* (bk)	Wright	Limerick	96
1840	05	*John Bell* (s)	Black	New Ross	175
1840	05	*Josephine* (bk)	McIntyre	Belfast	315

Quebec Mercury May 28: "In our last report we alluded to the quick passage made by the fine bark [sic] *Josephine*, from Belfast, and this morning we had a further proof of the excellent qualities of Captain McIntyre, of that vessel in the shape of a valuable snuff box, which his passengers — 315 in number — have unanimously presented to him with a highly complimentary address. The snuff box is of elegant workmanship and bears an appropriate inscription."

Year	Month	Vessel	Master	Departure Port	Passenger Numbers
1840	05	*Manlius* (s)	Hodge	Waterford	352
1840	05	*Marion* (s)	Bonnyman	Cork	263
1840	05	*Minstrel* (bg)	Outerbridge	Limerick	163
1840	05	*Nelson Village* (bk)	Barclay	Belfast	269

Three deaths and three sick of small pox.

Year	Month	Vessel	Master	Departure Port	Passenger Numbers
1840	05	*Ocean* (bk)	King	Waterford	82
1840	05	*Robert Kerr* (s)	Agnew	Belfast	253
1840	05	*Sarah Stewart* (bk)	Simpson	Belfast	276
1840	05	*Tottenham* (bk)	Brown	Waterford	83
1840	05	*Tryagain* (bk)	Heacock	Cork	189
1840	05	*Undinus* (sr)	Fudge	Limerick	147
1840	05	*Urania* (bk)	Clark	Cork	157
1840	06	*Blanche* (bg)	Henderson	Donegal	31
1840	06	*Ceres* (bg)	Lade	Sligo	152

Year	Month	Vessel	Master	Departure Port	Passenger Numbers
1840	06	*Chieftain* (s)	Power	Belfast	160
1840	06	*Doris* (bg)	Matthews	Limerick	145
1840	06	*Edwin* (bg)	Skelton	Killala	377
1840	06	*Eliza Ann* (bg)	Carruthers	Sligo	159
1840	06	*Elizabeth* (bg)	Wilson	Dublin	126
1840	06	*Emerald* (bg)	Figg	Westport	236
1840	06	*Henry* (bg)	McFee	Killala	148
1840	06	*Industry* (bk)	Stephens	Dublin	301

Three deaths during the voyage, eight sent to hospital.

Year	Month	Vessel	Master	Departure Port	Passenger Numbers
1840	06	*James Cook* (sr)	Follie	Limerick	137

Col. Wyndham's tenants.

Year	Month	Vessel	Master	Departure Port	Passenger Numbers
1840	06	*Jessie* (bg)	Jackson	Sligo	132
1840	06	*John & Jane* (bg)	Harvey	Sligo	190
1840	06	*Lord Oakley* (bg)	Crow	Westport	162
1840	06	*Louise* (bk)	Davies	Cork	108
1840	06	*Margaret Balfour* (bg)	Fitzsimmonds	Limerick	169
1840	06	*Mary* (bg)	Coxon	Cork	176
1840	06	*Mary Rowe* (bg)	Humphrey	Dublin	154
1840	06	*McDonnugh* (bg)	n/k	Cork	209
1840	06	*Nestor* (bg)	Clark	Sligo	150
1840	06	*Nicholson* (bg)	Key	Sligo	98
1840	06	*Quintin Leitch* (s, 485 tns)	Hunter	Newry	344
1840	06	*Recovery* (bg)	Conway	Sligo	215
1840	06	*Susan Jane* (bg)	Strong	Donegal	71
1840	06	*Thetis* (bg)	Champion	Limerick	185

Col. Wyndham's tenants.

Year	Month	Vessel	Master	Departure Port	Passenger Numbers
1840	06	*Thistle* (bg)	Thomas	Waterford	101
1840	06	*Thomas Gelston* (s)	Donald	Belfast	299
1840	06	*Thompson* (bg)	Barton	Killala	137
1840	06	*Tom* (bg)	Coulthard	Dublin	139

Quebec Mercury June 11: The *Tom* took on board 119 passengers from the *Emerald* from Westport, which foundered on the banks of Newfoundland. Captain Coulthard was commended for his kindness and gentlemanly conduct during the whole of the passage.

Year	Month	Vessel	Master	Departure Port	Passenger Numbers
1840	06	*Wilkinson* (bg)	Gateskill	Sligo	135
1840	07	*Aisthorpe* (bg)	Murphy	Sligo	137

Year	Month	Vessel	Master	Departure Port	Passenger Numbers
1840	07	*Carricks* (bg)	Dawes	Westport	134
1840	07	*Dolphin* (s)	Roche	Cork	196
1840	07	*Dumfriesshire* (s)	Gowan	Belfast	369
1840	07	*Elizabeth* (bg)	Wilson	Dublin	126
1840	07	*Elizabeth* (bg)	Downes	Cork	157

Fever and measles on board.

Year	Month	Vessel	Master	Departure Port	Passenger Numbers
1840	07	*Independence* (s)	McCappin	Belfast	343
1840	07	*Panoma* (bk)	Coyle	Dublin	226
1840	08	*Astrea* (bg)	Donovan	Dublin	142
1840	08	*Brown* (bg)	Jackson	Sligo	93
1840	08	*Creole* (bg)	Taylor	Cork	17
1840	08	*David Walter* (bg)	Faran	Waterford	59
1840	08	*Greenhow* (bk)	Hall	Newry	21
1840	08	*Henry Volant* (bg)	McEwing	Sligo	56
1840	08	*Hibernia* (bg)	Wedgwood	Sligo	127
1840	08	*Ireby* (bg)	Hindlow	Sligo	165

The captain got separated temporarily from the ship and was lost in the fog. However, the ship arrived safely and the passengers were in good health.

Year	Month	Vessel	Master	Departure Port	Passenger Numbers
1840	08	*Jane* (bg)	Toby	Sligo	165
1840	08	*Kingston* (bg)	Roe	Cork	93
1840	08	*Lotus* (bk)	Hammond	Cork	13
1840	08	*Mariner's Hope* (bg)	Lockly	Londonderry	73
1840	08	*Marquis of Normanby* (bg)	Gregg	Cork	111
1840	08	*St. James* (bg)	Crawford	Cork	134
1840	08	*Trial* (bg)	Davidson	Dublin	77
1840	08	*Viola* (bg)	Longstaff	Sligo	180
1840	09	*Ann* (bg)	O'Brien	Donegal	8
1840	09	*Barbara* (s)	Gorman	Limerick	24
1840	09	*Cherub* (bg)	Duggan	Londonderry	159
1840	09	*Chieftain* (s)	Sion	Belfast	36
1840	09	*Constitution* (s)	Neil	Belfast	27
1840	09	*Despatch* (bk)	Walsh	Waterford	8
1840	09	*Industry* (bg)	Barratt	Sligo	11
1840	09	*John & Mary* (bk)	Wright	Limerick	7

Year	Month	Vessel	Master	Departure Port	Passenger Numbers
1840	09	*John Bell* (s)	Black	New Ross	31
1840	09	*Lively* of Galway (bg, 299 tns)	McDonogh, Wm.	Cork	181

For the passenger list see theshipslist.com. The passengers included thirty-eight children.

Year	Month	Vessel	Master	Departure Port	Passenger Numbers
1840	09	*Spey* (bg)	Dobson	Killala	60
1840	09	*Thistle* (bg)	Thomas	Waterford	11

NOTES

Chapter 1: Mid-Canada's Appeal to the Irish

1. PRONI T1639/5: Charlotte Bacon to Alexander Kerr, her father, July 26, 1843.
2. John Francis Maguire, *The Irish in America* (New York, Montreal: D. and J. Sadler, 1868), 331.
3. Helen Cowan, *British Emigration to British North America: The First Hundred Years* (Toronto: University of Toronto Press, 1961), 179, 199. Oliver Macdonagh, *A Pattern of Government Growth 1800–1860: The Passengers Acts and Their Enforcement* (London: MacGibbon & Kee, 1961), 27–29.
4. Ninth Reports of the Colonial Land Emigration Commissioners, in BPP 1849(1082) XXII, 1–2.
5. Maguire, *The Irish in America*, 332.
6. PRONI T3081/1: Henry Johnson to his wife Jane in County Antrim, December 3, 1848.
7. LAC MG24 H7: Diary of William Graves, 22.
8. PRONI D1748/G/490.

9.   Irish emigration to all parts of the world, from the seventeenth century to the present, is covered in Patrick Fitzgerald and Brian Lambkin, *Migration in Irish History, 1607–2007* (New York: Palgrave Macmillan, 2008). For an overview of Irish emigration to North America, see Kerby A. Miller, *Emigrants and Exiles: Ireland and the Irish Exodus to North America* (Oxford: Oxford University Press, 1985). For an overall study of Irish emigration to Canada, see Cecil J. Houston and William J. Smyth, *Irish Emigration and Canadian Settlement: Patterns, Links and Letters* (Toronto: University of Toronto Press, 1990), and Donald MacKay, *Flight from Famine: The Coming of the Irish to Canada* (Toronto: Natural Heritage, 2009).

10. The rebellion of Irish Catholics was quelled by Oliver Cromwell's English army in 1649–50.

11. *Belfast Commercial Chronicle*, October 5, 1816; July 23, 1817.

12. *Sherbrooke Daily Record*, March 19, 1906. Peter Southam, *Irish Settlement and National Identity in the Lower St. Francis Valley* (Richmond, QC: St. Patrick's Society of Richmond and Vicinity, 2012), 178–83.

13. "The Society, in Connection with the Established Church of Scotland, for Promoting the Religious Interests of Scottish Settlers in British North America" was founded in 1825. Having been established by Glaswegians, it later came to be known by its condensed name — "The Glasgow Colonial Society."

14. For the work of the Society for the Propagation of the Gospel in promoting the interests of the Anglican Church in Ontario and Quebec, see Lucille H. Campey, *Seeking a Better Future: The English Pioneers of Ontario and Quebec* (Toronto: Dundurn, 2012), 32, 40, 63, 75, 78, 113, 212.

15. Aidan Manning, *Between the Runways: A History of Irish-Catholic Settlement in Southern Peel County and Etobicoke* (Etobicoke, ON: Author, 2009), 50–58.

16. Reverend Samuel J. Boddy, *A Brief Memoir of the Rev. Samuel B. Ardagh, A.M., T.C.D., Late Rector of Barrie and Incumbent of Shanty Bay, Lake Simcoe, Upper Canada*, edited by Samuel J. Boddy (Toronto: Rowsell and Hutchison, 1874), 26.

17. PRONI MIC205/1: Magrath family papers, 1769–1895. The Reverend Magrath was the Anglican minister at Erindale for twenty-two years until his death in 1851.

18. Miller, *Emigrants and Exiles*, 322–23.

19. Nicholas Flood Davin, *The Irishman in Canada* (London: Sampson Low, Marston & Co., 1877), 245.

Chapter 2: Early Arrivals

1. Robert J. Grace, *The Irish in Quebec: An Introduction to the Historiography* (Quebec: Institut québécois de recherche sur la culture, 1993), 24.

2. Ibid., 21–25.

3 New France had 2,500 families at this time. John O'Farrell, "Irish Families in Ancient Quebec," in *The Untold Story: The Irish in Canada*, edited by Robert O'Driscoll and Lorna Reynolds (Toronto: Celtic Arts of Canada, 1988), Vol. 1, 281–94.

4. BAnQ (Montreal), TL4, S1, D1535; BAnQ (Quebec) TL1, S11, SS1, D105A, P28, TL4, S1, D6194.

5. BAnQ (Quebec) TL5, D1300. The complaint was made by Ignace Gamelin and François Perrault, the probable owners of the forge. While the company selected its skilled workforce mainly from Burgundy in France, it also recruited a few Irishmen as general workers. The Forges du Saint-Maurice was the birthplace of Canada's iron industry and it is now a National Historic Site. For further details about the history of the forge, see Clare H. Pentland, *Labour and Capital in Canada 1650–1860* (Toronto: James Lorimer & Co., 1981), 34–48.

6. O'Farrell, "Irish Families in Ancient Quebec," 291–93.

7. St. Patrick's Day had been celebrated in Montreal in 1759 by Irish soldiers stationed at the Montreal Garrison.

8. Lower Canada was by far the largest of the British colonies, having a population of 250,000 by 1806. For population figures, see Joseph Bouchette, *The British Dominions in North America: A Topographical and Statistical Description of the Provinces of Lower and Upper Canada, New Brunswick, Nova Scotia, the Islands of Newfoundland, Prince*

Edward Island and Cape Breton (London: Longman, Rees, Orme, Brown, Green and Longman, 1832), Vol. II, 235.

9. Their ancestors had settled on land that had been confiscated from Irish Catholics, this being a manoeuvre carried out by the English Crown to strengthen its interests in Ireland. However, because of their Presbyterian faith, the Ulster arrivals suffered discrimination from the Irish Episcopal establishment and were denied civil and military office. For background information on the political, economic, and religious tensions in Ulster in the seventeenth and eighteenth centuries, see R.J. Dickson, *Ulster Emigration to Colonial America, 1718–1775* (London: Routledge & Kegan Paul, 1966), 1–17.

10. Between 1718 and 1775, the year when the American War of Independence began, a quarter of a million Ulster people immigrated to the North American colonies. Religious grievances dating back to the previous century had helped to propel this great exodus.

11. PRONI T/1970.

12. For details of the Irish Loyalists who settled in the Maritime region, see Lucille H. Campey, *Atlantic Canada's Irish Immigrants: A Fish and Timber Story* (Toronto: Dundurn, 2016), 37–50.

13. Fernand Ouellet, *Le Bas-Canada 1791–1840: Changements structuraux et crise* (Ottawa: Les Editions de l'Université d'Ottawa , 1976) [Translated and adapted: Patricia Claxton, *Lower Canada, 1791–1840: Social Change and Nationalism* (Toronto: McClelland & Stewart, 1980)], 22–36.

14. Robert Harvey, *A Few Bloody Noses: The American War of Independence* (London: John Murray, 2001), 179–82.

15. For servicemen, land was granted according to rank, ranging generally from 1,000 acres for officers to 100 acres for privates. Civilians usually got 100 acres for each head of family and 50 additional acres for every person belonging to the family. Cowan, *British Emigration to British North America*, 3–12.

16. The Volunteers of Ireland were also known as the 105th Regiment of Foot (British Army).

17. The eight townships were known as the Royal Townships. Angela E.M. Files, "Loyalist Settlement along the St. Lawrence in Upper

Canada," in *Grand River Branch (U.E.L. Association of Canada) Newsletter* 8, No. 1 (February. 1996): 9–12.

18. The additional five townships were known as the Cataraqui townships. They consisted of Kingston (Frontenac County), Ernestown (Addington County), Fredericksburg, and Adolphustown (Lennox County) and Marysburgh (Prince Edward County).

19. J.S. McGivern, "Catholic Loyalists in the American Revolution: A Sketch," in *Canadian Catholic Historical Association Study Sessions* 48 (1981): 91–99.

20. Glen Lockwood, "The Pattern of Settlement in Eastern Ontario," *Families* 30, No. 4 (1991): 235–57.

21. The regiment's former soldiers were granted land near Antigonish Harbour and clearly prospered. Campey, *Atlantic Canada's Irish Immigrants*, 49, 86.

22. Daniel Parkinson, "The American Heritage of Rawdon Township Lower Canada," *Connections* (Journal of the Quebec Family History Society) 29, No. 2 (Winter 2006): 22–28.

23. Joseph Bouchette was the Canadian surveyor general of British North America. His two "Topographical Dictionaries" *of Lower Canada* and his "Topographical Descriptions of the Provinces of Lower and Upper Canada,'" written between 1815 and 1832, are important sources of immigrant settlement data. Joseph Bouchette, *A Topographical Dictionary of the Province of Lower Canada* (London: Longman & Co, 1832). Entry for Kilkenny Township.

24. Hastings County in Upper Canada was also named after Sir Francis Rawdon. Having adopted his mother's name in 1790, his surname became Rawdon-Hastings from 1790.

25. Christopher Moore, *The Loyalists: Revolution, Exile, Settlement* (Toronto: McClelland & Stewart, 1994), 243–47.

26. Few immigrants arrived in Upper Canada from Britain until 1815. Bouchette, *The British Dominions in North America: A Topographical and Statistical Description*, Vol. II, 235.

27. John Clarke, "A Geographical Analysis of Colonial Settlement in the Western District of Upper Canada, 1788–1850" (Ph.D. thesis, University of Western Ontario, London, 1970), 37.

28. Hilda Marion Neatby, *Quebec, The Revolutionary Age, 1760–1791* (Toronto: McClelland & Stewart, 1966), 133–41; John A. Dickinson and Brian Young, *A Short History of Quebec*, 2nd edition (Toronto: Longman, 1993), 54–59.

29. The French militia took up arms to defend Quebec from the Americans in 1775 although none volunteered to join the British Army in attacking the American colonies.

30. Following later boundary changes Foucault (renamed Caldwell Manor) is now in the State of Vermont.

31. The Noyan seigneury was owned by Gabriel Christie and the St. Armand seigneury was owned by Thomas Dunn. Both were English-born. Wilbur Henry Siebert, "American Loyalists in the Eastern Seigneuries and Townships of the Province of Quebec." *Transactions of the Royal Society of Canada*, 3rd series (1913), Vol. VII, 3–41.

32. *Belfast Newsletter*, February 8–11, 1774.

33. Françoise Nöel, "Gabriel Christie's Seigneuries: Settlement and Seigneurial Administration in the Upper Richelieu Valley, 1764–1854" (Ph.D. thesis, McGill University, Montreal, 1985), 161, 203, 561, 625.

34. Siebert, "American Loyalists in the Eastern Seigneuries and Townships," 32–37.

35. Two systems of land tenure were now in place. The original French seigneuries stretched along the St. Lawrence River as far as the Gaspé Peninsula, and along the Ottawa, Chaudière, and Richelieu rivers.

36. There were 129 men, 52 women, and 132 children in the first group, followed by 56 people in a second group. Siebert, "Loyalist Settlements in the Gaspé Peninsula," 399–405.

37. Bouchette, *British Dominions in North America: A Topographical and Statistical Description*, Vol. I, 323–33; Siebert, "Loyalist Settlements in the Gaspé Peninsula," Register of Inhabitants in 1786, 403.

38. Michel Le Moignan, "Douglastown: Un rameau de la verte Erin en Gaspésie," *Revue d'Histoire de la Gaspésie* 5 (1967): 178–85.

39. Gilbert C. Patterson, *Land Settlement in Upper Canada, 1783–1840* (Toronto: Ontario Archives, 1921), 43–44.

40. LAC MG23 HII7 (m/f A-128): Peter Russell to Hugh Farmer, 1794–1803.

41. Cowan, *British Emigration to British North America*, 25–26. Selkirk argued that, after the United Irish Rebellion of 1798, it would be advantageous to the government to remove people to Canada who might otherwise become leaders of disaffection were they to remain in Ireland.
42. LAC MG24 I88: Maria Murney's Account of her Grandfather's Experiences, 1.
43. Ibid., 2.
44. Dickinson and Young, *Short History of Quebec*, 60–62.
45. PRONI T2410.
46. LAC MG24 D1: John William Wolsey and family.

Chapter 3: Quebec City and Rural Areas to the North and South

1. Raoul Blanchard, *Le Centre du Canada Français: Province de Québec* (Montreal: Librairie Beauchemin Limitée, 1948), 428.
2. *DCB*, Vol. VII (John Neilson).
3. *Select Committee on the Civil Government of Canada, 1828*, 275–76: evidence of John Neilson.
4. Ibid.
5. *Quebec Gazette*, November 11, 1831.
6. *Select Committee on the Civil Government of Canada, 1828*, 275–76: evidence of John Neilson.
7. Blanchard, *Le Centre du Canada Français*, 428.
8. Robert Grace, "The Irish in Mid-Nineteenth-Century Canada and the Case of Quebec: Immigration and Settlement in a Catholic City" (Ph.D. thesis, Laval University, Quebec, 1999), 44–72.
9. There were two Alexander Buchanans who served as Quebec immigration agents. Alexander, the elder, served as agent from 1828 to 1838. Alexander, the younger, his nephew, was agent from 1833 to 1862. From at least as early as 1833, Alexander, the younger, looked after the immigration office during the winter when his uncle took a leave of absence for health reasons.
10. Alexander Buchanan, *1832 Emigrants' Handbook for Arrivals at Québec*, reprinted in *Connections the Journal of the Quebec Family History Society* 29 (3) (Spring 2007): 9–13.

11. BPP 1831–32(724) XXXII.

12. BPP 1833(141) XXVII.

13. BPP "Annual Report on Emigration for 1832" and "Annual Report on Emigration for 1843," reported in Grace, "The Irish in Mid-Nineteenth-Century Canada," 73.

14. In spite of widespread and repeated complaints within Britain over the high cost of timber, the protective tariffs remained in place until 1860. Ralph Davis, *The Industrial Revolution and British Overseas Trade* (Leicester: Leicester University Press, 1979), 48–49. Duties increased from 25s. per load in 1804 to 54s. 6d. per load in 1811.

15. Marianna O'Gallagher, *The Shamrock Trail: Tracing the Irish in Quebec City* (Ste. Foy, QC: Carraig Books, 1997). The early Irish lived just to the south of Basin Louise.

16. BPP 1831–32(724) XXXII.

17. James O'Leary, *History of the Irish Catholics of Quebec: Saint Patrick's Church to the Death of Reverend P. McMahon* (Quebec, 1895), 7–13.

18. Nancy Schmitz, *Irish for a Day: Saint Patrick's Day Celebrations in Quebec City, 1765–1990* (Ste. Foy, QC: Carraig Books, 1991), 10–18.

19. Raoul Blanchard, *L'Est du Canada Français, "Province de Québec"* (Montreal: Publications de l'Institut Scientifique Franco-Canadien, 1935), 237.

20. John Neilson, *Select Committee on the Civil Government of Canada, 1828,* 275–76.

21. Marianna O'Gallagher, "Saint Patrick's, Quebec: The Building of a Church and of a Parish, 1827–1833" (M.A. thesis, University of Ottawa, 1976), 31–32.

22. John Neilson, *Select Committee on the Civil Government of Canada, 1828,* 271.

23. Lower Canada Census, 1851. By 1851, Valcartier and River aux Pins were part of St. Gabriel. In 1831, Buchanan had noted that Irish immigrants were settling in Tewkesbury close to Stoneham.

24. In 1828, John Neilson had reported that ninety-two Protestants lived at nearby Beauport. *Select Committee on the Civil Government of Canada, 1828,* 271.

25. BAnQ P351 P2452: Arthur Murray to Sir Henri-Gustave Joly de Lotbinière, the Quebec premier, October 15, 1879.

26. Shipping data reveals that just over half of the immigrant ships to arrive in Quebec in 1819 had left from ports in Ulster.

27. BAnQ E21, S64, SS5, SSS6: Petitioners seeking tracts of land in St. Gabriel seigneury, which had been owned formerly by the Jesuits. There were some Scottish petitioners but the Irish greatly outnumbered them.

28. BAnQ E21, S64, SS5, SSS6: D1005.

29. Ibid., D1004, D1006, D1010, D1012, D1013, D1014, D1037.

30. Ibid., D1184.

31. Ibid., D1043, D1056, D1121.

32. Ibid., D1137, D1200, D1221, D1222.

33. Ibid., D1123, D1226, D1259, D1842.

34. Bouchette, *Topographical Dictionary of Lower Canada*.

35. John Neilson, *Select Committee on the Civil Government of Canada, 1828*, 275–76.

36. Bouchette, *Topographical Dictionary of Lower Canada*, see entry for Portneuf.

37. Ibid. See entry for Gaudarville.

38. Blanchard, *Le Centre du Canada Français*, 428.

39. Lower Canada Census, 1851.

40. Pierre de Billy, "Forever Shannon: A Village Holds Fast to Its Irish Roots in the Heart of French Quebec," *Royal Canadian Geographical Society* (July/August 1999): 58–63.

41. BPP 1831–32(724) XXXII.

42. In 1851, Irish, Scottish, and English residents were only a tiny proportion of Cap Santé's population, which stood at 3,473. It had fifty Protestants at that time.

43. DERO D3349/3: Metcalfe family of Killarch correspondence. Letters to the Reverend J. Metcalfe, in Kilnmarsh, 3/1, July 10, 1908, and 3/2, September 27, 1909.

44. Ibid., 3/4, August 9, 1911.

45. The Quebec Seminary, a community of priests, was based in Quebec City. It was founded in 1663.

46. John Boylan, who died in 1948, quoted in Soeur Marie-Ursule, *Civilisation traditionnelle des Lavalois* (Quebec: Université Laval, 1951), 49.

47. Marie-Ursule, *Civilisation traditionnelle*, 17.

48. Archives de l'Archevêché de Québec, *Registre des lettres, 1836–1839*, quoted in Marie-Ursule, *Civilisation traditionnelle*, 24.

49. Ibid., 19–24.

50. Ibid., 17–29.

51. Archives de l'Archevêché de Québec, Registre des requêtes m/f 78, quoted in ibid., 23–24.

52. Mrs. John Boylan quoted in ibid., 53.

53. Settler recollections quoted in ibid., 37.

54. Ibid., 23–26.

55. Ibid., 32–35.

56. Craig's Road went on to the Gosford Road, which crossed the Eastern Townships.

57. BPP 1831–32(724) XXXII.

58. Buchanan, *1832 Emigrants' Handbook for Arrivals at Québec*.

59. BPP 1833(141) XVII. Buchanan also mentioned that the Irish were heading for nearby St. Giles seigneury. However, it only had a tiny Irish population in 1851.

60. Patrick M. Redmond, *Irish Life in Rural Quebec, A History of Frampton* (Montreal: Author, 1977), 4–9, 18. Colonel Jacques Voyer also owned a substantial amount of land on the west side.

61. Bouchette, *Topographical Dictionary of Lower Canada*.

62. Jules-Adrien Kirouac, *Histoire de la paroisse de Saint-Malachie* (Quebec: Typ. Laflamme & Proulx, 1909), 12–13, 29–30, 37, 46.

63. Ibid., 70.

64. Bouchette, *Topographical Dictionary of Lower Canada*.

65. Armine W. Mountain, *A Memoir of George Jehoshaphat Mountain, D.D., D.C.L., Late Bishop of Quebec/Compiled (at the Desire of the Synod of That Diocese) by Armine W. Mountain* (Montreal, J. Lovell, 1866), 128.

66. Ibid., 199.

67. Archives of the Archdiocese of Quebec, Frampton, 1–10, quoted in Redmond, *History of Frampton*, 14.

68. Redmond, *History of Frampton*, 42.

69. John Neilson, *Select Committee on the Civil Government of Canada, 1828*, 271.

70. Redmond, *History of Frampton*, 43, 44.

71. Anne-Marie Poulin, and Jean Simard, *An Anglican Heritage: Christ Church in Frampton* (Quebec: Corporation Culturelle de Frampton, 1989).

72. Redmond, *History of Frampton*, 18.

73. Maguire, *The Irish in America*, 266–67.

74. Beaurivage consisted of St. Sylvestre and St. Patrice parishes. St. Patrice appears separately for the first time in the 1881 Census.

75. D. Aidan McQuillan, "Beaurivage: The Development of an Irish Ethnic Identity in Rural Quebec, 1820–1860," in *The Untold Story: The Irish in Canada*, edited by Robert O'Driscoll and Lorna Reynolds (Toronto: Celtic Arts of Canada, 1988), Vol. 1, 263–79.

76. D. Aidan McQuillam, "Returns on Investment: Seigneurial Land Development in Nineteenth-Century Quebec," in *Mythic History and Symbolic Landscape*, edited by Serge Courville and Brian S. Osborne (Sainte-Foy, QC: Inter-University Centre for Quebec Studies, 1997), 46–51.

77. BAnQ M/F 117/13: Fonds famille Ross. Journal de la seigneurie Beaurivage, 1825–37.

78. Ibid.

79. Jacques Gagnée, "The Irish Catholics of Lower Canada and Quebec: Their Churches," PDF file dated 2014 compiled by gagne.jacques@ sympatico.ca. Belfast was established in 1829 by Protestant Irish at what is now the modern location of St. Patrice-de-Beaurivage. It no longer exists.

80. Schmitz, *Irish for a Day*, 193.

81. Most Irish-born settlers in the area were concentrated at St. Sylvestre in 1851. Nearby St. Giles had 104 Irish and Ste. Agathe had 225.

82. In 1871, St. Sylvestre had 2,228 Irish and only 1,287 French inhabitants.

83. Religious disputes, including those involving Orangemen, are discussed in Chapter 12.

84. *DCB*, Vol. VIII (James Godfrey Hanna).

85. St. Charles de la Belle Alliance was later renamed St. Georges de Beauce. The 1851 Lower Canada Census shows it to have had fifty-two Irish-born.

86. PRONI T2680/2/15: Edward Parks, February 6, 1871.

Chapter 4: The Eastern Townships

1. Dugald McKenzie McKillop, *Annals of Megantic County, Quebec* (Lynn, MA: Author, 1902), 211.

2. Gwen Rawlings Barry, *Ulster Protestant Emigration to Lower Canada* (Lower Sackville, NS: Evans Books, 2003), 23–28.

3. Summary data on ethnic origins and religious affiliations has been taken from the Lower Canada Census of 1851–52 (Vol. 1, Personal Census).

4. Ibid.

5. Françoise Noël, *Competing for Souls: Missionary Activity and Settlement in the Eastern Townships, 1784–1851* (Sherbrooke, QC: University of Sherbrook, 1988), 7–45.

6. Victor Eugene Morrill and Erastus Gardner Pierce, *Men of Today in the Eastern Townships* (Sherbrooke, QC: Reink Books, 1917), 116, 136.

7. Blanchard, *Le Centre du Canada Français*, 342.

8. *DCB*, Vol. VI (John Savage).

9. ETRC P028: John Savage fonds.

10. Mary Olive Vaudry, "A Sketch of the Life of Captain John Savage, J.P., First Settler in Shefford County, 1792" (United Empire Loyalists' Association of Canada Meeting, March, 1921). The original settlers included nine Loyalists.

11. ETRC P158/003.02/001: Hackett family fonds.

12. *Report from the Select Committee Appointed to Inquire into the Expediency of Encouraging Emigration from the United Kingdom*, 1826, 1861.

13. J.I. Little, "A.C. Buchanan and the Megantic Experiment: Promoting British Colonization in Lower Canada," *Social History*, Vol. XLVI, No. 92 (2013): 295–319.

14. Barry, *Ulster Protestant Emigration to Lower Canada*, 23.

15. Lucille H. Campey, *Les Écossais: The Pioneer Scots of Lower Canada, 1763–1855* (Toronto: Natural Heritage, 2006), 78–86.

16. Alexander Buchanan was a fellow Ulsterman having shipping interests in the Londonderry–British North American trade. His knowledge of the local timber trade and general living conditions in Lower Canada would have been highly persuasive to these Ulster people.

17. BPP 1831–32(724) XXXII.

18. Little, "A.C. Buchanan and the Megantic Experiment," 306, 308.

19. BPP 1831–32(724) XXXII.

20. Gwen Rawlings, *Pioneers of Inverness Township, Quebec: An Historical and Genealogical Story, 1800–1978*, edited by Elizabeth Harwood: cartography by R.A. Nutter (Cheltenham, ON.: Boston Mills Press, 1979), 110.

21. Sylvia Green-Guenette and Elizabeth Larrabee, "Patterson Family: Ireland to Megantic County, Lower Canada and our McNey Connection," *Quebec Family History Society* (2011).

22. *Strabane Morning Post*, February 9, 1830.

23. Buchanan, *1832 Emigrants' Handbook for Arrivals at Québec*, 3. The names of some of the families who settled in Inverness Township between 1825 and 1829 are given in Gwen Rawlings, "The English 180 Years in Rural Quebec Megantic County," *Canadian Genealogist* 3, 2 (1981): 74–83.

24. Bouchette, *The British Dominions in North America: A Topographical and Statistical Description*, 570.

25. McKillop, *Annals of Megantic County*, 139.

26. The work of the Society for the Propagation of the Gospel in promoting the interests of the Anglican Church in mid-Canada is discussed in Lucille H. Campey, *Seeking a Better Future: The English Pioneers of Ontario and Quebec* (Toronto: Dundurn, 2012), 31–32.

27. For details of the work of the Glasgow Colonial Society in Lower Canada, see Campey, *Les Écossais*, 17–18, 51, 66, 84, 103.

28. In 1881, the province of Ulster was nearly 50 percent Catholic, 22 percent Church of Ireland, and 26 percent Presbyterian. Munster and Connaught provinces were strongly Catholic (more than

90 percent), as was Leinster (86 percent). Angela McCarthy, *Irish Migrants in New Zealand, 1840–1937: "The Desired Haven"* (Belfast: The Boydell Press, 2005), 239–40.

29. In 1831, half of Megantic County's Protestants were Anglicans, while 10 percent were Presbyterians. The balance changed slightly by 1861, with 45 percent being Anglicans and 31 percent Presbyterians. See Barry, *Ulster Protestant Emigration to Lower Canada*, 31.

30. ETRC UC054/103: St. Andrews United Church, Inverness.

31. NAB CO 384/23, 573–74: John Richardson to George Murray, 1830.

32. Norman MacDonald, *Canada, Immigration and Settlement 1763–1841*. London: Longmans & Co., 1939, 327–28.

33. LAC (M-1353): Glasgow Colonial Society Correspondence, Rev. John Clugston to Rev. Burns, July 11, 1833.

34. BPP w/e August 7, 1841.

35. RHL USPG Series E, 1845–46 (LAC m/f A-221).

36. Barry, *Ulster Protestant Emigration to Lower Canada*, 23–33.

37. *Montreal Gazette*, January 23, 1908.

38. Robert Sellar, *The Tragedy of Quebec: The Expulsion of its Protestant Farmers* (Toronto: University of Toronto Press, 1907), 13–20, 123–28, 196–205.

39. "An Important Letter of a Resident of Quebec as to the Disabilities of Protestants in the Province of Quebec: The Parish System" (Toronto: Equal Rights Association for the Province of Ontario, 1890) typified the grievances being raised by Protestant farmers over the growing powers of the Catholic Church. Colonization societies were formed at this time to encourage French Canadians back from the United States to the Eastern Townships.

40. John Irvine Little, *Nationalism, Capitalism and Colonization in Nineteenth-Century Quebec: The Upper St. Francis District* (Kingston, ON: McGill-Queen's University Press, 1989), 36–63.

41. The Grand Trunk Railway was also known as the St. Lawrence and Atlantic Railway Line.

42. Reverend T.J. Walsh, "Pioneer English Catholics in the Eastern Townships," *Canadian Catholic Historical Association Report*, (1939–40): 55–70.

43. J.I. Little (ed.) *Love Strong as Death: Lucy Peel's Canadian Journal, 1833–1836* (Waterloo, ON: Wilfrid Laurier University Press, 2001), 201.

44. One section of the British American Land Company, having 596,000 acres, lay in the St. Francis Tract, between Lake Megantic and the St. Francis River, while the second section of 251,000 acres was scattered throughout Shefford, Stanstead, and Sherbrooke counties.

45. For details of the people from Norfolk and Suffolk who settled in Sherbrooke County and in the St. Francis Tract, see Campey, *Seeking a Better Future*, 85–97. For details of the people from the Isle of Lewis who settled in what became Compton, Frontenac, and Wolfe counties in Lower Canada, see Campey, *Les Écossais*, 98–110.

46. A colonization road linking Port St. Francis at the confluence of the St. Lawrence and St. Francis rivers with the town of Richmond was constructed by the British American Land Company in 1835. It gave immigrants ready access to townships in the Lower St. Francis Valley.

47. The distribution of Irish farms is taken from Peter Southam, *Irish Settlements and National Identity in the Lower St. Francis Valley. Richmond* (Quebec: St. Patrick's Society of Richmond and Vicinity, 2012), 18.

48. ETRC P141/002/1002B: 125th Celtic Cross Project, list of pioneers: Anderson, Bardon, Beattie, Bigger, Blaney, Boyce, Boyd, Boyle, Brady, Brighton, Britton, Brown, Brynan, Burke, Burton, Butler, Camden, Cameron, Campbell, Carroll, Carey, Cassidy, Chadwick, Choice, Clouston, Cogan, Connell, Conway, Corrigan, Costello, Cotter, Croke, Cross, Crozier, Cryan, Cumming, Cusick, Daly, Delaney, Denery, Donahue, Donovan, Dooley, Doonan, Doyle, Duffy, Duggan, Dunn, Dwyer, Egan, Fahey, Falls, Fanning, Feeney, Fitzgerald, Fitzpatrick, Flanagan, Flavin, Flynn, Fowler, Gallaher, Gavin, Gilmore, Goodspeed, Gorman, Gribben, Groves, Hagan, Hale, Handley, Henderson, Heney, Hill, Hilliard, Hogan, Horan, Houley, Hughes, Hutchison, Insley, Johns(t)on, Kallum, Kavanagh, Keating, Keenan, Kelly, Kerney, Kielly, Killeen, Langan, Largey, Laughrea, Leeds, Lennon, Lynch, Maguire, Malone, Maloney, Martin, Matheson, McGuire, McCabe, McCaffrey,

McCam, McCanney, McCauley, McCormick, McCourt, McCrea, McCullough, McDonnell, McGinley, McGoldrick, McGrain, McGrave, McInnelly, McKinnon, McKivery, McManus, McNamara, McNaughton, McVey, Meaney, Meehan, Melrose, Mimminaugh, Monaghan, Mooney, Moore, Moran, Moriarity, Mullen, Mulloy, Murphy, Murtagh, Nelligan, Nolan, Nuckley, Nugent, Nultey, Noonan, O'Donnell, O'Hara, O'Malley, O'Mara, O'Neill, O'Reilly, Pearcy, Penny, Pound, Powell, Power(s), Quinn, Ramsay, Richardson, Roach, Romney, Ryan, Scallion, Shea, Sheehey, Shortell, Small, Smith, Sullivan, Terrell, Timony, Travers, Tuite, Wallace, Whelan.

49. Southam, *Irish Settlements and National Identity in the Lower St. Francis Valley*, 245–48.

50. J.I. Little, "The Fostering Care of Government: Lord Dalhousie's Survey of the Eastern Townships," *Social History* 43, No. 8 (2010): 193–212.

51. Southam, *Irish Settlements and National Identity in the Lower St. Francis Valley*, 85.

52. Bouchette, *British Dominions in North America: A Topographical and Statistical Description*, 369.

53. Christianna Neill Stevens family memoir quoted in Southam, *Irish Settlements and National Identity in the Lower St. Francis Valley*, 75–76.

54. Frederick George Heriot, a Scottish military officer, supervised the Drummondville settlement.

55. Although nominally an English regiment, the 49th "Hertfordshire" Regiment of Foot included a large number of Irish troops.

56. Southam, *Irish Settlements and National Identity in the Lower St. Francis Valley*, 27–35.

57. The Enniskillen families were related to one another.

58. Walsh, "Pioneer English Catholics in the Eastern Townships," 61.

59. Ibid., 61–62.

60. J.I. Little, "Missionary Priests in Quebec's Eastern Townships: The Years of Hardship and Discontent, 1825–1853," *Canadian Catholic Historical Association* 45 (1978): 21–35.

61. RHL USPG Series E 1845–46 (LAC m/f A-221).

62. RHL USPG Series E 1854–55 (LAC m/f A-223).

63. Walsh, "Pioneer English Catholics in the Eastern Townships," 61–62.

64. Morrill and Pierce, *Men of Today in the Eastern Townships,* 206.

65. ETRC P141: St. Patrick's Society of Richmond Anniversary Booklet.

66. Southam, *Irish Settlements and National Identity in the Lower St. Francis Valley,* 79.

67. ETRC P076: Agnes Bradley Haddock fonds.

68. Ibid.

69. An 1835 advertisement in the *Belfast Newsletter* stated that the land company offered for sale "one million acres of land in farms of 100 acres and upwards, situated in the healthy and fertile Eastern Townships of Lower Canada." The agent was William McCorkell, founder of the shipping line named after him. PRONI T2125/31/2.

70. Southam, *Irish Settlements and National Identity in the Lower St. Francis Valley,* 10–18, 71.

71. In the 1830s, 290 Catholic families lived in the townships of Shipton, Melbourne, Tingwick, Windsor, Brompton, and points south of them, of whom three quarters were Irish. Southam, *Irish Settlements and National Identity in the Lower St. Francis Valley,* 97–98.

72. Southam, *Irish Settlements and National Identity in the Lower St. Francis Valley,* 85.

73. Walsh, "Pioneer English Catholics in the Eastern Townships," 65, 72.

74. Mrs. L.E. Codere, "The Establishment of St. Patrick's Church in Sherbrooke, Quebec: Its Development and Influence Throughout a Period of Fifty-Seven Years," *Canadian Catholic Historical Association Report* 11 (1943–44): 129–42.

75. The Dublin-born Richard William Heneker was commissioner of the British American Land Company by this time, and he was also involved in local railway development and was president of the Eastern Townships Bank. ETRC P073: Richard William Heneker fonds.

76. Bouchette, *Topographical Dictionary of Lower Canada* — Shipton Township entry.

77. Southam, *Irish Settlements and National Identity in the Lower St. Francis Valley,* 133–34. Because it lacked the water power to attract industry, Richmond itself grew relatively slowly. Most of the economic growth

associated with the arrival of the railway took place in its surrounding villages.

78. They sailed in the *Countess of Arran* in June 1851. Some of the women and children were assisted by the Canadian authorities to proceed to friends who lived mainly in the United States. Gerard Moran, *Sending Out Ireland's Poor: Assisted Emigration to North America in the Nineteenth Century* (Dublin: Four Courts Press, 2004), 120.

79. BPP 1852(1474) XXXIII, 26, 33.

80. Walsh, "Pioneer English Catholics in the Eastern Townships," 70. The settlers included: Edward Lamb, Patrick Daley, Ambrose Shea, Peter McManus, D.J. McKenty, Bernard and Patrick Conway, Thomas Todd, Dennis Gleason, John Maguire, John Keenan, Thomas McGee, and John Healy.

81. Southam, *Irish Settlements and National Identity in the Lower St. Francis Valley*, 83–85.

82. ETRC P141/002/1002B: St. Patrick's Society of Richmond and Vicinity.

Chapter 5: Montreal and Rural Areas to the North and South

1. Claude Bourguignon, *Saint-Colomban: Une épopée Irlandaise au Piémont des Laurentides* (Chambly, QC: Editions Passe Present, 1988), 41. Interview with Ernest McAndrews, 1983.

2. In 1831–32, Buchanan stated that "many respectable families have gone to the townships of Kildare, Kilkenny, and New Glasgow" and in 1836 he stated that "farming emigrants may settle to advantage" in the townships of Rawdon, Kildare, and Kilkenny. BPP 1831–32(724) XXXII; BPP 1836(76) XL.

3. Lower Canada Census, 1851.

4. Raoul Blanchard, *L'Ouest du Canada Français* (Montreal: Beauchemin, 1953–54), 257.

5. In 1851, Montreal had 41,000 Catholics of whom 26,000 were French Canadians. The remaining 15,000 must have been mainly Irish (either Irish-born or people with Irish-ancestry).

6. Montreal's upwardly mobile poor are discussed in Sherry Olson and Patricia A. Thornton, *Peopling the North American City: Montreal*

1840–1900 (Montreal: McGill-Queen's University Press, 2011), 350–52.

7. Maguire, *The Irish in America*, 100.

8. Ibid., 96.

9. Pentland, *Labour and Capital in Canada, 1650–1860*, 102–21.

10. William Forbes Adams, *Ireland and Irish Emigration to the New World from 1815 to the Famine* (New Haven, CT: Yale University Press, 1932), 354.

11. D'Arcy O'Connor, *Montreal's Irish Mafia: The True Story of the Infamous West End Gang* (Etobicoke, ON: John Wiley & Sons Canada, 2011), 12–16. Griffintown was not solely Irish, having a sizeable French Canadian population.

12. See especially Sharon Doyle Driedger, *An Irish Heart: How a Small Immigrant Community Shaped Canada* (Toronto: HarperCollins, 2010), which tells Griffintown's story in detail. Also see Herbert Brown Ames, *The City Below the Hill: A Sociological Study of a Portion of the City of Montreal, Canada* (Montreal: Bishop Engraving and Print Company, 1897).

13. Griffintown was later renamed Faubourg-des-Récollets, after the order of nuns who first held property there in the late eighteenth century.

14. Driedger, *An Irish Heart*, 8.

15. Stephen Leacock, *Montreal, Seaport and City* (Toronto: McClelland & Stewart, 1948), 172.

16. Maguire, *The Irish in America*, 97.

17. PRONI T3664/1: Marianne Gurd, Montreal to Fanny Payne, County Longford, May 4, 1850.

18. Driedger, *An Irish Heart*, 350.

19. BAnQ (Gatineau) P1000 S3 D16: Irish Settlement of St. Columban by Brother Jerome Hart, Daniel O'Connell School (1955).

20. Bouchette, *Topographical Dictionary of Lower Canada*.

21. NAS RHP 35156: 1838 plan of Lower Canada.

22. The names of the family heads who were present in 1825 have been recorded in Bourguignon, *Saint-Colomban*, 35. They included: Pierre Miron, Jean-Baptiste Miron, Michael Carthy, Michael Molloy, Patrick

Molloy, Thomas Keogh, Richard Power, Michael Murphy, François [illegible], Michael Ryan, Patrick Kelly, Patrick Shea, Peter Canfield, Anthony Dempsey, Edward Magher, James Qinlan, John Ryan, Edward Elliott, John O'Brien, Denis Carthy, John Murphy, [illegible] Howard, Brian Finegan [illegible] Casey, Owen Manning, Philip Reilly, John Reilly, Hugh Reilly, James Cowley, William McCormick, Michael Fahey, Cornelius Horan, Anthony Murphy, Michael Borden, James Murphy, Patrick [Murray?], John Murray, James Murphy, Duncan McNabb, François [Labroisse?] John Ryan, Richard Burke, Duncan [McDonald?] Joseph Houle [Houde?].

23. Driedger, *An Irish Heart*, 88.

24. Father Falvey died in 1885 and is buried in St. Columban Cemetery.

25. BAnQ (Gatineau) P1000 S3 D16. Sister Mary St. Patrick died in 1905 and is buried in St. Columban Cemetery.

26. Ibid.

27. Montcalm County appears as Leinster in the 1851 Census.

28. Blanchard, *Le Centre du Canada Français*, 427–29. Bourguignon, *Saint-Colomban*, 30.

29. Wexford was later renamed Entrelacs.

30. NAS RHP 35156: 1838 plan of Lower Canada.

31. Bouchette, *Topographical Dictionary of Lower Canada*.

32. New Glasgow appears as Lacorne in the 1851 Lower Canada Census.

33. Kilarney Lakes appears on the 1838 Lower Canada map (NAS RHP 35156) and Bouchette refers to it in his *Topographical Dictionary*.

34. Joliette County appears as Berthier County in the 1851 Census.

35. Grace, *The Irish in Quebec: An Introduction to the Historiography*, 72.

36. Joseph Bouchette, *General Report of an Official Tour Through the New Settlements of the Province of Lower Canada Performed in the Summer of 1824, in Obedience to the Commands and Instructions of His Excellency George Earl of Dalhousie, G.C.B., Captain General and Governor in Chief of British North-America* (Quebec: T. Carey, 1825), 15.

37. BPP w/e June 13, 1840.

38. Daniel B. Parkinson, "From Rawdon to Wellington County," *Connections* (The Journal of the Quebec Family History Society) 38, No. 2 (1999): 67–78.

39. Bouchette, *Topographical Dictionary of Lower Canada*.

40. "Irish Settlement" appears next to Kildare on the 1838 map.

41. Lanaudière Heritage Trail/Laurentian Heritage Web Magazine.

42. Blanchard, *Le Centre du Canada Français*, 428–29, 441.

43. Bouchette, *Topographical Dictionary of Lower Canada*.

44. Blanchard, *L'Ouest du Canada Français*, 68–69.

45. Bouchette outlined the area's attractions in his *Topographical Dictionary, Lower Canada* (entry for Beauharnois).

46. Buchanan, *1832 Emigrants' Handbook for Arrivals at Quebec*. BPP w/e Aug. 20, 1842. Running along the Richelieu River, the Chambly Canal was part of a waterway linking the St. Lawrence River with the Hudson River in the United States. Commenced in 1831, it was opened in 1843.

47. See Chapter 6.

48. Robert Sellar, *History of the County of Huntingdon and of the Seigniories of Chateauguay and Beauharnois from Their First Settlement to the Year 1838* (Huntingdon, QC: Canadian Gleaner, 1888), 201.

49. Ibid., 204–6.

50. Ibid., 367. The common load was 1 and 1/2 bushels — about ninety pounds.

51. Ibid., 367.

52. Ibid., 422–30.

53. RHL USPG Series E, 1845–46 (LAC m/f A-221).

54. RHL USPG Series E 1860 (LAC m/f A-228).

55. RHL USPG Series E, 1845–46 (LAC m/f A-221).

56. Sherrington appears in Huntingdon County in the 1851 Census.

57. Sellar, *History of the County of Huntingdon*, 490.

58. Ibid., 252.

59. *DCB* Vol. IX (Edward Ellice). A fur baron, merchant banker and major landowner, Ellice had considerable financial interests in North America.

60. The obligations and rights of tenants and seigneurs are outlined in Serge Courville [translated by Richard Howard], *Quebec: A Historical Geography* (Vancouver: University of British Columbia Press, 2008), 49–68, 132–38.

61. Bouchette, *Topographical Dictionary of Lower Canada*. Beauharnois entry.

62. Sellar, *History of the County of Huntingdon*, 294–97.

63. The old St. Malachie Cemetery was located on the north side of the Châteauguay River west of the village of Ormstown. All traces of it have disappeared.

64. Sellar, *History of the County of Huntingdon*, 299.

65. *Montreal Gazette*, March 19, 1855. Ormstown's first Anglican church was built in 1835.

66. RHL USPG Series E, 1845–46 (LAC m/f A-221).

67. Sellar, *History of the County of Huntingdon*, 309.

68. Ibid., 467.

69. Ibid., 263.

70. Ibid.

71. Ibid., 473–79.

72. Ibid., 474.

73. Ibid., 55.

74. *DCB*, Vol. V, Henry Caldwell.

75. Noël, "Gabriel Christie's Seigneuries," 161, 203.

76. Iberville County appears as Rouville County in the 1851 Census.

77. Campey, *Les Écossais*, 9, 56, 74, 96.

78. Bouchette, *Topographical Dictionary of Lower Canada*, Monnoir entry.

79. BPP 1831–32(724)XXXII. Buchanan refers to the people who were heading for "the neighbourhood of St. Césaire."

80. BAnQ Montreal *Cadastre Abrégé de la Seigneurie de Monnoir*, 1861, 50–51. The 1861 landholders included Daniel Boomhover, Joseph Arthur, Joseph Nolin, James Cogan, Joseph Harbeck, and Abel Taylor. The "Rang des Irlandais" location can still be seen in the present-day road atlas.

81. Father John Downs, "Sainte-Marthe et Ses Irlandais," *Quelques pages d'histoire de Sainte Marthe, comté de Vaudreuil*, publications généalogiques n.d., 8–13. Hudson Historical Society website.

Chapter 6: The Ottawa Valley

1. MacKay, *Flight from Famine*, 167.
2. Bruce S. Elliott, "Emigration from South Leinster to Eastern Upper Canada," *Canadian Papers in Rural History* 8, Gananoque (1991): 277–305.
3. Martin Doyle, *Hints on Emigration to Upper Canada Especially Addressed to the Middle and Lower Classes of Great Britain and Ireland* (Dublin: 1834), 71–74.
4. NAI CSO/RP/1818/403, 412: Petition of Thomas Lipsett, May 21, 1818. The other heads of household were: David, John, Gilbert, and Thomas Lipsett, William Mullan, Stuart Armstrong, Robert and John Johnston, Archibald Elliott, John Rogers, William Long, James Coulter, Charles Hogg, John Clark, Armstrong Elliott, William Dudgeon.
5. Lockwood, "The Pattern of Settlement in Eastern Ontario," 235–57, Bruce S. Elliott, *Irish Migrants in the Canadas: A New Approach* (Kingston, ON: McGill-Queen's University Press, 1988), 82–146. Ian Pringle & Enoch Padolsky, "The Irish Heritage of the English of the Ottawa Valley," *English Studies in Canada* 8, No. 3 (Fall 1981): 338–52.
6. Campey, *Seeking a Better Future*, 103–10.
7. Bruce. S. Elliott, "The Famous Township of Hull: Image and Aspirations of a Pioneer Quebec Community," *Social History*, Vol. 12 (1969): 339–67.
8. In spite of widespread and repeated complaints within Britain over the high cost of timber, the protective tariffs remained in place until 1860. Davis, *The Industrial Revolution and British Overseas Trade*, 48–49. Duties increased from 25s. per load in 1804 to 54s. 6d per load in 1811.
9. Donald MacKay, *The Lumberjacks* (Toronto: Natural Heritage, 1998), 40.
10. Richard Reid, (ed.), *The Upper Ottawa Valley to 1855: A Collection of Documents Edited with an Introduction by Richard Reid* (Toronto: Champlain Society, 1990). Also see R. Forbes Hirsch, *The Upper Ottawa Valley Timber Trade: A Sketch* (Ottawa: The Historical Society of Ottawa, Bytown Pamphlet series, No. 14, April 1985).

11. Pentland, *Labour and Capital in Canada 1650–1860*, 104, 116, 121. MacKay, *The Lumberjacks*, 28, 36.

12. *DCB* (Peter Aylen) Vol. IX. Michael S. Cross, "The Shiners' War: Social Violence in the Ottawa Valley in the 1830s," *Canadian Historical Review* 54, No. 1 (March 1973): 1–26.

13. NAB MPG 484(1): Sketch of the Rideau Settlement.

14. For further details of the Scots who settled in the Rideau Valley military settlements, see Lucille H. Campey, *The Scottish Pioneers of Upper Canada, 1784–1855: Glengarry and Beyond* (Toronto: Natural Heritage, 2005), 35–68. Also see Michael E. Vance, *Imperial Immigrants: Scottish Settlers in the Upper Ottawa Valley* (Toronto: Dundurn, 2012).

15. The British government's £10 emigration scheme, introduced in 1817, was used. Talbot, as group leader, was required to pay a £10 deposit for each settler, which was repayable later. Land grants were provided free of charge. For further details of Talbot's group, see Elliott, *Irish Migrants in the Canadas*, 61–81. For the list of the people in his group, see ibid., 246–47. The heads of households were mainly farmers, but they included a few shoemakers, bricklayers, and carpenters.

16. *DCB* (Richard Talbot) Vol. VIII. Talbot's group sailed in the *Brunswick*. Talbot's muddled thinking in planning and implementing his colonization scheme caused much disappointment and many setbacks. He lost the confidence of around half of his original recruits, who left his group. In all, he recruited a total of thirty-two families plus various single men, including his sons, servants, and labourers. Fifteen families settled in the Richmond military settlement, fifteen families went west to Middlesex County (see Chapter 8), and two went to Montreal. Elliott, *Irish Migrants in the Canadas*, 63–77.

17. LAC MG25 G300: Richardson family.

18. Michael S. Cross, "The Age of Gentility: The Formation of the Aristocracy in the Ottawa Valley," Canadian Historical Association: *Historical Papers* 2, No. 1 (1967): 105–17.

19. Report of the Reverend John Flood (Richmond) to the Society for the Propagation of the Gospel in RHL USPG Series E, 1854–55 (LAC m/f A-223).

20. Glen J. Lockwood, *The Rear of Leeds and Lansdowne: The Making of Community on the Gananoque River Frontier, 1796–1996* (Lyndhurst, Ontario: Corporation of the Township of Rear of Leeds and Lansdowne, 1996), 126.

21. NAB CO 384/1, 178–87: Families from counties Carlow and Wexford preparing to emigrate from New Ross in November, 1817.

22. Bruce S. Elliott, "Emigration from South Leinster to Eastern Upper Canada," *Canadian Papers in Rural History* 8, Gananoque (1991): 277–305. The two lists of Wexford and Carlow families can be found in theshipslist.com.

23. Lockwood, *The Rear of Leeds and Lansdowne*, 26.

24. Grace, "The Irish in Mid-Nineteenth-Century Canada," 73–80.

25. Remittances are discussed in Grace, "The Irish in Mid-Nineteenth-Century Canada," 73–76.

26. Oliver Macdonagh, *A Pattern of Government Growth, 1800–1860, The Passengers Acts and Their Enforcement* (London: MacGibbon & Kee, 1961), 27–31.

27. MacKay, *Flight from Famine*, 55–63.

28. Passenger lists for the *Hebe*, crossing in August 1823 with 288 passengers, and the *Stakesby*, crossing in September 1823 with 293 passengers, are in LAC MG24 B74 (m/f M-141). They name the immigrants and give details of their former residence in Ireland.

29. Andrew Haydon, *Pioneer Sketches in the District of Bathurst* (Toronto: Ryerson Press, 1925), 163.

30. *Report from the Select Committee Appointed to Inquire into the Expediency of Encouraging Emigration from the United Kingdom, 1826* (404) IV, Return of Irish Emigrants settled in the Bathurst District.

31. Letter from Michael Corkery, July 6, 1827, in: "Instructions Under the Direction of the Secretary of State for the Colonial Department Communicated to Lieut. Col. Cockburn by the Rt. Hon. R.W. Horton in a Letter Dated 26th January 1827, with a Letter and Appendix Addressed to R.W. Horton by Lieut. Col. Cockburn, Detailing the Execution of these Instructions" [electronic resource], 66.

32. Ibid., 65–66.

33. OA F61 (m/f524); Peter Robinson fonds, #8, 26–28.

34. NAB CO 384/12, 174–76.

35. Ibid., 345–48.

36. OA F61 (m/f524): Peter Robinson fonds, #8, 29–32.

37. NAB CO 384/12, 167–69.

38. Cowan, *British Emigration to British North America*, 65–84.

39. A major confrontation occurred between Orangemen and Irish Catholics in Beckwith Township on April 23, 1824, but only Irish Catholics were found guilty and convicted of rioting and assault. For further details see MacKay, *Flight from Famine*, 70–79.

40. See Chapter 7.

41. *Montreal Gazette*, June 11, 1829.

42. DERO D3155/WH 2867: letters from John Richards, 1830–31 to Rt. Hon Wilmot Horton, March 4, 1831.

43. William N.T. Wylie, *Poverty, Distress and Disease: Labour and the Construction of the Rideau Canal, 1826–32* in *Labourers on the Rideau Canal. 1826–1832: From Worksite to World Heritage Site*, edited by Katherine Mary Jean McKenna (Ottawa: Borealis Press, 2008), 31–40.

44. John MacTaggert, *Three Years in Canada: An Account of the Actual State of the Country in 1826-7-8 Comprehending Its Resources, Productions, Improvements and Capabilities and Including Sketches of the State of Society, Advice to Emigrants, Etc.* (London: 1829) Vol. I, 290; Vol. II, 242.

45. MacKay, *The Lumberjacks*, 13–16, 22–27, 40–45.

46. Reports from the Select Committee Appointed to Inquire into the Expediency of Encouraging Emigration from the United Kingdom, 1826 Abstract of Petitions.

47. Lord Clifden provided his tenants with funds to emigrate during the 1840s. Gerard Moran, *Sending Out Ireland's Poor: Assisted Emigration to North America in the Nineteenth Century* (Dublin: Four Courts Press, 2004), 38, 45, 53.

48. Report from the Select Committee Appointed to Inquire into the Expediency of Encouraging Emigration, 1826: Abstract of Petitions, 484, 497, 499.

49. The social mobility of the Irish in Huntley Township is discussed in J. Gwynn, "The Irish in Eastern Ontario: The Social Structure of Huntley Township in Carleton County, 1851–71," in *Exploring Our*

Heritage: The Ottawa Valley Experience, edited by Vrenia Ivonoffski and Sandra Campbell (Arnprior, ON: Arnprior and District Historical Society, 1980), 20–31.

50. Elliott, *Irish Migrants in the Canadas*, 116–17.
51. Glen J. Lockwood, *Montague: A Social History of an Irish Ontario Township, 1783–1980* (Smiths Falls, ON: Corporation of the Township of Montague, 1980), 107–10.
52. Glen J. Lockwood, "Irish Immigrants and the Critical Years in Eastern Ontario: Montague Township, 1821–81," *Canadian Papers in Rural History* Vol. IV (1984): 153–78.
53. Glen J. Lockwood, "Success and the Doubtful Image of Irish Immigrants in Upper Canada: The Case of Montague Township, 1820–1900," in *The Untold Story: The Irish in Canada*, edited by Robert O'Driscoll and Lorna Reynolds (Toronto: Celtic Arts of Canada, 1988) Vol. I, 319–41.
54. LAC (m/f) C-11733: South Elmsley Township Census, 1851, quoted in Lockwood, "Success and the Doubtful Image of Irish Immigrants in Upper Canada: The Case of Montague Township," 330.
55. LAC (m/f) C-11732: Montague Township Census, 1851, quoted in Ibid., 333.
56. Elliott, *Irish Migrants in the Canadas*, 161–70.
57. BAnQ (Gatineau) P11, D4: William H. Johnston and Ruby Dods. The Gibsons, Shouldices, and the Mahons came to Masham in 1836, as did Samuel Gibson and his wife, Ellen, both originating from County Monaghan.
58. John L. Gourlay, *History of the Ottawa Valley: A Collection of Facts, Events and Reminiscences for Over Half a Century* (Ottawa: Author, 1896), 197. Eardley, Hull, Masham, and Wakefield townships were later incorporated into Gatineau County.
59. Raoul Blanchard, "Les Pays de l'Ottawa," *Études Canadiennes Troisième Série*, Vol. 3 (Grenoble, France: Allier, 1949), 57–64.
60. Willard Vandine Smith, "The Evolution of a Fall Line Settlement, Buckingham, Quebec," (M.A. thesis, University of Ottawa, 1967), 19, 28, 33.
61. BAnQ P80, S1: Ruth Higginson collection, *Buckingham Post*, Jan. 5, 1899; Jan. 26, 1934.

62. Father R.P. Alexis De Barbezieux, *Histoire de la Province Ecclésiastique d'Ottawa et de la Colonisation dans la Vallée de l'Ottawa* (Ottawa: 1897), 118–20, 468.

63. Elliott, *Irish Migrants in the Canadas*, 9–35.

64. The 1851 Lower Canada census only shows Ottawa County, which includes entries for the later Pontiac County.

65. LAC 920 MD 154: Journal of James Moncrieff Wilson, 44–45.

66. LAC MG25 G347: Heney family.

67. The Grenville Canal was built to navigate the Long Sault Rapids on the Ottawa River.

68. Marjory Whitelaw (ed.), *The Dalhousie Journals* (Ottawa: Oberon Press, 1978–82) Vol. 2, 34.

69. C. Thomas, *History of the Counties of Argenteuil, Quebec, and Prescott, Ontario, from the Earliest Settlement to the Present* (Montreal: John Lovell, 1896), 208, 263.

70. BAnQ Gatineau, P48, B4D4: William McQuat Cottingham fonds.

71. Ibid.

72. New Ireland later became known as Laurel.

73. Thomas, *History of the Counties of Argenteuil, Quebec, and Prescott, Ontario*, 428.

74. *DCB*, Vol. VII (George Hamilton).

75. Dorothy Jane Smith, "The Community and the Fair: Vankleek Hill, West Hawkesbury Township and the Agricultural Fair, 1900–1950" (M.A. thesis, Carleton University, Ottawa, 2011), 65–66.

76. Thomas, *History of the Counties of Argenteuil, Quebec, and Prescott, Ontario*, 576.

77. LAC MG25 G271 Vol. 16 No. 11: Gertrude Maria Harkin.

78. OA F1237: Thomas Dick fonds.

79. Thomas, *History of the Counties of Argenteuil, Quebec, and Prescott, Ontario*, 647–49. The Irish Settlement was also known as "McDonald Hill" and the "Darragh Settlement." Robert McAuley is believed to have been the first settler. John McCrank arrived in around 1827, Daniel McCormick came in 1847, and Patrick McDonnell arrived in 1850.

80. BAnQ (Gatineau) P1000 S3 D4: *Rediscovering Our Past 1847–1997:*

A Celebration of Pontiac County's 150th Anniversary by Jo-Anne Brownlee (1998), 4–7.

81. LAC MG8-G49: Rev. Mary A. Dougherty, "Quyon Parish History," 1959, 1–5.

82. Kathleen Mennie-de Varennes, *Au Coeur de la Gatineau ou l'Histoire de la Paroisse de la Visitation de Gracefield* (Quebec: Ste Foy, 1985), 27–28. *DCB*, Vol. VIII (John Egan).

83. LAC MG8-G49: Rev. Mary A. Dougherty, "Quyon Parish History," 1959, 1–5.

84, LAC MG25 G271 Vol. 17/27: Rev. James Brown, "History of the Parish of Onslow" (1908) 1, 2, 5.

85. PRONI T2410.

86. LAC MG25 G271 Vol. 17/15.

87. Ibid. Some of the Tipperary settlers were migrants from other parts of the Ottawa Valley (Elliott, *Irish Migrants in the Canada*, 161–70).

88. LAC MG25 G271 Vol 17/21, 22. Before Falloon's arrival Protestant settlers had to rely on the Methodist ministry in the area.

89. Michel Pourbaix, *The History of a Christian Community: Eardley, Luskville, Pontiac* (Pontiac, QC: Corporation Culturelle de Frampton, 1999), 12, 28, 32. Daniel Pickett was the first Methodist pastor to visit Hull from the Upper Canada side of the river, and from 1823 Methodist preachers made regular visits. Hull's Methodist circuit founded in 1826 was the first to be established on the north side of the river. For details of the Perth Methodist circuit, founded in 1821, see James M. Neelin and Michael R. Neelin, *The Old Methodist Burying Ground in the Town of Perth, Lanark County, Ontario* (Ottawa Branch, Ontario Genealogical Society, 1978).

90. LAC MG25 G271, Vol. 17/17: Shawville. Mennie-de Varennes, *Au Coeur de la Gatineau*, 28.

91. Ibid. Religious notes.

92. Lockwood, "The Pattern of Settlement in Eastern Ontario," 252–54. Those settling in Stafford included Protestants from Wexford.

93. PRONI D4008/2.

94. Elliott, *Irish Migrants in the Canadas*, 119, 162–65, 239.

Chapter 7: The Rest of Eastern Ontario and the Peter Robinson Settlers

1. Maguire, *The Irish in America*, 109–10.

2. Ibid., 105.

3. James Buchanan, an Ulsterman, was the brother of Alexander Buchanan, the Quebec immigration agent.

4. H.J.M. Johnston, *British Emigration Policy, 1815–1830: Shovelling Out Paupers* (Oxford: Clarendon Press, 1972), 24.

5. Moran, *Sending Out Ireland's Poor*, 23. In selecting people for his 1825 scheme, Peter Robinson had allocated 100 places to Mountcashel's tenants.

6. In 1851, Peterborough, Victoria, Northumberland, Durham, and Hastings counties had around 26,500 Irish-born, of whom less than one quarter would have received assistance from the government or landlords.

7. MacKay, *Flight from Famine*, 80–117. Wendy Cameron, "Peter Robinson's Settlers in Peterborough," in *The Untold Story: The Irish in Canada*, edited by Robert O'Driscoll and Lorna Reynolds (Toronto: Celtic Arts of Canada, 1988), Vol. I, 343–53. Wendy Cameron, "Selecting Peter Robinson's Irish Emigrants," *Social History* 9 (1976): 29–46. Cowan, *British Emigration to British North America*, 77–84.

8. See Chapter 6 for the Ottawa Valley Peter Robinson settlers.

9. They sailed in nine naval transports from Cork: The *Fortitude* (282), *Resolution* (227), *Albion* (191), *Brunswick* (343), *Star* (214), *Amity* (147), *Regulus* (157), *Elizabeth* (210), and *John Barry* (253). There were several deaths during the voyages due to fever. For the passenger lists, see olivetree.com.

10. A.G. Brunger, "Geographical Propinquity Among Pre-Famine Catholic Irish Settlers in Upper Canada," *Journal of Historical Geography* 8, No. 3 (1982): 265–82.

11. Howard Pammett, "The Irish Emigrant Settler in the Pioneer Kawarthas," *Families* 17 (4) (1978): 154–74.

12. Moran, *Sending Out Ireland's Poor*, 24–25.

13. NAB CO 384/13 (1824–25), 541.

14. Charles Pelham Mulvany, C.M. Ryan, and C.R. Stewart, *History*

of the County of Peterborough, Ontario: Containing a History of the County, History of Haliburton County, Their Townships, Towns, Schools, Churches, Etc., General and Local Statistics, Biographical Sketches, and an Outline History of the Dominion of Canada, Etc., Etc* (Toronto: C.B. Robinson, 1884), 273.

15. For the questionnaire replies see LAC m/f M-141: Peter Robinson Papers, 1823–44. Also see Cameron, "Peter Robinson's Settlers in Peterborough," 350–51.

16. MacKay, *Flight from Famine*, 92–93.

17. Cowan, *British Emigration to British North America*, 78–79.

18. Edwin C. Guillet, *The Valley of the Trent*, edited with an Introduction and Notes by Edwin C. Guillet (Toronto: Champlain Society for the Government of Ontario, University of Toronto Press, 1957), 112, quoting Stewart's letter of January 20, 1826.

19. MacTaggert, *Three Years in Canada*, Vol. I, 192; Vol. II, 281.

20. Susanna Moodie, *Roughing It in the Bush, or, Forest Life in Canada* (Toronto: MacLear, 1871), 210.

21. Samuel Strickland, *Twenty-Seven Years in Canada West, or, The Experience of an Early Settler* (London: R. Bentley, 1853), Vol. I, 87.

22. Catharine Parr Traill, *Backwoods of Canada*, Letter VI.

23. Frances Stewart, *Our Forest Home: Being Extracts from the Correspondence of the Late Frances Stewart* (Montreal, 1902) 84–85.

24. Basil Hall to William Wilmot Horton (undersecretary of state for the colonies), printed in *The Belfast Commercial Chronicle*, January 26, 1828.

25. Basil Hall, *Travels in North America in the Years 1827 and 1828* (Edinburgh: Cadell, 1830), Vol. 1, 288.

26. Ibid., Vol. 1, 286.

27. Ibid., Vol. 2, 321–22.

28. Ibid., Vol. 1, 138.

29. LAC MG24 I59: John Langton and family fonds: letters to his father June 16, 28, August 12, 1835.

30. Report from the Select Committee Appointed to Inquire into the Expediency of Encouraging Emigration, 1826, Evidence of Dr. Strachan, 100.

31. Glasgow Colonial Society Correspondence (LAC M-1354): Rev. Thomas Alexander to Rev. James Gibson, April 1, 1835.

32. Cavan Township was in Durham County and Monaghan was in Peterborough County.

33. Houston and Smyth, *Irish Emigration and Canadian Settlement*, 48–50, 205–7. For details of the Buchanan group that settled west of Toronto, see Chapter 8.

34. John J. Mannion, *Irish Settlements in Eastern Canada: A Study of Cultural Transfer and Adaptation* (Toronto: University of Toronto Press, 1974), 15–54.

35. Mackay, *Flight from Famine*, 112.

36. Watson Kirkconnell, *Victoria County Centennial History* (Lindsay, ON: Waterman-Warder Press, 1921), 25. Irish immigrants, who sailed from Sligo in the *Eliza* in 1840, were said to be heading for their relatives already settled in Cavan Township. BPP w/e June 20.

37. Kirkconnell, *Victoria County Centennial History*, 11.

38. Guy Richard Ferguson, "The Peter Robinson Settlers in Emily Township, 1825–61" (M.A. thesis, Queen's University, Kingston, 1979).

39. Howard T. Pammett, *Lilies and Shamrocks: A History of Emily Township County of Victoria Ontario, 1818–1973* (Lindsay, ON: J. Deyell & Co., 1974), 25–38. For Robinson's list of settlers receiving lots in Emily Townships see 318–22.

40. The Wyndham tenants sailed in the *Waterloo* and arrived in Quebec in June "in excellent health." BPP w/e July 6, 1839.

41. Wendy Cameron and Mary McDougall Maude, *Assisting Emigration to Upper Canada: The Petworth Project, 1832–37* (Montreal: McGill-Queen's University Press, 2000), 191–92. Flannan P. Enright, "Pre-Famine Reform and Emigration on the Wyndham Estate in Clare," *The Other Clare*, Vol. 8 (1984): 33–36.

42. Wyndham Estate records (NAC m/f A-1642), quoted in MacKay, *Flight from Famine*, 183.

43. MacKay, *Flight from Famine*, 178–85. Moran, *Sending Out Ireland's Poor*, 56–57, 118.

44. Ibid.

45. For instance, in 1840 Wyndham paid the passages of 126 tenants from his County Clare estate who sailed in the *James Cook* from Limerick. They were said to be intending to settle in the Peterborough area. BPP w/e June 6.

46. NAI RLFC/3/1/950: George Wyndham to J.P. Kennedy, March 24, 1846.

47. Maguire, *The Irish in America*, 111.

48. Trains first arrived in Lindsay from Port Hope in 1857. Kirkconnell, *Victoria County Centennial History*, 145–47.

49. PRONI D3513/1/22: J. Collins to family members, June 22, 1863, August 1, 1864.

50. PRONI D1424/3/29, /30: Ellen Dunlop to Rev. Alexander Kirkpatrick, May 21, 1879, February 7, 1881.

51. PRONI D1604/289: Tom Hay to George Kirkpatrick, February 18, 1883.

52. Glasgow Colonial Society Correspondence (LAC M-1353): Rev. Matthew Miller to Rev. Burns, September 29, 1832.

53. Rev. Miller, Ibid.

54. Ibid.

55. Clara McFerran, "Catholic Pioneers of Tyendinaga and Neighbouring Townships," *Canadian Catholic Historical Association Report* 8 (1940–41): 77–94.

56. PRONI T3566/1: William Portt petition, April 1820.

57. In a letter home to his family in Fermanagh, Royal Keys, living in Marmora, also referred to Tyendinaga, stating that some of it was already settled but that the government had not yet had it surveyed. MCFMS: Letter from Royal and Mary Keys to William Keys, September 10, 1834.

58. PRONI T3566/1: William Portt was one of Richard Talbot's recruits arriving in 1819. Elliott, *Irish Migrants in the Canadas*, 92.

59. Gerald E. Boyce, *Historic Hastings* (Belleville, ON: Hastings County Council, 1967), 270–71.

60. Susanna Moodie, quoted in Boyce, *Historic Hastings*, 271.

61. bytown.net/hastingscounty.htm.

62. MacKay, *Flight from Famine*, 93.

63. In 1823, Charles Hayes set aside some land for the building of a Catholic church, which was completed in 1829. Boyce, *Historic Hastings*, 204, 300. Also see marmorahistory.ca/1821-pioneer-iron-town.

64. Marmora Historical Foundation (marmorahistory.ca).

65. MCFMS: Letter from Royal and Mary Keys to William Keys, September 10, 1834.

66. Boyce, *Historic Hastings*, 287.

67. One hundred of Fitzwilliam's tenants from County Wicklow, "all very poor," sailed from Liverpool to Quebec in 1841. BPP w/e August 7.

68. Pauline Ryan, "A Study of Irish Immigration to North Hastings County," *Ontario History*, Vol. LXXXIII, No. 1 (March 1991): 23–37. Gravestone inscriptions and death notices reveal that most Irish immigrants living in North Hastings County originated from Wicklow.

69. Boyce, *Historic Hastings*, 365–66.

70. Mulvany et al., *History of the County of Peterborough*, 456–57. Kirkconnell, *Victoria County Centennial History*, 10, 74–84. The economy was more mixed in the northern townships, with people being engaged in mining and lumbering in addition to farming.

71. Houston and Smyth, *Irish Emigration and Canadian Settlement*, 102–4, 127–32.

72. Boyce, *Historic Hastings*, 90. *DCB*, Vol. IX (William Hutton). William Hutton wrote *Canada: Its Present Conditions, Prospects and Resources, Fully Described for the Information of Intending Emigrants* (London: Stanfords, 1854).

73. Julian Gwyn, "The Irish in the Napanee River Valley: Camden East Township, 1851–1881," in *The Untold Story: The Irish in Canada*, edited by Robert O'Driscoll and Lorna Reynolds (Toronto: Celtic Arts of Canada, 1988), 355–75.

74. Catherine Anne Wilson, *A New Lease on Life: Landlords, Tenants, and Immigration in Ireland and Canada* (Montreal: McGill-Queen's University Press, 1994), 174–204.

75. PRONI D3817: Moore Hill Papers, documentation of the Amherst Island estate of Robert Perceval Maxwell.

76. The Ards settlers who took up this offer were not Lord Mountcashel's

tenants. He lost possession of Amherst Island in the 1840s and sold it to Major Robert Perceval Maxwell, a fellow Irishman.

77. In 1851, 50 percent of Wolfe Island's population was Roman Catholic. Given that there were very few French, most of them must have been Irish Catholics. Around one quarter of the population was Irish-born, indicating that a sizeable proportion of the Irish were recent arrivals.

78. Maguire, *The Irish in America*, 127.

79. The land was said to be particularly poor in Pittsburgh. Lockwood, *The Rear of Leeds and Lansdowne*, 30.

80. Settlement data taken from the 1871 Census indicates that these townships experienced a substantial intake of Irish immigrants during the famine period. Houston and Smyth, *Irish Emigration and Canadian Settlement*, 216–18.

81. The sick were taken to hastily constructed sheds as well as to the hospital at Kingston. The dead were buried in a mass grave on the hospital grounds. An Angel of Mercy stone monument was placed at the site in 1894.

82. Daniel Coleman Lyne, "The Irish in the Province of Canada in the Decade Leading to Confederation" (M.A. thesis, McGill University, Montreal, 1960), 65–67.

83. Clare F. Galvin, *The Holy Land: A History of Ennismore Township, County of Peterborough Ontario, 1825–1975* (Ennismore, ON: Corporation of the Township of Ennismore, 1978), 24–27, 47.

Chapter 8: North to Lake Simcoe and Westward to the Thames Valley

1. PRONI T1362/1: Richard Breathwaite to his parents, October 1, 1849.

2. RHL USPG Series E, 1854–56 (LAC m/f A-223): United Society for the Propagation of the Gospel, reports from missionaries.

3. Maguire, *The Irish in America*, 112.

4. *Report from the Select Committee Appointed to Inquire into the Expediency of Encouraging Emigration*, 1826. Evidence of Dr. Strachan, 100. The Buchanan families who went to the Peterborough region settled in Cavan and Monaghan townships.

5.   In 1881, Simcoe County had just over 32,000 people having Irish ancestry, who represented 42 percent of Simcoe's total population.

6.   Rama and Mara townships had experienced a large influx of Irish Catholics by 1851. J.E. Farewell, *County of Ontario: Short Notes as to the Early Settlement and Progress of the County and Brief References to the Pioneers and Some Ontario County Men Who Have Taken a Prominent Part in Provincial and Dominion Affairs* (Whitby, ON: Gazette-Chronicle Press, 1907).

7.   Maguire, *The Irish in America*, 113–14, 122.

8.   Andrew F. Hunter, *A History of Simcoe County* (Barrie: Historical Committee of Simcoe County, 1948), 40, 44, 50.

9.   The Palatine Irish were Protestant Germans who had been living in the Middle Rhine region of present-day Germany before severe economic hardships caused some to head for Ireland in the early eighteenth century in search of better living conditions. They were mostly from Limerick, but some also originated from counties Wexford and Kerry. Some relocated to Upper Canada in the early nineteenth century. Despite forming small clusters in Brock Township (Ontario County) and Blanshard Township (Perth County) as well as in the Ottawa Valley, they were scattered widely by 1871. Elliott, *Irish Migrants in the Canadas*, 85, 134–36, 251–53.

10. Some Irish families also went to Tiny Township (Simcoe County) beginning in 1879. Daniel Parkinson, "Settlers at Simcoe County from Rawdon Township QC," *Families* 43, No. 1 (2004): 11–18.

11. OA F725: James D. Stephens fonds. Hunter, *A History of Simcoe County*, 248.

12. Hunter, *A History of Simcoe County*, 65.

13. *Society for the Propagation of the Gospel Annual Report*, 1841, xcii–xciii.

14. Hunter, *A History of Simcoe County*, 40, 63, 65.

15. Reverend Samuel J. Boddy, *A Brief Memoir of the Rev. Samuel B. Ardagh, A.M., T.C.D., Late Rector of Barrie and Incumbent of Shanty Bay, Lake Simcoe, Upper Canada*, edited by Samuel J. Boddy (Toronto: Rowsell and Hutchison,1874), 26.

16. William Watson, *The Emigrants Guide to the Canadas* (Dublin: G. Bull, 1822), 10.

17. The Irish-born represented 35 percent of Toronto's population — significantly more than the English-/Scottish-born put together.

18. Alexander Macdonell, the Roman Catholic priest and future bishop who served at St. Raphael, Glengarry, from 1804, established St. Paul's in 1822, making it the first Roman Catholic parish to be formed between Kingston and Windsor.

19. Aidan Manning, *Between the Runways: A History of Irish-Catholic Settlement in Southern Peel County and Etobicoke* (Etobicoke, ON: Author, 2009), 50–58.

20. Marriage records indicate that Toronto's early Irish Catholics had hailed from all parts of southern Ireland, but most had originated from counties Clare, Limerick, Cork, Tipperary, Waterford, Kerry, and Wexford. Mark McGowan, "Irish Catholics" in *The Encyclopaedia of Canada's Peoples*, edited by Paul Robert Magocsi (Toronto: Published for the Multicultural History Society of Ontario by the University of Toronto Press, circa 1999), 742.

21. Corktown, located along the lakefront, was south of present-day Regent Park and north of the Gardiner Expressway.

22. Manning, *Between the Runways*, 108.

23. Henry Scadding, *Toronto of Old, Abridged and Edited by F.H. Armstrong* (Toronto: Oxford University Press, 1966), 106.

24. Pentland, *Labour and Capital in Canada, 1650–1860*, 102–13.

25. Robert F. Harney (ed.), *Gathering Place: Peoples and Neighbourhoods of Toronto, 1834–1945* (Toronto: Multicultural History Society of Ontario, 1985), 25–47.

26. Mark G. McGowan, *The Waning of the Green: Catholics, the Irish, and Identity in Toronto, 1887–1922* (Montreal: McGill-Queen's University Press, 1999), 16–21.

27. Ibid., 21.

28. PRONI T3534/2: James Humphrey to his father in County Tyrone, September 24, 1824.

29. Manning, *Between the Runways*, 61–62.

30. PRONI T2345/4A: Moses Staunton of Toronto to his mother, December 28, 1856.

31. PRONI: T3152/6.

32. Manning, *Between the Runways*, 4–19.

33. Ibid., 50–55. By 1881, most of Peel County's Catholics were concentrated in Toronto Township.

34. PRONI MIC205/1: Correspondence of James Magrath, 1769–1895. The Reverend Magrath was the Anglican minister at Erindale for twenty-two years until his death in 1851.

35. Erindale, Mississauga. Wikipedia.

36. Houston and Smyth, *Irish Emigration and Canadian Settlement*, 48, 64, 87–89, 205–6.

37. See Chapter 7 for details of the Irish communities founded by the Buchanan settlers in Cavan and Monaghan townships.

38. *Report from the Select Committee Appointed to Inquire into the Expediency of Encouraging Emigration from the United Kingdom*, 1826. Evidence of Dr. Strachan, 100.

39. Johnston, *British Emigration Policy*, 24. Johnston claims that James Buchanan helped 7,000 immigrants, who were mainly Irish, to relocate to Upper Canada. Also see Adams, *Ireland and Irish Emigration to the New World*, 263–66, and Houston and Smyth, *Irish Emigration and Canadian Settlement*, 64, 87–89.

40. John Lynch, *Directory of the County of Peel for 1873–4* (Mississauga, ON: Halton-Peel Branch O.G.S., 1998.). The Buchanan group used John Beatty and Joseph Graham as their agents.

41. Manning, *Between the Runways*, 18–19.

42. Ibid., 18.

43. Watson, *The Emigrants Guide to the Canadas*, 7.

44. The County Antrim families were: John Bell and his wife Eliza Ann Agnew, who arrived in 1820, William Agnew and his wife Mary in 1830, Thomas Storey and his wife in 1840, Robert Ritchie and his wife Agnes Dutton in 1840, John Kinard and his wife Elizabeth in 1863, and Hugh Brownlee and his wife Sarah Jane in 1873. James Lynn, "County Antrim Origins of Some Nassagaweya Settlers," *Families* 44 (2) (2005): 81–96.

45. Protestant settlers from Tipperary also went to live in Streetsville and in the 1830s relocated to Goderich Township (Huron County). Elliott, *Migrants in the Canadas*, 251–53.

46. Nicholas Flood Davin, *The Irishman in Canada* (London: Sampson Low, Marston & Co, 1877), 341–43.

47. Ibid., 72. Because there were so many Irish, the area on the west bank of the Credit River became known as Corktown.

48. There were three major canal works in the Hamilton area: the Welland Canal at Niagara (1824–33), the nearby Burlington Bay Canal (1826–30), and the Desjardins Canal at Dundas (1827–37). The canals provided uninterrupted navigation for ships carrying goods through the Great Lakes to the major seaports of Montreal and Quebec City.

49. Andrew Carl Holman, "Corktown, 1832–1847, The Founding of Hamilton's Pre-Famine Irish Settlement" (M.A. thesis, McMaster University, Hamilton, 1989), 27, 42.

50. Hamilton's Corktown is bounded by James Street on the west, Main Street on the north, and Wellington Street on the east.

51. Holman, "Corktown, 1832–1847," 127–30.

52. The Irish were the largest ethnic group in West and East Flamborough townships.

53. PRONI T3081/1: Henry Johnson to his wife Jane in County Antrim, December 3, 1848.

54. PRONI T3081/1: Alexander Mackay to Henry Johnson, May 29, 1849, Arthur McConnell to Jane Johnson, October 18, 1849.

55. PRONI T3081/1: Henry Johnson to his wife Jane in County Antrim, December 3, 1848.

56. PRONI T2018/6: Walker and Lowry emigrant papers: Martha Cranston to Andrew Lowry, December 21, 1886.

57. Richard Talbot also assisted fifteen Tipperary families to relocate to the Ottawa Valley (see Chapter 6). In addition, Talbot assisted ten other Tipperary families to relocate to York Township. Elliott, *Irish Migrants in the Canadas*, 92.

58. C.O. Ermatinger, *The Talbot Regime: Or, the First Half Century of the Talbot Settlement* (St. Thomas, ON: Municipal World, 1904), 121. Ermatinger states that the following men who came to the London area were recruited by Richard Talbot (those shown in italics were single): *Edward Allen Talbot, John Talbot*, William Geeris [Geary], *Thomas Brooks, Peter Rodgers*, Thomas Guest, Frank Lewis, Benjamin Lewis,

William Haskett, *William Mooney*, *William Evans*, *William O'Neil*, Edmunds Stoney, Joseph O'Brien, George Foster, *Thomas Howey, James Howey, John Phalen*, Joseph Hardy, *Joseph N. Hardy*, John Gray, *John Gray Jr.*, Foilet Gray, Robert Keys, Charles Gooding, *Robert Ralph*, John Gumes, *John Sifton, Charles Sifton*, and Thomas Howard.

59. Davin, *The Irishman in Canada*, 380.

60. In 1791, Lieutenant Colonel John Simcoe advocated making New London the capital of Upper Canada. W.A. Goodspeed and C.L. Goodspeed, *History of the County of Middlesex, Canada* (Toronto and London: Authors, 1889), 561.

61. Ibid., 513.

62. Ibid., 688–89.

63. NAB CO384/14, 925–6. The Reverend McEwen also asked that his father, John McEwen, a former quartermaster in the Royal Artillery, now on half pay, "may also accompany the little band of settlers, if his half pay could be paid in Canada as in Ireland, and the usual grant of land to half pay men be given to him."

64. Rev. T. Radcliff (ed.) *Authentic Letters from Upper Canada: With an Account of Canadian Field Sports* (London: Simpkin & Marshall, 1833), Letter XI, 178–89.

65. William Francis Dillon, "The Irish in London, Ontario, 1826–1861" (M.A. thesis, University of Western Ontario, London, 1963), 22, 55, 63, 112, 128–32.

66. PRONI D2784/16: Nathanial to his brother William, December 5, 1853.

67. Ibid.

68. With the discovery in the 1850s of significant oil deposits in Enniskillen Township, wells and refineries were established at Oil Springs and Petrolia as well as at Sarnia.

69. Christina Burr, "Oil Mania: Colonial Land Policy, Land Speculation and Settlement in Enniskillen Township, 1830s–1860s," *Social History* 38, No. 76 (2005): 267–306. Christina Burr, *Canada's Victorian Oil Town: The Transformation of Petrolia from Resource Town into a Victorian Community* (Montreal: McGill-Queen's University Press, 2006), 70, 256.

70. PRONI D2068/5. Helen Noble in Petrolia, to her uncle, 1888. Helen and John Noble were friends of Ellen and Henry Dunlop from County Antrim, who settled in the Peterborough region (PRONI D1424/3/23). See Chapter 7.

71. PRONI D4231/A/58.

72. Elliot, *Migrants in the Canadas*, 157, 167, 239. See Eleanor Nielson, "An Index of Lanark Families Who Migrated to Lambton," *Ontario Genealogical Society, Branch News* 15, No. 2 (September–October 1982): 59–61.

73. A "Scots Colony" also formed along the shore of Lake St. Clair.

74. countyofessex.on.ca.

75. PRONI T3724/1: Daniel Waide to his son Alexander, January 1, 1855.

Chapter 9: Ontario's Western Peninsula

1. E.L. Marsh, *A History of the County of Grey* (Owen Sound, ON: Fleming Publishing Co., 1931), 137.

2. W.M. Brown, *The Queen's Bush: A Tale of the Early Days of Bruce County* (London: John Bale, Sons and Danielsson Ltd., 1932), 2–6.

3. For the background to the setting up of the company, its operations and the key people who promoted and directed it, see Robert C. Lee, *The Canada Company and the Huron Tract, 1826–1853* (Toronto: Natural Heritage, 2004).

4. Anon., *Lands in Upper Canada to be Disposed of by the Canada Company* (London: The Company, 1828).

5. Chapter 8 provides details of these Irish settlements. Also see Maps 14 and 15.

6. James Scott, *The Settlement of Huron County* (Toronto: Ryerson Press, 1966), 53, 61.

7. BPP 1827, V (550), 461–63: "Prospectus of Terms Upon Which the Canada Company Proposes to Dispose of Their Lands."

8. The Canada Company's remaining holdings, consisting of 1.4 million acres of Crown Reserves, were scattered widely across the province. It was originally intended that the company would be offered 829,430 acres of Clergy Reserves but after opposition from the Church of

England they were withdrawn and the Huron Tract was substituted in their place. It had been purchased by the government from the Chippewa First Nation.

9.   Lillian Francis Gates, *Land Policies of Upper Canada* (Toronto: University of Toronto Press, 1968), 168–70. In 1829 the average price per acre in the Huron Tract was 7s. 6d. It rose steadily, and by 1840 the average price was 13s. 3d.

10. Lee, *The Canada Company*, 45–84. The town of Galt, later becoming part of Cambridge, was named after John Galt.

11. The Canada Company had begun its operations eight years before its main rival, the British American Land Company, whose land holdings were concentrated in the Eastern Townships of Lower Canada. For details of the latter company see Chapter 4.

12. Although the Canada Company succeeded in performing its stated function as a seller of land, the larger than life personalities associated with the company (e.g., its directors, politicians, and church leaders) meant that its activities were fraught with intrigue and controversy from its very inception.

13. Lee, *The Canada Company*, 205–12.

14. Cowan, *British Emigration to British North America*, 179.

15. Houston and Smyth, *Irish Emigration and Canadian Settlement*, 94–96.

16. Ruth Holt and Margaret Williams, *Genealogical Extractions and Index of the Canada Company Remittance Books, 1843–1847* (Weston, ON: R. Holt, 1990). The Canada Company "Remittance Books" provide details of the money received by named individuals and their location in the British Isles.

17. Assisted immigration schemes for the Irish during the famine period are discussed in Chapter 10.

18. A.B. Hawke, May 7, 1847, in *The Elgin-Grey Papers, 1823–50*, edited with notes and appendices by Sir Arthur G. Doughty (Ottawa: J.O. Patenaude, I.S.O., printer to the King, 1937), Vol. III, 1135–6.

19. BPP 1847(777) XXXIX, A.C. Buchanan, November 24, 1846.

20. Ibid.

21. PRONI D1195/3/11, September 22, 1856, D1195/3/18, August 27, 1858.

22. Houston and Smyth, *Irish Emigration and Canadian Settlement*, 287–301.
23. Scott, *The Settlement of Huron County*, 142.
24. PRONI D4343/1: John McCullagh to James, May 24, 1838.
25. PRONI D4343/4: John McCullagh to William McCullagh, September 17, 1842.
26. Anon., *A Statement of the Satisfactory Results Which Have Attended Emigration to Upper Canada from the Establishment of the Canada Company Until the Present Period* (London: Smith, Elder & Co., 1841), 3.
27. Ibid., 14–15, 17–18.
28. Robert Alling to the Commissioners of the Canada Company, December 10, 1840, reprinted in the [Guelph] *Mercury Centennial Edition*, July, 20, 1927.
29. Robert Fisher's letter in 1832 to his parents in Suffolk, quoted in Patterson, *Land Settlement in Upper Canada*, xii–xiii.
30. LAC MG25 G309: Eagan family fonds.
31. Lee, *The Canada Company*, 108.
32. Mary Rae Shantz, "The Irish Catholics in Guelph: A Study of Ethnic Group Identity, 1827–1861" (M.A. thesis, University of Guelph, 1986), 40–42, 100–101, 115–22. Although the Irish were the largest ethnic group among Guelph's Catholics, the town also had a substantial number of German Catholics.
33. churchofourlady.com.
34. Lyne, "The Irish in the Province of Canada in the Decade Leading to Confederation," 378.
35. Biddulph Township was in Huron County until 1865, and afterward became part of Middlesex County.
36. Blanshard Township acquired Irish Palatine families from counties Tipperary and Limerick in the 1840s. Elliott, *Irish Migrants in the Canadas*, 134–36.
37. While Stanley mainly attracted Scottish and Irish settlers during the 1840s, Hay Township immediately to the south of it acquired many Germans. They were the dominant ethnic group in 1881. Scott, *The Settlement of Huron County*, 170–71.

38. "Historical Papers of the Stewart Family: Early Years in Leeds County, Upper Canada, 1833–1854." I am grateful to Mr. and Mrs. Ken F. Stewart of Toronto for providing these papers and giving me permission to use them.

39. Scott, *The Settlement of Huron County*, 157–61. The Goshen Line and Babylon Line appear in the modern-day Ontario Road Atlas.

40. Stephen Township had more or less equal proportions of English, Irish, and German inhabitants by 1881. Susan Muriel Mack, *The History of Stephen Township* (Crediton, ON: Corporation of the Township of Stephen, 1992), 24, 258.

41. Biddulph's early settlers included fugitive slaves from the southern United States who formed the Wilberforce Settlement in about 1830. Jenifer Grainger, *Vanished Villages of Middlesex* (Toronto: Natural Heritage, 2002), 35–37.

42. Elliott, *Irish Migrants in the Canadas*, 132–42, 170–71.

43. Jennie Raycraft Lewis, *Sure An' This Is Biddulph* (Biddulph, ON: Biddulph Town Council, 1964), 21–43. Hodgins was Biddulph's first reeve.

44. W.S. Johnston and H.J.M. Johnston, *History of Perth County to 1967* (Stratford, ON: Corporation of the County of Perth, 1967), 150. William Johnston, *History of the County of Perth from 1825 to 1902* (Stratford, ON: Beacon Herald, 1976), 220.

45. Grainger, *Vanished Villages of Middlesex*, 17–23. Robine Lizars and Kathleen Macfarlane Lizars, *In the Days of the Canada Company: The Story of the Settlement of the Huron Tract and a View of the Social Life of the Period 1825–1850* (Toronto: W. Briggs, 1896), 272–73, 397.

46. Grainger, *Vanished Villages of Middlesex*, 156.

47. Scott, *The Settlement of Huron County*, 60, 162–65. Other early settlers included Dennis and John Downie, Patrick O'Sullivan, H. O'Neill, and a man called O'Connell.

48. Hibbert's Irishtown became known as St. Columban in 1865.

49. LAC MG25 G305: Storey family fonds.

50. Derek Nile Tucker, "Successful Pioneers: Irish Catholic Settlers in the Township of Hibbert Ontario, 1845–1887" (M.A. thesis, McMaster University, Hamilton, 2001), 106–10.

51. Johnston, *History of the County of Perth from 1825 to 1902*, H.J.M. Johnston, "Immigration to the Five Eastern Townships of the Huron Tract," *Ontario History* 54 (1962): 214, 221.

52. Wikipedia (Kingsbridge, ON). Some of Kingsbridge's early settlers also originated from counties Clare, Cork, and Tipperary.

53. Scott, *The Settlement of Huron County*, 190.

54. Ibid., 207–8.

55. Johnston and Johnston, *History of Perth County to 1967*, 15, 143, 148, 162–63.

56. Elliott, *Irish Migrants in the Canadas*, 161–62, 252. For details of the Halton and Peel Irish settlements see Chapter 8.

57. Daniel B. Parkinson, "From Rawdon to Wellington County" (Parts I, II, III) *Families* 38 (1999): (2): 67–78, (3): 131–41, (4): 195–205.

58. MCFMS "Emigration of Kells Family from Ireland to North America" provided by Dr. R.T.B McClean.

59. Ken Seiling, "The Early Settlement of Wellington County," *Families* 15 (4) 1976: 143–49.

60. For the building of the Garafraxa Road, see Paul White, *Owen Sound: The Port City* (Toronto: Natural Heritage, 2000), 15–16; for the Durham Road see Elliott, *Irish Migrants in the Canadas*, 172.

61. For details of the Irish Protestants who relocated from Rawdon in Lower Canada to frontier land in western Upper Canada see Daniel Parkinson, "To Huron's Shore: Rawdon, Quebec Families in Bruce, Grey, and Huron Counties," *Families* 44 (2) 2005: 67–80.

62. NAB CO 384/74: Letter dated March 24, 1843, from the Governor General.

63. Lyne, "The Irish in the Province of Canada in the Decade Leading to Confederation," 65–67.

64. Marsh, *A History of the County of Grey*, 213.

65. Elliott, *Irish Migrants in the Canadas*, 119.

66. Marsh, *A History of the County of Grey*, 121–23, 145.

67. Ibid., 68, 87, 125.

68. The town of Markdale was named after Mark Armstrong, who originated from County Fermanagh.

69. William Benson, *Life and Adventures of William Benson* (Toronto:

Author, 1876), 44, 130.

70. Anon., *History of Sydenham Township: Centennial Project* (Owen Sound, ON: Sydenham Township Council, 1967), 223–25. Catholics in the Irish Block had their first log church built by 1852.

71. Hunter, *A History of Simcoe County*, 33.

72. Elliott, *Irish Migrants in the Canadas*, 172–74.

Chapter 10: Irish Arrivals During the Great Famine of 1847

1. "Historical Papers of the Stewart Family," Hugh and Elizabeth Barkley to Adam Stewart, August 20, 1846.

2. OA F486 (MU3274): Kerr family papers, J. MacDonald to John Kerr, January 25, 1847.

3. PRONI T3168/1: Buchanan to the Governor General, May 1, 1847.

4. André Charbonneau and André Sevigny, *1847 Grosse Île: A Record of Daily Events* (Ottawa: Canadian Heritage, 1997), 1–32.

5. There had been a total potato crop failure in 1846. The fungus (*Phytophthora infestans*), which attacks the leaves and tubers of potatoes, destroyed the crops, making thousands of people vulnerable to malnutrition and severe destitution. This led to a sharp rise in emigration in 1847.

6. James S. Donnelly, Jr., *The Great Irish Potato Famine* (Stroud: The History Press, 2002). Kerby A. Miller, *Emigrants and Exiles: Ireland and the Irish Exodus to North America* (Oxford: Oxford University Press, 1985), 280–344.

7. The Irish Poor Law gave powers to parishes to collect a poor rate as a form of taxation to support local workhouses.

8. Irish immigrants predominated from at least 1825, when official figures first became available. In 1847 people arriving in Quebec from Irish ports accounted for some 60 percent of the total. N.H. Carrier and J.R. Jeffrey, *External Migration: A Study of the Available Statistics 1815–1950* (London: HMSO, 1953), 95–96.

9. Charbonneau and Sevigny, *1847 Grosse Île: A Record of Daily Events*, 23.

10. Lyne, "The Irish in the Province of Canada in the Decade Leading to Confederation," 22–28.

11. Merna M. Forster, "Quarantine at Grosse Île," *Canadian Family Physician* 41 (May 1995): 841–48.

12. *Journals of the Legislative Assembly of the Province of Canada (JLA)* (Montreal: Rollo Campbell), Vol. 6, May 21, 1847, No. 1, Appendix L.

13. BPP 1847–48 (50) XLVII.

14. Ibid.

15. Marianna O'Gallagher, *Grosse Île: Gateway to Canada 1832–1947* (Quebec: Carraig Books, 1984), 47–57.

16. Shipping services offered to the Irish are discussed in further detail in Chapter 11.

17. Edwin C. Guillet, *The Great Migration: The Atlantic Crossing by Sailing Ships Since 1770* (Toronto: University of Toronto Press, 1963), 19, 67.

18. *JLA*, Vol. 6, May 27, 1847, No. 1, Appendix L.

19. *JLA*, Vol. 6, June 8, 1847, No. 1, Appendix R.

20. O'Gallagher, *Grosse Île: Gateway to Canada 1832–1947*, 50–51.

21. Charbonneau and Sevigny, *1847 Grosse Île : A Record of Daily Events*, 74–75.

22. Moran, *Sending Out Ireland's Poor*, 36–39, 99.

23. There were also many smaller landowners who assisted their tenants to travel to Quebec, such as Lord Clifden from Kilkenny and George F. Colley from Cork. Moran, *Sending Out Ireland's Poor*, 123–42.

24. MacKay, *Flight from Famine*, 193.

25. British Parliamentary Papers, Colonies, Canada, Vol. 17, 385, quoted in MacKay, *Flight from Famine*, 286–87.

26. Dougherty (ed.), *Elgin Grey Papers, 1846–52*, quoted in MacKay, *Flight from Famine*, 295–96.

27. Jim Rees, *Surplus People: from Wicklow to Canada* (Cork: Collins Press, 2014), 42, 47, 59, 65–66. BPP 1847-48 (50) XLVII.

28. This figure includes those Irish who were assisted by landlords as well as those living in workhouses, the latter being helped by Poor Law Unions.

29. Moran, *Sending Out Ireland's Poor*, 101–16.

30. See ancestorsatreat.com/Ireland. "People from the Fitzwilliam Estate Who Settled in Ontario, 1847–55."

31. Moran, *Sending Out Ireland's Poor*, 96, 116.

32. See Chapter 7.

33. Ibid., 120.

34. Driedger, *An Irish Heart*, 59–102.

35. "Grosse Isle, Quebec": Wikipedia.org.

36. The sick were taken to hastily constructed sheds as well as to the hospital at Kingston. The dead were buried in a mass grave on the hospital grounds. An Angel of Mercy stone monument was placed at the site in 1894.

37. MacKay, *Flight from Famine*, 270–71.

38. A memorial to the Irish who died in Toronto in 1847 was erected in 2007 at Ireland Park. It is situated on the waterfront, east of the foot of Bathurst Street.

39. Kenneth Duncan, "Irish Famine Immigration and the Social Structure of Canada West," *Canadian Review of Sociology and Anthropology* 2 (1965): 19–40.

40. Thomas D'Arcy McGee, *The Irish Position in British and in Republican North America: A Letter to the Editors of the Irish Press Irrespective of Party* (Montreal: Author, 1866), 7.

41. Houston and Smyth, *Irish Emigration and Canadian Settlement*, 216–18. Using the 1871 Census, Houston and Smyth have determined where the famine and post-famine Irish were principally located. They did this by noting those areas where the Irish-born represented at least 30 percent of the total Irish population. Their study thus highlights where Irish migrants of the previous twenty-five years probably congregated.

42. Sectarian violence in the major cities and towns is discussed in further detail in Chapter 12.

Chapter 11: Sea Crossings

1. PRONI T2515/1: David McCloy Diary, 1847, 1–2.

2. Ibid. Because David's father was a freemason, local freemasons offered help and paid for his and his son's funerals. The McCloys were also supported by local Pennsylvania Dutch people, who became their "new-found friends."

3. Ibid., 3–4.

4. James Wilson, *Narrative of a Voyage from Dublin to Quebec in North America* (Dublin: T. Courtney, 1822), 2. Wilson was on his way to Brockville.

5. Ibid., 4.

6. LAC MG24 H7: Diary of William Graves, 7.

7. *Quebec Mercury*, June 11, 1840.

8. See Appendix I.

9. PRONI T3534/2: James Humphrey to his father in County Tyrone, September 24, 1824.

10. LAC MG24 H11: Journal of James Coulter.

11. PRONI D693/7/1: Dr. William Campbell to Rev. Robert Campbell, County Antrim, October 28, 1832.

12. PRONI D1859/1: John and Eliza Anderson to John Anderson, County Londonderry, July 1, 1832.

13. PRONI T3478/1/2: Henry Johnson to Jane, his wife, September 18, 1848. The ship carried between 400 and 500 Irish Catholics. Johnson was one of forty Irish Protestants who were also on board.

14. LAC MG24-J12: George Pashley fonds.

15. BPP 1843(109) XXXIV. As result of their ordeal, the passengers had consumed their food supplies. Alexander Buchanan gave them sufficient food for their onward journey once they reached Quebec.

16. PRONI T3789/1: A list of the passengers lost in the crossing of the *Exmouth* from Londonderry to Quebec in 1847 appeared in the *Londonderry Journal*, May 12, 1847. Only three crewmen survived.

17. *Quebec Gazette*, May 24, 1841. Four crew members and four passengers survived.

18. Macdonagh, *A Pattern of Government Growth 1800–1860, The Passenger Acts and Their Enforcement*, 58–59, 74–90, 148–51. In 1841 the passenger legislation required immigrants to have 3 quarts of water daily and 2 ½ lbs. biscuit, 1 lb. flour, 5 lbs. oatmeal, 2 lbs. rice, ¾ lb. sugar, and 2 ounces of tea per week.

19. PRONI T2515/1: McCloy Diary.

20. In the 1830s the price of a passage from the principal Irish ports to Quebec was between £2 and £2 10s. without provisions and £4 to £5

with provisions. Fares from Liverpool were normally lower. Anon., *Information Published by His Majesty's Commissioners for Emigration Respecting the British Colonies in North America* (London: HMSO, 1832) 5, 7–8.

21. The 1855 Act, containing 103 different clauses, could not realistically be enforced nor could the previous legislation, which had been passed in 1847, 1848, 1849, and 1852.

22. PRONI D693/7/1: Dr. William Campbell to Rev. Robert Campbell, County Antrim, October 28, 1832.

23. BPP 1844(181) XXXV.

24. BPP 1842(373) XXXI.

25. Oliver Macdonagh, "Emigration and the State, 1833–55: An Essay in Administrative History," *Transactions of the Royal Historical Society*, Fifth Series, Vol. 5 (London: The Royal Historical Society, 1955): 133–59. Guillet, *The Great Migration: The Atlantic Crossing by Sailing Ships Since 1770*, 13–19.

26. Macdonagh, *The Passenger Acts and Their Enforcement*, 154–55. The complaint was made by Francis Spaight, leader of the Limerick passenger trade. He was also a major landowner who assisted his tenants to immigrate to Upper Canada (see Chapter 10).

27. BPP 1842(373) XXXI.

28. Ibid.

29. BPP 1849(1025) XXXVIII.

30. Although the vessel was extremely old, having been built in 1763, it was given an E1 designation by Lloyd's, indicating that it was seaworthy.

31. BPP 1847(777) XXXIX.

32. Ibid.

33. Ibid.

34. *Quebec Mercury*, May 28, 1840.

35. The proceeds of the immigrant tax were divided into fourths: between the Quebec Emigrant Hospital, the Montreal General Hospital, the Quebec Emigrant Society, and the Montreal Emigrant Society. Cowan, *British Emigration to British North America*, 56–57, 152–53.

36. In 1832 there were 2,723 cholera-related deaths in Quebec City and 2,547 deaths in Montreal. Countless more died in the nearby

countryside. Dickinson and Young, *Short History of Quebec*, 113–14. Ouellet, *Le Bas Canada*, 215.

37. *Quebec Gazette*, August 1834.

38. Charbonneau and Sevigny, *1847 Grosse Île: A Record of Daily Events*, 72–73. Letter published in the *Quebec Morning Chronicle*, June 4, 1847.

39. Ibid., 76.

40. Charbonneau and Sevigny, *1847 Grosse Île: A Record of Daily Events*, 93.

41. See Chapter 10 for details of Irish immigrant arrivals at Grosse Île in 1847.

42. Charbonneau and Sevigny, *1847 Grosse Île: A Record of Daily Events*, 86–87.

43. NAB CO 188/102, Colebrooke to Grey, October 27, 1847, quoted in "Introduction" by Lorna Reynolds in Gerald Keegan, "Black '47: A Summer of Sorrow," in *The Untold Story: The Irish in Canada*, edited by Robert O'Driscoll and Lorna Reynolds (Toronto: Celtic Arts of Canada, 1988), Vol. I, 103–68.

44. These abuses led to the various protective measures that were introduced in the Passenger Act of 1828. Macdonagh, "Emigration and the State, 1833–55: An Essay in Administrative History," 134, 141–42.

45. Immigrant numbers rose steadily in the 1830s but plummeted suddenly in 1838–39 following the Upper and Lower Canada Rebellions. They rose again dramatically starting in 1840.

46. To complicate matters further, some immigrants who were bound for either Upper or Lower Canada did the reverse. They sailed via New York to gain access to its faster and more comfortable ships, despite having to pay higher fares.

47. The *Lloyd's Shipping Register* is available as a regular series from 1775 apart from the years 1785, 1788, and 1817.

48. Still in use today and run by a Classification Society with a worldwide network of offices and administrative staff, the *Lloyd's Register* continues to provide standard classifications of quality for shipbuilding and maintenance.

49. The number of years that a ship could hold the highest code varied according to where it was built. In time, rivalries developed between

shipowners and underwriters and this led to the publication of two registers between 1800 and 1833 — the *Ship Owners Register* (Red Book) and the *Underwriters Register* (Green Book). Their coverage was similar but not identical. By 1834, with bankruptcies facing both sides, the two registers joined forces to become the *Lloyd's Register of British and Foreign Shipping*.

50. The inability to find a Lloyd's Code does not necessarily cast doubt on the quality of a vessel. The bigger shipping firms could insure their ships and cargoes themselves and thus had no need for a Lloyd's survey. Some shipowners may have simply avoided the cost of a survey in the hope that nothing would go wrong, but they were probably in the minority.

51. BPP 1847–48 (50) XLVII.

52. The physical characteristics of a vessel greatly affected sailing performance as well as passenger comfort and safety. For an analysis of the different types of vessels that were used to take immigrants to North America, see Lucille H. Campey, *Fast Sailing and Copper-Bottomed: Aberdeen Sailing Ships and the Emigrant Scots They Carried to Canada* (Toronto: Natural Heritage, 2002), 80–98.

53. *Quebec Mercury*, May 21, 1836.

54. See individual ship crossings in Appendix.

55. Arthur R.M. Lower, *Colony to Nation: A History of Canada* (Toronto: Longmans, Green & Co., 1946), 98.

56. Macdonagh, *The Passenger Acts and Their Enforcement*, 194.

57. *First Report from the Select Committee of the House of Lords on Colonization from Ireland, 1847–48*, 45–46.

58. Macdonagh, *The Passenger Acts and Their Enforcement*, 193–96.

59. Mark McGowan, "Famine, Facts and Fabrication: An Examination of Diaries from the Irish Famine Migration to Canada," *Canadian Journal of Irish Studies* 3, No. 2 (Fall 2007): 48–55.

60. Sellars published the fabricated diary in serialized form under the title "The Summer of Sorrow." McGowan, "Famine, Facts and Fabrication," 50.

61. This fictionalized account was provided by Brother James J. Mangan, a native of Admaston, Ontario. See McGowan, "Famine, Facts and Fabrication," 50–52.

62. BPP 1847–48(50) XLVII.

63. *Belfast Newsletter*, February 22, 1834.

Chapter 12: The Irish in Ontario and Quebec

1. Davin, *The Irishman in Canada*, ix.

2. Grace, *The Irish in Quebec*, 54–70.

3. The Fenians, also known as the Irish Republican Brotherhood, formed in the 1850s.

4. *DCB*, Vol. IX, Thomas D'Arcy McGee.

5. Charles Murphy, *1825 — D'Arcy McGee — 1925: A Collection of Speeches and Addresses, Together with a Complete Report of the Centennial Celebration of the Birth of the Honourable Thomas D'Arcy McGee, at Ottawa, April 13th, 1925 Selected and Arranged by Charles Murphy* (Toronto: Macmillan, 1937).

6. MacKay, *Flight from Famine*, 330.

7. Driedger, *An Irish Heart*, 201.

8. Ibid., 202.

9. The repeal associations campaigned for the repeal of the 1801 Act of Union between Ireland and Great Britain.

10. For the Ontario repeal associations, see Michael Harrison, "Nominal List of Repealers from the *Toronto Mirror*, February, 1844," *Families* 36 (2) 1997: 111–16. For the Atlantic Canada repeal groups see Campey, *Atlantic Canada's Irish Immigrants*, 58, 217, 366.

11. *The Sherbrooke News*, March 25, 1875, quoted in Southam, *Irish Settlements and National Identity in the Lower St. Francis Valley*, 129.

12. Seamus J. King, *The Clash of the Ash in Foreign Fields: Hurling Abroad* (Cashel: S. King, 1998), 85.

13. Driedger, *An Irish Heart*, 141.

14. Schmitz, *Irish for a Day*, 188.

15. Ibid.

16. Ibid., 87.

17. Driedger, *An Irish Heart*, 96.

18. *DCB*, Vol. XII (William Beatty).

19. Anon., *Emigration to Canada: The Province of Ontario, Its Soil, Resources, Institutions, Free Grant Lands ... for the Information of Intending Emigrants* (Toronto: Hunter, Rose, 1871), 21–25.

20. *DCB*, Vol. XII (Thomas McMurray).

21. *Ottawa Tribune*, March 21, 1862.

22. Cecil J. Houston and William J. Smyth, *The Sash Canada Wore: A Historical Geography of the Orange Order in Canada* (Toronto: University of Toronto Press, 1980), 31–56.

23. Lyne, "The Irish in the Province of Canada in the Decade Leading to Confederation," 378. Alan C. Brunger, "The Distribution of Scots and Irish in Upper Canada, 1851–71," *The Canadian Geographer* 34, No. 3 (1990): 250–58.

24. PRONI T3534/2: James Humphrey to his father in County Tyrone, 1824.

25. Gregory S. Kealey, "The Orange Order in Toronto: Religious Riot and the Working Class," in *The Untold Story: The Irish in Canada*, edited by Robert O'Driscoll and Lorna Reynolds (Toronto: Celtic Arts of Canada, 1988), Vol. 2, 829–51.

26. Maguire, *The Irish in America*, 83.

27. LAC MG 24 I162: Walter O'Hara diary. Arriving in 1827, O'Hara purchased a 330-acre farm near Dundas (Hamilton) and ran a timber business, 45.

28. Maguire, *The Irish in America*, 1.

29. R. Bleasdale, "Irish Labourers on the Canals of Upper Canada in the 1840s" (M.A. thesis, University of Western Ontario, London, 1975), 144–50.

BIBLIOGRAPHY

PRIMARY SOURCES (MANUSCRIPTS)

Bibliothèque et Archives Nationales du Québec (BAnQ)

E21: Ministry of Lands and Forests (land petitions).
M/F 117/13: fonds Famille Ross.
P11: fonds William H. Johnston and Ruby Dodds.
P48: fonds William McQuat Cottingham.
P80, S1: Ruth Higginson collection.
P351: fonds famille Joly de Lotbinière.
P1000, S3 D4: Pontiac County's 150th Anniversary.
P1000 S3 D16: Irish Settlement of St. Columban by Brother Jerome Hart, Daniel O'Connell School (1955).
TL4, TL5: Provost Court of Quebec.

Derbyshire Record Office (DERO)

D3349/3 Metcalf family of Killarch correspondence.
D3155: Catton Collection.

Eastern Townships Resource Centre (ETRC)

P028: John Savage fonds.

P073: Richard William Heneker fonds.

P076: Agnes Bradley Haddock fonds.

P141: St. Patrick's Society of Richmond fonds.

P158/003.02/001: Hackett family fonds.

UC054/103: St. Andrew's United Church, Inverness.

Library and Archives of Canada (LAC)

MG8-G49: United Church (Wesleyan Methodist Circuit) fonds for Quyon (Pontiac County).

MG 23 H117: Hugh Hovell Farmer fonds.

MG24 B74: Peter Robinson fonds.

MG24 D1: John William Wolsey and family fonds.

MG24 H7: Diary of William Graves.

MG24 H11: Journal of James Coulter.

MG24 I88 Maria Murney's account of her grandfather's experiences.

MG24 I59: John Langton and family fonds.

MG24 I162: Diary of Walter O'Hara.

MG24 I199: James Ritchie fonds.

MG24 J12: George Pashley fonds.

MG25 G271 Genealogies/Family Studies.

MG25 G300: Richardson family.

MG25 G305: Storey family.

MG25 G309: Eagan family.

MG25 G347: Heney family.

920 MD 154: Journal of James Moncrieff Wilson.

M-1353, 1354 (microfilm reels): Glasgow Colonial Society Correspondence 1829–43.

Mellon Centre for Migration Studies, Omagh, Ireland (MCFMS)

"Emigration of Kells Family from Ireland to North America" provided by Dr. R.T.B. McClean.

Letter from Royal and Mary Keys to William Keys, 1834.

National Archives of Britain (NAB)

CO 188: New Brunswick Original Correspondence.

CO 384: Colonial Office Papers on emigration containing original correspondence concerning North American settlers.

MPG 484(1): Sketch of the Rideau Settlement.

National Archives of Ireland (NAI)

CSO/RP/1822/403: Petition of Thomas Lipsettt, 1822.

RLFC/3/1/950: George Wyndham to J.P. Kennedy, March 24th, 1846.

National Archives of Scotland (NAS)

RHP 35156/1-2: Plans of Upper and Lower Canada, 1838–39.

Ontario Archives (OA)

F61 (microfilm reel 524): Peter Robinson fonds.

F486 MU3274: Kerr family papers, 1819–87.

F709 (MU754): Series I-I Benjamin Crawford's trip to Upper Canada, 1801.

F725: James D. Stephens fonds.

F1237: Thomas Dick fonds.

Oxford University: Rhodes House Library (RHL)

United Society for the Propagation of the Gospel (USPG) Series E: Reports from Missionaries.

Public Record Office of Northern Ireland (PRONI)

D693: Accounts and correspondence relating principally to the Campbell, McKeown, Bannon, and Moore families, all of County Antrim.

D1195/3: Letter from Jane White, Goderich.

D1414/3/23-30: Letters from Ellen Dunlop, Peterborough, Ontario.

D1604/289: Letters from Tom Hay, Peterborough, Ontario, to his uncle George Kirkpatrick.

D1748/G/490: Johnston Neilson, Armagh, 1836.

D1859: Anderson emigrant papers.

D2068: Grattan family papers.

D3513/1/22: Letter from James Collins, Peterborough, Ontario.

D3817: Moor Hill papers.

D4008: Taylor family of Canada papers.

D4231/A: Correspondence of Anne and Isabella Weir with friends and relatives in the United States and friends and family in County Fermanagh.

D4343: McCulloch emigrant letters, Goderich, 1838–1901.

D7284/16: Emigrant letters from Joseph and Nathaniel Carrothers to their brother William.

MIC205/1: Blake Family Papers.

T1362/1: Richard Braithwaite, Cannington, 1849.

T1639: Charlotte Bacon to Alexander Kerr, her father, July 26, 1843.

T1970: Army Surgeon, 1814–15.

T2018/6: Alexander of Lowry and family of Caulfield, emigrant papers.

T2345/4A: Moses Staunton of Toronto to his mother, December 28, 1856.

T2410: Lieutenant James Prendergast, County Monaghan.

T2515/1: David McCloy, diary, 1847.

T2680: Edward Parks, St. Sylvestre, Quebec, 1871.

T308/1: McConnell emigrant papers, 1848–88.

T3152/6: Hugh Kennedy in Toronto, May 6, 1912.

T3534: Richardson and Humphrey documents.

T3566: William Portt, Hamilton.

T3168/1–3: Ship arrivals at Quebec from Ireland, May 1847.

T3478: Johnson emigrant letters.

T3534: Richardson and Humphrey documents.

T3724/1: Wade family letters. Daniel Wade, County Antrim, to his son in Ontario, 1855.

T3789/1: Crossing of *Exmouth* from Londonderry to Quebec, 1847.

PRINTED PRIMARY SOURCES AND
CONTEMPORARY PUBLICATIONS

Anonymous. "An Important Letter of a Resident of Quebec as to the Disabilities of Protestants in the Province of Quebec: The Parish System." Toronto: Equal Rights Association for the Province of Ontario, 1890.

———. *A Statement of the Satisfactory Results Which Have Attended Emigration to Upper Canada from the Establishment of the Canada Company until the Present Period.* London: Smith, Elder, 1841.

———. *Information Published by His Majesty's Commissioners for Emigration Respecting the British Colonies in North America.* London: HMSO, 1832.

———. Journals of the Legislative Assembly of the Province of Canada. Montréal: Rollo Campbell.

———. *Lands in Upper Canada to Be Disposed of by the Canada Company.* London: The Company, 1828.

Barbezieux, Father R.P. Alexis De. *Histoire de la Province Ecclésiastique d'Ottawa et de la Colonisation dans la Vallée de l'Ottawa.* Ottawa: 1897.

Benson, William. *Life and Adventures of William Benson.* Toronto: Author, 1876.

Boddy, Reverend Samuel J. *A Brief Memoir of the Rev. Samuel B. Ardagh, A.M., T.C.D., Late Rector of Barrie and Incumbent of Shanty Bay, Lake Simcoe, Upper Canada,* edited by Samuel J. Boddy. Toronto: Rowsell and Hutchison,1874.

Bouchette, Joseph. *A Topographical Dictionary of the Province of Lower Canada.* London: W. Faden, 1815.

———. *A Topographical Dictionary of the Province of Lower Canada.* London: Longman, 1832.

———. *General Report of an Official Tour through the New Settlements of the Province of Lower-Canada Performed in the Summer of 1824, in Obedience to the Commands and Instructions of His Excellency George Earl of Dalhousie, G.C.B., Captain General and Governor in Chief of British North-America.* Quebec: T. Carey, 1825.

————. *The British Dominions in North America: A Topographical and Statistical Description of the Provinces of Lower and Upper Canada, New Brunswick, Nova Scotia, the Islands of Newfoundland, Prince Edward Island, and Cape Breton*, vols. 1 and 2. London: Longman, Rees, Orme, Brown, Green and Longman, 1832.

British American Land Company. *Information Respecting the Eastern Townships of Lower Canada*. London: W.J. Ruffy, 1833.

Census of Lower Canada, 1851, 1871, 1881.

Census of Upper Canada, 1851, 1871, 1881.

Champion, Thomas Edward. *The Anglican Church in Canada*. Toronto: Hunter, Rose, 1898.

Davin, Nicholas Flood. *The Irishman in Canada*. London: Sampson Low, Marston, 1877.

Doyle, Martin. *Hints on Emigration to Upper Canada: Especially Addressed to the Middle and Lower Classes of Great Britain and Ireland*. Dublin: W. Curry, 1834.

Ermatinger, C.O. *The Talbot Regime: Or, the First Half Century of the Talbot Settlement*. St. Thomas: Municipal World, 1904.

Ermatinger, Edward. *Life of Colonel Talbot and the Talbot Settlement*. St. Thomas: A. McLachin's Home Journal Office, 1859.

Farewell, J.E. *County of Ontario: Short Notes as to the Early Settlement and Progress of the County and Brief References to the Pioneers and Some Ontario County Men Who Have Taken a Prominent Part in Provincial and Dominion Affairs*. Whitby, Ontario: Gazette-Chronicle Press, 1907.

Goodspeed, W.A. and C.L. Goodspeed. *History of the County of Middlesex Canada*. Toronto and London: Authors, 1889.

Gourlay, John L. *History of the Ottawa Valley, A Collection of Facts, Events and Reminiscences for over Half a Century*. Ottawa: Author, 1896.

Hall, Basil. *Travels in North America in the Years 1827 and 1828*. Edinburgh: Cadell, 1830.

Hutton William. *Canada: Its Present Conditions, Prospects and Resources, Fully Described for the Information of Intending Emigrants*. London: Stanfords, 1854.

Lizars, Robine, and Kathleen Macfarlane Lizars. *In the Days of the Canada Company: The Story of the Settlement of the Huron Tract and a View of the Social Life of the Period 1825–1850.* Toronto: W. Briggs, 1896.

Lloyd's Shipping Register 1775–1855.

MacTaggert, John. *Three Years in Canada, An Account of the Actual State of the Country in 1826–7–8 Comprehending Its Resources, Productions, Improvements and Capabilities and Including Sketches of the State of Society, Advice to Emigrants, etc. Two Volumes.* London: 1829.

Maguire, John Francis. *The Irish in America.* New York, Montreal: D. and J. Sadler, 1868.

McGee, Thomas D'Arcy. *The Irish Position in British and in Republican North America: A Letter to the Editors of the Irish Press Irrespective of Party.* Montreal: Author, 1866.

Moodie, Susanna. *Roughing It in the Bush, or, Forest Life in Canada.* Toronto: MacLear, 1871.

Mulvany, Charles Pelham, C.M. Ryan, and C.R. Stewart, *History of the County of Peterborough, Ontario: Containing a History of the County, History of Haliburton County, Their Townships, Towns, Schools, Churches, etc., General and Local Statistics, Biographical Sketches, and an Outline History of the Dominion of Canada, etc.* Toronto: C.B. Robinson, 1884.

Radcliff, Rev. T., ed. *Authentic Letters from Upper Canada: With an Account of Canadian Field Sports.* London: Simpkin and Marshall, 1833.

Sellar, Robert. *The History of the County of Huntingdon and of the Seigniories of Chateauguay and Beauharnois from Their First Settlement to the Year 1838.* Huntingdon, Quebec: Canadian Gleaner, 1888.

Society for the Propagation of the Gospel in Foreign Parts, *Annual Reports.*

Strickland, Samuel. *Twenty-Seven Years in Canada West, or, The Experience of an Early Settler.* London: R. Bentley, 1853.

Thomas, C. *History of the Counties of Argenteuil, Quebec, and Prescott, Ontario, from the Earliest Settlement to the Present.* Montreal: John Lovell, 1896.

Watson, William. *The Emigrants Guide to the Canadas.* Dublin: G. Bull, 1822.

Wilson, James. *Narrative of a Voyage from Dublin to Quebec in North America, 1822.* Dublin: T. Courtney, 1822.

PARLIAMENTARY PAPERS

Annual Reports of the Immigration Agent at Quebec

Colonial Land and Emigration Commissioners, Annual Reports

Papers Relative to Emigration to the British Provinces in North America

Report from the Select Committee Appointed to Inquire into the Expediency of Encouraging Emigration from the United Kingdom, 1826, 1826–27

Report from the Select Committee on the Civil Government of Canada, 1828

First Report from the Select Committee of the House of Lords on Colonization from Ireland, 1847–48

CONTEMPORARY NEWSPAPERS

Belfast Commercial Chronicle

Belfast Newsletter

Guelph Mercury

Montreal Gazette

Ottawa Tribune

Quebec Gazette

Quebec Mercury

Quebec Morning Chronicle

Sherbrooke Daily Record

Sherbrooke News

Strabane Morning Post

CONTEMPORARY MATERIAL OF LATER PRINTING

Bird, Isabella Lucy. *The Englishwoman in America*. Toronto: University of Toronto Press, 1966 (originally published in 1856).

Buchanan, Alexander. *1832 Emigrants' Handbook for Arrivals at Québec*. Reprinted in the journal of the Quebec Family History Society, *Connections* 29, no. 3 (Spring 2007): 9–13.

Doughty, Sir Arthur G., ed. *The Elgin-Grey Papers, 1823–50.* Ottawa: J.O. Patenaude, I.S.O., printer to the King, 1937.

Guillet, Edwin C. *The Valley of the Trent.* Edited with an introduction and notes by Edwin C. Guillet. Toronto: Champlain Society for the Government of Ontario, University of Toronto Press, 1957.

Lynch, John. *Directory of the County of Peel for 1873–4.* Mississauga: Halton-Peel Branch O.G.S., 1998.

Reid, Richard, ed. *The Upper Ottawa Valley to 1855: A Collection of Documents.* Edited with an introduction by Richard Reid. Toronto: Champlain Society, 1990.

Scadding, Henry. *Toronto of Old.* Abridged and edited by F. H. Armstrong. Toronto: Oxford University Press, 1966 (originally published in 1873).

Sellar, Robert. *The Tragedy of Quebec: The Expulsion of Its Protestant Farmers.* Toronto: University of Toronto Press, 1974 (originally published 1907).

Whitelaw, Marjory, ed. *The Dalhousie Journals (written 1820 to 1828).* Ottawa: Oberon, 1978–82.

SECONDARY SOURCES

Adams, William Forbes. *Ireland and Irish Emigration to the New World from 1815 to the Famine.* New Haven: Yale University Press, 1932.

Anon. *History of Sydenham Township: Centennial Project.* Owen Sound: Sydenham Township Council, 1967.

Barry, Gwen Rawlings. *A History of Megantic County: Downhomers of Quebec's Eastern Townships.* Lower Sackville: Evans Books, 1999.

———. *Ulster Protestant Emigration to Lower Canada: Megantic County & St-Sylvestre.* Lower Sackville: Evans Books, 2003.

Blake, George. *Lloyd's Register of Shipping 1760–1960.* London: Lloyds, 1960.

Blanchard, Raoul. *Le Centre du Canada Français Province de Québec.* Montreal: Librairie Beauchemin Limitée 1948.

———. "Les Pays de l'Ottawa." *Études Canadiennes Troisième Série 3.* Grenoble: Allier, 1949.

———. *L'Est du Canada Français, "Province de Quebec."* Montreal: Publications de l'Institut Scientifique Franco-Canadien, 1935.

————. *L'Ouest du Canada Français*. Montreal: Beauchemin, 1953–1954.

Bleasdale, R. "Irish Labourers on the Canals of Upper Canada in the 1840s." M.A. thesis, University of Western Ontario, 1975.

Bourguignon, Claude. *Saint-Colomban: Une épopée Irlandaise au Piémont des Laurentides*. Chambly: Editions Passe Present, 1988.

Boyce, Gerald E. *Historic Hastings*. Belleville: Hastings County Council, 1967.

Brown, W.M. *The Queen's Bush: A Tale of the Early Days of Bruce County*. London: John Bale, Sons & Danielsson Ltd., 1932.

Brunger, Alan C. "The Distribution of Scots and Irish in Upper Canada, 1851–71." *The Canadian Geographer* 34, no. 3 (1990): 250–8.

Brunger, A.G. "Geographical Propinquity among Pre-famine Catholic Irish Settlers in Upper Canada." *Journal of Historical Geography* 8, no. 3 (1982): 265–82.

Burr, Christina. *Canada's Victorian Oil Town: The Transformation of Petrolia from Resource Town into a Victorian Community*. Montreal: McGill-Queen's University Press, 2006.

————. "Oil Mania: Colonial Land Policy, Land Speculation and Settlement in Enniskillen Township, 1830s–1860s." *Social History* 38, no. 76 (2005): 267–306.

Cameron, Wendy. "Peter Robinson's Settlers in Peterborough." In *The Untold Story: The Irish in Canada*, vol. 1, edited by Robert O'Driscoll and Lorna Reynolds, 343–53. Toronto: Celtic Arts of Canada, 1988.

————. "Selecting Peter Robinson's Irish Emigrants." *Social History* 9 (1976): 29–46.

Cameron, Wendy, and Mary McDougall Maude. *Assisting Emigration to Upper Canada: The Petworth Project, 1832–37*. Montreal: McGill-Queen's University Press, 2000.

Campey, Lucille H. *Atlantic Canada's Irish Immigrants: A Fish and Timber Story*. Toronto: Dundurn, 2016.

————. *Fast Sailing and Copper-Bottomed: Aberdeen Sailing Ships and the Emigrant Scots They Carried to Canada*. Toronto: Natural Heritage, 2002.

————. *Les Écossais: The Pioneer Scots of Lower Canada, 1763–1855*. Toronto: Natural Heritage, 2006.

———. *Planters, Paupers and Pioneers: English Settlers in Atlantic Canada.* Toronto: Natural Heritage, 2010.

———. *Seeking a Better Future: The English Pioneers of Ontario and Quebec.* Toronto: Dundurn, 2012.

———. *The Scottish Pioneers of Upper Canada, 1784–1855: Glengarry and Beyond.* Toronto: Natural Heritage, 2005.

Carrier, N.H., and J.R. Jeffrey. *External Migration: A Study of the Available Statistics 1815–1950.* London: HMSO, 1953.

Charbonneau, André, and André Sevigny. *1847 Grosse Îsle: A Record of Daily Events.* Ottawa: Canadian Heritage, 1997.

Clarke, John. "A Geographical Analysis of Colonial Settlement in the Western District of Upper Canada, 1788–1850." Ph.D. diss., University of Western Ontario, 1970.

Courville, Serge. *Quebec: A Historical Geography.* Translated by Richard Howard. Vancouver: UBC Press, 2008.

Cowan, Helen. *British Emigration to British North America: The First Hundred Years.* Toronto: University of Toronto Press, 1961.

Craig, Gerald M. *Upper Canada: The Formative Years, 1784–1841.* Toronto: McClelland & Stewart, 1993.

Cross, Dorothy Suzanne. "The Irish in Montreal, 1867–1896." M.A. thesis, McGill University, 1969.

Cross, Michael S. "The Age of Gentility: The Formation of the Aristocracy in the Ottawa Valley." *Canadian Historical Association: Historical Paper* 2, no. 1 (1967): 105–17.

———. "The Shiners' War: Social Violence in the Ottawa Valley in the 1830s." *Canadian Historical Review* 54, no. 1 (March, 1973): 1–26.

Davis, Ralph. *The Industrial Revolution and British Overseas Trade.* Leicester: Leicester University Press, 1979.

De Billy, Pierre. "Forever Shannon: A Village Holds Fast to Its Irish Roots in the Heart of French Québec." *Royal Canadian Geographical Society* (July/August, 1999): 58–63.

Dickinson, John A., and Brian Young. *A Short History of Quebec.* 2nd edition. Toronto: Longman, 1993.

Dickson, R.J. *Ulster Emigration to Colonial America 1718–1775.* London: Routledge & Kegan Paul, 1966.

Dictionary of Canadian Biography. Toronto: University of Toronto Press, 1979–85.

Dillon, William Francis. "The Irish in London, Ontario, 1826–1861." M.A. thesis, University of Western Ontario, 1963.

Donnelly, James S. Jr. *The Great Irish Potato Famine*. Stroud: The History Press, 2002.

Downs, Father John. "Sainte-Marthe et ses Irlandais," *Quelques pages d'histoire de Sainte Marthe, comté de Vaudreuil*, publications généalogiques n.d., 8–13. Hudson Historical Society website.

Driedger, Sharon Doyle. *An Irish Heart: How a Small Immigrant Community Shaped Canada*. Toronto: HarperCollins, 2011.

Duncan, Kenneth. "Irish Famine Immigration and the Social Structure of Canada West." *Canadian Review of Sociology and Anthropology* 2 (1965): 19–40.

Elliott, Bruce S. "Emigration from South Leinster to Eastern Upper Canada." *Canadian Papers in Rural History* 8 (1991): 277–305.

———.*Irish Migrants in the Canadas: A New Approach*. Kingston: McGill-Queen's University Press, 1988.

———. "'The Famous Township of Hull': Image and Aspirations of a Pioneer Quebec Community." *Social History* 12 (1969): 339–67.

Enright, Flannan P. "Pre-Famine Reform and Emigration on the Wyndham Estate in Clare." *The Other Clare* 8 (1984): 33–36.

Ferguson, Guy Richard. "The Peter Robinson Settlers in Emily Township, 1825–61." M.A. thesis, Queen's University, 1979.

Files, Angela E.M. "Loyalist Settlement Along the St. Lawrence in Upper Canada." *Grand River Branch: U.E.L. Association of Canada Newsletter* 8, no. 1 (February 1996): 9–12.

Fitzgerald, Patrick, and Brian Lambkin, *Migration in Irish History, 1607–2007*. New York: Palgrave Macmillan, 2008.

Forster, Merna M. "Quarantine at Grosse Île." *Canadian Family Physician* 41 (May 1995): 841–8.

Gagnée, Jacques. "The Irish Catholics of Lower Canada and Québec: Their Churches." PDF file, 2014. (This online source describes the early Irish communities that were founded in Lower Canada and provides details of their churches and the priests who served them.) Galvin, Clare F. *The Holy Land: A History of Ennismore Township, County of Peterborough Ontario, 1825–1975.* Ennismore, ON: Corporation of the Township of Ennismore, 1978.

Gates, Lilian Francis. *Land Policies in Upper Canada.* Toronto: University of Toronto Press, 1968.

Grace, Robert. "The Irish in Mid-Nineteenth-Century Canada and the Case of Quebec: Immigration and Settlement in a Catholic City." Ph.D. diss., Laval University, 1999.

Grace, Robert J. *The Irish in Quebec: An Introduction to the Historiography.* Quebec: Institut québécois de recherche sur la culture, 1993.

Grainger, Jennifer. *Vanished Villages of Middlesex.* Toronto: Natural Heritage, 2002.

Gray, Charlotte. *Sisters in the Wilderness: The Lives of Susanna Moodie and Catharine Parr Traill.* Toronto: Penguin Books, 1999.

Green-Guenette, Sylvia, and Elizabeth Larrabee. "Patterson Family: Ireland to Megantic County, Lower Canada and Our McNey Connection." *Quebec Family History Society: Connections* (2011).

Guillet, Edwin. *Early Life in Upper Canada.* Toronto: University of Toronto Press, 1963. Reprint, original written in 1933.

Guillet, Edwin C. *The Great Migration: The Atlantic Crossing by Sailing-Ship since 1770.* Toronto: University of Toronto Press, 1963.

———. *The Pioneer Farmer and Backwoodsman.* Toronto: University of Toronto Press, 1963.

Gwynn, J. "The Irish in Eastern Ontario: The Social Structure of Huntley Township in Carleton County, 1851–71." In *Exploring Our Heritage: The Ottawa Valley Experience*, edited by Vrenia Ivonoffski and Sandra Campbell, 20–31. Arnprior, ON: Arnprior and District Historical Society, 1980.

Gwyn, Julian. "The Irish in the Napanee River Valley: Camden East Township, 1851–1881." In *The Untold Story: The Irish in Canada*, edited by Robert O'Driscoll and Lorna Reynolds, 355–75. Toronto: Celtic Arts of Canada, 1988.

Harney, Robert F., ed. *Gathering Place: Peoples and Neighbourhoods of Toronto, 1834–1945.* Toronto: Multicultural History Society of Ontario, 1985.

Harrison, Michael. "Nominal List of Repealers from the *Toronto Mirror* February, 1844." *Families* 36 no. 2 (1997): 111–6.

Harvey, Robert. *A Few Bloody Noses: The American War of Independence.* London: John Murray, 2001.

Haydon, Andrew. *Pioneer Sketches in the District of Bathurst.* Toronto: Ryerson Press, 1925.

Hirsch, R. Forbes. *The Upper Ottawa Valley Timber Trade: A Sketch.* Ottawa: The Historical Society of Ottawa, 1985.

Holman, Andrew Carl. "Corktown, 1832–1847: The Founding of Hamilton's Pre-Famine Irish Settlement." M.A. thesis, McMaster University, 1989.

Holt, Ruth, and Margaret Williams. *Genealogical Extraction and Index of the Canada Company Remittance Books, 1843–1847.* Weston, ON: R. Holt, 1990.

Houston, Cecil J., and William J. Smyth. *Irish Emigration and Canadian Settlement: Patterns, Links, and Letters.* Toronto: Toronto University Press, 1990.

———. *The Sash Canada Wore: A Historical Geography of the Orange Order in Canada.* Toronto: University of Toronto Press, 1980.

Hunter, Andrew F. *A History of Simcoe County.* Barrie: Historical Committee of Simcoe County, 1948.

Johnson, Stanley C. *A History of Emigration from the United Kingdom to North America, 1763–1912.* London: G. Routledge, 1913.

Johnston, H.J.M. *British Emigration Policy 1815–1830: "Shovelling Out Paupers".* Oxford: Clarendon Press, 1972.

———. "Immigration to the Five Eastern Townships of the Huron Tract." *Ontario History* 54 (1962): 207–24.

Johnston, William. *History of the County of Perth from 1825 to 1902.* Stratford, ON: Beacon Herald, 1976.

Johnston, W.S., and H.J.M. Johnston. *History of Perth County to 1967.* Stratford, ON: Corporation of the County of Perth, 1967.

Kealey, Gregory S. "The Orange Order in Toronto: Religious Riot and the Working Class." In *The Untold Story: The Irish in Canada*, vol. 2, edited by Robert O'Driscoll and Lorna Reynolds, 829–51. Toronto: Celtic Arts of Canada, 1988.

Keep, G.R.C. "Irish Migration to Montreal, 1847–67." M.A. thesis, McGill University, 1848.

King, Seamus J. *The Clash of the Ash in Foreign Fields: Hurling Abroad.* Cashel: S. King, 1998.

Kirkconnell, Watson. *Victoria County Centennial History.* Lindsay, ON: Waterman-Warder Press, 1921.

Kirouac, Jules-Adrien. *Histoire de la Paroisse de Saint-Malachie.* Quebec: Typ. Laflamme and Proulx, 1909.

Leacock, Stephen. *Montreal: Seaport and City.* Toronto: McClelland & Stewart, 1948.

Lee, Robert C. *The Canada Company and the Huron Tract, 1826–1853.* Toronto: Natural Heritage, 2004.

Le Moignan, Michel. "Douglastown, un Rameau de la Verte Erin en Gaspésie." *Revue d'Histoire de la Gaspésie* 5 (1967) 178–85.

Lewis, Jennie Raycraft. *Sure An' This Is Biddulph.* Biddulph ON: Biddulph Town Council, 1964.

Little, J.I. "A.C. Buchanan and the Megantic Experiment: Promoting British Colonization in Lower Canada." *Social History* 46, no. 92 (2013) 295–319.

———., ed. *Love Strong as Death: Lucy Peel's Canadian Journal, 1833–1836.* Waterloo, ON: Wilfred Laurier University Press, 2001.

———. *Nationalism, Capitalism and Colonization in Nineteenth Century Quebec: The Upper St. Francis District.* Kingston, ON: McGill-Queen's University Press, 1989.

Lockwood, Glen. "The Pattern of Settlement in Eastern Ontario." *Families* 30, no. 4 (1991): 235–57.

Lockwood, Glen J. "Irish Immigrants and the Critical Years in Eastern Ontario: Montague Township 1821–81." *Canadian Papers in Rural History* 4 (1984): 153–78.

———. *Montague: A Social History of an Irish Ontario Township, 1783–1980.* Smith Falls, ON: Corporation of the Township of Montague, 1980.

———. "Success and the Doubtful Image of Irish Immigrants in Upper Canada: The Case of Monatgue Township, 1820–1900." In *The Untold Story: The Irish in Canada,* vol. 1, edited by Robert O'Driscoll and Lorna Reynolds, 319–41. Toronto: Celtic Arts of Canada, 1988.

———. *The Rear of Leeds and Lansdowne: The Making of Community on the Gananoque River Frontier, 1796–1996.* Lyndhurst, ON: Corporation of the Township of Rear of Leeds and Lansdowne, 1996.

Lower, Arthur R.M. *Colony to Nation: A History of Canada.* Toronto: Longmans, Green, 1946.

———. "Immigration and Settlement in Canada, 1812–1820." *Canadian Historical Review* 3, (1922): 37–47.

Lyne, Daniel Coleman. "The Irish in the Province of Canada in the Decade Leading to Confederation." M.A. thesis, McGill University, 1960.

Lynn, James. "County Antrim Origins of Some Nassagaweya Settlers." *Families* 44 no. 2 (2005): 81–96.

MacDonagh, Oliver. *A Pattern of Government Growth 1800–1860: The Passenger Acts and Their Enforcement.* London: MacGibbon and Kee, 1961.

———. "Emigration and the State, 1833–55: An Essay in Administrative History." *Transactions of the Royal Historical Society* 5 (1955).

MacDonald, Norman. *Canada, Immigration and Settlement 1763–1841.* London: Longmans, 1939.

Mack, Susan Muriel. *The History of Stephen Township.* Crediton, ON: Corporation of the Township of Stephen, 1992.

MacKay, Donald. *Flight from Famine: The Coming of the Irish to Canada.* Toronto: Natural Heritage, 2009.

———. *The Lumberjacks.* Toronto: Natural Heritage, 1998.

Magocsi, Paul Robert, ed. *The Encyclopedia of Canada's Peoples.* Toronto: University of Toronto Press, 1999.

Manning, Aidan. *Between the Runways: A History of Irish-Catholic Settlement in Southern Peel County and Etobicoke.* Etobicoke: Author, 2009.

Mannion, John J. *Irish Settlements in Eastern Canada: A Study of Cultural Transfer and Adaptation.* Toronto: University of Toronto Press, 1974.

Marie-Ursule, Soeur. *Civilisation Traditionnelle des Lavalois.* Quebec: Université Laval, 1951.

Marsh, E.L. *A History of the County of Grey.* Owen Sound: Fleming, 1931.

McCarthy, Angela. *Irish Migrants in New Zealand, 1840–1937, 'The Desired Haven.'* Belfast: Boydell Press, 2005.

McFerran, Clara. "Catholic Pioneers of Tyendinaga and Neighbouring Townships." *Canadian Catholic Historical Association Report* 8 (1940–1941): 77–94.

McGivern, J.S. "Catholic Loyalists in the American Revolution: A Sketch." *Canadian Catholic Historical Association Study Sessions* 48 (1981): 91–99.

McGowan, Mark. "Famine, Facts and Fabrication: An Examination of Diaries from the Irish Famine Migration to Canada." *Canadian Journal of Irish Studies* 3, no. 2 (Fall, 2007): 48–55.

———. "Irish Catholics." In *The Encyclopaedia of Canada's Peoples*, edited by Paul Robert Magocsi, 734–63. Toronto: University of Toronto Press, 1999.

McGowan, Mark G. *The Waning of the Green: Catholics, the Irish, and Identity in Toronto, 1887–1922.* Montreal: McGill-Queen's University Press, 1999.

McKillop, Dugald McKenzie. *Annals of Megantic County, Quebec.* Lynn, MA: Author, 1902.

McQuillan, D. Aidan. "Beaurivage: The Development of an Irish Ethnic Identity in Rural Quebec, 1820–1860." In *The Untold Story: The Irish in Canada*, edited by Robert O'Driscoll and Lorna Reynolds, vol. 1, 263–79. Toronto: Celtic Arts of Canada, 1988.

———. "Returns on Investment: Seigneurial Land Development in Nineteenth Century Quebec." In *Mythic History and Symbolic Landscape*, edited by Serge Courville and Brian S. Osborne, 46–51. Sainte-Foy, QC: Inter-University Centre for Quebec Studies, 1997.

Mennie-de Varennes, Kathleen. *Au Coeur de la Gatineau ou l'Histoire de la Paroisse de la Visitation de Gracefield.* Quebec: Ste Foy, 1985.

Miller, Kerby A. *Emigrants and Exiles: Ireland and the Irish Exodus to North America.* Oxford: Oxford University Press, 1985.

Moodie, Susanna. *Roughing It in the Bush or Life in Canada.* London: Virago Press, 1986.

Moore, Christopher. *The Loyalists: Revolution, Exile, Settlement.* Toronto: McClelland & Stewart, 1994,

Moran, Gerard. *Sending Out Ireland's Poor: Assisted Emigration to North America in the Nineteenth Century.* Dublin: Four Courts Press, 2004.

Morrill, Victor Eugene, and Erastus Gardner Pierce. *Men of Today in the Eastern Townships.* Sherbrooke, QC: Reink Books, 1917.

Mountain, Armine W. *A Memoir of George Jehoshaphat Mountain, D.D., D.C.L., Late Bishop of Quebec.* Montreal: J. Lovell, 1866.

Murphy, Charles. *1825 — D'Arcy McGee — 1925: A Collection of Speeches and Addresses, Together with a Complete Report of the Centennial Celebration of the Birth of the Honourable Thomas D'Arcy McGee, at Ottawa, April 13th, 1925.* Toronto: Macmillan, 1937.

Neatby, Hilda Marion. *Quebec: The Revolutionary Age, 1760–1791.* Toronto: McClelland & Stewart, 1966.

Neelin, James M., and Michael R. Neelin. *The Old Methodist Burying Ground in the Town of Perth, Lanark County, Ontario.* Ottawa: Ontario Genealogical Society, 1978.

Nielson, Eleanor. "An Index of Lanark Families Who Migrated to Lambton." *Ontario Genealogical Society* 15, no. 2 (Sept.–Oct., 1982): 59–61.

Noël, Françoise. *Competing for Souls: Missionary Activity and Settlement in the Eastern Townships, 1784–1851.* Sherbrooke, QC: University of Sherbrooke, 1988.

———. "Gabriel Christie's Seigneuries: Settlement and Seigneurial Administration in the Upper Richelieu Valley, 1764–1854." Ph.D. diss., McGill University, 1985.

Nolte, William M. "The Irish in Canada, 1815–1867." Ph.D. diss., University of Maryland, 1975.

O'Farrell, John. "Irish Families in Ancient Quebec." In *The Untold Story: The Irish in Canada,* vol. 1, edited by Robert O'Driscoll and Lorna Reynolds, 281–94. Toronto: Celtic Arts of Canada, 1988.

O'Gallagher, Marianna. *Grosse Îsle: Gateway to Canada 1832–1947.* Quebec: Carraig Books, 1984.

———. *The Shamrock Trail: Tracing the Irish in Quebec City.* Ste. Foy, QC: Carraig Books, 1997.

O'Leary, James. *History of the Irish Catholics of Quebec: Saint Patrick's Church to the Death of Reverend P. McMahon.* Quebec: 1895.

Ouellet, Fernand. *Lower Canada, 1791–1840: Social Change and Nationalism.* Translated and adapted by Patricia Claxton. Toronto: McClelland & Stewart, 1980.

Pammett, Howard. *Lilies and Shamrocks: A History of Emily Township County of Victoria Ontario, 1818-1973.* Lindsay, ON: J. Deyell, 1974.

——. "The Irish Emigrant Settler in the Pioneer Kawarthas." *Families* 17 no. 4 1978: 154-74.

Parkinson, Daniel B. "From Rawdon to Wellington County," part 1, 2, 3. *Families* 38 (1999): 67-78, 131-41, 195-205.

——. "Settlers at Simcoe County from Rawdon Township QC." *Families* 43, no. 1 (2004): 11-18.

——. "The American Heritage of Rawdon Township Lower Canada." *Connections* 29, no.2 (Winter, 2006): 32-8.

——. "To Huron's Shore: Rawdon, Quebec Families in Bruce, Grey and Huron Counties." *Families* 44, no. 2 (2005): 67-80.

Patterson, Gilbert C. *Land Settlement in Upper Canada, 1783-1840.* Toronto: Ontario Archives, 1921.

Pentland, Clare H. *Labour and Capital in Canada 1650-1860.* Toronto: James Lorimer, 1981.

Poulin, Anne-Marie, and Jean Simard. *An Anglican Heritage: Christ Church in Frampton, Quebec.* Corporation Culturelle de Frampton, 1989.

Pourbaix, Michel. *The History of a Christian Community: Eardley, Luskville, Pontiac.* Pontiac, QC: 1999.

Pringle, Ian, and Enoch Padolsky. "The Irish Heritage of the English of the Ottawa Valley." *English Studies in Canada* 8, no. 3 (Fall, 1981): 338-52.

Rawlings, Gwen. *Pioneers of Inverness Township, Quebec: An Historical and Genealogical Story, 1800-1978,* edited by Elizabeth Harwood, cartography by R.A. Nutter. Cheltenham, ON: Boston Mills Press, 1979.

——. "The English 180 Years in Rural Quebec Megantic County." *Canadian Genealogist* 3, no. 2 (1981): 74-83.

Read, Colin. *The Rising in Western Upper Canada: The Duncombe Revolt and After.* Toronto: University of Toronto Press, 1982.

Redmond, Patrick M. *Irish Life in Rural Quebec: A History of Frampton.* Montreal: Author, 1977.

Rees, Jim. *Surplus People: from Wicklow to Canada.* Cork: Collins Press, 2014.

Reynolds, Lorna. "Black '47: A Summer of Sorrow." In *The Untold Story: The Irish in Canada,* vol. 1, edited by Robert O'Driscoll and Lorna Reynolds, 103-68. Toronto: Celtic Arts of Canada, 1988.

Robertson, Norman. *History of the County of Bruce*. Toronto: William Briggs, 1906.

Ryan, Pauline. "A Study of Irish Immigration to North Hastings County." *Ontario History* 83, no. 1, (March, 1991): 23–37.

Schmitz, Nancy. *Irish for a Day: Saint Patrick's Day Celebrations in Quebec City, 1765–1990*. Ste Foy, QC: Carraig Books, 1991.

Scott, James. *The Settlement of Huron County*. Toronto: Ryerson Press, 1966.

Seiling, Ken. "The Early Settlement of Wellington County." *Families* 15, no. 4 (1976): 143–9.

Shantz, Mary Rae. "The Irish Catholics in Guelph: A Study of Ethnic Group Identity, 1827–1861." M.A. thesis, University of Guelph, 1986.

Shepperson, W.S. *British Emigration to North America: Projects and Opinions in the Early Victorian Period*. Oxford: Blackwell, 1957.

Siebert, Wilbur Henry. "American Loyalists in the Eastern Seigneuries and Townships of the Province of Quebec." *Transactions of the Royal Society of Canada* 7, 3rd series (1913): 3–41.

———. "Loyalist Settlements in the Gaspé Peninsula." *Transactions of the Royal Society of Canada* 8, 3rd Series (1914): 399–405.

Smith, Dorothy Jane. "Vancleek Hill, West Hawkesbury Township, 1900–1950." M.A. thesis, Carleton University, 2011.

Smith, Willard Vandine. "The Evolution of a Fall Line Settlement, Buckingham, Quebec." M.A. thesis, University of Ottawa, 1967.

Southam, Peter. *Irish Settlement and National Identity in the Lower St. Francis Valley*. Richmond, QC: St. Patrick's Society of Richmond and Vicinity, 2012.

Traill, Catharine Parr. *The Backwoods of Canada*. Ottawa: Carleton University Press, 1997.

Tucker, Derek Nile. "Successful Pioneers: Irish Catholic Settlers in the Township of Hibbert Ontario, 1845–1887." M.A. thesis, McMaster University, 2001.

Vance, Michael E. *Imperial Immigrants: Scottish Settlers in the Upper Ottawa Valley*. Toronto: Dundurn, 2012.

Vaudry, Mary Olive. "A Sketch of the Life of Captain John Savage, J.P., First Settler in Shefford County, 1792." United Empire Loyalists' Association of Canada Meeting, March 1921.

Walsh, Reverend T.J. "Pioneer English Catholics in the Eastern Townships." *Canadian Catholic Historical Association Report* (1939–40): 55–70.

White, Paul. *Owen Sound: The Port City*. Toronto: Natural Heritage, 2000.

Wilson, Catherine Anne. *A New Lease on Life: Landlords, Tenants and Immigration in Ireland and Canada*. Montreal: McGill-Queen's University Press, 1994.

Wylie, William N.T. *Poverty, Distress and Disease: Labour and the Construction of the Rideau Canal, 1826–32*. In *Labourers on the Rideau Canal, 1826–1832: From Worksite to World Heritage Site*, edited by Katherine Mary Jean McKenna, 31–40. Ottawa: Borealis, 2008.

IMAGE CREDITS

✦

65 Courtesy Beauce 1977 at English Wikipedia.

75 © Dominic R. Labbé, McMasterville, Quebec. Reproduced by permission.

76 Courtesy Jeangagnon, 2014, at English Wikipedia.

79 Photograph by Geoff Campey.

84 Courtesy Eastern Townships Resource Centre CA E001 P049–013.

90 Courtesy McCord Museum II–146359.

92 Courtesy Diego Delso, delso.photo, Licence CC-BY-SA.

94 Photograph by Geoff Campey.

99 © Dominic R. Labbé, McMasterville, Quebec. Reproduced by permission.

106 Courtesy Library and Archives Canada, Acc. No. 1970-188-2150 W.H. Coverdale Collection of Canadiana.

108 Courtesy Library and Archives Canada, W.H. Coverdale Collection of Canadiana.

112 Courtesy Library and Archives Canada, Acc. No. 1979–12–17. Mr. R.W. Henwood, Montreal, Quebec.

114 Photograph by Geoff Campey.

128 Courtesy Toronto Reference Library, Special Collections, Baldwin Collection Ref: C 2-23b.

131 Courtesy Library and Archives Canada, Acc. No. 1957–60–23.

133 © Kevin Derrick, Peterborough, Ontario. Reproduced by permission.

136 Courtesy C.P. Meredith/Library and Archives Canada/PA.

147 Courtesy C.P. Meredith/Library and Archives Canada/PA.

148 Courtesy AG25 and licensed under GNU Free Documentation Licence, Version 2.1.

152 Courtesy Library and Archives Canada Acc. No. 1934–402.

156 Courtesy Library and Archives Canada.

164 Courtesy Library and Archives Canada Acc. No. R0266-403. Peter Winkworth Collection of Canadiana.

167 Courtesy Library and Archives Canada, Acc. No. 1956–62–123.

169 © John Vetterli, 2008. Used by permission under the Wikipedia Creative Commons attribution-Share Alike 2.0 Generic Licence.

173 Courtesy Library and Archives Canada, Acc. No. 1981–42–29R. Source: Dr. Nigel Davies, Gelati, Mexico.

179 Courtesy Jules-Ernest Livernois/Library and Archives Canada/ PA-024001.

183 Courtesy Laurier Press Clippings/Library and Archives Canada/ C-066298.

184 Courtesy Library and Archives Canada Acc. No. 1934–286–1.

186 Courtesy Bibliothèque et Archives nationales du Quebec P.585, D13, P7.

207 Courtesy Library and Archives Canada.

208 Public domain.

213 Public domain.

216 Public domain.

218 Courtesy Library and Archives Canada, Acc. No. 1965–76–18.

231 Courtesy McCord Museum I–7383–1.

232 Courtesy James Inglis/Library and Archives Canada/C–083423.

235 Courtesy McCord Museum II–83373.

236 Courtesy McCord Museum M930.50.3.186.

238 Courtesy Reverend Woodhouse / Library and Archives Canada/ C-003007.

239 Courtesy Toronto Reference Library, Special Collections ARTS–PC–43.

413 Photograph by The Portrait Place, Priory Square, Salisbury U.K.

INDEX

ABOUT THE AUTHOR

Ottawa-born Lucille Campey began her career in Canada as a scientist, having obtained an honours degree in chemistry from Ottawa University. Following her marriage to Geoff, she moved to England, obtaining a master's degree at Leeds University in 1987 in medieval history, and ten years later a doctorate at Aberdeen University on Scottish emigration to Canada. Having worked for the British Conservative Party, she became a special advisor to a cabinet minister in John's Major's government. This gave her an understanding of the inner workings of the government, which she has put to good use in her immigration studies.

BOOK CREDITS

Acquiring Editor: J. Kirk Howard
Editor: Allison Hirst
Project Editor: Elena Radic
Proofreader: Tara Tovell

Designer: Jennifer Gallinger

Publicist: Kendra Martin/Michelle Melski

DUNDURN

Publisher: J. Kirk Howard
Vice-President: Carl A. Brand
Editorial Director: Kathryn Lane
Artistic Director: Laura Boyle
Director of Sales and Marketing: Synora Van Drine
Publicty Manager: Michelle Melski

Editorial: Allison Hirst, Dominic Farrell, Jenny McWha, Rachel Spence, Elena Radic
Marketing and Publicity: Kendra Martin, Kathryn Bassett, Elham Ali